A
MORE PERFECT
UNION
Documents in U.S. History

SECOND EDITION

VOLUME II: SINCE 1865

Paul F. Boller, Jr.

Ronald Story

University of Massachusetts, Amherst

HOUGHTON MIFFLIN COMPANY • BOSTON

Dallas   Geneva, Illinois   Palo Alto   Princeton, New Jersey

——— To Martin and Eliza

Printed in the U.S.A.

Library of Congress Catalog Card Number: 87-81489

ISBN: 0-395-45690-8

ABCDEFGHIJ-B-9543210-8987

CONTENTS

CHAPTER ONE
Reconstructing the Union

CHAPTER TWO
The Minorities

CHAPTER THREE

The Age of Progress

CHAPTER FOUR

The Big Stick

CHAPTER SEVEN

Contemporary America

A STATISTICAL APPENDIX
(after page 324)

PREFACE

Our two-volume reader, **A More Perfect Union: Documents in U.S. History,** presents key documents chosen to provide students with the original words of speeches, political and legal writings, and literature that reflected, precipitated, and implemented developments and events during America's past four centuries. The readings in Volume I cover the era from the founding of the Virginia and Massachusetts Bay colonies to Reconstruction; Volume II begins with the post–Civil War period, repeating some of the first volume's final readings, and concludes with selections that concern contemporary issues. We are pleased with the reception that **A More Perfect Union** has received, and we have worked toward refining the contents in this second edition.

About a third of the material is new to this second edition, which contains more documents and Counterpoint source data than the first edition. New selections include such readings as Samuel Parris's "Christ Knows How Many Devils There Are" (from the Salem witch-trial period), Meriwether Lewis's "Report on the Missouri and Columbia Rivers," and Margaret Fuller's "Woman in the Nineteenth Century," all in Volume I, and "Report of the Joint Committee on Reconstruction" (in both volumes, on Klansmen of the Carolinas), Knute Rockne's "A Sales Promotion Address," and Ronald Reagan's "Address on Lebanon and Grenada." The Counterpoints have been closely integrated with the documents' subject matter. The introductions to the Counterpoints have been completely revised; they explain what facts and trends can be gleaned from the data presented in the tables and figures drawn from historians' original research. These tables and figures are, for the most part, new to this edition.

The readings in these volumes represent what we believe to be an attractive blend of social and political history, together with cultural and economic trends, suitable for introductory courses in American history. Three considerations guided our selection of items. First, we looked for famous documents with a lustrous place in the American tradition. These—the Mayflower Compact, for example, or the Gettysburg Address, or Franklin Roosevelt's first inaugural address—we chose for their great mythic quality, as expressions of fundamental ideals with which students should be familiar. Second, we searched out writings that had immediate impact and caused something to happen. Examples from this very large group include the Virginia slave statutes, Thomas Paine's

The Crisis, the Emancipation Proclamation, and Earl Warren's decision in **Brown** v. **The Board of Education of Topeka**—all famous pieces and influential as well. Finally, we included documents that seemed to reflect important attitudes or developments. Into this group fall Thomas Hart Benton's racial views as well as the writings of Upton Sinclair on industrial Chicago and Martin Luther King, Jr., on Vietnam. In this category, where the need for careful selection from a wide field was most apparent, we looked especially for thoughtful pieces with a measure of fame and influence. Horace Mann's statement on schools reflected common attitudes; it also caused something to happen and is a well-known statement of reformist concern. We have also intermixed familiar documents with unexpected ones (Andrew Jackson, say, and T. S. Arthur, or Woodrow Wilson and Margaret Sanger).

Once a document was chosen, we did not hesitate to edit it severely when the selection seemed too long. This consideration obviously affected book-length works but also was applicable to such pieces as John Peter Zenger's account of his trial for libel or Joseph McCarthy's speech on Communist subversion. In some cases, particularly with writings from the colonial era, we have modernized spelling and punctuation.

With the documents are pedagogical features to aid students in comprehending the role and significance of these readings. Each document has a lengthy headnote that summarizes the relevant trends of the era, provides a specific setting for the document, and sketches the life of the author. The headnotes are followed by study questions to guide students through the prose and suggest ways of thinking about the selections. The headnotes, and especially the study questions, contain many cross-references to other documents in the collection to provide perspective and encourage comparative analysis.

Each chapter concludes with a Counterpoint, a group of tables and sometimes charts and figures that deal with some aspect of American society relevant to the era and theme of that chapter's documents. Generally the work of distinguished modern historians, often "classic" studies in their own right, the Counterpoints touch on issues raised in different ways by the documents—such as the Jacksonian assault on privilege, or difficulties faced by blacks and immigrants in industrial America. The Counterpoints expose students to historical statistical evidence, which provides a contrast to the historical record of documents and speeches; they also add a further flavor of social history to what, given our concern with the famous and influential, is still a predominantly political, constitutional, and diplomatic collection. All Counterpoints have introductions and cross-references, similar to those for the documents.

The Statistical Appendix, comprising statistics on population, government, and the economy spanning the life of the nation, is offered in the same spirit as the Counterpoints are—as an alternative way, or in some instances perhaps the only way, of seeing important long-term historical trends. The documents are creations of particular moments; the Counterpoints provide close-ups of particular eras; the Appendix offers, in its fashion, the whole sweep of American history. The Statistical Appendix thus supplies a background for both the documents and the Counterpoints.

We would like to thank the following people who reviewed the manuscript for one or both volumes:

William Breitenbach, University of Puget Sound
Terry A. Cooney, University of Puget Sound
Anne Day, Clarion University of Pennsylvania
Joseph Ellis, Trenton State College
Ronald Lora, University of Toledo
Roderick Nimtz, Miami University
Margaret Patoski, Texas Wesleyan College
Eldon R. Turner, University of Florida

We also wish to thank the staff of Houghton Mifflin Company for their encouragement and assistance in the preparation of this work.

P. F. B.
R. S.

INTRODUCTION

The two volumes of **A More Perfect Union: Documents in U.S. History** bring together a wide variety of documents illustrating political, social, economic, cultural, constitutional, and intellectual history for use in college courses in American history and culture. Volume I begins with the Virginia Ordinance of 1621 and ends with a post-Reconstruction speech by Frederick Douglass (1883). Volume II starts with the Reconstruction period and Abraham Lincoln's second inaugural address (1865) and continues to the present time, concluding with a speech by Ronald Reagan (1983).

The documentary readings cover the major themes in American history. In Volume I these include: the strides toward freedom and independence during the colonial period; the growth of nationalism during the early nineteenth century; the reform movements during the first half of that century; the sectional conflict at mid-century; and the perennial American racial dilemma. Volume II repeats the last theme and adds these three: the responses to the periodic crises faced by the American economy since the late nineteenth century; the impetus toward humanitarian reform at every period of our national history; and the development of the United States into a superpower in the twentieth century. Both volumes also portray the perpetual tension throughout our history between freedom and security, individual enterprise and social justice, popular democracy and responsible leadership. The documents encompass a great deal of political history, but also contain social and economic developments. In the charters, laws, treaties, speeches, announcements, and reports—together with the end-of-chapter Counterpoint sections, which present statistics covering trends in American life—it is possible to observe American history in the making.

History, a multifaceted enterprise, at its most basic level is a collection of facts. Historians keep records of treaties, elections, legislative acts, conferences, battles, legal decisions, and other significant happenings so that these are available to lawyers, diplomats, public officials, journalists, and other interested parties to consult. Some collections of documents are little more than reference books. Our volumes are not intended to be used in this way, but they do contain many fundamental records of American history for ready reference: the Declaration of Independence, the Monroe Doctrine, the **Dred Scott** decision, the Emancipation Proclamation, Franklin Roosevelt's first inaugural address, the Supreme Court decision in **Brown** v. **Board of Education**, and Dwight D. Eisenhower's warning about the military-industrial complex.

But history is more than encyclopedia; history is also story. American history is filled with dramatic events: America's Declaration of Independence in 1776; Mississippi's secession cry in 1860; Lincoln's signing of the Emancipation Proclamation in 1863; Franklin Roosevelt's call for war on Japan after the attack on Pearl Harbor; the Woodstock Festival in 1969; the Watergate crisis in 1972–1974. **A More Perfect Union** is an anthology, not narrative history, so it does not recount any of these stories. Nevertheless, the basic materials from which narrative historians do reconstruct such stories are contained in these volumes: John Peter Zenger's trial in 1735; David Walker's appeal for justice for American blacks in 1829; Woodrow Wilson's impassioned call for war on Germany in 1917; and Richard Nixon's surprise visit to the People's Republic of China in 1972 after years of U.S. hostility toward the Chinese Communists.

Original records often make more fascinating reading than mere summaries of events written by persons who were not on the scene. Who can read David Walker's appeal today and not be deeply moved by what he said about the plight of blacks in the United States in 1829? Or read the description of the treatment of the Cheyenne and not be filled with indignation? Or read Jefferson's first inaugural address and not be filled with hope? Written records form the very substance of narrative history.

History is not, however, merely story, not merely a collection of facts. It is more than a series of dramatic moments. Life for most people of every era consists largely of habit, ritual, convention, schedule, and routine. One of the historian's primary tasks is to reconstruct life as it was lived at times and in places enormously different from our own: colonial Massachusetts, antebellum Philadelphia, Chicago at the turn of the century, American society at the time of the Great Depression. **A More Perfect Union** supplies ample materials—statistics as well as documents—for recapturing life in both the near and distant past in this country.

The how and the why behind historical developments are more fascinating than the dates when events occurred. To encourage you to think about the how and the why, the authors have provided questions throughout **A More Perfect Union**. In the introduction to each document, after a general commentary and biographical information where it is appropriate, the last paragraph contains questions to consider. The end-of-chapter Counterpoint sections also have questions pertaining to the tables, and some queries appear in the Statistical Appendix.

We are all culture-bound. We tend to judge other peoples, places, and periods by our own standards, and it is hard for us to comprehend other cultures in their deepest reaches. But if, after mastering the records of a past culture, we succeed in overcoming the parochialism of the present and in penetrating the central vision of societies quite different from our own, we can become wiser about what human beings have accomplished in other times and places and can be more realistic about our own achievements. The documents in these volumes will enable readers to enter the lives of Americans whose experiences were totally different from their own: people in Pennsylvania in the middle of the eighteenth century, Cherokee Indians in Georgia in the 1830s, chattel slaves in colonial Virginia, emancipated blacks after the Civil War, Chicago stockyard workers in the early twentieth century, and young people at the Woodstock Festival in 1969 at the height of the countercul-ture movement. Variety, not uniformity, has been the spice of life in America since the very first settlements after Columbus.

But history is more than the study of past cultures. Students who want to understand the American past cannot stop with descriptions of what people did in earlier times; they will want to know why Americans acted as they did, and why, at critical junctures in our history, they took actions laden with momentous consequences for the future. A histo-rian's most challenging task is to find out why social change occurred. Why did colonial Americans decide to strike for independence in 1776? What brought on the Civil War? Why did the United States decide to go to war in 1898, 1917, 1941, and 1950? What caused the Great De-pression of the 1930s? What brought about the Great Inflation of the 1970s and 1980s?

Students of history search for factors that cause change. Are technological innovations at the root of historical change, or are new ways of producing and distributing material goods the basic developers? Or is it novelty of outlook—the appearance of new ideas—that trans-forms society? Undoubtedly, ideas and economic interests are both at work. At the same time there is much that is accidental and unexpected in human affairs.

One purpose of **A More Perfect Union** is to stimulate you to think about the tremendous changes that have taken place on the American scene and to try to account for these changes. Original documents form a good basis for such an inquiry. They supply information about why Americans thought and acted as they did at particular points in time. In addition, many records in this anthology explain why Americans be-haved as they did at decisive moments. The Declaration of Indepen-dence gives reasons why the American people decided on revolution in 1776. **The Federalist,** Number Ten, contains a theory of how societies in general, and American society in particular, operate. Woodrow Wil-son's address to Congress on the eve of war with Germany in 1917 contains a theory about the relation of nations to each other.

Past, present, and future are co-implicated in the documents in
A More Perfect Union. Historical records contain factual data, material
for dramatic stories, descriptions of bygone cultures, and suggestions for
understanding social change. But the records also contain guidelines
for action. The Declaration of Independence sets forth ideals, goals, and
aspirations for the American people to act upon, as well as explanations
of actions taken. Thomas Jefferson's first inaugural address and Andrew
Jackson's Bank Veto Message do the same. Franklin Roosevelt's first
inaugural address in the midst of the Great Depression and his war
message to Congress after the attack on Pearl Harbor also combine
ideals and actions. The basic documents in these volumes contain pre-
scriptions as well as descriptions: manifestoes, appeals, recommendations, suggestions, and calls to action.

The written word continues, of course, to be the major source for
those seeking to understand the American past. But a striking development in historical scholarship during the past twenty years is the extensive use of nonverbal evidence, such as art work and statistical data, to
illuminate the past. These sources can enhance, modify, or explain the
written record. Cartoons of Andrew Jackson, for example, tell us something about his popular reputation; photographs from the Great Depression reveal the forces behind the birth of Social Security. In other
cases, nonverbal sources, particularly statistical ones, have a story of
their own to tell.

The Counterpoints and Statistical Appendix offer samples of the
kind of statistical data that historians are relying on increasingly. The
Counterpoint section at the end of each chapter is based upon a series
of statistics. These concern mainly the American population, economy,
and government—obviously important areas in which statistics are
abundantly available. The purpose of these Counterpoints is to give you
an opportunity to discover how historians draw conclusions from raw
data. An introduction alerts you to the principal issues to think about
and gives some guidance in reading the tables and charts and extracting
their information. You are encouraged to study them carefully, and to
consider the implications of the data. The effort will be repaid by an
insight into the nature of the historical enterprise, by a sense of how
history is extracted out of the documents of the past.

At the conclusion of each volume is a Statistical Appendix (the
same Statistical Appendix appears in both volumes). The information in
this Appendix, which spans periods up to the current decade, reveals a
great deal about the America of earlier times, just as the Counterpoint
tables do. Statistics on population, on changes in wages and consumer
prices for different economic sectors, on religious affiliations, and on
federal expenditures for defense, debt service, the postal service, and
veterans' benefits, all have much to tell about the ways Americans have

led their lives. As in the Counterpoints, an introduction to each table explains its relevance and guides the reader toward an understanding of the table's data.

We do not believe numbers will ever supplant words as the basic stuff of historical study. Nevertheless, with the aid of literary records, such figures, stark and ambiguous though they may seem, reveal trends in industry and labor, social and economic problems, and patterns of mobility, to mention only a few possibilities. Quantitative material has become indispensable to fully comprehending the past, and it will become even more significant in the future. Thus, in the two volumes of **A More Perfect Union**, a combination of numbers and original words is presented to give depth to the images of America's past and to shed light on its future.

Reconstruction after the post–Civil War era.   Reconstruction meant rebuilding after the devastation of war, embodied in this photograph of a rolling mill and ordnance trains destroyed during General Sherman's march through Georgia; it also meant changing a way of life. (Library of Congress)

CHAPTER ONE

Reconstructing the Union

1.

BINDING WOUNDS

In June 1864, when the Republicans nominated Abraham Lincoln for a second term, the end of the war seemed as far away as ever. Northerners were shocked at the heavy casualties reported from battlefields in Virginia, and criticism of the administration had become so harsh that in mid-August Lincoln was convinced he would not be re-elected. The Radical Republicans, who spoke for the antislavery faction of the party, condemned him as "politically, militarily, and financially a failure" and for a time backed John C. Frémont for the presidency. The Northern Democrats nominated General George. B. McClellan, a former federal commander, and adopted a platform calling for the immediate cessation of hostilities and the restoration of the Union by a negotiated peace. Lincoln was so sure McClellan would defeat him that he wrote a secret memorandum explaining how he would cooperate with the new president after the election in order to save the Union.

But a series of federal victories—the closing of Mobile Bay, the capture of Atlanta, and the routing of Southern forces in the Shenandoah Valley—led public opinion to swing back rapidly to Lincoln. Republican newspapers began ridiculing the "war-is-a-failure" platform of the Democrats, and Frémont decided to drop out of the campaign. Lincoln's prediction that he would not be re-elected proved wrong. On election day he won a plurality of nearly half a million votes and carried every state in the Union except Kentucky, Delaware, and New Jersey.

In his second inaugural address on March 4, 1865, Lincoln singled out slavery as the cause of the Civil War and stated that its eradication was inevitable. He expressed hope for a speedy end to the conflict, called for "malice toward none" and "charity for all," and looked forward to the day when Americans would achieve a "just and lasting peace" among themselves and with all nations. On April 9, Robert E. Lee surrendered to Ulysses S. Grant at Appomattox; two days later Lincoln made his last public address, outlining his reconstruction policy. He had never considered the South to be outside of the Union and hoped for a speedy reconciliation. On April 14, at his last cabinet meeting, he urged the cabinet members to put aside all thoughts of hatred and revenge.

Born to a frontier farming family in Kentucky in 1809, Abraham Lincoln grew up in Indiana and Illinois. As a young man he worked as a farmer, rail-splitter, boatsman, and storekeeper before turning to law and politics. He became enormously successful as a lawyer and served several years in the Illinois legislature and one term in the House of Representatives. Lincoln was largely self-educated; he read and reread such books as the Bible, Aesop's fables, the works of Shakespeare, and the poems of Robert Burns, and developed great skill as a writer. In 1858 his debates with Illinois Senator Stephen Douglas over slavery brought him national prominence and helped win him the Republican nomination for president in 1860. During the Civil War he made restoration of the Union his primary objective, but he also made it clear it must be a Union without slavery. On April 14, while attending a performance at Ford's Theatre in Washington, he was shot by actor John Wilkes Booth, a Confederate sympathizer. He died the next morning.

Questions to consider. Lincoln's second inaugural address is commonly regarded as one of the greatest addresses ever made by an American president. Why do you think this is so? What did he regard as the basic issue of the Civil War? What irony did he see in the attitude of the contestants? What use of the Bible did he make? Do you think this was likely to appeal to Americans in 1865?

Second Inaugural Address (1865)
Abraham Lincoln

FELLOW-COUNTRYMEN:—At this second appearing to take the oath of the presidential office there is less occasion for an extended address than there was at the first. Then a statement somewhat in detail of a course to be pursued seemed fitting and proper. Now, at the expiration of four years, during which public declarations have been constantly called forth on every point and phase of the great contest which still absorbs the attention and engrosses the energies of the nation, little that is new could be presented. The progress of our arms, upon which all else chiefly depends, is as well known to the public as to myself, and it is, I trust, reasonably satisfactory and encouraging to all. With high hope for the future, no prediction in regard to it is ventured.

On the occasion corresponding to this four years ago all thoughts were anxiously directed to an impending civil war. All dreaded it, all sought to avert it. While the inaugural address was being delivered from this place, devoted altogether to *saving* the Union without war, insurgent agents were in the city seeking to *destroy* it without war—seeking to dissolve the Union and

From James D. Richardson, ed., **A Compilation of the Messages and Papers of the Presidents** (Government Printing Office, Washington, D.C., 1897–1907), VIII: 3477–3478.

divide effects by negotiation. Both parties deprecated war, but one of them would *make* war rather than let the nation survive, and the other would *accept* war rather than let it perish, and the war came.

One eighth of the whole population was colored slaves, not distributed generally over the Union, but localized in the southern part of it. These slaves constituted a peculiar and powerful interest. All knew that this interest was somehow the cause of the war. To strengthen, perpetuate, and extend this interest was the object for which the insurgents would rend the Union even by war, while the Government claimed no right to do more than to restrict the territorial enlargement of it. Neither party expected for the war the magnitude nor the duration which it has already attained. Neither anticipated that the *cause* of the conflict might cease with or even before the conflict itself should cease. Each looked for an easier triumph, and a result less fundamental and astounding. Both read the same Bible and pray to the same God, and each invokes His aid against the other. It may seem strange that any men should dare to ask a just God's assistance in wringing their bread from the sweat of other men's faces, but let us judge not, that we be not judged. The prayers of both could not be answered. That of neither has been answered fully. The Almighty has His own purposes. "Woe unto the world because of offenses; for it must needs be that offenses come, but woe to that man by whom the offense cometh." If we shall suppose that American slavery is one of those offenses which, in the providence of God, must needs come, but which, having continued through His appointed time, He now wills to remove, and that He gives to both North and South this terrible war as the woe due to those by whom the offense came, shall we discern therein any departure from those divine attributes which the believers in a living God always ascribe to Him? Fondly do we hope, fervently do we pray, that this mighty scourge of war may speedily pass away. Yet, if God wills that it continue until all the wealth piled by the bondsman's two hundred and fifty years of unrequited toil shall be sunk, and until every drop of blood drawn with the lash shall be paid by another drawn with the sword, as was said three thousand years ago, so still it must be said, "The judgments of the Lord are true and righteous altogether."

With malice toward none, with charity for all, with firmness in the right as God gives us to see the right, let us strive on to finish the work we are in, to bind up the nation's wounds, to care for him who shall have borne the battle and for his widow and his orphan, to do all which may achieve and cherish a just and lasting peace among ourselves and with all nations.

2.

A HELPING HAND

The Thirteenth Amendment, which became part of the Constitution in 1865, freed about four million slaves in the South. But with freedom came uncertainty, insecurity, and perplexity. Unlike the peasants of France and Russia, who stayed on the land on which they had been working when they were freed from serfdom, the former American slaves were cast adrift at the end of the Civil War with no means of livelihood. They found themselves without property, legal rights, education, training, and any experience as independent farmers or laborers. Thousands began roaming the countryside looking for work and ways to survive. The first year of freedom brought hunger, disease, suffering, and death.

The freedmen did receive some assistance from the federal government after the war. In March 1865, Congress established the Bureau of Refugees, Freedmen, and Abandoned Lands (commonly called the Freedmen's Bureau) to provide them with food, clothing, shelter, and medical aid. Under the direction of General Oliver O. Howard (the "Christian General"), the Freedmen's Bureau also established schools and colleges for young blacks, founded savings banks, set up courts to protect their civil rights, and tried to get them jobs and fair contracts of employment. During its seven years of existence (1865–1872), the bureau spent more than fifteen million dollars for food and other aid and over six million dollars on schools and educational work, and gave medical attention to nearly half a million patients. Bureau agents also registered black voters and encouraged political participation. The hostility of Southern whites and the growing indifference of whites in the North, however, negated much of the bureau's work.

The report excerpted below was written by Colonel Eliphalet Whittlesey, assistant bureau commissioner for North Carolina, in October 1865. Whittlesey later became a general and moved to Washington, where he served as a trustee of the national Freedman's Savings Bank. In North Carolina where blacks made up only a third of the population and therefore only a third of the potential voters, the Republican party and the national government soon began to lose political control. By 1871 the white Democratic party once again controlled the state, ending Reconstruction there.

Questions to consider. Southern whites argued repeatedly that the fundamental objective of the Freedmen's Bureau was not to help the needy but to punish its foes by transforming Southern racial and economic relations. Does Whittlesey's report support this contention? Who received federal assistance in 1865? On what grounds was assistance given? Who made the decisions? What staff was available to the bureau? In what ways did Whittlesey sound like the commander of an occupying army? Of the bureau's four goals, which did he seem to feel were most urgent? Do you agree with his priorities? Was he genuinely committed to them? Was he optimistic? Which of its goals was the bureau most likely to achieve in the short run? In the long run?

Report on the Freedmen's Bureau (1865)

On the 22d of June I arrived at Raleigh with instructions from you to take the control of all subjects relating to "refugees, freedmen, and the abandoned lands" within this State. I found these subjects in much confusion. Hundreds of white refugees and thousands of blacks were collected about this and other towns, occupying every hovel and shanty, living upon government rations, without employment and without comfort, many dying for want of proper food and medical supplies. A much larger number, both white and black, were crowding into the towns, and literally swarming about every depot of supplies to receive their rations. My first effort was to reduce this class of suffering and idle humanity to order, and to discover how large a proportion of these applicants were really deserving of help. The whites, excepting "loyal refugees," were referred to the military authorities. To investigate the condition of refugees and freedmen and minister to the wants of the destitute, I saw at once would require the services of a large number of efficient officers. As fast as suitable persons could be selected, application was made to the department and district commanders for their detail, in accordance with General Order No. 102, War Department, May 31, 1865. In many cases these applications were unsuccessful because the officers asked for could not be spared. The difficulties and delays experienced in obtaining the help needed for a proper organization of my work will be seen from the fact that upon thirty-four written requests, in due form, only eleven officers have been detailed by the department and district commanders. . . .

With this brief history of my efforts to organize the bureau, I proceed to state

From **Report of the Joint Committee on Reconstruction,** 1st Session, 39th Congress (Government Printing Office, Washington, D.C., 1866), II: 186–192.

The Design and Work Proposed

In my circulars Nos. 1 and 2 (copies of which are herewith enclosed) the objects to be attained are fully stated. All officers of the bureau are instructed—

1. To aid the destitutes, yet in such a way as not to encourage dependence.
2. To protect freedmen from injustice.
3. To assist freedmen in obtaining employment and fair wages for their labor.
4. To encourage education, intellectual and moral.

Under these four divisions the operations of the bureau can best be presented.

Relief Afforded

It was evident at the outset that large numbers were drawing rations who might support themselves. The street in front of the post commissary's office was blocked up with vehicles of all the descriptions peculiar to North Carolina, and with people who had come from the country around, in some instances from a distance of sixty miles, for government rations. These were destitute whites, and were supplied by order of the department commander. Our own headquarters, and every office of the bureau, was besieged from morning till night by freedmen, some coming many miles on foot, others in wagons and carts. The rations issued would scarcely last till they reached home, and in many instances they were sold before leaving the town, in exchange for luxuries. To correct these evils, orders were issued that no able-bodied man or woman should receive supplies, except such as were known to be industrious, and to be entirely destitute. Great care was needed to protect the bureau from imposition, and at the same time to relieve the really deserving. By constant inquiry and effort the throng of beggars was gradually removed. The homeless and helpless were gathered in camps, where shelter and food could be furnished, and the sick collected in hospitals, where they could receive proper care. . . .

Protection

Regarding this bureau as the appointed instrument for redeeming the solemn pledge of the nation, through its Chief Magistrate, to secure the rights of freedmen, I have made every effort to protect them from wrong. Suddenly set free, they were at first exhilarated by the air of liberty, and committed some excesses. To be sure of their freedom, many thought they must leave the old scenes of oppression and seek new homes. Others regarded the property accumulated by their labor as in part their own, and demanded a share of it. On the other hand, the former masters, suddenly stripped of their wealth, at first looked upon the freedmen with a mixture of hate and fear. In these circumstances some collisions were inevitable. The negroes were complained of as idle, insolent, and dishonest; while they complained that they were treated with more cruelty than when they were slaves. Some were tied up and whipped without trial; some were driven from their homes without pay for their labor, without clothing or means of support; others were forbidden to leave on pain of death, and a few were shot or otherwise murdered. All officers of the bureau were directed, in accordance with your circular No. 5, to investigate these difficulties between the two classes, to settle them by counsel and arbitration as far as possible, to punish light offences by fines or otherwise, and to report more serious cases of crime to the military authorities for trial. The exact number of cases heard and decided cannot be given; they have been so numerous that no complete record could be kept; one officer reported that he had heard and disposed of as many as 180 complaints in a single day. The method pursued may be best presented by citing a few cases and the action thereon. From the report of Captain James, for August, I quote the following:

"I forward to you, in his own language, a report of a case which occurred in Gates county, on the northern border of the State, far away from any influence of troops, and where the military power of the government had been little felt. No doubt it illustrates others in similar localities far from garrisons and northern influences. The report will repay perusal, and appears to have been managed with admirable tact on the part of Captain Hill. Reports had reached me of the way in which David Parker, of Gates county, treated his colored people, and I determined to ascertain for myself their truth. Accordingly, last Monday, August 20, accompanied by a guard of six men from this post, (Elizabeth City,) I proceeded to his residence, about forty miles distant. He is very wealthy. I ascertained, after due investigation, and after convincing his colored people that I was really their friend, that the worst reports in regard to him were true. He had twenty-three negroes on his farm, large and small. Of these, fourteen were fieldhands; they all bore unmistakable evidence of the way they had been worked; very much undersized, rarely exceeding, man or women, 4 feet 6 inches—men and women of thirty and forty years of age looking like boys and girls. It has been his habit for years to work them from sunrise to sunset, and often long after, only stopping one hour for dinner—food always cooked for them to save time. He had, and has had for many years, an old colored man, one-eyed and worn out in the service, for an overseer or 'over-looker,' as he called himself. In addition, he has two sons at home, one of whom has made it a point to be with them all summer long—not so much to superintend as to drive. The old colored overseer always went behind the gang with a cane or whip, and woe betide the unlucky wretch who did not continually do his part; he had been brought up to work, and had not the least pity for any one who could not work as well as he.

"Mr. Parker told me that he had hired his people for the season: that directly after the surrender of General Lee he called them up and told them they were free; that he was better used to them than to others, and would prefer hiring them; that he would give them board and two suits of clothing to stay with him till the 1st day of January, 1866, and one Sunday suit at the end of that time; that they consented willingly—in fact, preferred to remain with him, &c. But from his people I learned that though he did call them up, as stated, yet when one of them demurred at the offer his son James flew at him and cuffed and kicked him; that after that they were all 'perfectly willing to stay'; they were watched night and day; that Bob, one of the men, had been kept chained nights; that they were actually afraid to try to get away. There was no complaint of the food nor much of the clothing, but they were in constant terror of the whip. Only three days before my arrival, Bob had been stripped in the field and given fifty lashes for hitting Adam, the colored over-looker, while James Parker stood by with a gun, and told him to run if he wanted to, he had a gun there. About four weeks before, four of them who went to church and returned before sunset were treated to twenty-five lashes each. Some were beaten or whipped almost every day. Having ascertained these and other similar facts, I directed him to call them up and pay them for the first of May last up to the present time. I investigated each case, taking into consideration age, family, physical condition, &c., estimating their work from $8 down, and saw him pay them off then and there, allowing for clothing and medical bill. I then arrested him and his two sons, and brought them here, except Dr. Joseph Parker, whose sister is very sick, with all the colored people I thought necessary as witnesses, intending to send them to Newbern for trial. But on account of the want of immediate transportation I concluded to release them on their giving a bond in the sum of $2,000 to Colonel E. Whittlesey, assistant commissioner for the State of North Carolina, and to his successors in office, conditioned as follows:

"That whereas David Parker and James Parker have heretofore maltreated their colored people, and have enforced the compulsory system instead of the free labor system: Now, therefore, if they, each of them, shall hereafter well and kindly treat, and cause to be treated, the hired laborers under their or his charge, and shall adopt the free labor system in lieu of the compulsory system, then this bond to be void and of no effect; otherwise to remain in full force and effect, with good security."

Lieutenant Colonel Clapp, superintendent central district, reports three cases of cruel beating, which have been investigated, and the offenders turned over to the military authorities for trial; besides very many instances of defrauding freedmen of their wages.

From the reports of Major Wickersham, superintendent of southern district, I quote the following:

"August 25.—A. S. Miller, Bladen county, states that Henry Miller (colored) neglects to support his family. Action: required Henry Miller to use his wages for the support of his wife and children, who have no claims on their former master, and can look to no one else than the husband and father for support.

"27th.—Betsy Powell (colored) states that Mrs. Frank Powell, Columbus county, has driven her away without pay for her labor. Gave letter to Mrs. Powell directing her to pay Betsy for her labor since April 27, 1865.

"29th.—Len Shiner (colored) states that he made an agreement with Mr. David Russell, of Robeson county, to work and gather his crop, for which he was to receive subsistence and one-third of the crop, when gathered. Mr. Russell has driven him off and refuses to pay. Wrote to Mr. Russell directing him to comply with terms of agreement, or furnish satisfactory reasons for not doing so. These are but examples of hundreds of complaints heard and acted upon by Major Wickersham and other officers in the southern district."

The following cases are taken from the report of Captain Barritt, assistant commissioner, at Charlotte:

"Morrison Miller charged with whipping a girl Hannah (colored.) Found guilty. Action: ordered to pay said Hannah fifty bushels of corn towards supporting herself and children, two of said children being the offspring of Miller.

"Wm. Wallace charged with whipping Martha (colored.) Plead guilty. Action: fined said Wallace $15, with assurance that if the above offence was repeated, the fine would be doubled.

"Council Best attempts to defraud six families of their summer labor, by offering to sell at auction the crop on his leased plantation. Action: sent military force and stopped the sale until contract with laborers was complied with."

A hundred pages of similar reports might be copied, showing, on the one side, that many freedmen need the presence of some authority to enforce upon them their new duties; and on the other, that so far from being true that "there is no county in which a freedman can be imposed upon," there is no county in which he is not oftener wronged; and these wrongs increase just in proportion to their distance from United States authorities. There has been great improvement, during the quarter, in this respect. The efforts of the bureau to protect the freedmen have done much to restrain violence and injustice. Such efforts must be continued until civil government is fully restored, just laws enacted, or great suffering and serious disturbance will be the result.

Industry

Contrary to the fears and predictions of many, the great mass of colored people have remained quietly at work upon the plantations of their former masters during the entire summer. The crowds seen about the towns in the early part of the season had followed in the wake of the Union army, to escape from slavery. After hostilities ceased these refugees returned to their homes, so that but few vagrants can now be found. In truth, a much larger amount of vagrancy exists among the whites than among the blacks. It is the almost uniform report of officers of the bureau that freedmen are industrious.

The report is confirmed by the fact that out of a colored population of nearly 350,000 in the State, only about 5,000 are now receiving support from the government. Probably some others are receiving aid from kind-hearted men who have enjoyed the benefit of their services from childhood. To the general quiet and industry of this people there can be no doubt that the efforts of the bureau have contributed greatly. I have visited some of the larger towns, as Wilmington, Newbern, Goldsborough, and both by public addresses and private instructions counselled the freedmen to secure employment and maintain themselves. Captain James has made an extensive tour through the eastern district for the same purpose, and has exerted a most happy influence. Lieutenant Colonel Clapp has spent much of his time in visiting the county seats of the central district, and everywhere been listened to by all classes with deep interest. Other officers have done much good in this way. They have visited plantations, explained the difference between slave and free labor, the nature and the solemn obligation of contracts. The chief difficulty met with has been a want of confidence between the two parties. The employer, accustomed only to the system of compulsory labor, is slow to believe that he can secure fruitful services by the stimulus of wages. The laborer is unwilling to trust the promises of those for whom he had toiled all his days without pay; hence but few contracts for long periods have been effected. The bargains for the present year are generally vague, and their settlement as the crops are gathered in requires much labor. In a great majority of cases the landowners seem disposed to do justly, and even generously; and when this year's work is done, and the proceeds divided, it is hoped that a large number of freedmen will enter into contracts for the coming year. They will, however, labor much more cheerfully for money, with prompt and frequent payments, than for a share of the crop, for which they must wait twelve months. A large farmer in Pitt county hires hands by the job, and states that he never saw negroes work so well. Another in Lenoir county pays monthly, and is satisfied so far with the experiment of free labor. Another obstacle to long contracts was found in the impression which had become prevalent to some degree, *i.e.,* that lands were to be given to freedmen by the government. To correct this false impression I published a circular, No. 3, and directed all officers of the bureau to make it as widely known as possible. From the statistical reports enclosed, it will be seen that during the quarter 257 written contracts for labor have been prepared and witnessed; that the average rate of wages, when paid in money, is from $8 to $10 per month; that 128 farms are under the control of the bureau and cultivated for the benefit of freedmen; that 8,540 acres are under cultivation, and 6,102 are employed. Many of the farms were rented by agents of the treasury as abandoned lands, previous to the establishing of this bureau, and were transferred to us with the leases upon them. Nearly all have been restored to their owners, under the President's proclamation of amnesty, and our tenure of the few that remain is so uncertain that I have not deemed it prudent to set apart any for use of refugees and freedmen, in accordance with the act of Congress approved March 3, 1865. But many freedmen are taking this matter into their own hands, and renting lands from the owners for one or more years. . . .

I am also endeavoring to purchase or rent, for a long period, the lands upon which houses have been erected by freedmen, so that they may not lose

Former slave children at a Freedmen's Bureau school. The Freedmen's Bureau, created by Congress in March 1865 to help the former slaves adjust to freedom, provided emergency food and shelter at first. Later on it helped the freedmen obtain work, conducted military courts to hear complaints, established schools at both the elementary and college levels, and registered black voters. By 1872, when the bureau was abolished, it had spent more than $15 million in aiding the freedmen and had established many schools and colleges for educating blacks. (Valentine Museum, Cook Collection)

what has been expended. The most important local interest of this kind is the Trent river settlement. The village was carefully laid out by Captain James, and now contains a population of nearly 3,000, all but about 300 self-supporting. "Although," says Captain James, "in interest a part of the city of Newbern, it lies outside of the corporate limits, and therefore came under no municipal regulations." I therefore issued an order erecting it into a separate municipality. I imposed a small tax upon the trades and occupations of the people, and a very moderate ground rent upon the lots, to raise a fund for meeting the necessary expenses of maintaining the settlement. They pay these sums with pleasure, deeming them an evidence of citizenship. From the fund thus raised the superintendent, assistant superintendent, a clerk, six nurses in hospital, and some fifteen mechanics and laborers employed about the settlement, are paid. A good market is now nearly completed, the stalls of which have been taken up beforehand at high rates. It needs only the power to sell these people their lots of land to induce them to put more permanent improvements on them. The settlement, as such, is by all confessed to be well ordered, quiet, healthy, and better regulated than the city proper.

Education

The quarter has been one of vacation rather than active work in this department. Still some progress has been made, and much done to prepare for the coming autumn and winter. Rev. F. A. Fiske, a Massachusetts teacher, has been appointed superintendent of education, and has devoted himself with energy to his duties. From his report it will be seen that the whole number of schools, during the whole or any part of the quarter, is 63, the number of teachers 85, and the number of scholars 5,624. A few of the schools are self-supporting, and taught by colored teachers, but the majority are sustained by northern societies and northern teachers. The officers of the bureau have, as far as practicable, assigned buildings for their use, and assisted in making them suitable; but the time is nearly past when such facilities can be given. The societies will be obliged hereafter to pay rent for school-rooms and for teachers' homes. The teachers are engaged in a noble and self-denying work. They report a surprising thirst for knowledge among the colored people—children giving earnest attention and learning rapidly, and adults, after the day's work is done, devoting the evening to study. In this connexion it may be mentioned, as a result of moral instruction, that 512 marriages have been reported and registered, and 42 orphans provided with good homes.

3.

KLANSMEN OF THE CAROLINAS

Reconstruction developed in a series of moves and countermoves. In a white Southern backlash to Union victory and emancipation came the "black codes" for coercing black laborers and President Andrew Johnson's pardon of Confederate landowners. Then in a Northern backlash to these codes and pardons came the Civil Rights bills, the sweeping Reconstruction Acts of 1867, and the Fourteenth and Fifteenth Amendments, all designed to guarantee black political rights. White Southerners reacted to these impositions in turn with secret night-time terrorist or "night rider" organizations designed to shatter Republican political power. Congress tried to protect Republican voters and the freedmen with the Force Acts of 1870 allowing the use of the army to prevent physical assaults, but Northern willingness to commit troops and resources to the struggle was waning. By the mid-1870s only three states remained in Republican hands, and within three years racist Democrats controlled these, too. The night riders had turned the tide.

Although numerous secret societies for whites appeared in the Reconstruction South—including the Order of the White Camelia (Louisiana), the Pale Faces (Tennessee), the White Brotherhood (North Carolina), and the Invisible Circle (South Carolina)—the largest and most influential society, and the one that spawned these imitators, was the Ku Klux Klan, the so-called Invisible Empire. The Klan began in Tennessee in 1866 as a young men's social club with secret costumes and rituals similar to those of the Masons, the Odd-Fellows, and other popular societies. In 1867, however, following passage of the Reconstruction Acts, anti-Republican racists began to see the usefulness of such a spookily secret order, and the Klan was reorganized to provide for "dens," "provinces" (counties), and "realms" (states), all under the authority of a "Grand Wizard," who in 1867 was believed to have been Nathan B. Forrest, a former slave trader and Confederate general.

The Klan structure was probably never fully established because of the disorganized conditions of the postwar South. Other societies with different names emerged, and the Reconstruction-era "Ku-Klux" may have disbanded as a formal entity in the early 1870s. But it clearly survived in spirit and in loosely formed groups, continuing to terrorize Republicans and their allies among the newly enfranchised freedmen into the 1870s and sowing fear among the black families who composed, after all, the labor force on which the white planters still depended. The excerpt reprinted below includes congressional testimony by David

Schenck, a member of the North Carolina Klan seeking to portray it in the best possible light, followed by testimony from Elias Hill, a South Carolina black man victimized by a local "den" of the Klan. Schenck and Hill were testifying before a joint Senate-House committee concerned with anti-black terrorism.

Questions to consider. The oath taken by David Schenck emphasizes the Klan's religious, constitutional, and benevolent qualities, whereas Elias Hill's story reveals its terrorist features. Are there elements in the Klan oath that seem to hint at or justify the use of violence? Why does the oath contain the phrases "original purity," "pecuniary embarrassments," and "traitor's doom"? What "secrets of this order" could deserve death? Klansmen later claimed that because they could terrorize the superstitious freedmen simply by using masks, odd voices, and ghostly sheets, no real violence was necessary. Opponents have claimed, on the other hand, that Klansmen were basically sadists acting out sexual phobias and deep paranoia. What light does Elias Hill's testimony shed on these conflicting claims? What position did Hill seem to hold in the black community? Did the Klansmen seem to be assaulting him because of his condition or because of his position in the black community? Why did they ask Hill to pray for them? Would it be fair or accurate to call the Ku Klux Klan an example of a political terrorist organization that succeeded?

Report of the Joint Committee on Reconstruction (1872)

A select committee of the Senate, upon the 10th of March, 1871, made a report of the result of their investigation into the security of person and property in the State of North Carolina. . . . A sub-committee of their number proceeded to the State of South Carolina, and examined witnesses in that State until July 29. . . .

David Schenck, esq., a member of the bar of Lincoln County, North Carolina . . . was initiated in October, 1868, as a member of the Invisible Empire. . . . In his own words: "We were in favor of constitutional liberty as handed down to us by our forefathers. I think the idea incorporated was that we were opposed to the [fourteenth and fifteenth] amendments to the

From **Report of the Joint Select Committee to Inquire into the Condition of Affairs in the Late Insurrectionary States** (Government Printing Office, Washington, D.C., 1872), 25–27, 44–47.

Constitution. I desire to explain in regard to that that it was not to be—at least, I did not intend by that that it should be—forcible resistance, but a political principle."

The oath itself is as follows:

I, (name,) before the great immaculate Judge of heaven and earth, and upon the Holy Evangelist of Almighty God, do, of my own free will and accord, subscribe to the following sacred, binding obligation:

I. I am on the side of justice and humanity and constitutional liberty, as bequeathed to us by our forefathers in its original purity.

II. I reject and oppose the principles of the radical [Republican] party.

III. I pledge aid to a brother of the Ku-Klux Klan in sickness, distress, or pecuniary embarrassments. Females, friends, widows, and their households shall be the special objects of my care and protection.

IV. Should I ever divulge, or cause to be divulged, any of the secrets of this order, or any of the foregoing obligations, I must meet with the fearful punishment of death and traitor's doom, which is death, death, death, at the hands of the brethren. . . .

Elias Hill of York County, South Carolina, is a remarkable character. He is crippled in both legs and arms, which are shriveled by rheumatism; he cannot walk, cannot help himself . . .; was in early life a slave, whose freedom was purchased by his father. . . . He learned his letters and to read by calling the school children into the cabin as they passed, and also learned to write. He became a Baptist preacher, and after the war engaged in teaching colored children, and conducted the business correspondence of many of his colored neighbors. . . . We put the story of his wrongs in his own language:

"On the night of the 5th of May, after I had heard a great deal of what they had done in that neighborhood, they came . . . to my brother's door, which is in the same yard, and broke open the door and attacked his wife, and I heard her screaming and mourning. I could not understand what they said, for they were talking in an outlandish and unnatural tone, which I had heard they generally used at a negro's house. They said, 'Where's Elias?' She said, 'He doesn't stay here; yon is his house.' I had heard them strike her five or six licks. Someone then hit my door. . . .

"They carried me into the yard between the houses, my brother's and mine, and put me on the ground. . . . 'Who did that burning? Who burned our houses?' I told them it was not me. I could not burn houses. Then they hit me with their fists, and said I did it, I ordered it. They went on asking me didn't I tell the black men to ravish all the white women. No, I answered them. They struck me again. . . . 'Haven't you been preaching and praying about the Ku-Klux? Haven't you been preaching political sermons? Doesn't a [Republican Party newspaper] come to your house? Haven't you written letters?' Generally one asked me all the questions, but the rest were squatting over me—some six men I counted as I lay there. . . . I told them if they would

A visit of the Ku Klux Klan.   This popular drawing from the early 1870s renders its black subjects with exaggerated, stereotyped features. But the one-room cabin—small, sparsely furnished, with food dangling from the ceiling—rings true to life. The illustrator effectively captured the aura of invasion without warning and the startled terror that accompanied Ku Klux Klan raids. These succeeded so well partly because they reached directly into black homes in this way. Faced with assaults on their children as well as themselves and lacking weaponry and military or police protection, the freedmen eventually buckled to Klan terror, although total segregation and disfranchisement did not take place until the 1890s. (Library of Congress)

take me back into the house, and lay me in the bed, which was close adjoining my books and papers, I would try and get it. They said I would never go back to that bed, for they were going to kill me. . . . They caught my leg and pulled me over the yard, and then left me there, knowing I could not walk nor crawl. . . .

"After they had stayed in the house for a considerable time, they came back to where I lay and asked if I wasn't afraid at all. They pointed pistols at me all around my head once or twice, as if they were going to shoot me. . . . One caught me by the leg and hurt me, for my leg for forty years has been drawn each year, more and more, and I made moan when it hurt so. One said, 'G-d d—n it, hush!' He had a horsewhip, [and] I reckon he struck me eight cuts right on the hip bone; it was almost the only place he could hit my body, my legs are so short. They all had disguises. . . . One of them then took a strap, and buckled it around my neck and said, 'Let's take him to the river and drown him.' . . .

"Then they said, 'Look here! Will you put a card in the paper to renounce all republicanism? Will you quit preaching?' I told them I did not know. I said that to save my life. . . . They said if I did not they would come back the next week and kill me. [After more licks with the strap] one of them went into the house where my brother and sister-in-law lived, and brought her to pick me up. As she stooped down to pick me up one of them struck her, and as she was carrying me into the house another struck her with a strap. . . . They said, 'Don't you pray against Ku-Klux, but pray that God may forgive Ku-Klux. Pray that God may bless and save us.' I was so chilled with cold lying out of doors so long and in such pain I could not speak to pray, but I tried to, and they said that would do very well, and all went out of the house. . . ."

Satisfied that he could no longer live in that community, Hill wrote to make inquiry about the means of going to Liberia. Hearing this, many of his neighbors desired to go also. . . . Others are still hoping for relief, through the means of this sub-committee.

4.

THE GREAT RETREAT

During the election of 1876 both parties resorted to fraud. Two sets of electoral returns came in from Southern states still occupied by federal troops, and it was necessary for Congress to set up an electoral commission to decide whether Rutherford B. Hayes, the Republican candidate, or Samuel J. Tilden, the Democratic standard-bearer, had won. Seven commission members were Republicans and seven were Democrats. The fifteenth member was to have been an independent, but as it turned out, he voted with the Republicans. By a strict party vote of 8 to 7, the commission awarded all 20 of the disputed electoral votes to the Republicans, and Hayes became president with 185 votes to Tilden's 184. Most Democrats felt they had been cheated out of victory; some of them even talked of rejecting the commission's decision and trying to block Hayes's inauguration. Had they done so, the quarrel over the election would have continued far beyond Inauguration Day, with grave consequences for the nation.

In the end, Southern Democrats reached a compromise with Northern Republicans. At a series of secret meetings between party leaders the Southern Democrats agreed to accept the electoral commission's decision. In return, the Republicans promised that Hayes would withdraw the remaining federal troops from the South, appoint at least one Southerner to his cabinet, and see to it that the South received federal aid to promote industrialization. The Compromise of 1877 brought the crisis to an end, and Hayes became the new president. After his inauguration in March 1877, Hayes took prompt action to fulfill the promises made to the Southern Democrats: he appointed a Tennessee Democrat to his cabinet, he withdrew the last of the federal soldiers from the South, and he began supporting federal-aid bills to benefit the South. The withdrawal of federal troops from Louisiana and South Carolina in April 1877 led to the demise of Republican governments in the South and the end of Reconstruction.

In his first annual message to Congress in December 1877, Hayes recalled the 1876 crisis and expressed satisfaction that it had been peacefully resolved. He also reminded Congress of the plea he had made at his inauguration that love of country would mute the racial and sectional tensions agitating the nation. He went on to mention his efforts to reduce antagonisms between North and South and ventured the opinion that they had had "beneficent results." He was especially pleased with the consequences of ending military reconstruction. Returning the

Southern states to local self-government had ended political turmoil and lawlessness there, he declared, and had produced a general restoration of order and "the orderly administration of justice." He did not mention the freedmen.

Hayes was born in Delaware, Ohio, in 1822. After he was graduated from Kenyon College, he studied law at Harvard and later established a successful law practice in Cincinnati. When the Civil War came, he joined a volunteer unit, rising to the rank of brevet major-general. He was wounded several times in action. After the war he served two terms in Congress, supporting Radical Reconstruction measures over President Johnson's veto and voting for Johnson's impeachment. He went on to serve as governor of Ohio and was elected to that office three times. In the Republican convention of 1876 he was a dark horse; he did not receive the presidential nomination until the seventh ballot. Though his presidency was generally undistinguished, he did please bankers by his sound money policies, and civil service reformers by his efforts to combat the spoils system. After leaving the White House he quickly dropped into obscurity. He died in 1893.

Questions to consider. Some Northern Democrats bitterly resented the electoral commission's decision for Hayes. They called him His Fraudulency, the Usurper, and Ruther-fraud B. Hayes. Was Hayes's first annual message to Congress, reproduced here, likely to win them over? To what "recent amendments" to the Constitution was he referring? What actions to restore national harmony did he emphasize? What policies did he fail to mention?

═══════

First Annual Message to Congress (1877)
Rutherford B. Hayes

To complete and make permanent the pacification of the country continues to be, and until it is fully accomplished must remain, the most important of all our national interests. The earnest purpose of good citizens generally to unite their efforts in this endeavor is evident. It found decided expression in the resolutions announced in 1876 by the national conventions of the leading political parties of the country. There was a widespread apprehension that the

From James D. Richardson, ed., **A Compilation of the Messages and Papers of the Presidents** (Government Printing Office, Washington, D.C., 1897–1907), IX: 4394–4397.

"Great Acrobatic Feat of Rutherford B. Hayes."   Hayes had a difficult acrobatic act to perform if he was to succeed as president. It had taken an Electoral Commission set up by Congress to declare him a winner by one electoral vote over Samuel J. Tilden, even though he won fewer popular votes than Tilden. Even after his inauguration on March 4, 1877, some people continued to jeer at him as "His Fraudulency" and "Ruther-fraud B. Hayes." As president, Hayes had to show people he was determined to end the graft and corruption that had discredited the Grant administration. He did reasonably well: he appointed reformers to his cabinet, launched a cleanup of the civil service, and removed several notorious spoilsmen from office. But while he was president, the Republican party for all practical purposes abandoned the cause of civil rights for blacks. (Library of Congress)

momentous results in our progress as a nation marked by the recent amendments to the Constitution were in imminent jeopardy; that the good understanding which prompted their adoption, in the interest of a loyal devotion to the general welfare, might prove a barren truce, and that the two sections of the country, once engaged in civil strife, might be again almost as widely severed and disunited as they were when arrayed in arms against each other.

The course to be pursued, which, in my judgment, seemed wisest in the presence of this emergency, was plainly indicated in my inaugural address. It pointed to the time, which all our people desire to see, when a genuine love of our whole country and of all that concerns its true welfare shall supplant the destructive forces of the mutual animosity of races and of sectional hostility. Opinions have differed widely as to the measures best calculated to secure this great end. This was to be expected. The measures adopted by the Administration have been subjected to severe and varied criticism. Any course whatever which might have been entered upon would certainly have encountered distrust and opposition. These measures were, in my judgment, such as were most in harmony with the Constitution and with the genius of our people, and best adapted, under all the circumstances, to attain the end in view. Beneficent results, already apparent, prove that these endeavors are not to be regarded as a mere experiment, and should sustain and encourage us in our efforts. Already, in the brief period which has elapsed, the immediate effectiveness, no less than the justice, of the course pursued is demonstrated, and I have an abiding faith that time will furnish its ample vindication in the minds of the great majority of my fellow-citizens. The discontinuance of the use of the Army for the purpose of upholding local governments in two States of the Union was no less a constitutional duty and requirement, under the circumstances existing at the time, than it was a much-needed measure for the restoration of local self-government and the promotion of national harmony. The withdrawal of the troops from such employment was effected deliberately, and with solicitous care for the peace and good order of society and the protection of the property and persons and every right of all classes of citizens.

The results that have followed are indeed significant and encouraging. All apprehension of danger from remitting those States to local self-government is dispelled, and a most salutary change in the minds of the people has begun and is in progress in every part of that section of the country once the theater of unhappy civil strife, substituting for suspicion, distrust, and aversion, concord, friendship, and patriotic attachment to the Union. No unprejudiced mind will deny that the terrible and often fatal collisions which for several years have been of frequent occurrence and have agitated and alarmed the public mind have almost entirely ceased, and that a spirit of mutual forbearance and hearty national interest has succeeded. There has been a general reestablishment of order and of the orderly administration of justice. Instances of remaining lawlessness have become of rare occurrence; political turmoil and turbulence have disappeared; useful industries have been resumed; public credit in the Southern States has been greatly strengthened, and the encouraging benefits of a revival of commerce between the sections of the country lately embroiled in civil war are fully enjoyed. Such are some of the results already attained, upon which the country is to be congratulated. They are of such importance that we may with confidence patiently await the desired consummation that will surely come with the natural progress of events. . . .

5.

AFTERMATH

Frederick Douglass regarded the Declaration of Independence as a "watchword of freedom." But he was tempted to turn it to the wall, he said, because its human rights principles were so shamelessly violated. A former slave himself, Douglass knew what he was talking about. Douglass thought that enslaving blacks fettered whites as well and that the United States would never be truly free until it ended chattel slavery. During the Civil War, he had several conversations with Lincoln, urging him to make emancipation his major aim. He also put unremitting pressure on the Union army to accept black volunteers, and after resistance to admitting blacks into the army gave way, he toured the country encouraging blacks to enlist and imploring the government to treat black and white solders equally in matters of pay and promotion.

Douglass had great hopes for his fellow blacks after the Civil War. He demanded they be given full rights—political, legal, educational, and economic—as citizens. He also wanted to see the wall of separation between the races crumble and see "the colored people of this country, enjoying the same freedom [as whites], voting at the same ballot-box, using the same cartridge-box, going to the same schools, attending the same churches, travelling in the same street cars, in the same railroad cars, on the same steam-boats, proud of the same country, fighting the same war, and enjoying the same peace and all its advantages." He regarded the Republican party as the "party of progress, justice and freedom" and at election time took to the stump and rallied black votes for the party. He was rewarded for these services by appointment as marshal of the District of Columbia in 1877, as recorder of deeds for the District in 1881, and as minister to Haiti in 1889. But he was also asked by Republican leaders to keep a low profile, was omitted from White House guest lists, and was excluded from presidential receptions even though one duty of the District marshal was to introduce the guests at White House state occasions.

Douglass was puzzled and then upset by the increasing indifference of Republican leaders to conditions among blacks after the Civil War. In 1883 he attended a convention of blacks in Louisville, Kentucky, which met to discuss their plight and reaffirm their demand for full civil rights. In his keynote address, which is reprinted here, Douglass vividly portrayed the discrimination and persecution his people encountered, but he continued to believe that "prejudice, with all its malign accomplishments, may yet be removed by peaceful means."

Born into slavery in Maryland in 1817, Frederick Augustus Washington Bailey learned to read and write despite efforts to keep him illiterate. In 1838 he managed to escape to freedom and adopted the name Frederick Douglass. Shortly afterward he became associated with William Lloyd Garrison and developed into such an articulate spokesman for the antislavery cause that people doubted he had ever been a slave. In 1845 he published his **Narrative of the Life of Frederick Douglass, an American Slave,** naming names, places, dates, and precise events to convince people he had been born in bondage. Douglass continued to be an articulate spokesman for the black cause throughout his life. Shortly before his death in 1895 a college student asked him what a young black could do to help the cause. "Agitate! Agitate! Agitate!" Douglass is supposed to have told him.

Questions to consider. In the following address Douglass was speaking to a convention of blacks in Louisville, but his appeal was primarily to American whites. How did he try to convince them that blacks deserved the same rights and opportunities as all Americans? How powerful did he think the color line was? What outrages against his people did he report? What was his attitude toward the Republican party, which he had so faithfully served? Were the grievances he cited largely economic or were they social and political in nature?

―――――

Address to the Louisville Convention (1883)
Frederick Douglass

Born on American soil in common with yourselves, deriving our bodies and our minds from its dust, centuries having passed away since our ancestors were torn from the shores of Africa, we, like yourselves, hold ourselves to be in every sense Americans, and that we may, therefore, venture to speak to you in a tone not lower than that which becomes earnest men and American citizens. Having watered your soil with our tears, enriched it with our blood, performed its roughest labor in time of peace, defended it against enemies in time of war, and at all times been loyal and true to its best interests, we deem it no arrogance or presumption to manifest now a common concern with you for its welfare, prosperity, honor and glory. . . .

From Philip Foner, ed., **The Life and Writings of Frederick Douglass** (4 v., International Publishers, New York, 1955), IV: 373–392. Reprinted by permission.

It is our lot to live among a people whose laws, traditions, and prejudices have been against us for centuries, and from these they are not yet free. To assume that they are free from these evils simply because they have changed their laws is to assume what is utterly unreasonable and contrary to facts. Large bodies move slowly. Individuals may be converted on the instant and change their whole course of life. Nations never. Time and events are required for the conversion of nations. Not even the character of a great political organization can be changed by a new platform. It will be the same old snake though in a new skin. Though we have had war, reconstruction and abolition as a nation, we still linger in the shadow and blight of an extinct institution. Though the colored man is no longer subject to be bought and sold, he is still surrounded by an adverse sentiment which fetters all his movements. In his downward course he meets with no resistance, but his course upward is resented and resisted at every step of his progress. If he comes in ignorance, rags, and wretchedness, he conforms to the popular belief of his character, and in that character he is welcome. But if he shall come as a gentleman, a scholar, and a statesman, he is hailed as a contradiction to the national faith concerning his race, and his coming is resented as impudence. In the one case he may provoke contempt and derision, but in the other he is an affront to pride, and provokes malice. Let him do what he will, there is at present, therefore, no escape for him. The color line meets him everywhere, and in a measure shuts him out from all respectable and profitable trades and callings. In spite of all your religion and laws he is a rejected man.

He is rejected by trade unions, of every trade, and refused work while he lives, and burial when he dies, and yet he is asked to forget his color, and forget that which everybody else remembers. If he offers himself to a builder as a mechanic, to a client as a lawyer, to a patient as a physician, to a college as a professor, to a firm as a clerk, to a Government Department as an agent, or an officer, he is sternly met on the color line, and his claim to consideration in some way is disputed on the ground of color.

Not even our churches, whose members profess to follow the despised Nazarene, whose home, when on earth, was among the lowly and despised, have yet conquered this feeling of color madness, and what is true of our churches is also true of our courts of law. Neither is free from this all-pervading atmosphere of color hate. The one describes the Deity as impartial, no respecter of persons, and the other the Goddess of Justice as blindfolded, with sword by her side and scales in her hand held evenly between high and low, rich and low, white and black, but both are the images of American imagination, rather than American practices.

Taking advantage of the general disposition in this country to impute crime to color, white men *color* their faces to commit crime and wash off the hated color to escape punishment. In many places where the commission of crime is alleged against one of our color, the ordinary processes of law are set aside as too slow for the impetuous justice of the infuriated populace. They take the law into their own bloody hands and proceed to whip, stab, shoot, hang, or burn the alleged culprit, without the intervention of courts, counsel, judges, juries, or witnesses. In such cases it is not the business of the accusers to prove guilt, but it is for the accused to prove his innocence, a thing hard for him to do in these infernal Lynch courts. A man accused, surprised, frightened and captured by a motley crowd, dragged with a rope about his neck in midnight-darkness to the nearest tree, and told in the coarsest terms of profanity to prepare for death, would be more than human if he did not, in his terror-stricken appearance, more confirm suspicion of guilt than the contrary. Worse still, in the presence of such hell-black outrages, the pulpit is usually dumb, and the press in the neighborhood is silent or openly takes side with the mob. There are occasional cases in which white men are lynched, but one sparrow does not make a summer. Every one knows that what is called Lynch law is peculiarly the law for colored people and for nobody else. If there were no other grievance than this horrible and barbarous Lynch law custom, we should be justified in assembling, as we have now done, to expose and denounce it. But this is not all. Even now, after twenty years of so-called emancipation, we are subject to lawless raids of midnight riders, who, with blackened faces, invade our homes and perpetrate the foulest of crimes upon us and our families. This condition of things is too flagrant and notorious to require specifications or proof. Thus in all the relations of life and death we are met by the color line. We cannot ignore it if we would, and ought not if we could. It hunts us at midnight, it denies us accommodation in hotels and justice in the courts; excludes our children from schools, refuses our sons the chance to learn trades, and compels us to pursue only such labor as will bring the least reward. While we recognize the color line as a hurtful force, a mountain barrier to our progress, wounding our bleeding feet with its flinty rocks at every step, we do not despair. We are a hopeful people. This convention is a proof of our faith in you, in reason, in truth and justice—our belief that prejudice, with all its malign accomplishments, may yet be removed by peaceful means; that, assisted by time and events and the growing enlightenment of both races, the color line will ultimately become harmless. When this shall come it will then only be used, as it should be, to distinguish one variety of the human family from another. It will cease to have any civil, political, or moral significance, and colored conventions will then be dispensed with as anachronisms, wholly out of place, but not till then. Do not marvel that we are discouraged. The faith within us has a rational basis, and is confirmed by facts. When we consider how deep-seated this feeling against us is; the long centuries it has been forming; the forces of avarice which have been marshaled to sustain it; how the language and literature of the country have been pervaded with it; how the church, the press, the play-house, and other influences of the country have been arrayed in its support, the progress toward its extinction must be considered vast and wonderful. . . .

We do not believe, as we are often told, that the Negro is the ugly child of the national family, and the more he is kept out of sight the better it will

Frederick Douglass.   Douglass's greatest work came before and during the Civil War. One of the most eloquent and magnetic of all the abolitionist leaders, he contributed enormously to the antislavery cause. During the Civil War he pressed hard for the enlistment of blacks to fight in the Union armies on an equal footing with whites. After the war he continued his efforts for civil rights, including black suffrage. For his services to the Republican party he received appointments as secretary to the Santo Domingo commission, marshal and recorder of deeds for the District of Columbia, and U.S. minister to Haiti. (National Portrait Gallery, Smithsonian Institution, Washington, D.C.)

be for him. You know that liberty given is never so precious as liberty sought for and fought for. The man outraged is the man to make the outcry. Depend upon it, men will not care much for a people who do not care for themselves. Our meeting here was opposed by some of our members, because it would disturb the peace of the Republican party. The suggestion came from coward lips and misapprehended the character of that party. If the Republican party cannot stand a demand for justice and fair play, it ought to go down. We were men before that party was born, and our manhood is more sacred than any party can be. Parties were made for men, not men for parties.

The colored people of the South are the laboring people of the South. The labor of a country is the source of its wealth; without the colored laborer to-day the South would be a howling wilderness, given up to bats, owls, wolves, and bears. He was the source of its wealth before the war, and has been the source of its prosperity since the war. He almost alone is visible in her fields, with implements of toil in his hands, and laboriously using them to-day.

Let us look candidly at the matter. While we see and hear that the South is more prosperous than it ever was before and rapidly recovering from the waste of war, while we read that it raises more cotton, sugar, rice, tobacco, corn, and other valuable products than it ever produced before, how happens it, we sternly ask, that the houses of its laborers are miserable huts, that their clothes are rags, and their food the coarsest and scantiest? How happens it that the land-owner is becoming richer and the laborer poorer?

The implication is irresistible—that where the landlord is prosperous the laborer ought to share his prosperity, and whenever and wherever we find this is not the case there is manifestly wrong somewhere. . . .

Flagrant as have been the outrages committed upon colored citizens in respect to their civil rights, more flagrant, shocking, and scandalous still have been the outrages committed upon our political rights by means of bull-dozing and Kukluxing, Mississippi plans, fraudulent courts, tissue ballots, and the like devices. Three States in which the colored people outnumber the white population are without colored representation and their political voice suppressed. The colored citizens in those States are virtually disfranchised, the Constitution held in utter contempt and its provisions nullified. This has been done in the face of the Republican party and successive Republican administrations. . . .

This is no question of party. It is a question of law and government. It is a question whether men shall be protected by law, or be left to the mercy of cyclones of anarchy and bloodshed. It is whether the Government or the mob shall rule this land; whether the promises solemnly made to us in the constitution be manfully kept or meanly and flagrantly broken. Upon this vital point we ask the whole people of the United States to take notice that whatever of political power we have shall be exerted for no man of any party who will not, in advance of election, promise to use every power given him by the Government, State or National, to make the black man's path to the ballot-box as straight, smooth and safe as that of any other American citizen. . . .

We hold it to be self-evident that no class or color should be the exclusive rulers of this country. If there is such a ruling class, there must of course be a subject class, and when this condition is once established this Government of the people, by the people, and for the people, will have perished from the earth.

COUNTERPOINT I

Emancipation and Achievement

What did black Americans do with their freedom following emancipation? Most, naturally enough, remained on the land, the South being an agricultural section. Large numbers, however, exercised their newly gained freedom by streaming to the towns and cities of the region. How did these blacks fare? How did they organize themselves? Were the schools, economic measures, and labor standards of the new Freedmen's Bureau as crucial to black progress as supporters and officers of the bureau asserted?

Historians have long combed the testimony of bureau officials and the letters and statements of Southern whites and the ex-slaves themselves for evidence regarding post–Civil War conditions for blacks. Recently historians have also combed census records, court documents, trade figures, and the like for statistical evidence. Carl Osthaus has unearthed exciting material in the records of the Freedman's Savings Bank, a major initiative of the bureau itself. Congress chartered the bank in 1865, almost as soon as the war had ended. Headquartered in Washington, by 1871 the bank had established branches in towns all across the South; the branches together had $4 million in assets and sixty thousand depositors.

In records from 1867 of the Louisville, Kentucky, bank, one of the largest early branches, Osthaus has found (table A) some patterns that might be expected. All the Louisville depositors were blacks and about two-thirds were illiterate; a majority were men, farmers, and ex-slaves; about 55 percent (probably farmers) lived outside of town. But there are surprises, too. Eighty percent of the depositors were ex-soldiers, presumably in the Union army, which had mustered in Kentucky in 1861. Moreover, the opening deposits were not minuscule. Most were over $50 and a third were over $100, both significant amounts in the nineteenth century. Had the depositors somehow saved while they were still slaves? Had they earned that much since emancipation, possibly with help from the Freedmen's Bureau? Had they perhaps banked their military pay?

Partly with these questions in mind, Osthaus has also studied (table B) early records from the bank branch in Mobile, Alabama, in the Deep South, where the black population was larger than in border states like Kentucky and where fewer freedmen had been able to join the Union army. The occupations of depositors in the Mobile Branch, as it turns out, were indeed different. Although 63 were laborers (about

15 percent of the total number of depositors), possibly on farms, there were no farmers in the group and few soldiers. Most depositors were petty shopkeepers and skilled or service workers, and a few had professional standing—attorneys, clergymen, and teachers. The high totals of cooks, domestics, seamstresses, and washers indicate that there was probably a higher percentage of women investors than at the Louisville bank. The Mobile savers, therefore, were predominantly an urban wage-earning group with few visible ties to the countryside. Some may not have been ex-slaves. Women depositors may have been so numerous because they could find steady domestic work in this postwar town when men often could not.

The Louisville patterns reveal an encouraging development: the emergence of a new, male-dominant, black farming class able to save significant amounts. The Mobile figures reveal few, if any, similar ties to the countryside, where most ex-slaves lived. But Mobile was a port city that was unlikely to have many farmers. In the northern Alabama town of Huntsville (table C), where Osthaus has also studied bank records, the Louisville patterns reappear: a majority of the depositors during the three periods shown were illiterate male farmers, many of them ex-soldiers living outside of town. But the total percentage of ex-soldiers was lower than in Louisville (29 percent as opposed to 80 percent), and the non-agricultural percentage higher (over 50 percent compared with 34 percent). Also, the Huntsville figures extend into the 1870s, showing that the proportion of depositors who were male declines, as does the proportion who were rural and black. Soldiers vanish from the records almost entirely. As Huntsville moved further into the Reconstruction period, the figures indicate that Huntsville's depositors resembled Louisville's less and Mobile's more—diverse, perhaps, but also less connected to the section's vast rural population.

Do other Freedman's Savings Bank branches show the same configuration in the 1870s? In Charleston, South Carolina, another port city, the answer is definitely yes. A third of the Charleston depositors (table D.1) were women; almost three-fourths lived in town; and nine-tenths did nonagricultural work (all occupations other than farmers). Some whites used the Charleston bank, as did some children. One out of every three depositors could write, and a fair number, perhaps one in four, were over 40 years old. Charleston savers, then, were diverse, if poor, and they represented a broad urban base while retaining some connection to the black farm population—precisely what Congress had hoped for when it chartered the bank.

Not all new bank depositors were individuals. Some were societies and associations. It is in this list (table D.2), Osthaus argues, that the leadership and organizational impulses of the black community show most clearly. Of the 75 Charleston organizations with deposits, for example, at least 20 were religious, 12 insured against "sickness and death," and another 10 were "charitable"—proof that Charleston blacks were people of faith concerned with mutual assistance and benevolence of a type familiar in Northern immigrant communities. There were also occupational and business groups, political and veterans' associations, and women's societies. The list attests, in fact, to a remarkably rich associational life among urban freedmen. It suggests, too, that the community's real leaders were the churches and ministers and not (with some exceptions) farmers, workers, or entrepreneurs. Whatever the nature of the societies, moreover, the depositors all trusted their money to the bank.

Unfortunately, this confidence was misplaced. In the mid-1870s a combination of economic depression, bad loans, and graft in the national headquarters had driven the Freedman's Savings Bank into bankruptcy. When the bank vanished, so did the meager savings of thousands of its depositors. In this way a Freedmen's Bureau initiative that provided genuine service in the short run eventually led to economic disaster.

A. Description of Every Tenth Louisville Depositor, 1867

Characteristics	Number	Percentage
Sex		
Male	45	88%
Female	6	12
Ability to write name		
Signature	4	8
Weak signature	1	2
Signed with an "X"	34	67
Unknown	12	23
Race		
Negro	51	100
Caucasian	0	0
Unknown	0	0
Residence		
Louisville	19	37
Non-Louisville	28	55
Unknown	4	8
Status at birth		
Slave	26	51
Freeborn	1	2
Unknown	24	47
Military experience		
Soldiers	41	80
Nonsoldiers	6	12
Unknown	4	8
Occupation (1866–1867) (32 only)		
Farmers	21	66
Laborers	3	
Servants	3	
Waiters	1	34
Teamsters	2	
Boatmen	1	
Ministers	1	
Amount of opening deposit in dollars (1866–1867) (28 only)		
$0–50	5	
51–100	12	
101–150	6	
151–200	4	
201–250	1	
251 +		

SOURCE: From Carl R. Osthaus, *Freedmen, Philanthropy, and Fraud: A History of the Freedman's Savings Bank* (University of Illinois Press, Urbana, 1976), pp. 114–119. Copyright © 1976 by the Board of Trustees of the University of Illinois.

B. Occupations of Persons for Whom Accounts Were Opened in the Mobile Bank, January 1, 1866–April 15, 1867

Agents	1	Cotton weighers	5	Sextons	2
Attorneys	2	Domestics	28	Shoemakers	2
Bakers	3	Draymen	24	Shopkeepers	4
Barbers	12	Gardeners	5	Slaters	1
Blacksmiths	1	Grocers	14	Stewards	2
Boatmen	16	Hairdressers	3	Stonecutters	1
Bootblacks	1	Janitors	4	Tailors	5
Butchers	2	Laborers	63	Teachers	4
Carpenters	21	Machinists	1	Tinners	3
Cartmen	5	Masons	12	Undertakers	2
Clergymen	1	Millers	1	Varnishers	1
Clerks	1	Nurses	2	Washers	26
Coachmen	6	Ostlers	2	Societies	13
Compositors	2	Oystermen	2		
Cooks	29	Painters	2	No occupation	
Coopers	2	Porters	4	(married	
Cotton markers	6	Printers	1	women,	
Cotton pressmen	3	Saddlers	Unknown	minors, etc.)	122
Cotton samplers	2	Seamstresses	17	Soldiers	11
				Total	505

SOURCE: From Carl R. Osthaus, *Freedmen, Philanthropy, and Fraud: A History of the Freedman's Savings Bank* (University of Illinois Press, Urbana, 1976), pp. 114–119. Copyright © 1976 by the Board of Trustees of the University of Illinois.

C. Description of Every Tenth Huntsville Depositor, Selected Periods

Characteristics	Number 1867–68	1869–70	1872–73	Total	Percentage
Sex					
Male	18	46	18	82	85%
Female	0	7	7	14	15
Ability to write name					
Signature	2	11	4	17	18
Weak signature	4	1	4	9	9
Signed with an "X"	11	36	17	64	67
Unknown	1	5	0	6	6
Race					
Negro	17	50	21	88	92
Caucasian	1	2	3	6	6
Unknown	0	1	1	2	2
Residence					
Huntsville	5	25	16	46	48
Non-Huntsville	12	26	9	47	49
Unknown	1	2	0	3	3
Age					
1–10	0	1	1	2	2
11–15	0	1	3	4	4
16–19	0	3	2	5	5
20–29	4	18	6	28	29
30–39	6	10	4	20	21
40–49	1	8	5	14	15
50–59	2	8	3	13	14
60–69	0	1	0	1	1
70+	0	1	1	2	2
Unknown	5	2	0	7	7
Military experience					
Soldiers	10	18	0	28	29
Nonsoldiers	0	7	10	17	18
Unknown	8	28	15	51	53
Occupation					
Professional and white collar				6	6.3
Artisans				14	14.6
Farmers				40	41.7
Cooks, washers, domestics				8	8.3
Waiters, butlers, porters, steward class				7	7.3
Laborers				8	8.3
Housewives				1	1.0
School children				4	4.2
Miscellaneous				2	2.1
Unknown				6	6.3

SOURCE: From Carl R. Osthaus, *Freedmen, Philanthropy, and Fraud: A History of the Freedman's Savings Bank* (University of Illinois Press, Urbana, 1976), pp. 114–119. Copyright © 1976 by the Board of Trustees of the University of Illinois.

D. Characteristics of Charleston Depositors and Societies and Businesses with Bank Accounts

1. Description of Every Tenth Charleston Depositor, July 1870–June 1871

Characteristics	Number	Percentage
Sex		
Male	126	67%
Female	61	33
Ability to write name		
Signature	63	34
Weak signature	19	10
Signed with an "X"	97	52
Unknown	8	4
Race		
Negro	162	87
Caucasian	10	5
Unknown	15	8
Residence		
Charleston	135	72
Non-Charleston	42	23
Unknown	10	5
Age		
1–10	11	6
11–15	15	8
16–19	11	6
20–29	60	32
30–39	27	14
40–49	23	12
50–59	17	9
60–69	4	2
70–79	1	1
Unknown	18	10
Occupation		
Professional and white collar	9	5
Artisans (includes 12 carpenters)	30	16
Farmers (farming for others, 9; farming for selves, 12)	21	11
Cooks, washers, domestics (may include one or two cooks who worked for city restaurants and who, therefore, should be added to artisan class)	31	17
Waiters, butlers, porters, steward class	17	9
Laborers (unskilled)	39	21
School children	12	6
Unknown	28	15

2. Charleston Societies and Businesses That Opened Bank Accounts, July 1870–June 1871

Acct. No.	Organization
5038	Veterans Republican Brotherhood
5039	Daughters of Jerusalem (sickness and death benefits)
5087	Lincoln Branch (charitable society)
5088	Union Lodge No. 1
5113	Daughters of Emanuel Watchman (sickness and death benefits)
5137	Young Calvary Union No. 2 (sickness and death benefits)
5165	Zion's Watchman Society
5183	Emanuel Sabbath School
5200	St. Theresa Charitable Association
5219	Israel Branch Society (charitable society)
5221	Benevolent Sociable Society (charitable society)
5231	United Fire Company
5319	Angel March Branch No. 2
5326	Good Hope Society (charitable society)
5346	Baptist Faith Society
5354	Young Watchman of Charleston Neck No. 2
5381	Christian Professor Society
5391	Faith, Hope, and Love (sickness and death benefits)
5456	Benford and Masyck "Ethiopia Troop"
5460	Young Centenary Branch No. 2 (sickness and death benefits)
5463	United Benevolent Compact and Sisters
5466	Emanuel Branch (sickness and death benefits)
5496	Charitable Home Association
5497	Club of the Sons of Jacob
5551	Young Interested Branch No. 2
5581	Liberia Branch Society (sickness and death benefits)
5610	Leaders Board of the Methodist Protestant Church
5635	Union Society No. 1 of the A.M.E. Church (sickness and death benefits)
5666	Lincoln Republican Guard
5670	Delany Rifles—Military Company of the City of Charleston
5672	Sons and Daughters of Daniel
5685	Class Union No. 19 (sickness and death benefits)
5708	Class Union No. 8 of Emanuel Church
5710	Ladies Historical Association
5716	Longshore Cooperative Association
5804	Class Union No. 17
5843	Sons and Daughters of Waymond
5852	Ladies Benevolent Society
5880	Zion Presbyterian Union No. 3
5909	Lincoln Tabernacle No. 1

(continued)

Table D.2 continued

Acct. No.	Organization
5911	Laboring Union No. 2
5922	Young Wesley Branch No. 2
5933	Ladies Companion
5943	Young Mens Christian Aid
6051	The Emanuel Branch
6087	Charleston Branch Joint Stock Company
6233	Wesley's Band
6243	Christian Social Nursery
6258	John Simmons Fish Company
6573	Sons and Daughters of Zareptha (sickness and death benefits)
6764	Class Union No. 9, Centenary M.E. Church
6778	Sons and Daughters of the Crops (sickness and death benefits)
6782	Ola Society of John the Baptist
6860	Lot Fund, Plymouth Church
6905	Class Union, Emanuel Church
6908	Class Union No. 9
6925	Lincoln Harp Society (sickness and death benefits)
6939	Protestant Gospel Society
6960	Beaufort Sons and Daughters of Love
7029	Plymouth Congregational Church
7059	Presbyterian Church, Wadisdo Island, S.C.
7065	Edisto Island Presbyterian Church
7111	Wesley Watchman Class No. 2
7116	Charleston Joint Stock and Jobbing Company (construction company)
7158	Spring Cart Association
7319	Charleston Land Company
7432	Good Samaritan Society
7440	Young Shebra Association
7500	Joshua Branch No. 2
7530	A.M.E. Church, Mt. Pleasant
7964	African M.E. Church, Edisto Island
8055	Mt. Olivet Independent Branch
8066	Union Star Fire Engine Company
8091	Enquiring Joshua Society
8181	Class Union No. 4

SOURCE: From Carl R. Osthaus, *Freedmen, Philanthropy, and Fraud: A History of the Freedman's Savings Bank* (University of Illinois Press, Urbana, 1976), pp. 114–119. Copyright © 1976 by the Board of Trustees of the University of Illinois.

East Europeans debarking in New York City, 1905. (International Museum of Photography at George Eastman House)

CHAPTER TWO

The Minorities

6.

CHEYENNE AUTUMN

Conflict between whites and Indians began with the first colonial land-ings and continued undiminished into the late nineteenth century. At that time the United States finally completed its conquest of the conti-nent and extended its authority over all the lands formerly belonging to the Indians. After the Civil War, as whites began moving in large num-bers along the new rail lines into areas west of the Mississippi River, the U.S. Army fought a series of wars against the larger and more combative of the Indian nations, notably the Comanche, the Apache, the Kiowa, the Cheyenne, and the Sioux. The Indians won occasional victories, such as the one over former Civil War General George A. Custer at the Little Bighorn in 1876, but most of the time they fell victim to the superior organization, supplies, and firepower of the whites. Whites' slaughter of the vast buffalo herds on which the Indians had based their lives—thirteen million buffalo had been killed by 1883—virtually assured the crushing of the tribes.

The Plains Indians were confined almost entirely to reservations, large tracts of land where, with the protection and economic aid of the Indian Office, it was thought that they might continue their nomadic, communal ways. But this policy was a failure. Tribal ranks, already se-verely depleted by the Plains wars, were further thinned by the growing scarcity of buffalo. Moreover, large tribes were often divided on widely scattered reservations, where resident (white) Indian agents usually proved unwilling or unable to prevent looting by settlers and the theft of funds earmarked for Indian assistance.

The excerpt from Helen Hunt Jackson's **Century of Dishonor** re-printed below illustrates the plight by the 1870s of the Cheyenne, who had been separated into two reservations, one in Oklahoma and the other in Montana-Wyoming, and who also had been victims of one of the period's most brutal massacres, at Sand Creek, Colorado, in 1864. **A Century of Dishonor** helped move government policy from subjugation and control of Indians toward their acculturation into white society by way of education and individual land ownership. An 1887 act of Con-gress distributed reservation lands as Indian farming plots and also re-leased millions of acres for white settlement. The last major military clash between the government and the Indians came with the slaughter of scores of Sioux families in 1890 at Wounded Knee, South Dakota.

Helen Hunt Jackson, born in Amherst, Massachusetts, in 1830, was the daughter of a professor and was a childhood friend of poet Emily

Dickinson. After the death in 1863 of Jackson's first husband, a Union army officer, she earned her living by writing poems, stories, and travel pieces. In 1872 she moved to Colorado, where she married a financier, grew concerned over the plight of the Indians, and wrote **A Century of Dishonor,** published in 1881, which she sent to every member of Congress at her own expense. Jackson soon became a best-selling novelist and a forceful advocate for the new policy of Indian assimilation. Her life embodied two great ironies. Though an Indian sympathizer, she was married to a man who helped build the railroads that destroyed the habitat of the Plains tribes. And even though she was a famous writer, much of her early work remained wrapped in obscurity because sexual prejudice had sometimes forced her to assume masculine pen names. She died in San Francisco, at the peak of her fame, in 1885.

Questions to consider. Jackson's narrative should be considered from several angles. Observe, first, how the government's Indian policy had changed since President Andrew Jackson's "removal" of the Cherokees in the 1830s (Vol. 1, Document 23). Why did the change occur? Was it at all connected with the closing of the frontier that some writers announced in the 1890s? Second, note that the Indian Office, like the Freedmen's Bureau (Document 2), was a federal welfare agency established to deal with a needy nonwhite population. What were the differences between these two programs? Did they result mainly from differences between freedmen and Indians, between the types of officials that ran the programs, or in congressional attitudes toward the West and the South? Also, consider the narrative in light of Andrew Carnegie's praise of democratic capitalist individualism just a few years later (Document 14). How compatible were Carnegie's values with either Cheyenne tribalism or government welfare activities?

A Century of Dishonor (1881)

Helen Hunt Jackson

The winter of 1877 and summer of 1878 were terrible seasons for the Cheyennes. Their fall hunt had proved unsuccessful. Indians from other reservations had hunted the ground over before them, and driven the buffalo off; and the Cheyennes made their way home again in straggling parties, destitute and

From Helen Hunt Jackson, **A Century of Dishonor** (Harper and Brothers, New York, 1881), 92–102.

hungry. Their agent reports that the result of this hunt has clearly proved that "in the future the Indian must rely on tilling the ground as the principal means of support; and if this conviction can be firmly established, the greatest obstacle to advancement in agriculture will be overcome. With the buffalo gone, and their pony herds being constantly decimated by the inroads of horse-thieves, they must soon adopt, in all its varieties, the way of the white man."

The ration allowed to these Indians is reported as being "reduced and insufficient," and the small sums they have been able to earn by selling buffalo-hides are said to have been "of material assistance" to them in "supplementing" this ration. But in this year there have been sold only $657 worth of skins by the Cheyennes and Arapahoes together. In 1876 they sold $17,600 worth. Here is a falling off enough to cause very great suffering in a little community of five thousand people. But this was only the beginning of their troubles. The summer proved one of unusual heat. Extreme heat, chills and fever, and "a reduced and insufficient ration," all combined, resulted in an amount of sickness heart-rending to read of. "It is no exaggeration estimate," says the agent, "to place the number of sick people on the reservation at two thousand. Many deaths occurred which might have been obviated had there been a proper supply of anti-malarial remedies at hand. Hundreds applying for treatment have been refused medicine."

The Northern Cheyennes grew more and more restless and unhappy. "In council and elsewhere they profess an intense desire to be sent North, where they say they will settle down as the others have done," says the report; adding, with an obtuseness which is inexplicable, that "no difference has been made in the treatment of the Indians," but that the "compliance" of these Northern Cheyennes has been "of an entirely different nature from that of the other Indians," and that it may be "necessary in the future to compel what so far we have been unable to effect by kindness and appeal to their better natures."

If it is "an appeal to men's better natures" to remove them by force from a healthful Northern climate, which they love and thrive in, to a malarial Southern one, where they are struck down by chills and fever—refuse them medicine which can combat chills and fever, and finally starve them—there indeed, might be said to have been most forcible appeals made to the "better natures" of these Northern Cheyennes. What might have been predicted followed.

Early in the autumn, after this terrible summer, a band of some three hundred of these Northern Cheyennes took the desperate step of running off and attempting to make their way back to Dakota. They were pursued, fought desperately, but were finally overpowered, and surrendered. They surrendered, however, only on the condition that they should be taken to Dakota. They were unanimous in declaring that they would rather die than go back to the Indian Territory. This was nothing more, in fact, than saying that they would rather die by bullets than of chills and fever and starvation.

These Indians were taken to Fort Robinson, Nebraska. Here they were confined as prisoners of war, and held subject to the orders of the Department

Indian camp.   This photograph depicts a Sioux camp at the Pine Ridge Agency, South Dakota, soon after the battle of Wounded Knee in December 1891. Reservation agents, fearful of the Indians' emotional and visionary "ghost dances," had called for cavalry to maintain order. When some Indians fled to the Badlands, the soldiers followed; in the ensuing melee, 40 soldiers and more than 200 Indians died. In 1972, members of the American Indian Movement occupied the Wounded Knee site to protest government policies and to assert Indian rights. (National Archives)

of the Interior. The department was informed of the Indians' determination never to be taken back alive to Indian Territory. The army officers in charge reiterated these statements, and implored the department to permit them to remain at the North; but it was of no avail. Orders came—explicit, repeated, finally stern—insisting on the return of these Indians to their agency. The commanding officer at Fort Robinson has been censured severely for the course he pursued in his effort to carry out those orders. It is difficult to see what else he could have done, except to have resigned his post. He could not take three hundred Indians by sheer brute force and carry them hundreds of miles, especially when they were so desperate that they had broken up the iron stoves in their quarters, and wrought and twisted them into weapons with which to resist. He thought perhaps he could starve them into submission. He stopped the issue of food; he also stopped the issue of fuel to them.

It was midwinter; the mercury froze in that month at Fort Robinson. At the end of two days he asked the Indians to let their women and children come out that he might feed them. Not a woman would come out. On the night of the fourth day—or, according to some accounts, the sixth—these starving, freezing Indians broke prison, overpowered the guards, and fled, carrying their women and children with them. They held the pursuing troops at bay for several days; finally made a last stand in a deep ravine, and were shot down—men, women, and children together. Out of the whole band there were left alive some fifty women and children and seven men, who, having been confined in another part of the fort, had not had the good fortune to share in this outbreak and meet their death in the ravine. These, with their wives and children, were sent to Fort Leavenworth to be put in prison; the men to be tried for murders committed in their skirmishes in Kansas on their way to the north. Red Cloud, a Sioux chief, came to Fort Robinson immediately after this massacre and entreated to be allowed to take the Cheyenne widows and orphans into his tribe to be cared for. The Government, therefore, kindly permitted twenty-two Cheyenne widows and thirty-two Cheyenne children—many of them orphans—to be received into the band of the Ogallalla Sioux.

An attempt was made by the Commissioner of Indian Affairs, in his Report for 1879, to show by tables and figures that these Indians were not starving at the time of their flight from Indian Territory. The attempt only redounded to his own disgrace; it being proved, by the testimony given by a former clerk of the Indian Bureau before the Senate committee appointed to investigate the case of the Northern Cheyennes, that the commissioner had been guilty of absolute dishonesty in his estimates, and that the quantity of beef actually issued to the Cheyenne Agency was hundreds of pounds less than he had reported it, and that the Indians were actually, as they had claimed, "starving."

The testimony given before this committee by some of the Cheyenne prisoners themselves is heart-rending. One must have a callous heart who can read it unmoved.

When asked by Senator [John T.] Morgan [of Alabama], "Did you ever really suffer from hunger?" one of the chiefs replied. "We were always hungry; we never had enough. When they that were sick once in awhile felt as though they could eat something, we had nothing to give them."

"Did you not go out on the plains sometimes and hunt buffalo, with the consent of the agent?"

"We went out on a buffalo-hunt, and nearly starved while out; we could not find any buffalo hardly; we could hardly get back with our ponies; we had to kill a good many of our ponies to eat, to save ourselves from starving."

"How many children got sick and died?"

"Between the fall of 1877 and 1878 we lost fifty children. A great many of our finest young men died, as well as many women."

"Old Crow," a chief who served faithfully as Indian scout and ally under General [George] Crook [commander of Far Western troops since 1868] for years, said: "I did not feel like doing anything for awhile, because I had no heart. I did not want to be in this country. I was all the time wanting to get back to the better country where I was born, and where my children are buried, and where my mother and sister yet live. So I have laid in my lodge most of the time with nothing to think about but that, and the affair up north at Fort Robinson, and my relatives and friends who were killed there. But now I feel as though, if I had a wagon and a horse or two, and some land, I would try to work. If I had something, so that I could do something, I might not think so much about these other things. As it is now, I feel as though I would just as soon be asleep with the rest."

The wife of one of the chiefs confined at Fort Leavenworth testified before the committee as follows: "The main thing I complained of was that we didn't get enough to eat; my children nearly starved to death; then sickness came, and there was nothing good for them to eat; for a long time the most they had to eat was corn-meal and salt. Three or four children died every day for awhile, and that frightened us."

When asked if there were anything she would like to say to the committee, the poor woman replied: "I wish you would do what you can to get my husband released. I am very poor here, and do not know what is to become of me. If he were released he would come down here, and we would live together quietly, and do no harm to anybody, and make no trouble. But I should never get over my desire to get back north; I should always want to get back where my children were born, and died, and were buried. That country is better than this in every respect. There is plenty of good, cool water there—pure water—while here the water is not good. It is not hot there, nor so sickly. Are you going where my husband is? Can you tell when he is likely to be released?" . . .

It is stated also that there was not sufficient clothing to furnish each Indian with a warm suit of clothing, "as promised by the treaty," and that, "by reference to official correspondence, the fact is established that the Cheyennes and Arapahoes are judged as having no legal rights to any lands, having forfeited their treaty reservation by a failure to settle thereon," and their "present reservation not having been, as yet, confirmed by Congress. Inasmuch as the Indians fully understood, and were assured that this reservation was given to them in lieu of their treaty reservation, and have commenced farming in the belief that there was no uncertainty about the matter it is but common justice that definite action be had at an early day, securing to them what is their right."

It would seem that there could be found nowhere in the melancholy record of the experiences of our Indians a more glaring instance of confused multiplication of injustices than this. The Cheyennes were pursued and slain for venturing to leave this very reservation, which, it appears, is not their reservation at all, and they have no legal right to it. Are there any words to fitly characterize such treatment as this from a great, powerful, rich nation, to a handful of helpless people?

7.

YELLOW PERIL

In 1882, Congress passed the Chinese Exclusion Act, prohibiting Chinese workers from entering this country for a period of ten years. As the date of expiration approached, however, pressure from powerful sources mounted for renewing the law. Leading the fight was the Immigration Committee of the House of Representatives, under the chairmanship of Representative Herman Stump of Maryland, who produced a stream of witnesses describing how the Chinese used drugs, committed crimes, and lusted after American women. Stump distilled the most important parts of this testimony in the report, reprinted below, that accompanied the committee's recommendation that the exclusion act be renewed.

The committee and its witnesses were persuasive. Not only did Congress extend the law for another ten years, but in 1893 President Grover Cleveland named Representative Stump Superintendent of Immigration. The exclusion act and Stump's appointment in turn set the stage for a treaty between the United States and China, signed in 1894, barring the immigration of Chinese laborers for ten years from the date of the exchange of ratifications. Those who had left the United States were permitted to return, provided they had wives, children, parents, or property worth $1,000 in this country. The treaty gave China the right to exclude American workers (of which there were none in China), but not American merchants and officials (who were numerous and important there). Chinese were thus all but barred from American soil, even as the Statue of Liberty (a gift of France) was unveiled in 1886 to welcome immigrants from Europe.

By 1900, Japanese workers, too, were entering the United States in sizable numbers; outcries against the "yellow peril" were again raised in the West. The so-called Gentleman's Agreement of 1907 between Washington and Tokyo instantly reduced the flow of unskilled Japanese laborers into the United States.

Questions to consider. The congressional report of 1892 argued that the Chinese presence in the United States was a threat to American "institutions." What institutions did the Immigration Committee seem most concerned about? Why does the report mention the "vegetable" diets of the Chinese? One aim of the committee was evidently to reduce the "smuggling" of Chinese aliens into the country. Why might such smuggling have taken place, and why did immigration officers seem unable to prevent it? From what source did the committee appear to receive the bulk of its evidence? The committee based much of its argument on the idea that the Chinese either could not or would not assimilate. Assuming that this lack of assimilation was a genuine problem, what alternatives might the committee have explored besides exclusion?

In studying the United States–China Treaty of 1894, consider the following points. First, although the document has racist overtones, it did not expel the Chinese already living in the United States or deny them citizenship rights; nor did it prevent all Chinese from entering this country. Compare this variety of racism with that depicted by Helen Hunt Jackson (Document 6) toward the Cheyenne, who were attacked and sequestered, and by Frederick Douglass (Document 5) and W. E. B. Du Bois (Document 10) toward blacks, who were exploited and disfranchised. What factors prevented a similar sequestration, disfranchisement, or exclusion of the Chinese? Second, what forces seem to have produced this treaty? Was it chiefly a result of working-class influence or of West Coast influence? Compare it with the Knights of Labor statement of 1878 (Document 13); refer also to Table A.3 in the Statistical Appendix. Does the 1894 treaty indicate real or merely symbolic gains in working-class and Western influence in Congress?

Congressional Report on Immigration (1892)

There is urgent necessity for prompt legislation on the subject of Chinese immigration. The exclusion act approved May 6, 1882, and its supplement expires by limitation of time on May 6, 1892, and after that time there will be no law to prevent the Chinese hordes from invading our country in number so vast, as soon to outnumber the present population of our flourishing States on the Pacific slope. . . .

The popular demand for legislation excluding the Chinese from this country is urgent and imperative and almost universal. Their presence here is inimical to our institutions and is deemed injurious and a source of danger. They are a distinct race, saving from their earnings a few hundred dollars and returning to China. This they succeed in doing in from five to ten years by living in the most miserable manner, when in cities and towns in crowded tenement houses, surrounded by dirt, filth, corruption, pollution, and prostitution; and gambling houses and opium joints abound. When used as cooks,

From U.S. Congress, House of Representatives, Report No. 255, February 10, 1892.

Anti-Chinese riot.   This wood engraving from **Frank Leslie's Illustrated Newspaper** depicts the anti-Chinese riot in Denver, Colorado, on October 31, 1880. Seen as a threat to the employment and living standards of white Americans, immigrants from China became objects of intense hostility during the 1870s. (Library of Congress)

farm-hands, servants, and gardeners, they are more cleanly in habits and manners. They, as a rule, have no families here; all are men, save a few women, usually prostitutes. They have no attachment to our country, its laws or its institutions, nor are they interested in its prosperity. They never assimilate with our people, our manners, tastes, religion, or ideas. With us they have nothing in common.

Living on the cheapest diet (mostly vegetable), wearing the poorest clothing, with no family to support, they enter the field of labor in competition with the American workman. In San Francisco, and in fact throughout the whole Pacific slope, we learn from the testimony heretofore alluded to, that the Chinamen have invaded almost every branch of industry; manufacturers of cigars, cigar boxes, brooms, tailors, laundrymen, cooks, servants, farm-hands, fishermen, miners and all departments of manual labor, for wages and prices at which white men and women could not support themselves and those dependent upon them. Recently this was a new country, and the Chinese may have been a necessity at one time, but now our own people are fast filling up and developing this rich and highly favored land, and American citizens will not and can not afford to stand idly by and see this undesirable race carry away the fruits of the labor which justly belongs to them. A war of races would soon be inaugurated; several times it has broken out, and bloodshed has followed. The town of Tacoma, in 1887, banished some 3,000 Chinamen on twenty-four hours' notice, and no Chinaman has ever been permitted to return.

Our people are willing, however, that those now here may remain, protected by the laws which they do not appreciate or obey, provided strong provision be made that no more shall be allowed to come, and that the smuggling of Chinese across the frontiers be scrupulously guarded against, so that gradually, by voluntary departures, death by sickness, accident, or old age, this race may be eliminated from this country, and the white race fill their places without inconvenience to our own people or to the Chinese, and thus a desirable change be happily and peacefully accomplished. It was thought that the exclusion act of 1882 would bring about this result; but it now appears that although at San Francisco the departures largely exceed the arrivals, yet the business of smuggling Chinese persons across the lines from the British Possessions and Mexico has so greatly increased that the number of arrivals now exceed the departures. This must be effectually stopped.

The United States–China Treaty of 1894

Whereas, On the 17th day of November, A.D. 1880, and of Kwanghali the sixth year, tenth moon, fifteenth day, a treaty was concluded between the United States and China for the purpose of regulating, limiting, or suspending the coming of Chinese laborers to, and their residence in, the United States; and

Whereas, The two Governments desire to cooperate in prohibiting such emigration and to strengthen in other ways the bonds of friendship between the two countries; and,

Whereas, The two Governments are desirous of adopting reciprocal measures for the better protection of the citizens or subjects of each within the jurisdiction of the other. . . .

Article I The high-contracting parties agree that for a period of ten years beginning with the date of the exchange of the ratifications of this convention, the coming, except under the conditions hereinafter specified, of Chinese laborers to the United States shall be absolutely prohibited.

Article II The preceding article shall not apply to the return to the United States of any registered Chinese laborer who has a lawful wife, child, or parent in the United States, or property therein of the value of $1,000, or debts of like amount due him and pending settlement. Nevertheless, every such Chinese laborer shall, before leaving the United States, deposit, as a condition of his return, with the Collector of Customs of the district from which he departs, a full description in writing of his family, or property, or debts, as aforesaid, and shall be furnished by said Collector with such certificate of his right to return under this treaty as the laws of the United States may now or hereafter prescribe and not inconsistent with the provisions of this treaty, and should the written description aforesaid be proved to be false, the right of return thereunder, or of continued residence after return, shall in each case be forfeited. And such right of return to the United States shall be exercised within one year from the date of leaving the United States, but such right of return to the United States may be extended for an additional period, not to exceed one year in cases where, by reason of sickness or other cause of disability beyond his control, such Chinese laborer shall be rendered unable sooner to return, which facts shall be fully reported to the Chinese Consul at the port of departure, and by him certified, to the satisfaction of the Collector of the port at which such Chinese subjects shall land in the United States. And no such Chinese laborer shall be permitted to enter the United States by land or sea without producing to the proper officer of the customs the return certificate herein required.

Article III The provisions of this convention shall not affect the right at present enjoyed of Chinese subjects, being officials, teachers, students, merchants, or travelers for curiosity or pleasure, but not laborers, of coming to

From the **New York Times**, November 19, 1894.

the United States and residing therein. To entitle such Chinese subjects as are above described to admission into the United States, they may produce a certificate from their Government or the Government where they last resided, vizéd [endorsed] by the diplomatic or Consular representative of the United States in the country or port whence they depart. It is also agreed that Chinese laborers shall continue to enjoy the privilege of transit across the territory of the United States in the course of their journey to or from other countries, subject to such regulations by the Government of the United States as may be necessary to prevent said privilege of transit from being abused.

Article IV   In pursuance of Article III, of the immigration treaty between the United States and China, signed at Pekin [Beijing] of the 17th day of November, 1880, (the 15th day of the tenth moon of Kwanghali, sixth year,) it is hereby understood and agreed that Chinese laborers or Chinese of any other class, either permanently or temporarily residing in the United States, shall have for the protection of their persons and property all rights that are given by the laws of the United States to citizens of the most favored nation, excepting the right to become naturalized citizens. And the Government of the United States reaffirms its obligations, as stated in said Article III, to exert all its power to secure protection to the person and property of all Chinese subjects in the United States.

Article V   The Government of the United States, having, by an act of Congress, approved May 5, 1892, as amended by an act approved Nov. 3, 1893, required all Chinese laborers lawfully within the limits of the United States before the passage of the first named act to be registered as in said acts provided, with a view of affording them better protection, the Chinese Government will not object to the enforcement of such acts, and reciprocally the Government of the United States recognizes the right of the Government of China to enact and enforce similar laws or regulations for the registration, free of charge, of all laborers, skilled or unskilled, (not merchants as defined by said acts of Congress,) citizens of the United States in China, whether residing within or without the treaty ports. And the Government of the United States agrees that within twelve months from the date of the exchange of the ratifications of this convention, and annually thereafter, it will furnish to the Government of China registers or reports showing the full name, age, occupation, and number or place of residence of all other citizens of the United States, including missionaries, residing both within and without the treaty ports of China, not including, however, diplomatic and other officers of the United States residing or traveling in China upon official business, together with their body and household servants.

Article VI   This convention shall remain in force for a period of ten years, beginning with the date of the exchange of ratifications, and if six months before the expiration of the said period of ten years neither Government shall have formally given notice of its final termination to the other, it shall remain in full force for another like period of ten years.

8.

BLACKS AND THE NEW SOUTH

The South suffered two ordeals following the Civil War: racism and poverty. The problem of race touched all Southerners, from oppressed former slaves to anxious white farmers and city dwellers. Poverty, especially the bleak agricultural poverty characteristic of the South, intensified the already severe problem of race. These twin cauldrons finally boiled over in the 1890s, when there were over one hundred fifty black lynchings per year and collapsing farm prices drove many thousands of families, black and white, into bankruptcy.

The Cotton States Exposition of Industry and the Arts, held in Atlanta in 1895, was designed to address the problem of poverty. Mainly the brainchild of Atlanta publishers and bankers, the exposition made much of the prospects for railroad expansion, iron and textile manufacturing, and lumber and tobacco processing; it was hoped that the success of these would reduce the South's unhappy dependence on agriculture and tie it to the rest of capitalistic America. But there was also the explosive issue of race. To address this, the exposition organizers, almost as an afterthought, invited Booker T. Washington, head of the Tuskegee Institute, a black vocational school in Tuskegee, Alabama, to speak to the mostly white exposition gathering. The exposition produced only a slight effect on Southern industrialization—manufacturing there did not become widespread until the 1920s and industrial prosperity has not really arrived even today. Washington's speech, on the other hand, was of major importance. What he said, in general, pleased his listeners, and they marked him as a worthy spokesman for his race. His reputation soon spread to the white North and to blacks as well. Thus, almost overnight, Washington became a prominent figure whose message mattered to everyone, especially to those in the South.

Booker T. Washington was born a slave in Virginia in 1856, and worked from the age of nine in West Virginia salt furnaces and coal mines. He later worked his way through Hampton Institute, a black school in Virginia, established by philanthropists following the Civil War. He graduated in 1875, briefly attended a theological seminary in Washington, D.C., and in 1881 accepted the headship of Tuskegee Institute, which he built up from two small buildings and 40 pupils to a hundred buildings, 1,500 students, and a million-dollar endowment a quarter-century later. Washington was successful at attracting funds from Northern tycoons and was tolerated, at least, by Southern politicians. His years of greatest fame came after the Atlanta speech and especially after President Theodore Roosevelt's invitation to dine at the White House in 1901. It was in these years that Washington developed what detractors called a "Tuskegee machine," based on the support of Tuskegee graduates and black businesspeople and the willingness of Northern charities and politicians to seek his advice on donations and appointments. His well-known autobiography, **Up from Slavery,** appeared in 1901. He died, exhausted from overwork, in Tuskegee, Alabama, in 1915.

Questions to consider. In reading Washington's Atlanta speech, consider especially the times in which it was delivered. Two strands weave through it: black rights and black work. Was Washington, as many have said, trading one for the other? Or was he attempting to use the leverage of black labor to achieve something even more precious in the turbulent 1890s: black safety. Are there particular reasons why 1895 might have seemed an especially good time to move whites in this way? What did Washington mean when he said, "Cast down your bucket where you are"? Was he speaking mainly to whites or to blacks? Were there population movements in the 1890s that might have prompted him to address both groups?

═════════

Atlanta Exposition Address (1895)
Booker T. Washington

Mr. President and Gentlemen of the Board of Directors and Citizens: One-third of the population of the South is of the Negro race. No enterprise seeking the material, civil, or moral welfare of this section can disregard this element of our population and reach the highest success. I but convey to you, Mr. President and Directors, the sentiment of the masses of my race when I say that in no way have the value and manhood of the American Negro been more fittingly and generously recognized than by the managers of this magnificent Exposition at every stage of its progress. It is a recognition that will do more to cement the friendship of the two races than any occurrence since the dawn of our freedom.

Not only this, but the opportunity here afforded will awaken among us a new era of industrial progress. Ignorant and inexperienced, it is not strange that in the first years of our new life we began at the top instead of at the

From Booker T. Washington, **Up from Slavery: A Biography** (Doubleday, Page and Co., New York, 1901), 218–225.

bottom; that a seat in Congress or the state legislature was more sought than real estate or industrial skill; that the political convention or stump speaking had more attractions than starting a dairy farm or truck garden.

A ship lost at sea for many days suddenly sighted a friendly vessel. From the mast of the unfortunate vessel was seen a signal, "Water, water; we die of thirst!" The answer from the friendly vessel at once came back, "Cast down your bucket where you are." A second time the signal, "Water, water; send us water!" ran up from the distressed vessel, and was answered, "Cast down your bucket where you are." And a third and fourth signal for water was answered, "Cast down your bucket where you are." The captain of the distressed vessel, at last heeding the injunction, cast down his bucket, and it came up full of fresh, sparkling water from the mouth of the Amazon River. To those of my race who depend on bettering their condition in a foreign land or who underestimate the importance of cultivating friendly relations with the Southern white man, who is their next-door neighbour, I would say: "Cast down your bucket where you are"—cast it down in making friends in every manly way of the people of all races by whom we are surrounded.

Cast it down in agriculture, mechanics, in commerce, in domestic service, and in the professions. And in this connection it is well to bear in mind that whatever other sins the South may be called to bear, when it comes to business, pure and simple, it is in the South that the Negro is given a man's chance in the commercial world, and in nothing is this Exposition more eloquent than in emphasizing this chance. Our greatest danger is that in the great leap from slavery to freedom we may overlook the fact that the masses of us are to live by the productions of our hands, and fail to keep in mind that we shall prosper in proportion as we learn to dignify and glorify common labour, and put brains and skill into the common occupations of life; shall prosper in proportion as we learn to draw the line between the superficial and the substantial, the ornamental gewgaws of life and the useful. No race can prosper till it learns that there is as much dignity in tilling a field as in writing a poem. It is at the bottom of life we must begin, and not at the top. Nor should we permit our grievances to overshadow our opportunities.

To those of the white race who look to the incoming of those of foreign birth and strange tongue and habits for the prosperity of the South, were I permitted I would repeat what I say to my own race, "Cast down your bucket where you are." Cast it down among the eight millions of Negroes whose habits you know, whose fidelity and love you have tested in days when to have proved treacherous meant the ruin of your firesides. Cast down your bucket among these people who have, without strikes and labour wars, tilled your fields, cleared your forests, builded your railroads and cities, and brought forth treasures from the bowels of the earth, and helped make possible this magnificent representation of the progress of the South. Casting down your bucket among my people, helping and encouraging them as you are doing on these grounds, and to education of head, hand, and heart, you will find that they will buy your surplus land, make blossom the waste places in your fields,

Tuskegee Institute Band, 1903. The brass band was by far the most typical form of outdoor musical entertainment in turn-of-the-century America, from circuses and patriotic parades to graduation days and Sundays in the park. When the Spanish-American War ended, the Army sold most of its surplus instruments, many of which wound up in the hands of black musicians, who used them to develop the most exciting new musical form of the twentieth century—jazz. (Library of Congress)

and run your factories. While doing this, you can be sure in the future, as in the past, that you and your families will be surrounded by the most patient, faithful, law-abiding, and unresentful people that the world has seen. As we have proved our loyalty to you in the past, in nursing your children, watching by the sick-bed of your mothers and fathers, and often following them with tear-dimmed eyes to their graves, so in the future, in our humble way, we shall stand by you with a devotion that no foreigner can approach, ready to lay down our lives, if need be, in defense of yours, interlacing our industrial, commercial, civil, and religious life with yours in a way that shall make the interests of both races one. In all things that are purely social we can be as separate as the fingers, yet one as the hand in all things essential to mutual progress.

There is no defense or security for any of us except in the highest intelligence and development of all. If anywhere there are efforts tending to curtail the fullest growth of the Negro, let these efforts be turned into stimulating, encouraging, and making him the most useful and intelligent citizen. Effort or means so invested will pay a thousand per cent interest. These efforts will be twice blessed—"blessing him that gives and him that takes."

There is no escape through law of man or God from the inevitable:—

"The laws of changeless justice bind
    Oppressor with oppressed;
And close as sin and suffering joined
    We march to fate abreast."

Nearly sixteen millions of hands will aid you in pulling the load upward, or they will pull against you the load downward. We shall constitute one-third and more of the ignorance and crime of the South, or one-third its intelligence and progress; we shall contribute one-third to the business and industrial prosperity of the South, or we shall prove a veritable body of death, stagnating, depressing, retarding every effort to advance the body politic.

Gentlemen of the Exposition, as we present to you our humble effort at an exhibition of our progress, you must not expect overmuch. Starting thirty years ago with ownership here and there in a few quilts and pumpkins and chickens (gathered from miscellaneous sources), remember the path that has led from these to the inventions and production of agricultural implements, buggies, steam-engines, newspapers, books, statuary, carving, paintings, the management of drug stores and banks, has not been trodden without contact with thorns and thistles. While we take pride in what we exhibit as a result of our independent efforts, we do not for a moment forget that our part in this exhibition would fall far short of your expectations but for the constant help that has come to our educational life, not only from the Southern states, but especially from Northern philanthropists, who have made their gifts a constant stream of blessing and encouragement.

The wisest among my race understand that the agitation of questions of social equality is the extremest folly, and that progress in the enjoyment of all the privileges that will come to us must be the result of severe and constant struggle rather than of artificial forcing. No race that has anything to contribute to the markets of the world is long in any degree ostracized. It is important and right that all privileges of the law be ours, but it is vastly more important that we be prepared for the exercise of these privileges. The opportunity to earn a dollar in a factory just now is worth infinitely more than the opportunity to spend a dollar in an opera-house.

In conclusion, may I repeat that nothing in thirty years has given us more hope and encouragement, and drawn us so near to you of the white race, as this opportunity offered by the Exposition; and here bending, as it were, over the altar that represents the results of the struggles of your race and mine, both starting practically empty-handed three decades ago, I pledge that in your effort to work out the great and intricate problem which God has laid at the doors of the South, you shall have at all times the patient, sympathetic help of my race; only let this be constantly in mind, that, while from representations in these buildings of the product of field, of forest, of mine, of factory, letters, and art, much good will come, yet far above and beyond material benefits will be that higher good, that, let us pray God, will come, in a blotting out of sectional differences and racial animosities and suspicions, in a determination to administer absolute justice, in a willing obedience among all classes to the mandates of law. This, coupled with our material prosperity, will bring into our beloved South a new heaven and a new earth.

9.

THE SEGREGATED SOUTH

After the **Dred Scott** decision in 1857 (Vol. 1, Document 31), the tide of federal decision making turned, becoming more favorable for blacks, at least through 1870 when the ratification of the Fifteenth Amendment to the Constitution guaranteed them the right to vote. But with President Rutherford B. Hayes's withdrawal of federal troops from the South in 1877, the current gradually shifted once more toward disfranchisement, exploitation, and, increasingly, segregation. In the **Plessy** v. **Ferguson** case in 1896, the Supreme Court upheld a Louisiana law requiring separate railroad cars for blacks and whites.

Homer Plessy was one-eighth black; by sitting in the white section of a railway car en route from New Orleans to Covington, Louisiana, he violated a Louisiana "Jim Crow" (racial separation) law. He was arrested for refusing to move into a black section, and John H. Ferguson, the Louisiana judge who tried the case, found him guilty. Believing that the Jim Crow law violated the Fourteenth Amendment, Plessy appealed the decision. But the Supreme Court upheld the Louisiana law, stating that the Fourteenth Amendment, which forbids states to abridge the civil rights and liberties of citizens, requires only that separate facilities be equal.

This "separate but equal" doctrine allowed segregation not only of private commercial facilities like hotels, but also of public schools and even towns and cities. In practice it permitted the creation of facilities that were surely separate, but hardly equal. The decision stood until 1954, when it was overturned by the Supreme Court in the landmark decision in **Brown** v. **The Board of Education of Topeka** (Document 38).

Henry Billings Brown, the author of the **Plessy** decision, was born to wealthy parents in Massachusetts in 1836. He attended Yale College and set up a law practice in Detroit. Appointed to the Supreme Court by President Benjamin Harrison in 1890, Brown retired from the Court in 1906 and lived in New York until his death in 1913. His chief opinion besides **Plessy** was a concurrence in the decision in **Dawson** v. **Bidwell** (1901) that inhabitants of annexed territories, such as Puerto Rico, had no constitutional rights.

Questions to consider. Several aspects of the **Plessy** opinion merit special attention. Note, for example, the dual themes of racism and growth. Henry Billings Brown clearly did not believe that his decision would segregate facilities in the South. Why not? Was it not, in fact, Southern industrial progress—new railroads, streetcars, hotels, and schools—and its effect on race relations that had brought the issue before the Court in the first place? Note, too, that Brown stood somewhere between Roger B. Taney, who had openly accepted African inferiority a half-century earlier (Vol. 1, Document 31), and Earl Warren, who a half-century later worried about psychological damage to segregated children (Document 38). Brown stated, rather, that although all citizens have a kind of "property" interest in their reputations because these can affect their future, segregation will not harm blacks' reputations unless they allow it to hurt their self-esteem. Whites in a minority position, said Brown, would not suffer diminished self-esteem; neither should blacks. What evidence is cited for this opinion? Note, finally, Brown's narrow view of the scope of the law. Law, he argued, can neither equalize nor unify society. In its **Plessy** decision, therefore, the Supreme Court declared actual racial experience—slavery, terrorism, and exploitation—to be irrelevant to the legal consideration of race relations. Do you agree with this reasoning?

Plessy *v*. Ferguson (1896)

This case turns upon the constitutionality of an act of the general assembly of the state of Louisiana, passed in 1890, providing for separate railway carriages for the white and colored races. . . .

The constitutionality of this act is attacked upon the ground that it conflicts both with the 13th Amendment of the Constitution, abolishing slavery, and the 14th Amendment, which prohibits certain restrictive legislation on the part of the states.

That it does not conflict with the 13th Amendment, which abolished slavery and involuntary servitude, except as a punishment for crime, is too clear for argument. . . .

The object of the [14th] amendment was undoubtedly to enforce the absolute equality of the two races before the law, but in the nature of things it could not have been intended to abolish distinctions based upon color, or to enforce social, as distinguished from political, equality, or a commingling of the two races upon terms unsatisfactory to either. Laws permitting, and even requiring their separation in places where they are liable to be brought

Plessy v. **Ferguson**, 163 U.S. 537 (1896).

into contact do not necessarily imply the inferiority of either race to the other, and have been generally, if not universally, recognized as within the competency of the state legislatures in the exercise of their police power. The most common instance of this is connected with the establishment of separate schools for white and colored children, which have been held to be a valid exercise of the legislative power even by courts of states where the political rights of the colored race have been longest and most earnestly enforced. . . .

It is claimed by the plaintiff in error that, in any mixed community, the reputation of belonging to the dominant race, in this instance the white race, is property, in the same sense that a right of action, or of inheritance, is property. Conceding this to be so, for the purposes of this case, we are unable to see how this statute deprives him of, or in any way affects his right to, such property. If he be a white man and assigned to a colored coach, he may have his action for damages against the company for being deprived of his so-called property. Upon the other hand, if he be a colored man and be so assigned, he has been deprived of no property, since he is not lawfully entitled to the reputation of being a white man. . . .

So far, then, as a conflict with the 14th Amendment is concerned, the case reduces itself to the question whether the statute of Louisiana is a reasonable regulation, and with respect to this there must necessarily be a large discretion on the part of the legislature. In determining the question of reasonableness it is at liberty to act with reference to the established usages, customs, and traditions of the people, and with a view to the promotion of their comfort, and the preservation of the public peace and good order. Gauged by this standard, we cannot say that a law which authorizes or even requires the separation of the two races in public conveyances is unreasonable or more obnoxious to the 14th Amendment than the acts of Congress requiring separate schools for colored children in the District of Columbia, the constitutionality of which does not seem to have been questioned, or the corresponding acts of state legislatures.

We consider the underlying fallacy of the plaintiff's argument to consist in the assumption that the enforced separation of the two races stamps the colored race with a badge of inferiority. If this be so, it is not by reason of anything found in the act, but solely because the colored race chooses to put that construction upon it. The argument necessarily assumes that if, as has been more than once the case, and is not unlikely to be so again, the colored race should become the dominant power in the state legislature, and should enact a law in precisely similar terms, it would thereby relegate the white race to an inferior position. We imagine that the white race, at least, would not acquiesce in this assumption. The argument also assumes that social prejudice may be overcome by legislation, and that equal rights cannot be secured to the Negro except by an enforced commingling of the two races. We cannot accept this proposition. If the two races are to meet on terms of social equality, it must be the result of natural affinities, a mutual appreciation of each other's merits and a voluntary consent of individuals. . . .

Legislation is powerless to eradicate racial instincts or to abolish distinctions based upon physical differences, and the attempt to do so can only result in accentuating the difficulties of the present situation. If the civil and political right of both races be equal, one cannot be inferior to the other civilly or politically. If one race be inferior to the other socially, the Constitution of the United States cannot put them upon the same plane.

10.

A LIBERAL RESPONSE

The first important black challenge to the Tuskegee machine of Booker T. Washington came with the formation of the Niagara Movement in 1905. The initial Niagara meeting was organized by W. E. B. Du Bois, who opposed Washington's policy of accommodation and gradualism and his emphasis on vocational education. The meeting took place in Niagara Falls, Ontario, because Du Bois and his colleagues were refused lodging on the American side of the border. Later meetings of the Niagara Movement were held in such symbolic towns as Harpers Ferry (famous for John Brown's raid) and Oberlin, Ohio (an abolitionist center before the Civil War). The movement soon picked up biracial support and established branches and committees throughout the country. By 1908, however, the organization had shriveled, largely due to lack of funds and political direction, together with Washington's implacable hostility. The movement served, nonetheless, as a significant forum for black intellectuals, and its leaders were instrumental in founding the larger and more durable National Association for the Advancement of Colored People (NAACP) in 1909.

The address reprinted below is chiefly the work of W. E. B. Du Bois, who was born in Massachusetts in 1868, attended Fisk and Harvard Universities, and joined the faculty of Atlanta University in 1897. His **Souls of Black Folk** (1903) sounded the intellectual revolt against Washington's program. Du Bois joined the faculty of the University of Pennsylvania in 1910, and served as publicity director for the NAACP and editor of the association's journal, **Crisis,** from 1909 until 1932. A creative scholar who published numerous books and articles, Du Bois espoused at different times liberal, black nationalist, and Marxist views. In 1961 he joined the American Communist party and moved to the African nation of Ghana, where he died in 1963.

Questions to consider. Compare the Niagara Movement manifesto of 1905 with Booker T. Washington's Atlanta speech of 1895 (Document 8). What are the most striking differences in the two statements? Do they have anything in common? Are the disagreements great enough in themselves to have divided black leaders? Does any single point of contention seem of overriding importance—the one point, perhaps, on which no compromise would be possible? The Niagarans were, of course, meeting in a Northern state ten years after Washington's speech. How does their statement seem to reflect the national experience of the intervening years? How does it seem to reflect national as opposed to merely Southern concerns? Consider, finally, the audience to which the manifesto seems to be addressed. In view of its critique of American society, what allies could the Niagara Movement (and later the NAACP) hope to attract, and what, if anything, did this desire imply about its future aims, tactics, and success?

Niagara Movement Address (1905)
W. E. B. Du Bois

. . . We believe that [Negro] American citizens should protest emphatically and continually against the curtailment of their political rights. We believe in manhood suffrage: we believe that no man is so good, intelligent or wealthy as to be entrusted wholly with the welfare of his neighbor.

We believe also in protest against the curtailment of our civil rights. All American citizens have the right to equal treatment in places of public entertainment according to their behavior and deserts.

We especially complain against the denial of equal opportunities to us in economic life; in the rural districts of the south this amounts to peonage and virtual slavery; all over the south it tends to crush labor and small business enterprises: and everywhere American prejudice, helped often by iniquitous laws is making it more difficult for Negro-Americans to earn a decent living.

Common school education should be free to all American children and compulsory. High school training should be adequately provided for all, and college training should be the monopoly of no class or race in any section of our common country. We believe that in defense of its own institutions, the United States should aid common school education, particularly in the south, and we especially recommend concerted agitation to this end. We urge an increase in public high school facilities in the south, where the Negro-Americans are almost wholly without such provisions. We favor well-equipped trade and technical schools for the training of artisans, and the need of adequate and liberal endowment for a few institutions of higher education must be patent to sincere well-wishers of the race.

We demand upright judges in courts, juries selected without discrimination on account of color and the same measure of punishment, and the same efforts at reformation for black as for white offenders. We need orphanages and farm schools for dependent children, juvenile reformatories for delinquents, and the abolition of the dehumanizing convict-lease system. . . .

From the **Cleveland Gazette**, July 22, 1905.

Dr. W. E. B. Du Bois. One of the great intellectuals of the twentieth century, Du Bois not only edited **The Crisis,** the publication of the NAACP, for twenty-two years and wrote nine books, but also led in the fight against colonialism in Africa and for a united African voice against exploitation and white supremacy. He was, in addition, a brilliant public speaker and a pathbreaking sociologist whose **Black Reconstruction** (1935) was the first study of that era to be grounded heavily on statistical evidence. (**Crisis** photo)

We hold up for public execration the conduct of two opposite classes of men; the practice among employers of importing ignorant Negro-American laborers in emergencies, and then affording them neither protection nor permanent employment; and the practice of labor unions of proscribing and boycotting and oppressing thousands of their fellow-toilers, simply because they are black. These methods have accentuated and will accentuate the war of labor and capital, and they are disgraceful to both sides. . . .

We regret that this nation has never seen fit adequately to reward the black soldiers who in its five wars, have defended their country with their blood, and yet have been systematically denied the promotions which their abilities deserve. And we regard as unjust, the exclusion of black boys from the military and navy training schools. . . .

The Negro race in America, stolen, ravished and degraded, struggling up through difficulties and oppression, needs sympathy and receives criticism; needs help and is given hindrance, needs protection and is given mob-violence, needs justice and is given charity, needs leadership and is given cowardice and apology, needs bread and is given a stone. This nation will never stand justified before God until these things are changed.

Especially are we surprised and astonished at the recent attitude of the church of Christ—on the increase of a desire to bow to racial prejudice, to narrow the bounds of human brotherhood, and to segregate black men in some outer sanctuary. This is wrong, unchristian and disgraceful to twentieth century civilization. . . .

And while we are demanding, and ought to demand, and will continue to demand the rights enumerated above, God forbid that we should ever forget to urge corresponding duties upon our people.

The duty to vote.
The duty to respect the rights of others.
The duty to work.
The duty to obey the laws.
The duty to be clean and orderly.
The duty to send our children to school.
The duty to respect ourselves, even as we respect others. . . .

11.

SOME URBAN BIGOTS

Anti-Semitism was a powerful current that reached from czarist Russia to democratic America in the late nineteenth century. In the United States, hostility to Jewish families was not common before the beginning of large-scale Jewish immigration in the 1880s. Thereafter, however, it emerged in all regions, classes, and parties. Resort hotels and exclusive men's clubs barred Jewish businessmen, and upper-class colleges established quota systems. Small-town Midwesterners and Southern farmers criticized not just Wall Street bankers but international Jewish bankers as well. Radical writers like Jack London cast a racist net that snared Jews as well as blacks. Even urban Catholic immigrants, who themselves experienced religious and nativist discrimination, harassed the "Christ-killers" and "Shylocks" who shared their ethnic slums.

The passage reprinted below is from James T. Farrell's **Young Lonigan,** a novel published in 1932 about the Chicago Irish community in 1915. Farrell was born in Chicago in 1904. After attending parochial school and the University of Chicago, he held temporary jobs while perfecting his literary skills. **Young Lonigan** was part of a trilogy, completed in 1935, portraying the youth, coming of age, and adulthood of Studs Lonigan. Farrell followed his acclaimed Lonigan trilogy with five novels about Danny O'Neill, another representative Chicago Irishman. A realist in literary technique and a radical in politics, Farrell published additional works after World War II, perhaps never approaching his earlier achievement but still leaving a remarkable record of acute social description.

Questions to consider. **Young Lonigan** illustrates how religion and race created urban tensions and suggests the basis of the ethnic pecking order in 1915. Did "Old Man O'Brien" have the same attitudes toward Jews as toward blacks? Were these attitudes based more on personal experience or on folklore and conventional wisdom? What did O'Brien mean by saying that "Jews killed all the other games"? What was he actually revealing about Chicago race relations in his story about the wrestling tournament? What different ways would Studs and Johnny, watching and listening to O'Brien, learn to use in dealing with "sheenies" and "shades"? Are any forces evident in this scene—worker solidarity, the ethnic melting pot, mass commercial culture—that might eventually serve to mitigate this kind of animosity?

Young Lonigan (1932)
James T. Farrell

Old Man O'Brien talked on:

"But I ain't so much interested in sports as I used to be. Baseball's the only clean game we got left. The Jews killed all the other games. The kikes dirty up everything. I say the kikes ain't square. There never was a white Jew, or a Jew that wasn't yellow. And there'll never be one. Why, they even killed their own God. . . . And now I'll be damned if they ain't comin' in spoiling our neighborhood. It used to be a good Irish neighborhood, but pretty soon a man will be afraid to wear a shamrock on St. Patrick's day, because there are so many noodle-soup drinkers around. We got them on our block. I even got one next door to me. I'd never have bought my property if I knew I'd have to live next door to that Jew, Glass's his name. But I don't speak to him anyway. And he's tryin' to make a gentleman of that four eyed kid of his. . . . as if a Jew could be a gentleman."

Johnny and Studs laughed, and told him that the Glass kid was nothing but a sissy. They had nothing to do with him.

"Well, don't . . . unless it's maybe to paste him one."

A pause.

"And say, Studs, you got 'em over your way, too. What does your old man think of 'em?"

"Well, he's always talking of selling. My father thinks they are ruling the neighborhood."

"They are . . . only, say . . . listen . . . can that my father stuff. Both of you kids know damn well that when you're alone you say . . . my old man . . . Come on, act natural. . . ."

Studs told himself that Johnny's old man was like a regular pal to a kid.

They stopped in an alley at Fifty-second and Prairie. Old Man O'Brien bawled hell out of a sweating Negro who was putting in a load of coal. The Negro was grimed with coal dust, and perspiration came out of him in rivers. He worked slowly but steadily, shoveling the coal into a wheelbarrow, pushing it down a board and emptying it down a chute through a basement window.

They drove on, and Mr. O'Brien said:

"You got to put pepper on the tails of these eight-balls. They're lazy as you make 'em. A Jew and a nigger. Never trust 'em farther than you can see 'em. But some niggers are all right. These southern ones that know their place are only lazy. But these northern bucks are dangerous. They are getting too spry here in Chicago, and one of these days we're gonna have a race riot, and then all the Irish from back of the yards will go into the black belt, and there'll be a lot of niggers strung up on lampposts with their gizzards cut out. . . . My kid here wanted to wrestle in that tournament over at Carter Playground last winter, and I'da let him, but he'd of had to wrestle with niggers. So I made him stay out. You got to keep these smokes in their place and not let 'em get gay."

They stopped for sodas, and Mr. O'Brien bought them each two. Studs could have caught his old man buying a kid two sodas like that. While they were sitting with their sodas, Old Man O'Brien told them of the things of yesteryear, and of plays he'd taken Johnny's mother to. One was called *Soudan,* given way back in about 1903, and was it a humdinger! They killed forty-five men in the first act. Was it a play! They had shipwrecks at sea, and what not, and when the shooting started half of the audience held their heads under the seats until it ended, and when the villain came on the stage everyone kept going *ss*! And the dime novels, and Nick Carter! But times had changed. Times had changed. Even kids weren't like they used to be, they had none of the old feeling of other times, they didn't have that old barefoot-boy attitude, and they weren't as tough, either, and they didn't hang around knotholes at the ball park to see the great players, not the old ones around Indiana anyway. Times had changed.

They drove around. At one place, Mr. O'Brien had to see a sheeny and explain why the coal delivery had been late. The fellow talked like a regular Oi Yoi Yoi, waving his arms in front of him like he was in the signal corps of the U.S. Army. He protested, but Old Man O'Brien gave him a long spiel, and as they were leaving, the guy all but kissed Johnny's father. When they drove on, O'Brien said to the kids:

"You got to soft soap some of these Abie Kabbibles."

He winked at them and they laughed. Studs kept thinking of his old man and Johnny's and dreaming of being a kid like Mr. O'Brien had been and wishing that his gaffer was more like Mr. O'Brien. . . .

It had been a great afternoon, though.

12.

CLOSING THE DOORS

For a half-century after the Civil War the United States maintained a relatively unrestrictive policy toward immigration from Europe. Yet the coming of so many millions of immigrants, particularly so many who were neither Protestant nor northern Europeans, caused growing alarm among "old-stock" Americans, who associated the newcomers with saloons, political corruption, and other "ills" of urban society. Labor leaders feared such floods of uncontrollable cheap labor; upper-class spokesmen were concerned about the possible "mongrelization" of the country.

The first broad effort to restrict immigration was the Literacy Test of 1917, which actually had little effect because most immigrants could in fact read and write. In 1921, Congress limited immigration from any country to 3 percent of that country's proportion of the American population as of 1910. By 1924 the public favored even more restrictive measures. The sweeping National Origins Act, excerpted below, brought the tradition of unrestricted entry by Europeans to a definitive close. Only people from the Western Hemisphere could come freely now. (A separate Oriental Exclusion Act later banned Asians altogether.) The national-origins standard, though modified, persisted until 1965, when the emphasis shifted from national origin to refugees, relatives, and occupational skills.

Questions to consider. The Immigration Act of 1924 shows how American society rated the different nationalities at that time. According to the quotas listed in the act, for example, a Czech was worth thirty Chinese, a Swiss equaled twenty Syrians, and an Irishman ten Italians. Is this a fair interpretation of the act? Of course, the act was not purely racial legislation. Not even at this peak of feverish nationalism did the U.S. government discriminate arbitrarily between nationalities or allot immigration space on a random basis. With the notable exception of the Orientals, national quotas were figured on a percentage basis: limiting Armenians also meant limiting Austrians. Most of the Western Hemisphere, moreover, was exempt from the act. Nevertheless, by basing quotas on the 1890 rather than the 1910 census, the act did embody clear racial preferences. Why, then, was such care taken to employ percentages rather than absolute numbers? Ironically, it was the Republicans, not the Southern-dominated Democrats (Woodrow Wilson, a well-known segregationist, twice vetoed immigrant literacy legislation), who perceived mass immigration as a grave national danger. What accounted for this seeming anomaly?

─────────

The Immigration Act of 1924

It will be remembered that the quota limit act of May 1921, provided that the number of aliens of any nationality admissible to the United States in any fiscal year should be limited to 3 per cent of the number of persons of such nationality who were resident in the United States according to the census of 1910, it being also provided that not more than 20 per cent of any annual quota could be admitted in any one month. Under the act of 1924 the number of each nationality who may be admitted annually is limited to 2 per cent of the population of such nationality resident in the United States according to the census of 1890, and not more than 10 per cent of any annual quota may be admitted in any month except in cases where such quota is less than 300 for the entire year.

Under the act of May, 1921, the quota area was limited to Europe, the Near East, Africa, and Australasia. The countries of North and South America, with adjacent islands, and countries immigration from which was otherwise regulated, such as China, Japan, and countries within the Asiatic barred zone, were not within the scope of the quota law. Under the new act, however, immigration from the entire world, with the exception of the Dominion of Canada, Newfoundland, the Republic of Mexico, the Republic of Cuba, the Republic of Haiti, the Dominican Republic, the Canal Zone, and independent countries of Central and South America, is subject to quota limitations. The various quotas established under the new law are shown in the . . . proclamation of the President, issued on the last day of the present fiscal year: . . .

Country or Area of Birth	Quota 1924–1925
Afghanistan	100
Albania	100
Andorra	100
Arabian peninsula	100
Armenia	124

[continued on page 80]

From **Annual Report of the Commissioner-General of Immigration** (Government Printing Office, Washington, D.C., 1924).

"The Only Way to Handle It."   This 1921 cartoon from the **Providence Evening Bulletin** urged support for measures to restrict immigration according to the size of resident nationality groups. New England Yankees, such as the readers of the **Bulletin,** helped lead the restrictionist movement, with considerable assistance from Midwesterners and Californians. Restrictionists felt especially threatened by the renewal of mass European migration to America following the end of World War I. (Library of Congress)

Country or Area of Birth	Quota 1924–1925
Australia, including Papua, Tasmania, and all islands appertaining to Australia	121
Austria	785
Belgium	512
Bhutan	100
Bulgaria	100
Cameroon (proposed British mandate)	100
Cameroon (French mandate)	100
China	100
Czechoslovakia	3,073
Danzig, Free City of	228
Denmark	2,789
Egypt	100
Estonia	124
Ethiopia (Abyssinia)	100
Finland	170
France	3,954
Germany	51,227
Great Britain and Northern Ireland	34,007
Greece	100
Hungary	473
Iceland	100
India	100
Iraq (Mesopotamia)	100
Irish Free State	28,567
Italy, including Rhodes, Dodekanesia, and Castellorizzo	3,845
Japan	100
Latvia	142
Liberia	100
Liechtenstein	100
Lithuania	344
Luxemburg	100
Monaco	100
Morocco (French and Spanish Zones and Tangier)	100
Muscat (Oman)	100
Nauru (Proposed British mandate)	100
Nepal	100
Netherlands	1,648
New Zealand (including appertaining islands)	100
Norway	6,453
New Guinea, and other Pacific Islands under proposed Australian mandate	100

Country or Area of Birth	Quota 1924–1925
Palestine (with Trans-Jordan, proposed British mandate)	100
Persia	100
Poland	5,982
Portugal	503
Ruanda and Urundi (Belgium mandate)	100
Rumania	603
Russia, European and Asiatic	2,248
Samoa, Western (proposed mandate of New Zealand)	100
San Marino	100
Siam	100
South Africa, Union of	100
South West Africa (proposed mandate of Union of South Africa)	100
Spain	131
Sweden	9,561
Switzerland	2,081
Syria and The Lebanon (French mandate)	100
Tanganyika (proposed British mandate)	100
Togoland (proposed British mandate)	100
Togoland (French mandate)	100
Turkey	100
Yap and other Pacific islands (under Japanese mandate)	100
Yugoslavia	671

COUNTERPOINT II

Urbanization and Ethnicity

Beginning in the late nineteenth century, poverty, oppression, and hope for a better life produced a massive migration of eastern and southern Europeans to this country. Most settled in the urban-industrial centers of the Northeast and Midwest, where they were joined by a growing number of blacks who had departed the South for similar reasons.

Every migrant group arrived impoverished, encountered prejudice, and had to struggle to preserve a semblance of orderly and familiar family life. But did they suffer equally? Were their coping strategies similar? And did families remain intact and serve as an economic support, or did they weaken and find economic progress even tougher? How, more specifically, did black migrants with a history of racial persecution compare with Jewish migrants with a similar history? How did both compare with another impoverished group, the Italians?

Partly with these questions in mind, Herbert Gutman has sifted 1905 New York State census data for information on blacks, Jews, and Italians in Manhattan. Similarities among groups are immediately discernible from his figures. Every group (table A) had sizable contingents between the ages of 20 and 39, the prime years for arduous labor. At every age level, however, there were about as many women as men, suggesting that in none of these ethnic groups did large numbers of men arrive alone to make money and then return "home." Home was now in New York City. No group had more than a handful in the 50-and-over age bracket. As for differences, two are particularly striking. First, comparison of the family groups shows that the Jewish and Italian family groups contained about twice the percentage of children under age 15 that black families had. Young people did migrate from the South. But frequently they were childless young adults, and often, it seems, they remained that way. Europeans brought children with them and may have had more upon arrival. Second, comparison of male adults with total adults shows that there were fewer males in the black population than among Jews and Italians—a reflection, perhaps, of differing job prospects among male migrants.

Household structures (table B) are, again, both similar and dissimilar. Black and Jewish households were about half nuclear (parents and children only), about a tenth extended (nuclear plus other relatives), and about two-fifths augmented (nuclear or extended plus unrelated subfamilies—that is, boarders). Blacks had a lot more subfamilies than Jews, however, indicating more people, or at least adults, per dwelling. While almost all families in both groups had a husband or father present, this was a little less common for black families than for Jewish. Most Italian families, like their Jewish counterparts, had a husband or father present. But Italian households included more nuclear families and many more extended families than blacks or Jews. So, although we can assume that the Italians were more crowded than the Jews (though not so crowded as the blacks), much of this crowding resulted from sharing space with nonnuclear relatives rather than with boarders, as in the black households.

What, finally, of earning power? Here (table C) are the biggest disparities of all, the only really major ones. Almost all blacks held un-skilled labor and service jobs; there were almost no professional or businessmen (the enterprise category) and no small proprietors (petty enterprise) at all. The Italians, too, had a large unskilled and service group, almost 20 percent more than the Jews. But there were plenty of skilled workers to give heft to Italian earning power and also a sizable smattering of white-collar, petty-enterprise, professional occupations to provide community leadership. Jews in turn had not only numerous skilled workers but twice as many white-collar, professional, and business positions. Italians and Jews, then, came to America poor and remained poor, at least for awhile, after they were settled—hence the crowding and the need for boarders. But the black migrants, lacking skills and meeting racial as opposed to simply ethnic prejudice, were poorer still because they held the worst-paying jobs—thus the extremes of both crowding and boarding. Moreover, the lack of higher-status and skilled occupations boded ill for their future.

So while all new urbanites suffered, not all suffered equally. There was a bottom rung, and the blacks, for all their adaptations and family resiliency, were on it.

A. Age and Sex of Black, Jewish, and Italian Family Groups and Adults, New York City, 1905

Age	Black Family Groups		Jewish Family Groups		Italian Family Groups	
	Male	Female	Male	Female	Male	Female
Under 15	17%	18%	33%	35%	34%	38%
15–19	6	7	12	17	10	12
20–29	32	34	25	22	22	21
30–39	27	23	15	11	16	13
40–49	12	11	9	9	10	9
50+	6	7	6	6	8	7
Number	7,004	7,364	11,199	10,263	7,968	6,825

Age	Black Adults Only		Jewish Adults Only		Italian Adults Only	
	Male	Female	Male	Female	Male	Female
20–29	42%	45%	45%	45%	40%	42%
30–39	35	31	28	23	28	26
40–49	15	15	15	18	18	18
50+	8	9	12	14	14	14
Number	5,346	5,486	6,246	4,882	4,542	3,428

SOURCE: From *The Black Family in Slavery and Freedom, 1750–1925* by Herbert G. Gutman. Copyright © 1969, 1976 by Herbert G. Gutman. Reprinted by permission of Pantheon Books, a Division of Random House, Inc., and Sterling Lord Literistic, Inc.

B. Household Structures of Blacks, Jews, and Italians, New York City, 1905

Type of Household	Blacks	Jews	Italians
Nuclear	49%	49%	60%
Extended	16%	12%	23%
Augmented	42%	43%	21%
Number of subfamilies	437	159	262
Husband or father present, households and subfamilies	83%	93%	93%
Number	3,014	3,584	2,945

SOURCE: From *The Black Family in Slavery and Freedom, 1750–1925* by Herbert G. Gutman. Copyright © 1969, 1976 by Herbert G. Gutman. Reprinted by permission of Pantheon Books, a Division of Random House, Inc., and Sterling Lord Literistic, Inc.

C. Occupations of Black, Jewish, and Italian Males (Aged 20 and Older), New York City, 1905

Occupation	Blacks	Jews	Italians
Laborer, unskilled	86%	7%	38%
Clothing	0	45	18
Skilled	9	21	30
White collar	3	8	4
Petty enterprise	0	12	9
Professional	1	4	1
Enterprise	1	3	0.4
Number	5,267	5,990	4,469
Composite Occupations	**Blacks**	**Jews**	**Italians**
Unskilled labor and service	86%	30%	47%
Skilled workers	9	43	39
Other	5	27	14
Number	5,267	5,990	4,469

SOURCE: From *The Black Family in Slavery and Freedom, 1750–1925* by Herbert G. Gutman. Copyright © 1969, 1976 by Herbert G. Gutman. Reprinted by permission of Pantheon Books, a Division of Random House, Inc., and Sterling Lord Literistic, Inc.

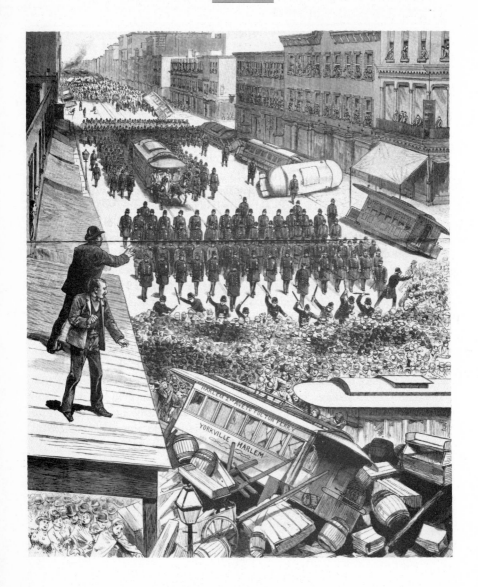

Police provide safe conduct to a streetcar during a New York City streetcar workers' strike, March 1883.   (Library of Congress)

CHAPTER THREE

The Age of Progress

13.

WORKER RESISTANCE

The decades following the Civil War brought an enormous expansion of activity in railroads, coal, steel, and other basic industries. This rapid rise in the development of America's natural resources meant a sharp rise in the country's per capita wealth and income and, in the long run, a higher standard of living for most people. But at the same time it meant other things as well: greater wealth and power for "capitalists," as the new leaders of industry were called; a deterioration in conditions for many workers; and a society repeatedly torn by class conflict.

The Noble Order of the Knights of Labor, formed as a secret workingmen's lodge in 1869, represented an early response to these trends. Secrecy seemed essential at first because of the hostility of employers toward labor unions. Not until 1881 did the Knights of Labor abandon secrecy and announce its objectives to the world. Its slogan was "An injury to one is the concern of all." The Knights took pride in the admission of all workers regardless of race, sex, or level of skill and in their moderate, public-spirited vision of a cooperative economic order. These factors, together with their support of succcesful railroad strikes, swelled the Knights' membership rolls to nearly 800,000 by 1886. After that, however, a wave of antiradicalism combined with internal problems and the loss of several bitter industrial struggles to send membership plummeting. By 1900 the organization was gone, to be replaced by two other labor organizations: the American Federation of Labor (AFL), founded in 1886, which organized skilled labor and struck for higher wages, and the Industrial Workers of the World (IWW), founded in 1905, which appealed to the unskilled and stood for industrial reorganization. The AFL, which opposed most of the Knights' principles, endured; the IWW, which shared many of them, did not.

Because the Knights of Labor was at first a secret organization, the preamble to its constitution, reprinted below, uses asterisks instead of the organization's name. The author of the preamble was Terence V. Powderly, Grand Master Workman of the Knights from 1879 to 1893. Powderly was born in Carbondale, Pennsylvania, in 1849, to Irish immigrant parents. After ten years as a railroad laborer and machinist, he became active in union affairs, joining the Knights in 1874 and rising rapidly in the organization. He was also a political activist during these years, serving as mayor of Scranton, Pennsylvania, and supporting many prolabor candidates in the 1880s, though refusing like most American labor leaders to support a separate labor party. After the Knights' decline,

Powderly studied law and then served in the Federal Bureau of Immigration. He died in Washington, D.C., in 1924.

Questions to consider. What general objectives did the preamble set forth? What practical demands? What do the Knights' demands reveal about working conditions in America during the Gilded Age (the period from 1870 to 1890)? To what extent was the preamble idealistic? How radical was it? The Knights barred doctors, lawyers, bankers, gamblers, and liquor dealers from membership, but did allow farmers, merchants, and small capitalists to join. Is there anything in the Knights' preamble that helps explain this policy? If you wanted to quote something from the preamble giving the gist of the Knights' philosophy, which passage would you select? Which of the Knights' goals have been achieved since the preamble was written?

Preamble to the Constitution of the Knights of Labor (1878)

The recent alarming development and aggression of aggregated wealth, which, unless checked, will invariably lead to the pauperization and hopeless degradation of the toiling masses, render it imperative, if we desire to enjoy the blessings of life, that a check should be placed upon its power and upon unjust accumulation, and a system adopted which will secure to the laborer the fruits of his toil; and as this much-desired object can only be accomplished by the thorough unification of labor, and the united efforts of those who obey the divine injunction that "In the sweat of thy brow shalt thou eat bread," we have formed the ***** with a view of securing the organization and direction, by co-operative effort, of the power of the industrial classes; and we submit to the world the object sought to be accomplished by our organization, calling upon all who believe in securing "the greatest good to the greatest number" to aid and assist us:—

I. To bring within the folds of organization every department of productive industry, making knowledge a standpoint for action, and industrial and moral worth, not wealth, the true standard of individual and national greatness.

II. To secure to the toilers a proper share of the wealth that they create; more of the leisure that rightfully belongs to them; more societary advantages;

From Terence V. Powderly, **Thirty Years of Labor** (Excelsior Publishing House, Columbus, Ohio, 1890), 243–246.

Strikebreakers dragged from a train in Pittsburgh, 1877. The 1877 railroad strike was the first nationwide strike. Two weeks of fierce fighting left hundreds dead and damage in the millions of dollars. Industrial conflicts continued to convulse the industry in the 1880s, with workers sometimes winning concessions and sometimes losing them.

more of the benefits, privileges, and emoluments of the world; in word, all those rights and privileges necessary to make them capable of enjoying, appreciating, defending, and perpetuating the blessing of good government.

III. To arrive at the true condition of the producing masses in their educational, moral, and financial condition, by demanding from the various governments the establishment of bureaus of Labor Statistics.

IV. The establishment of co-operative institutions, productive and distributive.

V. The reserving of the public lands—the heritage of the people—for the actual settler;—not another acre for railroads or speculators.

VI. The abrogation of all laws that do not bear equally upon capital and labor, the removal of unjust technicalities, delays, and discriminations in the administration of justice, and the adopting of measures providing for the health and safety of those engaged in mining, manufacturing, or building pursuits.

VII. The enactment of laws to compel chartered corporations to pay their employees weekly, in full, for labor performed during the preceding week, in the lawful money of the country.

VIII. The enactment of laws giving mechanics and laborers a first lien on their work for their full wages.

IX. The abolishment of the contract system on national, state, and municipal work.

X. The substitution of arbitration for strikes, whenever and wherever employers and employees are willing to meet on equitable grounds.

XI. The prohibition of the employment of children in workshops, mines, and factories before attaining their fourteenth year.

XII. To abolish the system of letting out by contract the labor of convicts in our prisons and reformatory institutions.

XIII. To secure for both sexes equal pay for equal work.

XIV. The reduction of the hours of labor to eight per day, so that the laborers may have more time for social enjoyment and intellectual improvement, and be enabled to reap the advantages conferred by the labor-saving machinery which their brains have created.

XV. To prevail upon governments to establish a purely national circulating medium, based upon the faith and resources of the nation, and issued directly to the people, without the intervention of any system of banking corporations, which money shall be a legal tender in payment of all debts, public or private.

14.

THE GOSPEL OF PRODUCTION

During the last part of the nineteenth century the United States experienced remarkable industrial development. In 1860 it was largely a nation of farms, villages, small businesses, and small-scale manufacturing establishments; by 1900 it had become a nation of cities, machines, factories, offices, shops, and powerful business combinations. Between 1860 and 1900, railroad trackage increased, annual production of coal rose steadily, iron and steel production soared, oil refining flourished, and development of electric power proceeded apace. "There has never been in the history of civilization," observed economist Edward Atkinson in 1891, "a period, or a place, or a section of the earth in which science and invention have worked such progress or have created such opportunity for material welfare as in these United States in the period which has elapsed since the end of the Civil War." By the end of the century, America's industrial production exceeded that of Great Britain and Germany combined, and the United States was exporting huge quantities of farm and factory goods to all parts of the world. The country had become one of the richest and most powerful nations in history.

Andrew Carnegie, "the King of Steel," was proud of American productivity. He liked to boast of the accomplishments of efficient business organization in the steel industry. "Two pounds of ironstone mined upon Lake Superior and transported 900 miles to Pittsburgh; one pound and a half of coal, mined and manufactured into coke, and transported to Pittsburgh; one-half pound of lime, mined and transported to Pittsburgh, a small amount of manganese ore mined in Virginia and brought to Pittsburgh—and these four pounds of materials manufactured into one pound of steel, for which the consumer pays one cent." Carnegie preached what he called a "gospel of wealth." His gospel emphasized individual initiative, private property, competition, and the accumulation of wealth in the hands of those with superior ability and energy. Carnegie failed to recognize the crucial role that government policies played in helping captains of industry like himself rise to the top; he also overlooked the fact that lack of opportunity rather than lack of initiative explained why many people stayed behind in what he thought of as the "race of life." Still, he did acknowledge that wealth was the product of society as well as of individual effort and maintained that rich people had the obligation to spend their surplus wealth for the good of the community. The "man who dies rich," he asserted, "dies disgraced."

Andrew Carnegie, the son of a handloom weaver, was born in Dunfermline, Scotland, in 1835. He moved with his family to Allegheny, Pennsylvania, at the age of twelve and got a job in a textile mill at $1.20 a week. At age fourteen he became a messenger in the Pittsburgh telegraph office. He was later promoted to telegraph operator, and finally, in a big jump forward, to private secretary and personal telegrapher for Thomas A. Scott, a Pennsylvania Railroad executive. Carnegie's rise thereafter was rapid. He became a railroad executive himself for a time and then amassed a fortune selling bonds, dealing in oil, and building bridges. In 1873 he decided to concentrate on steel. By adopting new technology and acquiring the best equipment available he was able to improve the quality of steel and to reduce its price. He was a master organizer. He gradually built his Carnegie Steel Company into a massive industry that controlled every phase of making steel: raw materials, transportation, manufacturing, and distribution. In 1901 he sold his company to financier J. P. Morgan, who merged it with his own steel holdings to form the United States Steel Corporation, the first billion-dollar corporation in the world. Carnegie spent the rest of his life in philanthropic work; by the time of his death in 1919 in Lenox, Massachusetts, he had spent some $350 million.

Questions to consider. Carnegie wrote many articles and books celebrating the American system. He thought that America's republican institutions were far more favorable to economic progress than the monarchical institutions of the Old World. The excerpt reprinted below from **Triumphant Democracy** (1886), a best seller, is typical. Why did Carnegie think that life "has become vastly better worth living" than it was a century before? What particular aspects of American life did he single out for special mention? In what ways did he think life in the United States was better than life in Europe? Was he writing mainly about the life of the average American or about that of the well-to-do? How did he relate America's economic achievements to democracy? How would Upton Sinclair (Document 16) or John L. Lewis (Document 28) have responded to Carnegie's effusions?

Triumphant Democracy (1886)
Andrew Carnegie

A community of toilers with an undeveloped continent before them, and destitute of the refinements and elegancies of life—such was the picture presented by the Republic sixty years ago. Contrasted with that of to-day, we might almost conclude that we were upon another planet and subject to different primary conditions. The development of an unequaled transportation system brings the products of one section to the doors of another, the tropical fruits of Florida and California to Maine, and the ice of New England to the Gulf States. Altogether life has become vastly better worth living than it was a century ago.

Among the rural communities, the change in the conditions is mainly seen in the presence of labor-saving devices, lessening the work in house and field. Mowing and reaping machines, horse rakes, steam plows and threshers, render man's part easy and increase his productive power. Railroads and highways connect him with the rest of the world, and he is no longer isolated or dependent upon his petty village. Markets for his produce are easy of access, and transportation swift and cheap. If the roads throughout the country are yet poor compared with those of Europe, the need of good roads has been rendered less imperative by the omnipresent railroad. It is the superiority of the iron highway in America which has diverted attention from the country roads. It is a matter of congratulation, however, that this subject is at last attracting attention. Nothing would contribute so much to the happiness of life in the country as such perfect roads as those of Scotland. It is a difficult problem, but its solution will well repay any amount of expenditure necessary. [British historian Thomas] Macaulay's test of the civilization of a people—the condition of their roads—must be interpreted, in this age of steam, to include railroads. Communication between great cities is now cheaper and more comfortable than in any other country. Upon the principal railway lines, the cars—luxurious drawing-rooms by day, and sleeping chambers by night—are ventilated by air, warmed and filtered in winter, and cooled in summer. Passenger steamers upon the lakes and rivers are of gigantic size, and models of elegance.

It is in the cities that the change from colonial conditions is greatest. Most of these—indeed all, excepting those upon the Atlantic coast—have been in great measure the result of design instead of being allowed, like Topsy, to "just grow." In these modern days cities are laid out under definite, far-seeing plans; consequently the modern city presents symmetry of form unknown in mediaeval ages. The difference is seen by contrasting the crooked cowpaths of old Boston with the symmetrical, broad streets of Washington or Denver. These are provided with parks at intervals for breathing spaces; amply supplied with pure water, in some cases at enormous expense; the most modern ideas

From Andrew Carnegie, Triumphant Democracy (Scribners, New York, 1886), 164–183.

Andrew Carnegie.   Carnegie was perhaps the country's most famous industrialist of the late 1800s. Certainly he was its richest, with a fortune of a half-billion dollars. But he was also its most articulate spokesman, producing widely read books and articles. Furthermore, as an immigrant's son who later endowed hundreds of public libraries, Carnegie exemplified two cherished American ideals: self-help in the accumulation of wealth, and stewardship in the disposal of it.

are embodied in their sanitary arrangements; they are well lighted, well policed, and the fire departments are very efficient. In these modern cities an extensive fire is rare. The lessening danger of this risk is indicated by the steady fall in the rate of fire insurance.

The variety and quality of the food of the people of America excels that found elsewhere, and is a constant surprise to Europeans visiting the States. The Americans are the best-fed people on the globe. Their dress is now of the richest character—far beyond that of any other people, compared class for class. The comforts of the average American home compare favorably with those of other lands, while the residences of the wealthy classes are unequaled. The first-class American residence of to-day in all its appointments excites the envy of the foreigner. One touch of the electric button calls a messenger; two bring a telegraph boy; three summon a policeman; four give the alarm of fire. Telephones are used to an extent undreamt of in Europe, the stables and other out-buildings being connected with the mansion; and the houses of friends are joined by the talking wire almost as often as houses of business. Speaking-tubes connect the drawing-room with the kitchen; and the dinner is brought up "piping hot" by a lift. Hot air and steam pipes are carried all over the house; and by the turning of a tap the temperature of any room is regulated to suit the convenience of the occupant. A passenger lift is common. The electric light is an additional home comfort. Indeed, there is no palace or great mansion in Europe with half the conveniences and scientific appliances which characterize the best American mansions. New York Central Park is no unworthy rival of Hyde Park and the Bois de Boulogne in its display of fine equipages; and in winter the hundreds of graceful sleighs dashing along the drives form a picture. The opera-houses, theatres, and public halls of the country excel in magnificence those of other lands, if we except the latter constructions in Paris and Vienna, with which the New York, Philadelphia and Chicago opera-houses rank. The commercial exchanges, and the imposing structures of the life insurance companies, newspaper buildings, hotels, and many edifices built by wealthy firms, not only in New York but in the cities of the West, never fail to excite the Europeans' surprise. The postal system is equal in every respect to that of Europe. Mails are taken up by express trains, sorted on board, and dropped at all important points without stopping. Letters are delivered several times a day in every considerable town, and a ten-cent special delivery stamp insures delivery at once by special messenger in the large cities. The uniform rate of postage for all distances, often exceeding three thousand miles, is only two cents . . . per ounce.

In short, the conditions of life in American cities may be said to have approximated those of Europe during the sixty years of which we are speaking. Year by year, as the population advances, the general standard of comfort in the smaller Western cities rises to that of the East. Herbert Spencer [an English philosopher] was astonished beyond measure at what he saw in American cities. "Such books as I had looked into," said he, "had given me no adequate idea of the immense developments of material civilization which I have found everywhere. The extent, wealth, and magnificence of your cities, and especially the splendors of New York, have altogether astonished me. Though I have not visited the wonder of the West, Chicago, yet some of your minor modern places, such as Cleveland, have sufficiently amazed me by the marvelous results of one generation's activity. Occasionally, when I have been in places of some ten thousand inhabitants, where the telephone is in general use, I have felt somewhat ashamed of our own unenterprising towns, many of which, of fifty thousand inhabitants and more, make no use of it."

Such is the Democracy; such its conditions of life. In the presence of such a picture can it be maintained that the rule of the people is subversive of government and religion? Where have monarchical institutions developed a community so delightful in itself, so intelligent, so free from crime or pauperism—a community in which the greatest good of the greatest number is so fully attained, and one so well calculated to foster the growth of self-respecting men—which is the end civilization seeks?

> "For ere man made us citizens
> God made us men."

The republican is necessarily self-respecting, for the laws of his country begin by making him a man indeed, the equal of other men. The man who most respects himself will always be found the man who most respects the rights and feelings of others.

The rural democracy of America could be as soon induced to sanction the confiscation of the property of its richer neighbors, or to vote for any violent or discreditable measure, as it could be led to surrender the President for a king. Equal laws and privileges develop all the best and noblest characteristics, and these always lead in the direction of the Golden Rule. These honest, pure, contented, industrious, patriotic people really do consider what they would have others do to them. They ask themselves what is fair and right. Nor is there elsewhere in the world so conservative a body of men; but then it is the equality of the citizen—just and equal laws—republicanism, they are resolved to conserve. To conserve these they are at all times ready to fight and, if need be, to die; for, to men who have once tasted the elixir of political equality, life under unequal conditions could possess no charm.

To every man is committed in some degree, as a sacred trust, the manhood of man. This he may not himself infringe or permit to be infringed by others. Hereditary dignities, political inequalities, do infringe the right of man, and hence are not to be tolerated. The true democrat must live the peer of his fellows, or die struggling to become so.

The American citizen has no further need to struggle, being in possession of equality under the laws in every particular. He has not travelled far in the path of genuine Democracy who would not scorn to enjoy a privilege which was not the common birthright of all his fellows.

15.

RURAL REVOLT

Rapid agricultural expansion was a crucial part of the nation's amazing economic growth in the late nineteenth century. Yet in this expansive era, average farm income went down and the farmer gradually lost pre-eminent status in American society. Farmers in the Midwest suffered from bad weather, and farmers in the South, from weevils and other pests. Everywhere growers received lower prices because of overproduction but paid higher borrowing and shipping costs because of what they saw as greedy and unresponsive banks and railroads. This network of "capitalist" transportation and finance quickly became a target of rural frustration, and farmers joined organizations such as the Grange and the Farmers' Alliance to promote their own interests.

In 1890, state alliances in the Midwest formed political parties to challenge the Republicans and Democrats; in the South, alliance members, faced with the difficult problem of race relations, sought to take over the Democratic party. Encouraged by local victories, however, the alliances created a national People's, or Populist, party in 1892 and ran James B. Weaver of Iowa for president. The Populists promised to restore the government (which they charged was controlled by the captains of industry and finance) "to the hands of the plain people." In their 1892 platform they called for a series of political reforms that would democratize the American system: the popular election of senators, the initiative, the referendum, and the secret ballot. They also made economic demands: government ownership of the railroad, telegraph, and telephone industries; a graduated income tax; shorter working hours for labor (to win urban allies); and an increase in the amount of money circulating in the country (particularly by means of the free coinage of silver), which, by producing inflation, would raise farm prices and ease the farmers' debt burdens.

The People's party did remarkably well for a new party. Weaver carried four states (for a total of twenty-two electoral votes) in 1892 and received over a million popular votes. The Populists also succeeded in electing a number of congressmen and some state officials. Although most Populist officeholders were in the Midwest and Rocky Mountain states, the achievement of the Southern wing of the party was perhaps the more remarkable because it was biracial. Indeed, despite widespread violence against them, the Populists in the South gained a significant black following on the basis of such appeals as the one by Thomas E.

Watson of Georgia reprinted below. By 1896, however, the party found its Southern supporters being harassed and murdered and its banking and currency program everywhere being taken over by the Democrats. Thus the People's party, like the Knights of Labor (Document 13), soon ceased to exist.

Thomas E. Watson, the Populists' foremost Southern leader, was born near Thomson, Georgia, in 1856. A schoolteacher and later a successful lawyer, Watson entered politics as a Democrat, but was elected to Congress in 1890 as a Farmers' Alliance candidate. He lost his re-election bid as a Populist in 1892, but remained active in the party's affairs and served as its vice-presidential candidate in 1896. In-creasingly disillusioned with the prospects for agrarian reform, Watson grew more intolerant with age and eventually supported black dis-franchisement and segregation. He died in Washington, D.C., in 1922, two years after his election to the U.S. Senate.

Questions to consider. In "The Negro Question in the South," which appeared in a national journal in 1892, Watson asked both races to leave their old party affiliations. What were these affiliations and how do you explain them? What did Watson think the two races had in common economically? How much validity was there in his contention that the two races "are kept apart" so that they "may be separately fleeced of [their] earnings" or in his insistence that material self-interest would bring them together? What sectional appeal did he make? What position did he take on the question of social equality? How much truth is there in his assumption that class interests cut across racial lines?

The Negro Question in the South (1892)
Thomas E. Watson

The key to the new political movement called the People's Party has been that the Democratic farmer was as ready to leave the Democratic ranks as the Republican farmer was to leave the Republican ranks. In exact proportion as the West received the assurance that the South was ready for a new party, it has moved. In exact proportion to the proof we could bring that the West had broken Republican ties, the South has moved. Without a decided break in both sections, neither would move. With that decided break, both moved.

From Thomas E. Watson, "The Negro Question in the South," **Arena** 35 (1892), 541–544, 548–550.

The very same principle governs the race question in the South. The two races can never act together permanently, harmoniously, beneficially, till each race demonstrates to the other a readiness to leave old party affiliations and to form new ones, based upon the profound conviction that, in acting together, both races are seeking new laws which will benefit both. On no other basis under heaven can the "Negro Question" be solved. . . .

The white tenant lives adjoining the colored tenant. Their houses are almost equally destitute of comforts. Their living is confined to bare necessities. They are equally burdened with heavy taxes. They pay the same high rent for gullied and impoverished land.

They pay the same enormous prices for farm supplies. Christmas finds them both without any satisfactory return for a year's toil. Dull and heavy and unhappy, they both start the plows again when "New Year's" passes.

Now the People's Party says to these two men, "You are kept apart that you may be separately fleeced of your earnings. You are made to hate each other because upon that hatred is rested the keystone of the arch of financial despotism which enslaves you both. You are deceived and blinded that you may not see how this race antagonism perpetuates a monetary system which beggars both."

This is so obviously true it is no wonder both these unhappy laborers stop to listen. No wonder they begin to realize that no change of law can benefit the white tenant which does not benefit the black one likewise; that no system which now does injustice to one of them can fail to injure both. Their every material interest is identical. The moment this becomes a conviction, mere selfishness, the mere desire to better their conditions, escape onerous taxes, avoid usurious charges, lighten their rents, or change their precarious tenements into smiling, happy homes, will drive these two men together, just as their mutually inflamed prejudices now drive them apart.

Suppose these two men now to have become fully imbued with the idea that their material welfare depends upon the reforms we demand. Then they act together to secure them. Every white reformer finds it to the vital interest of his home, his family, his fortune, to see to it that the vote of the colored reformer is freely cast and fairly counted.

Then what? Every colored voter will be thereafter a subject of industrial education and political teaching.

Concede that in the final event, a colored man will vote where his material interests dictate that he should vote; concede that in the South the accident of color can make no possible difference in the interests of farmers, croppers, and laborers; concede that under full and fair discussion the people can be depended upon to ascertain where their interests lie—and we reach the conclusion that the Southern race question can be solved by the People's Party on the simple proposition that each race will be led by self-interest to support that which benefits it, when so presented that neither is hindered by the bitter party antagonisms of the past.

Let the colored laborer realize that our platform gives him a better guaranty for political independence; for a fair return for his work; a better chance to buy a home and keep it; a better chance to educate his children and see them profitably employed; a better chance to have public life freed from race collisions; a better chance for every citizen to be considered as a *citizen* regardless of color in the making and enforcing of laws,—let all this be fully realized, and the race question in the South will have settled itself through the evolution of a political movement in which both whites and blacks recognize their surest way out of wretchedness into comfort and independence.

The illustration could be made quite as clearly from other planks in the People's Party platform. On questions of land, transportation and finance, especially, the welfare of the two races so clearly depends upon that which benefits either, that intelligent discussion would necessarily lead to just conclusions.

Why should the colored man always be taught that the white man of his neighborhood hates him, while a Northern man, who taxes every rag on his back, loves him? Why should not my tenant come to regard me as his friend rather than the manufacturer who plunders us both? Why should we perpetuate a policy which drives the black man into the arms of the Northern politician? . . .

To the emasculated individual who cries "Negro supremacy!" there is little to be said. His cowardice shows him to be a degeneration from the race which has never yet feared any other race. Existing under such conditions as they now do in this country, there is no earthly chance for Negro domination, unless we are ready to admit that the colored man is our superior in will power, courage, and intellect.

Not being prepared to make any such admission in favor of any race the sun ever shone on, I have no words which can portray my contempt for the white men, Anglo-Saxons, who can knock their knees together, and through their chattering teeth and pale lips admit that they are afraid the Negroes will "dominate us."

The question of social equality does not enter into the calculation at all. That is a thing each citizen decides for himself. No statute ever yet drew the latch of the humblest home—or ever will. Each citizen regulates his own visiting list—and always will.

The conclusion, then, seems to me to be this: the crushing burdens which now oppress both races in the South will cause each to make an effort to cast them off. They will see a similarity of cause and a similarity of remedy. They will recognize that each should help the other in the work of repealing bad laws and enacting good ones. They will become political allies, and neither can injure the other without weakening both. It will be to the interest of both that each should have justice. And on these broad lines of mutual interest, mutual forbearance, and mutual support the present will be made the stepping-stone to future peace and prosperity.

16.

SIDE EFFECTS

Industrialization brought, among other things, the factory system: big machines in large buildings where thousands of workers did specialized tasks under strict supervision. The factory system vastly increased America's output of such products as glass, machinery, newspapers, soap, cigarettes, beef, and beer. Factories thus provided innumerable new goods for American consumers and millions of new jobs for American workers. But factories also reduced workers' control over their place of work, made the conditions of labor more dangerous, and played no small part in destroying the dignity of that labor. The first part of the following excerpt from Upton Sinclair's novel **The Jungle** offers a glimpse into the factory system as it operated in a Chicago meat-packing plant around 1905.

Industrialization produced not only big factories but also big cities, particularly in the Northeast and Midwest. Sinclair therefore took pains to show the role of industry and new production techniques in creating urban transportation and other services. The second part of the excerpt suggests a few of the links between industrial growth and Chicago's leaders—the so-called gray wolves who controlled the city's government and businesses. Here again, Sinclair indicates the high toll in human life exacted by unrestrained development.

The Jungle caused a sensation when it was first published. The pages describing conditions in Chicago's meat-packing plants aroused horror, disgust, and fury, and sales of meat dropped precipitously. "I aimed at the public's heart," said Sinclair ruefully, "and hit it in the stomach." President Theodore Roosevelt ordered a congressional investigation of meat-packing plants in the nation, and subsequently Congress passed the Meat Inspection Act to remedy the situation. But Sinclair, a socialist, did not seek to inspire reform legislation. He was mainly concerned with dramatizing the misery of workers under the capitalist mode of production and winning recruits to socialism.

Upton Sinclair was born in Baltimore, Maryland, in 1878. After attending college in New York City, he began to write essays and fiction, experiencing his first real success with the publication of **The Jungle** in 1906. Dozens of novels on similar subjects—the coal and oil industries, newspapers, the liquor business, the persecution of radicals, the threat of dictatorship—poured from his pen in the following years, though none had the immediate impact of **The Jungle.** Sinclair's style, with its emphasis on the details of everyday life, resembles the realism of James T. Farrell (Document 11) and other writers of the time. But he also wrote as a "muckraker" (as Theodore Roosevelt called journalists who wrote exposés), trying to alert readers to the deceit and corruption then prevalent in American life. Unlike most muckrakers, however, he was politically active, running in California in the 1920s as a socialist candidate for the U.S. Congress. In 1934 he won the Democratic nomination for governor with the slogan "End Poverty in California" (EPIC), but he lost the election. During World War II he was a warm supporter of President Franklin D. Roosevelt and wrote novels about the war, one of which won a Pulitzer Prize. Not long before Sinclair's death in 1968 in Bound Brook, New Jersey, President Lyndon Johnson invited him to the White House to be present at the signing of the Wholesome Meat Act.

Questions to consider. The Jungle has been regarded as propaganda, not literature, and has been placed second only to Harriet Beecher Stowe's **Uncle Tom's Cabin** in its effectiveness as a propagandistic novel. Why do you think the novel caused demands for reform rather than converts to socialism? What seems more shocking in the passages from the novel reprinted below, the life of immigrant workers in Chicago in the early twentieth century or the filthy conditions under which meat was prepared for America's dining tables? What did Sinclair reveal about the organization of the work force in Chicago's meat-packing plants? Sinclair centered his story on a Lithuanian worker named Jurgis Rudkus and his wife, Ona. How convincing a character did he make Jurgis? In what ways did he make Jurgis's plight seem typical of urban workers of his time? Why did Jurgis deny that he had ever worked in Chicago before? What did Sinclair reveal about the attitude of employers toward labor unions at that time? About the alliance of business and government in American cities?

The Jungle (1906)
Upton Sinclair

There was another interesting set of statistics that a person might have gathered in Packingtown—those of the various afflictions of the workers. When Jurgis had first inspected the packing plants with Szedvilas, he had marveled while he listened to the tale of all the things that were made out of the carcasses of animals and of all the lesser industries that were maintained

From Upton Sinclair, **The Jungle** (Doubleday, Page and Co., New York, 1906), 116–117, 265–269. Published in the British Commonwealth by Penguin Books, Ltd. Reprinted by permission of the Estate of Upton Sinclair.

there; now he found that each one of these lesser industries was a separate little inferno, in its way as horrible as the killing-beds, the source and fountain of them all. The workers in each of them had their own peculiar diseases. And the wandering visitor might be skeptical about all the swindles, but he could not be skeptical about these, for the worker bore the evidence of them about on his own person—generally he had only to hold out his hand.

There were the men in the pickle rooms, for instance, where old Antanas had gotten his death; scarce a one of these had not some spot of horror on his person. Let a man so much as scrape his finger pushing a truck in the pickle rooms, and he might have a sore that would put him out of the world; all the joints in his fingers might be eaten by the acid, one by one. Of the butchers and floormen, the beef boners and trimmers, and all those who used knives, you could scarcely find a person who had the use of his thumb; time and time again the base of it had been slashed, till it was a mere lump of flesh against which the man pressed the knife to hold it. The hands of these men would be criss-crossed with cuts, until you could no longer pretend to count them or to trace them. They would have no nails,—they had worn them off pulling hides; their knuckles were swollen so that their fingers spread out like a fan. There were men who worked in the cooking rooms, in the midst of steam and sickening odors, by artificial light; in these rooms the germs of tuberculosis might live for two years, but the supply was renewed every hour. There were the beef luggers, who carried two-hundred-pound quarters into the refrigerator cars, a fearful kind of work, that began at four o'clock in the morning, and that wore out the most powerful man in a few years. There were those who worked in the chilling rooms, and whose special disease was rheumatism; the time limit that a man could work in the chilling rooms was said to be five years. There were the wool pluckers, whose hands went to pieces even sooner than the hands of the pickle men; for the pelts of the sheep had to be painted with acid to loosen the wool, and then the pluckers had to pull out this wool with their bare hands, till the acid had eaten their fingers off. There were those who made the tins for the canned meat, and their hands, too, were a maze of cuts, and each cut represented a chance for blood poisoning. Some worked at the stamping machines, and it was very seldom that one could work long there at the pace that was set, and not give out and forget himself, and have a part of his hand chopped off. There were the "hoisters," as they were called, whose task it was to press the lever which lifted the dead cattle off the floor. They ran along upon a rafter, peering down through the damp and the steam, and as old Durham's architects had not built the killing room for the convenience of the hoisters, at every few feet they would have to stoop under a beam, say four feet above the one they ran on, which got them into the habit of stooping, so that in a few years they would be walking like chimpanzees. Worst of any, however, were the fertilizer men, and those who served in the cooking rooms. These people could not be shown to the visitor—for the odor of a fertilizer man would scare any ordinary visitor at a hundred yards, and as for the other men, who worked in tank rooms full of steam and in some of which there were open vats near the level of the floor, their peculiar trouble was that they fell into the vats; and when they were fished out, there was never enough of them left to be worth exhibiting—sometimes they would be overlooked for days, till all but the bones of them had gone out to the world as Durham's Pure Leaf Lard!

*   *   *

Early in the fall Jurgis set out for Chicago again. All the joy went out of tramping as soon as a man could not keep warm in the hay; and, like many thousands of others, he deluded himself with the hope that by coming early he could avoid the rush. He brought fifteen dollars with him, hidden away in one of his shoes, a sum which had been saved from the saloon-keepers, not so much by his conscience, as by the fear which filled him at the thought of being out of work in the city in the wintertime.

He traveled upon the railroad with several other men, hiding in freight cars at night, and liable to be thrown off at any time, regardless of the speed of the train. When he reached the city he left the rest, for he had money and they did not, and he meant to save himself in this fight. He would bring to it all the skill that practice had brought him, and he would stand, whoever fell. On fair nights he would sleep in the park or on a truck or an empty barrel or box, and when it was rainy or cold he would stow himself upon a shelf in a ten-cent lodging-house, or pay three cents for the privileges of a "squatter" in a tenement hallway. He would eat at free lunches, five cents a meal, and never a cent more—so he might keep alive for two months and more, and in that time he would surely find a job. He would have to bid farewell to his summer cleanliness, of course, for he would come out of the first night's lodging with his clothes alive with vermin. There was no place in the city where he could wash even his face, unless he went down to the lake front—and there it would soon be all ice.

First he went to the steel mill and the harvester works, and found that his places there had been filled long ago. He was careful to keep away from the stockyards—he was a single man now, he told himself, and he meant to stay one, to have his wages for his own when he got a job. He began the long, weary round of factories and warehouses, tramping all day, from one end of the city to the other, finding everywhere from ten to a hundred men ahead of him. He watched the newspapers, too—but no longer was he to be taken in by the smooth-spoken agents. He had been told of all those tricks while "on the road."

In the end it was through a newspaper that he got a job, after nearly a month of seeking. It was a call for a hundred laborers, and though he thought it was a "fake," he went because the place was near by. He found a line of men a block long, but as a wagon chanced to come out of an alley and break the line, he saw his chance and sprang to seize a place. Men threatened him and tried to throw him out, but he cursed and made a disturbance to attract a policeman, upon which they subsided, knowing that if the latter interfered it would be to "fire" them all.

Cotton mill doffers. The textile industry was a major employer of women and children, as in this Roanoke, Virginia, mill in 1911. Their wages were low, and they were even more difficult than men to organize into unions. By 1915, many states had laws to regulate hours and working conditions for women and children. But in the South, where labor unions and the reform spirit were weak, such laws were rare. "I was working from 6 in the morning till 7 at night," a millboy said, "with time out for meals. Lifting a hundred pounds, and I only weighed 65 myself." (Library of Congress)

An hour or two later he entered a room and confronted a big Irishman behind a desk.

"Ever worked in Chicago before?" the man inquired; and whether it was a good angel that put it into Jurgis's mind, or an intuition of his sharpened wits, he was moved to answer, "no, sir."

"Where do you come from?"

"Kansas City, sir."

"Any references?"

"No, sir. I'm just an unskilled man, I've got good arms."

"I want men for hard work—it's all underground, digging tunnels for telephones. Maybe it won't suit you."

"I'm willing, sir—anything for me. What's the pay?"

"Fifteen cents an hour."

"I'm willing, sir."

"All right; go back there and give your name."

So within half an hour he was at work, far underneath the streets of the city. The tunnel was a peculiar one for telephone wires; it was about eight feet high, and with a level floor nearly as wide. It had innumerable branches—a perfect spider-web beneath the city; Jurgis walked over half a mile with his gang to the place where they were to work. Stranger yet, the tunnel was lighted by electricity, and upon it was laid a double-tracked, narrow gauge railroad!

But Jurgis was not there to ask questions, and he did not give the matter a thought. It was nearly a year afterward that he finally learned the meaning of this whole affair. The City Council had passed a quiet and innocent little bill allowing a company to construct telephone conduits under the city streets; and upon the strength of this, a great corporation had proceeded to tunnel all Chicago with a system of railway freight subways. In the city there was a combination of employers, representing hundreds of millions of capital, and formed for the purpose of crushing the labor unions. The chief union which troubled it was the teamsters'; and when these freight tunnels were completed, connecting all the big factories and stores with the railroad depots, they would have the teamsters' union by the throat. Now and then there were rumors and murmurs in the Board of Aldermen, and once there was a committee to investigate—but each time another small fortune was paid over, and the rumors died away; until at last the city woke up with a start to find the work completed. There was a tremendous scandal, of course; it was found that the city records had been falsified and other crimes committed, and some of Chicago's big capitalists got into jail—figuratively speaking. The aldermen declared that they had had no idea of it all, in spite of the fact that the main entrance to the work had been in the rear of the saloon of one of them. . . .

In a work thus carried out, not much thought was given to the welfare of the laborers. On an average, the tunnelling cost a life a day and several manglings; it was seldom, however, that more than a dozen or two men heard of any one accident. The work was all done by the new boring-machinery, with as little blasting as possible; but there would be falling rocks and crushed supports and premature explosions—and in addition all the dangers of rail-roading. So it was that one night, as Jurgis was on his way out with his gang, an engine and a loaded car dashed round one of the innumerable right-angle branches and struck him upon the shoulder, hurling him against the concrete wall and knocking him senseless.

When he opened his eyes again it was to the clanging of the bell of an ambulance. He was lying in it, covered by a blanket, and it was heading its way slowly through the holiday-shopping crowds. They took him to the county hospital, where a young surgeon set his arm, then he was washed and laid upon a bed in a ward with a score or two more of maimed and mangled men.

═══════

17.

CITY LIGHTS

Progressivism was a powerful force in turn-of-the-century America. Progressives believed in efficiency, so they fought to reform the civil service and to make government as effective and accountable as private business. They believed that capital, labor, and government should work together, so they urged the mediation of labor conflicts and the regulation of giant corporations. Believing in citizen participation, Progressives pioneered woman suffrage, the secret ballot, and the removal from office of corrupt officials by popular vote. Concerned with the suffering poor, Progressives promoted charity work, better public schools, university extension service, and better housing; they thought saloons and liquor caused trouble, so they struggled for prohibition. Most Progressives were educated, middle-class, native-born Protestants who felt uneasy around corporate greed and slum violence; they could be both self-righteous and narrow-minded. But they cared about the country. They were confident they could change things, and tried energetically to do just that. As President Theodore Roosevelt once cried on their behalf, "We stand at Armageddon and do battle for the Lord."

Settlement houses were quintessential Progressive institutions, places where the Progressive flame burned brightest. Established throughout urban America between 1880 and 1920, settlement houses —largely the handiwork of women reformers—arose to serve the vast swarm of newcomers to the country's great cities; these new "settlers" were European immigrants for the most part, but also included recent arrivals, black and white, from the rural South. The settlement houses provided meeting halls; the staffs sponsored lectures, encouraged political participation and sometimes union activity, taught English classes, agitated for tighter health codes, and held citizenship and naturalization classes. These early social workers paid special attention to the problems of poor women and inevitably, therefore, to the problems of immigrant families.

Urban youth were a particular concern of the settlements. Settlement workers labored ceaselessly for child labor laws, more playgrounds, better schools; they worked to heal the generation gap between immigrant parents clinging to older ways and children rejecting everything old and old-fashioned, including the parents. The social workers tried to explain the new land to these children and to give them a smattering of self-improvement and urban survival skills. The following excerpt was written by Jane Addams, founder of Chicago's Hull House and in 1909 probably the country's most illustrious woman—almost certainly its most famous reformer. In this work, as in all her writing and lectures, Addams used her experience at Hull House with characteristic brilliance. She did settlement work to benefit local Chicagoans. She then used local Chicagoans as case studies to demonstrate how badly the industrial system was damaging urban youth and how the system might be counteracted. This approach understandably brought great credit to the settlement houses and also great prestige to the reformers. Eventually their influence spread from neighborhood to city to state to, at last, nation.

Jane Addams was born in 1860 into a small-town middle-class Illinois family. After her graduation from college in 1881, Addams visited Europe, where she became inspired by a pioneer English settlement house that worked with the London poor. By 1889 she had founded a similar house in a ramshackle Chicago mansion. Addams attracted numerous bright, dedicated young women to work with her, including Florence Kelley, later an Illinois factory inspector, and Mary Kenny, a labor organizer. Together the three made Hull House famous. Addams's writings and speeches helped spread its reputation. **The Spirit of Youth and the City Streets** alone sold twenty thousand copies, and Addams's autobiography far more. She received the Nobel Peace Prize in 1931, four years before her death.

Questions to consider. Why did Addams see the theater as a serious urban problem, and how did she propose to combat it? Does her distinction between baseball and theater seem valid? How did she account for the popularity of saloons among youth? What would she offer as a substitute? What role did factory labor play in the lives of the urban youth described by Addams? How did factory labor affect their behavior? Did she propose fundamental changes? Do her alternatives seem realistic? Would the problems of the theater, the saloon, and the factory have affected small-town youth, too?

The Spirit of Youth (1909)
Jane Addams

This spring a group of young girls accustomed to the life of a five-cent theater, reluctantly refused an invitation to go to the country for a day's outing because the return on a late train would compel them to miss one evening's perform- ance. They found it impossible to tear themselves away not only from the excitements of the theater itself but from the gaiety of the crowd of young men and girls invariably gathered outside discussing the sensational posters.

A steady English shopkeeper lately complained that unless he provided his four daughters with the money for the five-cent theaters every evening they would steal it from his till, and he feared that they might be driven to procure it in even more illicit ways. Because his entire family life had been thus disrupted he gloomily asserted that "this cheap show had ruined his 'ome and was the curse of America." This father was able to formulate the anxiety of many immigrant parents who are absolutely bewildered by the keen absorp- tion of their children in the cheap theater. This anxiety is not, indeed, without foundation. An eminent alienist of Chicago states that he has had a number of patients among neurotic children whose emotional natures have been so over-wrought by the crude appeal to which they had been so constantly sub- jected in the theaters, that they have become victims of hallucination and mental disorder. The statement of this physician may be the first note of alarm which will awaken the city to its duty in regard to the theater, so that it shall at least be made safe and sane for the city child whose senses are already so abnormally developed.

This testimony of a physician that the conditions are actually pathological, may at last induce us to bestir ourselves in regard to procuring a more whole- some form of public recreation. Many efforts in social amelioration have been undertaken only after such exposures; in the meantime, while the occasional child is driven distraught, a hundred children permanently injure their eyes watching the moving films, and hundreds more seriously model their conduct upon the standards set before them on this mimic stage.

Three boys, aged nine, eleven and thirteen years, who had recently seen depicted the adventures of frontier life including the holding up of a stage coach and the lassoing of the driver, spent weeks planning to lasso, murder, and rob a neighborhood milkman, who started on his route at four o'clock in the morning. They made their headquarters in a barn and saved enough money to buy a revolver, adopting as their watchword the phrase "Dead Men Tell no Tales." One spring morning the conspirators, with their faces covered with black cloth, lay "in ambush" for the milkman. Fortunately for him, as the lariat was thrown the horse shied, and, although the shot was appropriately

From Jane Addams, **The Spirit of Youth and the City Streets** (The Macmillan Company, New York, 1909).

Jane Addams.   Addams's first concern was the immigrants and their acculturation in the United States. From this starting point she moved in a logical progres-
sion to the problems of industrial workers and urban youth. She never used the
words "adolescent" or "teenager." She thought the first too dry and academic;
the second was slang. Still, this was the age group that most concerned her, as
indeed it worried many other adults of that period. But they often wanted to
pound delinquency out of the young by finger-wagging, confinement, and force.
"Saint Jane" hoped to bury the bad tendencies of young people by giving their
good ones a fighting ʰance. (Photograph by Wallace Kirkland, Jane Addams
Memorial Collection, University of Illinois at Chicago Library)

fired, the milkman's life was saved. Such a direct influence of the theater is
by no means rare, even among older boys. Thirteen young lads were brought
into the Municipal Court in Chicago during the first week that "Raffles,
the Amateur Cracksman" was upon the stage, each one with an outfit of
burglar's tools in his possession, and each one shamefacedly admitting that

the gentlemanly burglar in the play had suggested to him a career of similar adventure.

In so far as the illusions of the theater succeed in giving youth the rest and recreation which comes from following a more primitive code of morality, it has a close relation to the function performed by public games. It is, of course, less valuable because the sense of participation is largely confined to the emotions and the imagination, and does not involve the entire nature.

We might illustrate by the "Wild West Show" in which the onlooking boy imagines himself an active participant. The scouts, the Indians, the bucking ponies, are his real intimate companions and occupy his entire mind. In contrast with this we have the omnipresent game of tag which is, doubtless, also founded upon the chase. It gives the boy exercise and momentary echoes of the old excitement, but it is barren of suggestion and quickly degenerates into horse-play.

Well considered public games easily carried out in a park or athletic field, might both fill the mind with the imaginative material constantly supplied by the theater, and also afford the activity which the cramped muscles of the town dweller so sorely need. Even the unquestioned ability which the theater possesses to bring men together into a common mood and to afford them a mutual topic of conversation, is better accomplished with the one national game which we already possess, and might be infinitely extended through the organization of other public games.

The theater even now by no means competes with the baseball league games which are attended by thousands of men and boys who, during the entire summer, discuss the respective standing of each nine and the relative merits of every player. During the noon hour all the employees of a city factory gather in the nearest vacant lot to cheer their own home team in its practice for the next game with the nine of a neighboring manufacturing establishment and on a Saturday afternoon the entire male population of the city betakes itself to the baseball field; the ordinary means of transportation are supplemented by gay stage-coaches and huge automobiles, noisy with blowing horns and decked with gay pennants. The enormous crowd of cheering men and boys are talkative, good-natured, full of the holiday spirit, and absolutely released from the grind of life. They are lifted out of their individual affairs and so fused together that a man cannot tell whether it is his own shout or another's that fills his ears; whether it is his own coat or another's that he is wildly waving to celebrate a victory. He does not call the stranger who sits next to him his "brother" but he unconsciously embraces him in an overwhelming outburst of kindly feeling when the favorite player makes a home run. Does not this contain a suggestion of the undoubted power of public recreation to bring together all classes of a community in the modern city unhappily so full of devices for keeping men apart? . . .

. . . In the saloon halls the young people were obliged to "pass money freely over the bar," and in order to make the most of the occasion they usually stayed until morning. At such times the economic necessity itself would override the counsels of the more temperate, and the thrifty door keeper would not insist upon invitations but would take in any one who had the "price of a ticket."[1] The free rent in the park hall, the good food in the park restaurant, supplied at cost, have made three parties closing at eleven o'clock no more expensive than one party breaking up at daylight, too often in disorder.

Is not this an argument that the drinking, the late hours, the lack of decorum, are directly traceable to the commercial enterprise which ministers to pleasure in order to drag it into excess because excess is more profitable? To thus commercialize pleasure is as monstrous as it is to commercialize art. It is intolerable that the city does not take over this function of making provision for pleasure, as wise communities in Sweden and South Carolina have taken the sale of alcohol out of the hands of enterprising publicans.

We are only beginning to understand what might be done through the festival, the street procession, the band of marching musicians, orchestral music in public squares or parks, with the magic power they all possess to formulate the sense of companionship and solidarity. . . .

As it is possible to establish a connection between the lack of public recreation and the vicious excitements and trivial amusements which become their substitutes, so it may be illuminating to trace the connection between the monotony and dullness of factory work and the petty immoralities which are often the youth's protest against them.

There are many city neighborhoods in which practically every young person who has attained the age of fourteen years enters a factory. When the work itself offers nothing of interest, and when no public provision is made for recreation, the situation becomes almost insupportable to the youth whose ancestors have been rough-working and hard-playing peasants.

In such neighborhoods the joy of youth is well nigh extinguished; and in that long procession of factory workers, each morning and evening, the young walk almost as wearily and listlessly as the old. Young people working in modern factories situated in cities still dominated by the ideals of Puritanism face a combination which tends almost irresistibly to overwhelm the spirit of youth. When the Puritan repression of pleasure was in the ascendant in America the people it dealt with lived on farms and villages where, although youthful pleasures might be frowned upon and crushed out, the young people still had a chance to find self-expression in their work. Plowing the field and spinning the flax could be carried on with a certain joyousness and vigor which the organization of modern industry too often precludes. Present industry based upon the inventions of the nineteenth century has little connection with the old patterns in which men have worked for generations. The modern factory calls for an expenditure of nervous energy almost more than it demands muscular effort, or at least machinery so far performs the work of the massive muscles, that greater stress is laid upon fine and exact movements

---

[1] Addams is describing special occasions or celebrations where people were admitted by either an invitation or a "cover charge" and could then remain as long as they continued to buy drinks (at a reduced price).—Eds.

necessarily involving nervous strain. But these movements are exactly of the type to which the muscles of a growing boy least readily respond, quite as the admonition to be accurate and faithful is that which appeals the least to his big primitive emotions. . . .

In vast regions of the city which are completely dominated by the factory, it is as if the development of industry had outrun all the educational and social arrangements.

The revolt of youth against uniformity and the necessity of following careful directions laid down by some one else, many times results in such nervous irritability that the youth, in spite of all sorts of prudential reasons, "throws up his job," if only to get outside the factory walls into the freer street, just as the narrowness of the school inclosure induces many a boy to jump the fence.

When the boy is on the street, however, and is "standing around on the corner" with the gang to which he mysteriously attaches himself, he finds the difficulties of direct untrammeled action almost as great there as they were in the factory, but for an entirely different set of reasons. The necessity so strongly felt in the factory for an outlet to his sudden and furious bursts of energy, his overmastering desire to prove that he could do things "without being bossed all the time," finds little chance for expression, for he discovers that in whatever really active pursuit he tries to engage, he is promptly suppressed by the police. . . .

The unjustifiable lack of educational supervision during the first years of factory work makes it quite impossible for the modern educator to offer any real assistance to young people during that trying transitional period between school and industry. The young people themselves who fail to conform can do little but rebel against the entire situation.

There are many touching stories by which this might be illustrated. One of them comes from a large steel mill of a boy of fifteen whose business it was to throw a lever when a small tank became filled with molten metal. During the few moments when the tank was filling it was his foolish custom to catch the reflection of the metal upon a piece of looking-glass, and to throw the bit of light into the eyes of his fellow workmen. Although an exasperated foreman had twice dispossessed him of his mirror, with a third fragment he was one day flicking the gloom of the shop when the neglected tank overflowed, almost instantly burning off both his legs. Boys working in the stock yards, during their moments of wrestling and rough play, often slash each other painfully with the short knives which they use in their work, but in spite of this the play impulse is too irrepressible to be denied. . . .

The discovery of the labor power of youth was to our age like the discovery of a new natural resource, although it was merely incidental to the invention of modern machinery and the consequent subdivision of labor. In utilizing it thus ruthlessly we are not only in danger of quenching the divine fire of youth, but we are imperiling industry itself when we venture to ignore these very sources of beauty, of variety and of suggestion.

18.

MONEY AND MERCY

Side by side with Progressive reform stood the gospel of wealth, and not merely Andrew Carnegie's national wealth, product of industrial progress, but individual wealth, product of private striving and ambition. The louder the call for reform, it seemed, the more alluring the appeal of getting and having money. Joining the voices of Carnegie and John D. Rockefeller (who made his fortune by monopolizing oil production and refining) were those of Horatio Alger, who wrote novels showing how the "plucky" found fortune, and the Reverend Henry Ward Beecher, whose Brooklyn pulpit echoed to the praises of financial success. And for every reformer thundering against "big business" was a Russell Conwell urging people to "get rich quick." The tension between reform and avarice was a theme song of the Progressive era.

Also typical of the period were the vehicles used by these figures to publicize their views. The mass-circulation magazines and such general-interest publications as **The Saturday Evening Post,** which sold for a nickel or a dime a copy, reached hundreds of thousands of readers in the early 1900s. Another medium, the lecture circuit or "Chautauqua," had its origins in summer programs for Sunday-school teachers in the 1870s in the New York resort area around Lake Chautauqua. Noticing that by the 1890s cheap railroad fares were enabling middle-class families to summer in the region, hotels and civic groups started sponsoring Chautauqua lectures on nonreligious subjects as well. Within a decade, recreational promoters had established more than two hundred Chautauqua-type resorts, all offering notable guest speakers. Thus a lecture circuit evolved where lecturers willing to keep traveling and talking could make significant amounts of money and spread their views, too. Here Jane Addams (Document 17) addressed the ordeal of the modern city. Here William Jennings Bryan gave his famous "Cross of Gold" speech assailing bankers (first delivered in 1896 at the Democratic Party convention) many thousands of times.

No one worked the Chautauqua circuit to better financial advantage than Russell Conwell. Born on a farm in western Massachusetts in 1843, Conwell studied at Yale and fought in the Civil War before embarking on short careers ranging from journalism to law to the ministry. In the 1880s he became interested in education, taught sporadically, and helped found what later became Temple University in Philadelphia. Philadelphia became his permanent home and also the setting for his fabulously successful lecture, "Acres of Diamonds." On the Chautauqua circuit of the 1890s, Conwell, thanks to the little speech excerpted below, finally achieved true fame and real fortune. He delivered it more than six thousand times before publishing it in a book of essays by the same name. By the time Conwell died in Philadelphia in 1925, the speech had earned him eight million dollars.

Questions to consider. Russell Conwell argued in his speech that making money is not just permissible but admirable. On what grounds did he make this claim? What sort of audience did he seem to be addressing? What concerns did he think his audience had about making money? How did he reconcile the existence of immense personal wealth with the existence of widespread poverty? What kind of evidence did he use to persuade his audience? Was he lecturing, perhaps, to the already converted? It has been said that Conwell reformulated the concept of charity from "Give What You Can" to "Get What You Give" and then neglected "Give" for "Get." Is this interpretation valid?

Acres of Diamonds (1915)
Russell Conwell

I have come to tell you what in God's sight I believe to be the truth, and if the years of life have been of any value to me in the attainment of common sense, I know I am right; that the men and women sitting here, who found it difficult perhaps to buy a ticket to this lecture or gathering to-night, have within their reach "acres of diamonds," opportunities to get largely wealthy. There never was a place on earth more adapted than the city of Philadelphia to-day, and never in the history of the world did a poor man without capital have such an opportunity to get rich quickly and honestly as he has now in our city. I say it is the truth, and I want you to accept it as such; for if you think I have come to simply recite something, then I would better not be here. I have no time to waste in any such talk, but to say the things I believe, and unless some of you get richer for what I am saying to-night my time is wasted.

I say that you ought to get rich, and it is your duty to get rich. How many of my pious brethren say to me, "Do you, a Christian minister, spend your time going up and down the country advising young people to get rich, to get money?" "Yes, of course I do." They say, "Isn't that awful! Why don't you preach the gospel instead of preaching about man's making

From Russell Conwell, **Acres of Diamonds** (Harper and Bros., New York, 1915), 18–21.

money?" "Because to make money honestly is to preach the gospel." That is
the reason. The men who get rich may be the most honest men you find in
the community.

"Oh," but says some young man here to-night, "I have been told all my
life that if a person has money he is very dishonest and dishonorable and mean
and contemptible." My friend, that is the reason why you have none, because
you have that idea of people. The foundation of your faith is altogether false.
Let me say here clearly, and say it briefly, though subject to discussion which
I have not time for here, ninety-eight out of one hundred of the rich men of
America are honest. That is why they are rich. That is why they are trusted
with money. That is why they carry on great enterprises and find plenty of
people to work with them. It is because they are honest men.

Says another young man, "I hear sometimes of men that get millions
of dollars dishonestly." Yes, of course you do, and so do I. But they are so
rare a thing in fact that the newspapers talk about them all the time as a
matter of news until you get the idea that all the other rich men got rich
dishonestly. . . .

My friend, you take and drive me—if you furnish the auto—out into the
suburbs of Philadelphia, and introduce me to the people who own their homes
around this great city, those beautiful homes with gardens and flowers, those
magnificent homes so lovely in their art, and I will introduce you to the very
best people in character as well as in enterprise in our city, and you know I
will. A man is not really a true man until he owns his own home, and they
that own their homes are made more honorable and honest and pure, and true
and economical and careful, by owning the home.

For a man to have money, even in large sums, is not an inconsistent
thing. We preach against covetousness, and you know we do, in the pulpit,
and oftentimes preach against it so long and use the terms about "filthy lucre"
so extremely that Christians get the idea that when we stand in the pulpit we
believe it is wicked for any man to have money—until the collection-basket
goes around, and then we almost swear at the people because they don't give
more money. Oh, the inconsistency of such doctrines as that!

Money is power, and you ought to be reasonably ambitious to have it.
You ought because you can do more good with it than you could without it.
Money printed your Bible, money builds your churches, money sends your
missionaries, and money pays your preachers, and you would not have many
of them, either, if you did not pay them. I am always willing that my church
should raise my salary, because the church that pays the largest salary always
raises it the easiest. You never knew an exception to it in your life. The man
who gets the largest salary can do the most good with the power that is
furnished to him. Of course he can if his spirit be right to use it for what it
is given to him.

I say, then, you ought to have money. If you can honestly attain unto
riches in Philadelphia, it is your Christian and godly duty to do so. It is an

awful mistake of these pious people to think you must be awfully poor in order to be pious.

Some men say, "Don't you sympathize with the poor people?" Of course I do, or else I would not have been lecturing these years. I won't give in but what I sympathize with the poor, but the number of poor who are to be sympathized with is very small. To sympathize with a man whom God has punished for his sins, thus to help him when God would still continue a just punishment, is to do wrong, no doubt about it, and we do that more than we help those who are deserving. While we should sympathize with God's poor—that is, those who cannot help themselves—let us remember there is not a poor person in the United States who was not made poor by his own shortcomings, or by the shortcomings of some one else. It is all wrong to be poor anyhow. Let us give in to that argument and pass that to one side.

A gentleman gets up back there, and says, "Don't you think there are some things in this world that are better than money?" Of course I do, but I am talking about money now. Of course there are some things higher than money. Oh yes, I know by the grave that has left me standing alone that there are some things in this world that are higher and sweeter and purer than money. Well do I know there are some things higher and grander than gold. Love is the grandest thing on God's earth, but fortunate the lover who has plenty of money. Money is power, money is force; money will do good.

19.

A PROGRESSIVE SPIRIT

The campaign for women's rights, which had begun before the Civil War, made painfully slow progress after the war. Most Americans continued to hold fast to the idea that a woman is weaker than a man and that her place is in the home caring for her husband and children. Age-old handicaps persisted: educational deprivation, legal discrimination, economic exploitation, and political disfranchisement. But veteran women's rights leaders like Elizabeth Cady Stanton (Vol. 1, Document 29) carried on the struggle for equal rights undaunted, and energetic new reformers like Anna Howard Shaw joined their ranks. There was some progress in education: women's colleges appeared and the new state universities opened their doors to women. There was also some improvement in the legal status of married women. Yet the inequalities remained great. The number of women entering professions like law and medicine remained minuscule, and whenever women did obtain work outside the home they were vastly underpaid.

Some feminists placed major emphasis on the right to vote. With the ballot in their hands, they argued, American women would have a powerful weapon with which to fight for all their other rights. The suffragists sought action at both the federal and the state levels. Congress began considering suffrage proposals as early as 1868 but failed to adopt any of them. The states did somewhat better. In 1890 Wyoming entered the Union with woman suffrage, and a few years later Colorado, Utah, and Idaho followed suit. By 1914, eleven states, all but one in the West, had given women the right to vote, and in 1916 Montana sent the first woman, Jeannette Rankin, to Congress. By this time, Carrie Chapman Catt, successor to Susan B. Anthony as president of the National Woman Suffrage Association, and other suffragists had renewed their struggle for federal action. In 1919, at long last, Congress passed an amendment to the Constitution stating that the right of citizens to vote could not "be denied or abridged by the United States or by any state on account of sex." Ratification of the Nineteenth Amendment by the states was complete by August 1920, and American women were able to vote in the presidential election that November.

Meanwhile, the struggle for women's economic and social, as well as political, rights continued. The General Federation of Women's Clubs, founded in 1889, devoted considerable energy toward improving working conditions for women and children in industry. At the same time radical feminists like Margaret H. Sanger and Emma Goldman began sponsoring unrestricted dissemination of birth-control information. The birth-control advocates at first stressed economics: the gradual reduction in the size of the working class by means of birth control, they insisted, would increase labor's ability to bargain with the capitalists. But the birth-control movement took root among middle-class rather than working-class women and centered on individual self-fulfillment rather than social reconstruction. The prospect of "free motherhood" and family planning appealed to middle-class women; it would, they realized, liberate them from many restrictions of the traditional American home. But it was not until after the adoption of the Nineteenth Amendment that feminists began devoting major energies to the birth-control crusade.

From almost the crusade's beginning, the name of Margaret Sanger and the cause of birth control were synonymous. Sanger and her friends, in fact, invented the term **birth control.** Sanger was not the first advocate of planned parenthood, nor was she the only influential leader in the movement. But her effectiveness, both as speaker and writer, soon won her fame both in the United States and abroad.

Margaret Sanger, the sixth of eleven children, was born in Corning, New York, in 1883. She studied nursing as a young woman and became a maternity nurse serving in New York City's crowded Lower East Side. There she became aware of the poverty, misery, illness, and even death produced by involuntary pregnancies and self-induced abortions. She gave up nursing in 1912 to devote her full attention to the cause of birth control. In 1914 she founded the National Birth Control League and began publishing a magazine called **Woman Rebel,** which had the slogan "No Gods, No Masters" on the masthead. The birth-control movement, Sanger contended, freed the mind from "sexual prejudice and taboo" and helped put women on an equal plane with men. In 1915 she was indicted for sending birth-control literature through the mails and in 1916 arrested for operating a birth-control clinic in Brooklyn. During her brief prison stay she started a new magazine called the **Birth Control Review,** which was dedicated to the scientific control of human reproduction. After World War I, she began achieving some of her objectives. With the relaxation of laws forbidding doctors to prescribe contraceptives and give instruction in birth-control methods she was able to open a birth-control clinic in Manhattan and to encourage the formation of similar clinics in other cities. She sponsored numerous national and international birth-control conferences and published many articles and books on birth control and sex education. She died in Tucson, Arizona, in 1966.

Questions to consider. Among Sanger's many writings was a book entitled **Happiness in Marriage,** published in 1926 and centered on transforming marriage into a voluntary association. In the excerpt from the book reprinted below, Sanger expanded on the ways in which "premature parenthood" could wreck marriage. How did she think the "position of womanhood" had changed in the past few years? What did she mean by saying that social equality complicates as well as ennobles the marriage relationship? What objectives did she seek for American women, and why did she think birth control would help them achieve those objectives? How convincing do you think her argument was for people (and there were still many in the early twentieth century) who thought birth-control literature was obscene? Sanger was considered a radical in her day. Would she be called one today?

Happiness in Marriage (1926)
Margaret H. Sanger

We must recognize that the whole position of womanhood has changed today. Not so many years ago it was assumed to be a just and natural state of affairs that marriage was considered as nothing but a preliminary to motherhood. A girl passed from the guardianship of her father or nearest male relative to that of her husband. She had no will, no wishes of her own. Hers not to question why, but merely to fulfil duties imposed upon her by the man into whose care she was given.

Marriage was synonymous with maternity. But the pain, the suffering, the wrecked lives of women and children that such a system caused, show us that it did not work successfully. Like all other professions, motherhood must serve its period of apprenticeship.

Today women are on the whole much more individual. They possess as strong likes and dislikes as men. They live more and more on the plane of social equality with men. They are better companions. We should be glad that there is more enjoyable companionship and real friendship between men and women.

This very fact, it is true, complicates the marriage relation, and at the same time ennobles it. Marriage no longer means the slavish subservience of the woman to the will of the man. It means, instead, the union of two strong and highly individualized natures. Their first problem is to find out just what the terms of this partnership are to be. Understanding full and complete cannot come all at once, in one revealing flash. It takes time to arrive at a full and

From Margaret Sanger, **Happiness in Marriage** (Blue Ribbon Books, New York, 1926), 83–97.

Margaret Sanger. Activists like Margaret Sanger provided a major impetus to social reform between 1900 and 1925. In these years, government spending on education and welfare at all levels rose by 1,000 percent to approximately $5 billion. The biggest increase came at the local level, and of this local increase, the bulk went for schooling. The number of child workers shrank drastically. So, too, did the burglary rate and the consumption of alcohol. Contraceptive use spread most rapidly among America's middle classes, whose symbol of the liberated woman became not the social activist but the flapper. This photograph shows Margaret Sanger (left) at the booth of the National Committee on Federal Legislation for Birth Control. (Library of Congress)

sympathetic understanding of each other, and mutually to arrange lives to increase this understanding. Out of the mutual adjustments, harmony must grow and discords gradually disappear.

These results cannot be obtained if the problem of parenthood is thrust upon the young husband and wife before they are spiritually and economically prepared to meet it. For naturally the coming of the first baby means that all other problems must be thrust aside. That baby is a great fact, a reality that must be met. Preparations must be made for its coming. The layette must be prepared. The doctor must be consulted. The health of the wife may need consideration. The young mother will probably prefer to go to the hospital. All of these preparations are small compared to the regime after the coming of the infant.

Now there is a proper moment for every human activity, a proper season for every step in self-development. The period for cementing the bond of love is no exception to this great truth. For only by the full and glorious living through these years of early marriage are the foundations of an enduring and happy married life rendered possible. By this period the woman attains a spiritual freedom. Her womanhood has a chance to bloom. She wins a mastery over her destiny; she acquires self-reliance, poise, strength, a youthful maturity. She abolishes fear. Incidentally, few of us realize, since the world keeps no record of this fact, how many human beings are conceived in fear and even in repugnance by young mothers who are the victims of undesired maternity. Nor has science yet determined the possibilities of a generation conceived and born of conscious desire.

In the wife who has lived through a happy marriage, for whom the bonds of passionate love have been fully cemented, maternal desire is intensified and matured. Motherhood becomes for such a woman not a penalty or a punishment, but the road by which she travels onward toward completely rounded self-development. Motherhood thus helps her toward the unfolding and realization of her higher nature.

Her children are not mere accidents, the outcome of chance. When motherhood is a mere accident, as so often it is in the early years of careless or reckless marriages, a constant fear of pregnancy may poison the days and nights of the young mother. Her marriage is thus converted into a tragedy. Motherhood becomes for her a horror instead of a joyfully fulfilled function.

Millions of marriages have been blighted, not because of any lack of love between the young husband and wife, but because children have come too soon. Often these brides become mothers before they have reached even physical maturity, before they have completed the period of adolescence. This period in our race is as a rule complete around the age of twenty-three. Motherhood is possible after the first menstruation. But what is physically possible is very often from every other point of view inadvisable. A young woman should be fully matured from every point of view—physically, mentally and psychically—before maternity is thrust upon her.

Those who advise early maternity neglect the spiritual foundation upon which marriage must inevitably be built. This takes time. They also ignore the financial responsibility a family brings.

The young couple begin to build a home. They may have just enough to get along together. The young wife, as in so many cases of early marriage these days, decides to continue her work. They are partners in every way—a commendable thing. The young man is just beginning his career—his salary is probably small. Nevertheless, they manage to get along, their hardships are amusing, and are looked upon as fun. Then suddenly one day, the young wife announces her pregnancy. The situation changes immediately. There are added expenses. The wife must give up her work. The husband must go into debt to pay the expenses of the new and joyfully received arrival. The novelty lasts for some time. The young wife assumes the household duties and the ever growing care of the infant. For a time the child seems to bring the couple closer together. But more often there ensues a concealed resentment on the part of the immature mother at the constant drudgery and slavery to the unfortunate child who has arrived too early upon the scene, which has interfered with her love life.

Two brothers I know married practically at the same time. They were both carpenters, living in the same neighborhood. The wife of the one gave birth to six children in a period of ten years. In spite of the efforts of the man to sustain the family, they were forced at the end of ten years to accept outside charity. The wife became a household drudge, nervous, broken, spiritless, neglected by her husband, despised by her children. The wife of the other brother did not become a mother until three years after marriage. This man remained throughout the ten years of my observation, clean, alert, honest, kind to his wife and two children. The wife kept up neat, tidy looks and was able to help her husband and children to advance themselves. Yet at the time of marriage both girls were equally attractive and intelligent.

The problem of premature parenthood is intensified and aggravated when a second infant follows too rapidly the advent of the first, and inevitably husband and wife are made the slaves of this undreamed of situation, bravely trying to stave off poverty, whipped to desperation by the heavy hand of chance and involuntary parenthood. How can they then recapture their early love? It is not surprising that more often they do not even trouble themselves to conceal the contempt which is the bitter fruit of that young and romantic passion.

For the unthinking husband, the "proud papa," the blushing bride is converted at once into the "mother of my children." It is not an unusual occurrence to find that three months after the birth of the baby, the parents are thinking and speaking to each other as "mumsy" and "daddy." The lover and sweetheart relation has disappeared forever and the "mama-papa" relation has taken its place.

Instead of being a self-determined and self-directing love, everything is henceforward determined by the sweet tyranny of the child. I have known of several young mothers, despite a great love for the child, to rebel against this intolerable situation. Vaguely feeling that this new maternity has rendered them unattractive to their husbands, slaves to a deadly routine of bottles, baths and washing, they have revolted. I know of innumerable marriages which have been wrecked by premature parenthood.

Love has ever been blighted by the coming of children before the real foundations of marriage have been established. Quite aside from the injustice done to the child who has been brought accidentally into the world, this lamentable fact sinks into insignificance when compared to the injustice inflicted by chance upon the young couple, and the irreparable blow to their love occasioned by premature or involuntary parenthood.

For these reasons, in order that harmonious and happy marriage may be established as the foundation for happy homes and the advent of healthy and desired children, premature parenthood must be avoided. Birth Control is the instrument by which this universal problem may be solved.

20.

ORGANIZATION MEN

Salesmanship and corporate organization were distinctive features of the U.S. economy by the 1920s. Giant factories produced such a river of goods that getting them distributed gave business considerable concern. Since distribution was ultimately a matter of selling, the salesperson became a key economic actor and therefore a familiar figure on the social landscape—the Fuller Brush man with his satchel of wares, the encyclopedia salesman peddling knowledge, the Hoover vacuum cleaner representative, and the real estate and insurance agents. Sinclair Lewis took their group snapshot in his novel **Babbitt**. Dale Carnegie wrote their standard "how-to" manuals in his series of pamphlets on **How to Win Friends and Influence People.**

But the era's principal sellers were not individuals; they were corporations. This era, after all, was the heyday of Ford, Kodak, Armour, General Electric, and U.S. Steel. The Hoover man and his fellow salesmen were cogs in large industrial enterprises with many functions and many layers of labor. Dale Carnegie taught people to sell themselves as well as their product, to "win friends," to "get along," and to appreciate teamwork. Corporations were in fact giant collectivities: huge teams working toward the common goal of corporate profit. Who better, then, to instruct and inspire them than the head of the winningest team of all?

The 1920s were the first golden age of big-time sports. Athletes such as Babe Ruth, Red Grange, Bill Tilden, and Jack Dempsey captivated the throngs with their exploits on the diamond, the gridiron, the court, and the canvas. Professional athletes became major entertainment figures, sometimes making staggering amounts of money, but amateurs like Tilden and golfer Bobby Jones were almost as famous. So great was the glory that everyone around the athletes shared it, from sports journalists such as Ring Lardner to franchise owners such as Charles Comiskey to managers and league officials such as Connie Mack and Kenesaw Mountain Landis. The sporting public indiscriminately lionized them all.

College football shared this big-time sporting scene. Fans, alumni, and students packed the oval stadiums week after week all across the country, and in a sizable arena with major rivals—Army and Navy, Harvard and Yale, Notre Dame and almost anyone—crowds could reach nearly a hundred thousand people. Understandably, college football coaches became celebrities in their own right, much sought after for charity events or after-dinner speeches. Walter Camp of Yale football was as big a draw as John McGraw of New York baseball.

Most celebrated of the college football coaches was Knute Rockne, head of the most dominant team, Notre Dame. A Norwegian by birth, Rockne emigrated to the United States in 1893, where he managed to obtain what all good Catholic boys aspired to: an education and a spot on the Notre Dame football team. By 1918, Rockne was head coach of the "Fighting Irish." Over the next thirteen years he compiled an amazing record: 105 wins and 12 losses, including five undefeated seasons, against the stiffest competition. From 1928 to his death in a plane crash in 1931, Rockne worked in the off-season for the Studebaker Corporation, giving sales talks like the one excerpted below. As he did in this talk, Rockne often invoked the memory of George Gipp, a player who died in mid-career. His famous line "Win one for the Gipper'" was later immortalized in a movie about his career; the part of Gipp was played by a young actor named Ronald Reagan.

Questions to consider. In this speech it appears that Rockne was instilling values rather than teaching techniques. Why might the Studebaker Corporation have felt the need to emphasize teamwork in the late 1920s? Which values was the company trying to combat? How would Andrew Carnegie (Document 14) or Russell Conwell (Document 18) have reacted to the speech? Note, also, how Rockne used anecdotes from the football field to illustrate general principles. Do you find the speech persuasive? Does playing on a football team resemble working for a corporation? Would running the team resemble running the corporation? Would another sport—baseball, say, or track and field—have worked as well? Or was football particularly appropriate?

═══════════

A Sales Promotion Address (1928)
Knute Rockne

I don't know anything about selling automobiles; I never sold one in my life; but perhaps a few remarks here on the psychology that is necessary for success in a football organization might not be out of place because it seems to me that the same psychology that makes for success in a football organization will make for success in any organization, and particularly in a selling organization.

From McCready Huston, **Salesman from the Sidelines: Being the Business Career of Knute K. Rockne** (New York: Ray Long and Richard R. Smith, 1932), 26–33. Reprinted by permission of Anne Huston Barron, Executor, Estate of McCready Huston, and Mary Jeanne Rockne Kochendorfer.

Now in the fall when we make our first call for the team, about three hundred and fifty lads assemble in a large room in the library; and it is my idea to talk to them on the correct psychology before I take them out on the field. I talk to them on ambition and I tell them that most of what I read about ambition is bunk. There is not plenty of room at the top. There is very little room at the top. There is room at the top only for the few who have the ability and the imagination and the daring and the personality and the energy that make them stand out from among their fellow men. But there is success for any man in his own job if he does it as well as it can be done. As far as I am able to observe the greatest satisfaction I can get on this earth is to do the particular job I am doing as well as it can be done; and I think that holds good for every one. There may be other things that are easier, but they generally leave a headache or a heartache the day after.

I tell the lads there are five types I do not want. And I say the first type I have in mind is the swelled head. The man who was a success a year ago and who is content to rest on his laurels, who wants to play on his reputation. Dry rot sets in and he ceases to make an effort. To that kind of boy there will come quite a shock because the chances are there will be someone playing in his place.

The second type is the chronic complainer. They crab at everyone but themselves. And I say no organization can afford to have that type of man among them because complaining is infectious. And I say the complainer is in for quite a shock, too, because as soon as I can find out who the complainers are, why some evening when they come out for practice there will be no suits in their lockers.

And third is the quitter. The quitter is the fellow who wishes he could play but who is not willing to pay the price; and I tell the boys if one of that type is here he might just as well quit now and not wear out the equipment.

I don't want boys to dissipate physically or emotionally. I tell them that I have no brief against playing pool long hours in the afternoon, dancing half the night, or learning to drive an automobile with one hand; but I tell them we have no time for it. If we are going to compete with organizations who do not do that sort of thing and who are saving all their energy for the contest, I say do not dissipate any energy emotionally. By that I mean they should not give way to emotions such as jealousy, hatred or anything of that sort. I say that this sort of thing destroys any organization; and then I tell them that we should look upon one another in a friendly way. Look for the good in one another and be inspired by the fine qualities in those around us and forget about their faults. I tell them that the chances are that I will notice their faults and won't stutter when I mention them to the particular individual who has them.

There is a sixth type of man who suffers from an inferiority complex. He generally comes from a small community and he says to himself, "What chances have I got to get on the first string of thirty-three men when there are 350 boys trying for it? I don't believe I've got a chance and I don't believe I can make it." If there are any among you who feel that way, forget about

Captain Knute Rockne, University of Notre Dame, 1913. Poor equipment, careless coaching, and plays like the "flying wedge" made turn-of-the-century college football a dangerous sport. In 1905, 18 players were killed and 160 seriously injured; several colleges dropped the sport. Authorities (led by none other than President Theodore Roosevelt, an avid fan) urged reforms. And reforms occurred. The introduction of the forward pass opened up the offense and made the game more interesting for spectators; the move to full-time coaches introduced longer, more intensive training schedules and thus fitter players. The National Collegiate Athletic Association was founded in 1910 to set stricter rules against fouls and keep colleges from secretly paying "students" to play football. Football deaths peaked at 30 in 1909, and steadily dwindled thereafter. (UPI/ Bettmann Newsphoto)

it and get a superiority complex. I say to them, "You are just as good as any man here. And by getting a superiority complex you can show the coach you belong at the top of the thirty-three men where you think you would like to be."

I remember one year about four years ago I divided the men on the field in groups,—the ends, tackles, guards, centers, quarterbacks, etc. I walked up to the group of guards. Now guard is a position demanding a certain amount of physical ruggedness. There were fifteen good-sized boys in the group and one little chap whose name was Metzger. I said to him, "Aren't you a little slight and small to be playing guard?" "Yes," he answered, "but I am a little rough." The same confidence enabled him, in spite of the fact that he weighed only 149 pounds, to hold his own against any opponent whether he weighed two hundred pounds or more.

In two weeks I call them together again and tell them that there are certain among them who have great potentialities but that they haven't shown any improvement. There are certain among them that I do not want unless they change.

The first is the chap who alibis, one who justifies his own failure, and I tell them that a boy who does this had better watch out or he will get into a second class, that of feeling sorry for himself, in which case the bony part of his spine turns into a soft substance known as soap and he is absolutely worthless.

The second class of lad—I generally have very few of them—is the slicker, the mucker, who tries to get by by playing unfair football. I tell that type of boy that we cannot afford to have him on the team for he will bring discredit on the school and on our organization. I also impress on him that slugging and unfairness do not pay either in a game or in life after leaving school.

Then, third, there is the boy who lacks courage, who is afraid. What is courage? Courage means to be afraid to do something and still going ahead and doing it. If a man has character, the right kind of energy, mental ability, he will learn that fear is something to overcome and not to run away from.

And before the first game of the year I talk to them along the same lines on ambition. I say ambition, the right kind of ambition, means that you must have the ability to co-operate with the men around you, men working with you; and it is my observation that ability to co-operate is more essential than individual technique. In this day and age no individual stands alone; he must be able to co-operate in every sense of the word; and that is not a very easy thing to do in football because I know in our college we often get boys who have been spoiled by the home press in their high school days. They kick the ball well, and pass pretty well, and once in a while they run with it. They are all pretty good—if you don't believe it they have clippings along with them to prove it. Teaching co-operation is not always the easiest thing in the world to do, especially to a group of boys. I remember one lad who looked good in practice, a sophomore, and we decided to start him the first game of the year.

Three times they called this chap's number and three times he made long runs for touchdowns, sixty, seventy, eighty yards in length; and, of course, on each of these runs he had excellent co-operation from his team mates. The next morning I picked up the paper to see if the local sport writer would give credit where credit was due. Did he say that the outstanding feature of the game was the wonderful blocking and tackling, unusual for so early in the season? No; this sport writer knew his public and he wrote what he thought the public would like. They had five columns telling all about the halfback and full-length pictures of him—front view, side view, and rear view.

Well, this young man never had anything like that happen to him before in his life, so the first thing we knew he was suffering from that disease which we call in athletics "elephantiasis of the occipital lobe." It is not a very danger-ous malady but it renders the victim useless for the time being. We gave him the usual serum treatment—ridicule from his team mates, the student body, and his best girl. That usually reduces the fever and swelling. . . .

A few weeks later we went East to play the Army, up there on the plains above the Hudson River. This, of course, was long before the Army games were moved to New York City. By that time we thought the young man had recovered from the malady so we decided to play him. We had a beautiful setting; clouds of variegated colors were floating in the sky; the boy's relatives were there to see him play. Anyhow, after a few minutes during which time this young man posed around evidently wondering how he looked from the grandstand, I put in the game a third string halfback who was anxious to go out and do his bit for the team and we were lucky enough to nose out the Army.

Monday, back in South Bend, we had our first practice after the game. The flash was sulking in a corner of the field. I did not pay any attention to him. Tuesday he was still sulking. I still ignored him. Wednesday he came to me and said, "Coach, I think I will turn in my suit." I replied, "I was just thinking of asking you for it." He said, "This is the most unfair treatment I ever received in my life. You disgraced and humiliated me in front of my folks." I said, "Don't you know why I took you out?" He did not seem to know. "I will refresh your memory," I said. "On two occasions when the Army kicked to us and after we failed three times to make any gain, George Gipp dropped back in punt formation and sent one of those long spirals soaring down the field. Every one of your team mates ran down the field just as fast as he could in order that the Army quarterback might not bring that ball back an inch. All but you. You were gamboling leisurely down the field. You were saving yourself for later on when they were to call your number. With the aid of your team mates you were going to get headlines in the New York papers. . . .

Well, that lad had character. He was well bred. He learned his lesson and came out and did his bit for the team. The next year he developed into an All-American halfback, if that means anything.

In any organization no one man can enjoy the spotlight all the time while the rest of the boys are doing the chores. Each one has to take a turn doing the chores. . . .

Now I want to impress the necessity of co-operation on the minds of you distributors, dealers, and sellers of automobiles and trucks. Unless you understand the problems of production, engineering, bookkeeping, service advertising and all departments that go to make up your organization, your organization cannot succeed. The failure of any one of them may cause you to fail.

Later on after a game or two, and particularly after a game where I have seen the lads give up, I talk to them further some noon on ambition. I tell them that there can be no ambition without perseverance. By perseverance I mean the ability to stick in there and keep giving the best of one's self. The ability to keep in there and keep trying when the going is tough and you are behind and everything seems hopeless. There can be no success, no reward, unless every man has the ability to stay in there until the last whistle blows. . . .

That applies to you automobile men out there on the firing line. You men are facing keen competition this year, perhaps facing more opposition that you ever faced in your lives, but I say that is the sort of thing you should thrill to—any kind of challenge. Any kind of organization ought to thrill to it. I think your organization, the Studebaker organization, has demonstrated that you can go better when the going is tough, so I say to you that this year you should thrill to this challenge.

COUNTERPOINT III

Getting and Spending

After the sustained explosion of industrial growth (described by Andrew Carnegie), Terence Powderly's toil in the vineyards of labor, Russell Conwell's admonitions to accumulate, Jane Addams's energetic reforms, and Knute Rockne's sales talks, who finally benefited? When the Roaring Twenties rolled around, did everyone ride the same financial merry-go-round? Did some individuals gain ground at the expense of others? Did some, perhaps, not gain at all? If not, then who bought Rockne's wares, watched Babe Ruth hit home runs, carried hip flasks and joined fraternities, attended sales conventions, used birth control, ran charities, staffed governments? Who were the people who really made the 1920s seem so vibrant, glittery, and well-heeled? What smashed the glitter?

Daniel Horowitz presents evidence that families at quite different economic levels did in fact participate in the consumer and leisure economy of the 1920s. The average typographer's family in 1921, for example, had to spend almost a third of the income for food and another third for clothing, shelter, and home operation (table A.1). But that left the remaining third—almost $900—for miscellaneous expenses, including 6 percent for recreation. A study of professional families in 1927 shows almost the same total proportion of average family income going for essentials and for miscellaneous consumption (table A.2). The amount spent on recreation was only 3.4 percent, but another 2 percent or so went for the related item of social entertainment, making the total recreation proportion about the same as for the average typographer's family. The professional families earned over twice as much money as their blue-collar counterparts, to be sure, but inflation and the passage of time from 1921 to 1927 accounted for a portion of this difference.

Typographers, however, were highly skilled workers, with considerably greater earning power than the average industrial or unskilled worker. Did the lesser ranks, too, fare well? Frank Stricker provides data suggesting that blue-collar workers' wages may have risen in absolute terms, but not to the degree that wages of middle-class workers rose. The real weekly earnings of all manufacturing hourly wage earners (table B.1) climbed over 8 percent from 1920 to 1926, and of female manufacturing wage earners over 12 percent. But unskilled factory workers did less well, gaining just a little over 2 percent in six years. All railroad workers, still a huge part of the labor force at that time, did somewhat better, gaining over 5 percent, but earnings of unskilled railroad workers actually fell by more than 10 percent.

White-collar and government workers (table B.2) meanwhile enjoyed tremendous gains in earnings—over 60 percent for professors and teachers; from 25 to 31 percent for service workers, salaried manufacturing employees, government workers, and salespeople; and even 13 percent for clerks for the beleaguered railroads! So yes, Stricker demonstrates, most (though not all) occupations advanced during the 1920s. But increases in wages of blue-collar workers were left far behind those for white-collar workers. Stricker's figures also suggest a possible answer to the question of why the 1920s appeared so prosperous to contemporary observers and to some historians. Wage increases for blue-collar workers leveled off after climbing rapidly from 1914 to 1920 (table B.1), but no one paid much attention because wage earners were not especially visible or significant to journalists and other commentators. By contrast, the precipitous climb of wages of white-collar employees came on the heels of six years of falling income (table B.2). The climb seemed all the more spectacular after the fall, and the climbers as a group, unlike workers, were highly visible and significant—like Knute Rockne.

The findings of Charles Holt (table C) might have given the consuming middle class itself pause, however, had the figures been available. Average real disposable income in the United States rose 28 percent from 1920 to 1929, and nonfarm income rose slightly less. But practically all this increase went to the top 1 percent of the population, whose income almost doubled in the ten years. The lower 93 percent of the nonfarm population experienced only a 6 percent rise in disposable income, similar to railroad workers' wage increase from 1920 to 1926 (table B.1). Prosperity, it seemed, produced radically maldistributed income. Given these distortions, even the free-spending professional and white-collar families of the period were hard-pressed to maintain the pace of consumption they had set for themselves.

Who gave the Roaring Twenties their consuming flavor? Blue-collar wage earners to a small degree. The middle classes to a significant degree. But most glittering, it would seem, was the economic elite, from Henry Ford to Yalies in raccoon coats, whose income soared far above the rest from the beginning of the decade to its bitter end.

A. Expenditures of Typographers' Families and Professionals' Families

1. Expenditures of Families of Typographers, 1921

Item	Average Amount per Family in Dollars	Percentage of Total Expenditures
Food	$ 879.14	31.8%
Clothing	313.14	11.4
Shelter	421.56	15.3
Home operation	260.71	9.4
Subtotal	1,874.55	67.9
Miscellaneous		
Recreation	167.43	6.1
Vehicles	65.96	2.4
Education	57.96	2.1
Tobacco	41.31	1.5
Church	11.69	0.4
Charity	9.62	0.3
Medical care	130.47	4.7
Union dues	146.61	5.3
Investments	164.37	6.0
Incidentals	91.45	3.3
Subtotal	886.87	32.1
Total	2,761.42	

2. Expenditures of Families of Professionals, 1927

Item	Average Amount per Family in Dollars	Percentage of Total Expenditures
Food	$1,043.28	16.0%
Clothing	893.44	13.7
Housing	1,343.30	20.7
House operation	991.98	15.3
Subtotal	4,272.00	65.7
Miscellaneous		
Savings, life insurance	620.00	9.6
Automobile	382.48	5.9
Medical care	275.00	4.2
Recreation	219.40	3.4
Education	136.80	2.1
Gifts	125.00	1.9
Social entertainment	123.00	1.9
Charity	60.00	0.9
Incidentals	60.00	0.9
Tobacco	54.00	0.8

(continued)

Table A.2 continued

Item	Average Amount per Family in Dollars	Percentage of Total Expenditures
Church	50.00	0.8
Barber, cosmetics	46.32	0.7
Carfare	40.00	0.6
Organization dues	36.00	0.6
Subtotal	2,228.00	34.3
Total	6,500.00	

SOURCE: From *The Morality of Spending* by Daniel Horowitz (The Johns Hopkins University Press, 1985). Reprinted by permission.

B. Changes in Earnings of Selected Categories of Blue-Collar and White-Collar Employees

1. Changes in Real Weekly Earnings for Selected Categories of Blue-Collar Workers

Occupation	World War I Period	Total Change	1920s Period	Total Change
All manufacturing wage earners	1914 to 1920	+20%	1920 to 1926	+ 8.3%
Male unskilled, manufacturing	1914 to 1920	+30	1920 to 1926	+ 2.3
Female, manufacturing	1914 to 1920	+18	1920 to 1926	+12.7
All railroad wage earners	1914 to 1920	+14	1920 to 1926	+ 5.3
Railroad workers, unskilled	1914 to 1920	+28	1920 to 1926	−10.9

2. Changes in Real Annual Earnings for Selected Categories of White-Collar Employees

Occupation	World War I Period	Total Change	1920s Period	Total Change
College professors	1914 to 1920	−35%	1920 to 1926	+63.8%
School teachers	1914 to 1920	−19	1920 to 1926	+60.5
Salaried in manufacturing	1914 to 1920	−18	1920 to 1926	+29.3
Clerical on railroads	1914 to 1920	− 1	1920 to 1926	+13.1
Salespeople (Ohio)	1915 to 1920	−16	1920 to 1926	+31.0
Service workers (Ohio)	1915 to 1920	− 3	1920 to 1926	+25.7
Government workers (District of Columbia)	1914 to 1920	−30	1920 to 1926	+30

SOURCE: From Frank Stricker, "Affluence for Whom?—Another Look at Prosperity and the Working Class in the 1920's" in Daniel V. Leab, editor, *The Labor History Reader* (University of Illinois Press, Urbana, 1985). © 1985 by the Board of Trustees of the University of Illinois.

C. Real Disposable Income per Capita, 1920–1929 (in 1929 Dollars)

Year	U.S. Average	Nonfarm Average	Top 1 Percent Nonfarm Average	Lower 93 Percent Nonfarm Average
1920	$543	$659	$ 7,962	$513
1921	477	599	8,397	435
1922	548	683	9,817	497
1923	613	754	9,641	566
1924	613	745	10,512	542
1925	633	761	12,719	521
1926	640	769	12,606	531
1927	649	775	13,563	525
1928	675	807	15,666	527
1929	693	825	15,721	544
Percent change 1920–1929	28%	25%	97%	6%

SOURCE: From Charles Holt, "Who Benefited from the Prosperity of the Twenties?" *Explorations in Economic History* 14 (July 1977). Reprinted by permission.

The return of the Great White Fleet after a victorious Spanish-American War. This painting by Fred Pansing shows Admiral Sampson's Flagship **New York** in the foreground. (Museum of the City of New York)

CHAPTER FOUR

The Big Stick

21.

THE OPEN DOOR

America's enlarged role in world affairs was not entirely military or co-
lonialist. Since before the Civil War a key principle of U.S. diplomacy had
been to expand the opportunities for American business abroad without
actually acquiring colonies. This view largely guided policy in Latin
America after the Monroe Doctrine and also in Asia after the beginning
of the China trade during the period of the American Revolution. By the
late nineteenth century, in fact, China had assumed such importance as
a potential market and investment area that the U.S. government felt
compelled to clarify its position to competing European powers. The
United States was afraid that the Great Powers (Great Britain, France,
Russia, and later Germany), which were carving "spheres of influence"
for themselves in China, would cut American merchants out of commercial opportunities there.

The American response to this threat was initially formulated by
William W. Rockhill, a diplomat with extensive Asian experience, in the
following memorandum to Secretary of State John M. Hay. Rockhill
counseled what he termed an Open Door policy for all countries seeking
trade and investment in China: recognition that spheres of influence did
exist but that opportunity to trade ought to be relatively equal. Rockhill's
analysis was the basis, in turn, of Hay's Open Door notes to Great
Britain, France, Germany, and Russia. This Open Door policy under-
scored the significance of China in American foreign policy and provided
considerable justification for acquiring Pacific territories that might be
used as way stations or staging areas. In 1900, in fact, twenty-five
hundred American troops helped European and Japanese forces suppress an antiforeign uprising in China, called the Boxer rebellion. The
policy also, of course, highlighted a general goal of American diplomacy:
achieving economic gain without colonial burdens. In the 1930s this
policy had severe consequences for relations between the United States
and Japan.

William W. Rockhill was born in Philadelphia in 1854 and graduated
from a French military academy in 1873. After three years in the French
army and eight years of world travel, Rockhill entered the U.S. diplomatic
corps with a particular interest in the Orient. After the Open Door
memorandum, he became Hay's chief Asian adviser, playing a major
role in moderating European reprisals during the Boxer rebellion and
serving as ambassador to China as well as to Russia, Turkey, and Greece.
A widely published authority on Asian history, Rockhill died in Hawaii

in 1914 while en route to China to become the personal adviser to the new Chinese president.

Questions to consider. Does the Open Door policy seem to have been a continuation of or a departure from previous American foreign policy? Does the formulation of the Open Door policy seem to have anticipated or followed the taking of Pacific territories, including the Philippines, by the United States? Note that Rockhill never urged the carving of an American sphere of influence in China. Why not? Also, was he concerned more with American trade or with the avoidance of serious conflict with the European powers? How did the Chinese and their government figure in his thinking? Finally, in what ways did the Open Door policy and the acquisition of the Philippines put the United States on a collision course with Japan a few decades later?

═══════

China Memorandum (1899)
William W. Rockhill

We find today in China that the policy of the "Open Door," the untrammeled exercise of the rights insured to Treaty Powers by the Treaty of Tientsin, and other treaties copied on it or under the most favoured nation clause, is claimed by the mercantile classes of the United States and other powers as essential to the healthy extension of trade in China. We see, on the other hand, that the political interests and the geographical relations of Great Britain, Russia, and France to China have forced those countries to divide up China proper into areas or spheres of interest (or influence) in which they enjoy special rights and privileges, the ultimate scope of which is not yet determined, and that at the same time Great Britain, in its desire not to sacrifice entirely its mercantile interests, is also endeavoring to preserve some of the undoubted benefits of the "open door" policy, but "spheres of influence" *are an accomplished fact,* this cannot be too much insisted upon. . . .

Such being the condition of things, and in view of the probability of complications soon arising between the interested powers in China, whereby it will become difficult, if not impossible, for the United States to retain the rights guaranteed them by treaties with China, what should be our immediate policy? To this question there can, it seems, be but one answer, we should at once initiate negotiations to obtain from these powers who have acquired

From **Foreign Relations of the United States: Diplomatic Papers** (Government Printing Office, Washington, D.C., 1900), 316–323.

"The Real Trouble Will Come with the 'Wake.'"   Joseph Keppler's lithograph for the August 15, 1900, issue of **Puck** depicts the Great Power struggle over economic concessions in China as a brawl among animals over a dragon's prostrate body. The chief adversaries are the bear, representing Russia's interests in northern China, and the lion, representing England's presence in Hong Kong and other coastal cities. Watching greedily are such lesser figures as the vulture, the hyena, and the jackal. The Open Door policy sought to limit the dismemberment of China and let the American eagle get its share. (Library of Congress)

zones of interest in China formal assurance that (1.) they will in no way interfere within their so-called spheres of interest with any treaty port or with vested rights in it of any nature; (2.) that all ports they may open in their respective spheres shall either be free ports, or that the Chinese treaty tariff at the time in force shall apply to all merchandise landed or shipped, no matter to what nationality belonging, and that the dues and duties provided for by treaty shall be collected by the Chinese Government; and (3.) that they will levy no higher harbor dues on vessels of other nationalities frequenting their ports in such spheres than shall be levied on their national vessels, and that they will also levy no higher railroad charges on merchandise belonging to or destined for subjects of other powers transported through their spheres than shall be levied on similar merchandise belonging to its own nationality.

In other words, we should insist on absolute equality of treatment in the various zones, for equality of opportunity with the citizens of the favored powers we cannot hope to have, in view of the well known method now in vogue for securing privileges and concessions, though we should continually, by every proper means, seek to gain this also.

Such understandings with the various Powers, and it is confidently believed that they could be reached at present, would secure an open market throughout China for our trade on terms of equality with all other foreigners, and would further remove dangerous sources of irritation and possible conflict between the contending powers, greatly tending to re-establish confidence, and prepare the way for concerted action by the Powers to bring about the reforms in Chinese administration and the strengthening of the Imperial Government, recognized on all sides as essential to the maintenance of peace.

22.

THE NEW EMPIRE

The United States went to war with Spain over Cuba in 1898. But the U.S. victory in the brief war brought acquisitions in the Pacific (the Philippines and Guam) as well as in the Caribbean (Puerto Rico); at this time the United States also got control of the Hawaiian islands and Wake Island. In part these acquisitions represented the resumption of a long tradition of westward territorial expansion that had been abandoned since the purchase of Alaska in 1867. In part they represented America's desire for "great power" status at a time when the European nations were winning colonies in Asia and Africa. But powerful economic forces were at work, too, as they had been in the formulation of the recent Open Door policy or, for that matter, in President James Monroe's assertion of his famous Doctrine in 1823.

At the beginning of the war, President William McKinley was unsure himself whether or not the United States should take over the Philippines, and if it did, whether its forces would take only Manila, or the whole island of Luzon, or the entire archipelago. Not until December 1898 did the president finally announce that the United States would pursue a policy of "benevolent assimilation" toward the whole territory. This decision gave rise to a small but vocal anti-imperialist movement at home and, more important, a strong Filipino resistance struggle against the American occupation.

At this point, however, forceful advocates of imperialism rose to defend the president in the most vigorous terms. Of these none was more forceful or more important than Senator Albert J. Beveridge. His Senate speech of January 1900 in support of a (successful) resolution urging colonial status for the Philippines, excerpted below, provided the broadest possible grounds for the president's policy. With the fight thus in hand at home, McKinley turned to winning the fight abroad. Having made his decision, moreover, he stuck doggedly with it, as the excerpt from his second inaugural address makes clear. In fact, the Americans overcame the insurgents only after another year's hard fighting and the death of more than a hundred thousand Filipinos.

William McKinley, who presided over what Secretary of State John Hay called the "splendid little war" with Spain, was born in Ohio in 1843, entered the House of Representatives as a Republican in 1876, and served four years as governor of Ohio. Strongly probusiness, McKinley won the presidency in 1896 amid a severe depression and was re-elected by large majorities in 1900. In September 1901, however, McKinley was shot at a reception in Buffalo, New York. Eight days later he became the third U.S. president to die from an assassin's bullet. McKinley's ally and fellow Ohioan, Albert Beveridge, was only thirty-seven at the time of his imperialist speech of 1900, but he was already known as a proponent of military strength and Anglo-Saxon supremacy. This speech further enhanced his standing in Republican circles. Beveridge left the Senate in 1912 to devote himself to writing. In 1919, eight years before his death in Indiana, his **Life of John Marshall** was awarded the Pulitzer Prize for historical biography.

Questions to consider. Beveridge's speech makes enormous claims for the strategic importance of the Philippines. On what grounds did Beveridge make these claims? Does the policy urged by Beveridge seem connected to the Open Door policy of William W. Rockhill (Document 21) and John Hay? Has history borne out Beveridge's predictions about the Pacific Ocean and world commerce? Did Beveridge think acquiring the Philippines would increase or reduce the chances of war? How did he seem to view the Declaration of Independence? The Constitution? Was Beveridge's main concern economics or race?

In McKinley's second inaugural address, note the government's ultimate objective: to provide the Filipinos with "self-government as fast as they were ready for it." What criteria did McKinley propose for determining readiness for self-government? Were there any implied criteria? Did they in any sense contradict the concept of self-government? Are McKinley's views here consonant with Beveridge's?

America's Destiny (1900)
Albert Beveridge

Mr. President, the times call for candor. The Philippines are ours forever, "territory belonging to the United States," as the Constitution calls them. And just beyond the Philippines are China's illimitable markets. We will not retreat from either. We will not repudiate our duty in the archipelago. We will not abandon our opportunity in the Orient. We will not renounce our part in the mission of our race, trustee, under God, of the civilization of the world. And we will move forward to our work, not howling out regrets like slaves whipped to their burdens, but with gratitude for a task worthy of our strength, and thanksgiving to Almighty God that He has marked us as His chosen people, henceforth to lead in the regeneration of the world.

From the **Congressional Record,** 56th Congress, 1st session, 704–712.

This island empire is the last land left in all the oceans. If it should prove a mistake to abandon it, the blunder once made would be irretrievable. If it proves a mistake to hold it, the error can be corrected when we will. Every other progressive nation stands ready to relieve us.

But to hold it will be no mistake. Our largest trade henceforth must be with Asia. The Pacific is our ocean. More and more Europe will manufacture the most it needs, secure from its colonies the most it consumes. Where shall we turn for consumers of our surplus? Geography answers the question. China is our natural customer. She is nearer to us than to England, Germany, or Russia, the commercial powers of the present and the future. They have moved nearer to China by securing permanent bases on her borders. The Philippines give us a base at the door of all the East.

Lines of navigation from our ports to the Orient and Australia; from the Isthmian Canal to Asia; from all Oriental ports to Australia, converge at and separate from the Philippines. They are a self-supporting, dividend-paying fleet, permanently anchored at a spot selected by the strategy of Providence, commanding the Pacific. And the Pacific is the ocean of the commerce of the future. Most future wars will be conflicts for commerce. The power that rules the Pacific, therefore, is the power that rules the world. And, with the Philippines, that power is and will forever be the American Republic. . . .

Nothing is so natural as trade with one's neighbors. The Philippines make us the nearest neighbors of all the East. Nothing is more natural than to trade with those you know. This is the philosophy of all advertising. The Philippines bring us permanently face to face with the most sought-for customers of the world. National prestige, national propinquity, these and commercial activity are the elements of commercial success. The Philippines give the first; the character of the American people supply the last. It is a providential conjunction of all the elements of trade, of duty, and of power. If we are willing to go to war rather than let England have a few feet of frozen Alaska, which affords no market and commands none, what should we not do rather than let England, Germany, Russia, or Japan have all the Philippines? And no man on the spot can fail to see that this would be their fate if we retired. . . .

Here, then, Senators, is the situation. Two years ago there was no land in all the world which we could occupy for any purpose. Our commerce was daily turning toward the Orient, and geography and trade developments made necessary our commercial empire over the Pacific. And in that ocean we had no commercial, naval, or military base. To-day we have one of the three great ocean possessions of the globe, located at the most commanding commercial, naval, and military points in the eastern seas, within hail of India, shoulder to shoulder with China, richer in its own resources than any equal body of land on the entire globe, and peopled by a race which civilization demands shall be improved. Shall we abandon it? That man little knows the common people of the Republic, little understands the instincts of our race, who thinks we will not hold it fast and hold it forever, administering just government by

American soldiers in the Philippines, 1899.   The United States had only 15,000 soldiers in the Philippines when the Spanish garrison surrendered in August 1898, and only a few thousand more by the time Spain transferred the islands to their new owner six months later. But the soldiers did not come home at the war's end because they had to suppress a nationalist revolt. By the end of the century, their number had doubled, and by 1902, 4,000 of them were dead. The Americans did finally kill almost 200,000 Filipino insurgents. Within forty years the Philippines became independent. (Library of Congress)

simplest methods. We may trick up devices to shift our burden and lessen our opportunity; they will avail us nothing but delay. We may tangle conditions by applying academic arrangements of self-government to a crude situation; their failure will drive us to our duty in the end. . . .

But, Senators, it would be better to abandon this combined garden and Gibraltar of the Pacific, and count our blood and treasure already spent a profitable loss, than to apply any academic arrangement of self-government to these children. They are not capable of self-government. How could they be? They are not of a self-governing race. They are Orientals, Malays, instructed by Spaniards in the latter's worst estate.

They know nothing of practical government except as they have witnessed the weak, corrupt, cruel, and capricious rule of Spain. What magic will anyone employ to dissolve in their minds and characters those impressions of governors and governed which three centuries of misrule have created? What alchemy will change the oriental quality of their blood and set the self-governing currents of the American pouring through their Malay veins? How shall they, in the twinkling of an eye, be exalted to the heights of self-governing peoples which required a thousand years for us to reach, Anglo-Saxon though we are . . . ?

The Declaration of Independence does not forbid us to do our part in the regeneration of the world. If it did, the Declaration would be wrong, just as the Articles of Confederation, drafted by the very same men who signed the Declaration, was found to be wrong. The Declaration has no application to the present situation. It was written by self-governing men for self-governing men. . . .

Senators in opposition are estopped from denying our constitutional power to govern the Philippines as circumstances may demand, for such power is admitted in the case of Florida, Louisiana, Alaska. How, then, is it denied in the Philippines? Is there a geographical interpretation to the Constitution? Do degrees of longitude fix constitutional limitations? Does a thousand miles of ocean diminish constitutional power more than a thousand miles of land . . . ?

No; the oceans are not limitations of the power which the Constitution expressly gives Congress to govern all territory the nation may acquire. The Constitution declares that "Congress shall have power to dispose of and make all needful rules and regulations respecting the territory belonging to the United States." . . .

Mr. President, this question is deeper than any question of party politics; deeper than any question of the isolated policy of our country even; deeper even than any question of constitutional power. It is elemental. It is racial. God has not been preparing the English-speaking and Teutonic peoples for a thousand years for nothing but vain and idle self-contemplation and self-admiration. No! He has made us the master organizers of the world to establish system where chaos reigns. He has given us the spirit of progress to overwhelm the forces of reaction throughout the earth. He has made us adepts in government that we may administer government among savage and senile peoples. Were it not for such a force as this the world would relapse into barbarism and night. And of all our race He has marked the American people as His chosen nation to finally lead in the regeneration of the world. This is the divine mission of America, and it holds for us all the profit, all the glory, all the happiness possible to man. We are trustees of the world's progress, guardians of its righteous peace. The judgment of the Master is upon us: "Ye have been faithful over a few things; I will make you ruler over many things."

What shall history say of us? Shall it say that we renounced that holy trust, left the savage to his base condition, the wilderness to the reign of waste, deserted duty, abandoned glory, forgot our sordid profit even, because we feared our strength and read the charter of our powers with the doubter's eye and the quibbler's mind? Shall it say that, called by events to captain and command the proudest, ablest, purest race of history in history's noblest work, we declined that great commission? Our fathers would not have had it so. No! They founded no paralytic government, incapable of the simplest acts of administration. They planted no sluggard people, passive while the world's work calls them. They established no reactionary nation. They unfurled no retreating flag. . . .

Mr. President and Senators, adopt the resolution offered, that peace may quickly come and that we may begin our saving, regenerating, and uplifting work. . . . Reject it, and the world, history, and the American people will know where to forever fix the awful responsibility for the consequences that will surely follow such failure to do our manifest duty. . . .

Second Inaugural Address (1901)
William McKinley

While the treaty of peace with Spain was ratified on the 6th of February, 1899, and ratifications were exchanged nearly two years ago, the Congress has indicated no form of government for the Philippine Islands. It has, however, provided an army to enable the Executive to suppress insurrection, restore peace, give security to the inhabitants, and establish the authority of the United States throughout the archipelago. It has authorized the organization of native troops as auxiliary to the regular force. It has been advised from time to time of the acts of the military and naval officers in the islands, of my action in appointing civil commissions, of the instructions with which they were charged, of their duties and powers, of their recommendations, and of their several acts under executive commission, together with the very complete general information they have submitted. These reports fully set forth the conditions, past and present, in the islands, and the instructions clearly show the principles which will guide the Executive until the Congress shall, as it is required to do by the treaty, determine "the civil rights and political status of

From James D. Richardson, ed., **A Compilation of the Messages and Papers of the Presidents** (Government Printing Office, Washington, D.C., 1897–1907), XIV: 6468–6469.

the native inhabitants." The Congress having added the sanction of its authority to the powers already possessed and exercised by the Executive under the Constitution, thereby leaving with the Executive the responsibility for the government of the Philippines, I shall continue the efforts already begun until order shall be restored throughout the islands, and as fast as conditions permit will establish local governments, in the formation of which the full co-operation of the people has been already invited, and when established will encourage the people to administer them. The settled purpose, long ago proclaimed, to afford the inhabitants of the islands self-government as fast as they were ready for it will be pursued with earnestness and fidelity. Already something has been accomplished in this direction. The Government's representatives, civil and military, are doing faithful and noble work in their mission of emancipation and merit the approval and support of their countrymen. The most liberal terms of amnesty have already been communicated to the insurgents, and the way is still open for those who have raised their arms against the Government for honorable submission to its authority. Our countrymen should not be deceived. We are not waging war against the inhabitants of the Philippine Islands. A portion of them are making war against the United States. By far the greater part of the inhabitants recognize American sovereignty and welcome it as a guaranty of order and of security for life, property, liberty, freedom of conscience, and the pursuit of happiness. To them full protection will be given. They shall not be abandoned. We will not leave the destiny of the loyal millions in the islands to the disloyal thousands who are in rebellion against the United States. Order under civil institutions will come as soon as those who now break the peace shall keep it. Force will not be needed or used when those who make war against us shall make it no more. May it end without further bloodshed, and there be ushered in the reign of peace to be made permanent by a government of liberty under law!

23.

GUNBOAT DIPLOMACY

Although the Monroe Doctrine of 1823 (Vol. 1, Document 20) had proclaimed a special interest in Latin American affairs, it was neither
militaristic nor especially interventionist in spirit. But the Open Door
policy and the Spanish-American War signaled a new military and
economic aggressiveness in Washington and a new determination to
assert the country's ambitions. It was probably inevitable, therefore, that
President Theodore Roosevelt should modify the Monroe Doctrine to
provide a rationale for direct intervention by armed force on behalf of
"progress" and "responsible government." A hero of the U.S. Army's
recent Cuban campaign against Spain and an admirer of Admiral
George Dewey, Roosevelt, who had succeeded the slain McKinley as
president, urged a policy of expanding the country's military might.
Advising the United States to "speak softly and carry a big stick,"
Roosevelt believed the United States should act as the policeman of
Central America and the Caribbean. Between Roosevelt's and Coolidge's
administrations the United States sent warships and soldiers to several
Caribbean countries, usually to protect U.S. investments.

Theodore Roosevelt, who inaugurated this era of gunboat diplomacy, was born to well-to-do parents in New York City in 1858. After
college he juggled politics, writing, and ranching and hunting, until
McKinley appointed him assistant secretary of the navy in 1897. He
resigned in 1898 to lead a cavalry unit called the Rough Riders in Cuba,
but returned to win the governorship of New York in 1899 and 1900.
He moved on to the vice presidency in 1901, and in that same year to
the presidency when McKinley was killed. Over the next ten years
Roosevelt promised a "square deal" and a "new nationalism," both em-
bodying his notions of social and military progress. In 1912 he bolted
the Republican party to head a Progressive ticket that lost to Woodrow
Wilson, a Democrat, whose internationalism Roosevelt relentlessly casti-
gated until his death in 1919.

Questions to consider. Compare Roosevelt's corollary with the
original Monroe Doctrine of 1823 (Vol. 1, Document 20). What are
the most important differences? Did they derive more from changes in
the world at large or from changes within the United States itself? Compare the corollary also with Rockhill's attitudes toward China (Document
21) and McKinley's attitudes toward the Philippines (Document 22).
What does the corollary have in common with the Open Door policy

and colonialism? In what ways does it differ? How does the corollary compare with the European spheres of influence in China? Note, finally, Roosevelt's remark about interference only in the "last resort." What did he mean by this? On the evidence of both his rhetoric and his actions, was he concerned most with U.S. economic interests, the well-being of the Latin American republics, or the potential behavior of the European powers? Did the corollary place any limits on the possible magnitude or duration of American intervention?

———

Monroe Doctrine Corollary (1904)
Theodore Roosevelt

It is not true that the United States feels any land hunger or entertains any projects as regards the other nations of the Western Hemisphere save such as are for their welfare. All that this country desires is to see the neighboring countries stable, orderly, and prosperous. Any country whose people conduct themselves well can count upon our hearty friendship. If a nation shows that it knows how to act with reasonable efficiency and decency in social and political matters, if it keeps order and pays its obligations, it need fear no interference from the United States. Chronic wrongdoing, or an impotence which results in a general loosening of the ties of civilized society, may in America, as elsewhere, ultimately require intervention by some civilized nation, and in the Western Hemisphere the adherence of the United States to the Monroe Doctrine may lead the United States, however reluctantly, in flagrant cases of such wrongdoing or impotence, to the exercise of an international police power. If every country washed by the Caribbean Sea would show the progress in stable and just civilization which with the aid of the Platt amendment Cuba has shown since our troops left the island, and which so many of the republics in both Americas are constantly and brilliantly showing, all question of interference by this Nation with their affairs would be at an end. Our interests and those of our southern neighbors are in reality identical. They have great natural riches, and if within their borders the reign of law and justice obtains, prosperity is sure to come to them. While they thus obey the primary laws of civilized society they may rest assured that they will be treated by us in a spirit of cordial and helpful sympathy. We would interfere with them only in the last resort, and then only if it became evident that their inability or unwillingness to do justice at home and abroad had violated the

From James D. Richardson, ed., A **Compilation of the Messages and Papers of the Presidents** (Government Printing Office, Washington, D.C., 1897–1907), XVI: 7371–7377.

Theodore Roosevelt. No turn-of-the-century American did more to popularize the idea of aggressive masculinity than Teddy Roosevelt. Sickly as a child, T.R. relished being photographed as a policeman, prize fighter, or big-game hunter. In the war with Spain he appeared as a soldier at the head of his volunteer unit of Rough Riders; in this 1902 picture he displays his prowess as a horseman. Republican boss Mark Hanna called him "that damned cowboy." Some scholars see his advocacy of a militant foreign policy as stemming in part from this commitment to the strenuous life. (Library of Congress)

rights of the United States or had invited foreign aggression to the detriment of the entire body of American nations. It is a mere truism to say that every nation, whether in America or anywhere else, which desires to maintain its freedom, its independence, must ultimately realize that the right of such independence can not be separated from the responsibility of making good use of it.

In asserting the Monroe Doctrine, in taking such steps as we have taken in regard to Cuba, Venezuela, and Panama, and in endeavoring to circumscribe the theater of war in the Far East, and to secure the open door in China, we have acted in our own interest as well as in the interest of humanity at large. There are, however, cases in which, while our own interests are not greatly involved, strong appeal is made to our sympathies. . . . In extreme cases action may be justifiable and proper. What form the action shall take must depend upon the circumstances of the case; that is, upon the degree of the atrocity and upon our power to remedy it.

24.

THE WAR FOR DEMOCRACY

Woodrow Wilson won the presidency in 1912 on behalf of a "new freedom," a program involving lower tariffs, banking reform, antitrust legislation, and, in foreign policy, the repudiation of Theodore Roosevelt's gunboat diplomacy. Even after sending troops to various Caribbean countries and to Mexico, Wilson claimed that his main concern was to promote peace and democracy in the world. When World War I erupted in Europe, Wilson saw the war as the result of imperialistic rivalries ("a war with which we have nothing to do") and urged, despite personal sympathy with Great Britain, that the United States stay neutral so as to influence the peace negotiations. Wilson won re-election in 1916 largely on a promise to keep the country out of war. But a combination of pro-British propaganda in American newspapers and German submarine attacks on American ships proved formidable, and in April 1917, Wilson finally requested a declaration of war in the following address to Congress. The sweeping, visionary arguments of this remarkable speech shaped not only America's expectations about the war itself but also attitudes about the proper U.S. role in international affairs for years to come.

Born in 1856 in Virginia, Woodrow Wilson grew up in the South; his father was a Presbyterian minister. He attended Princeton and Johns Hopkins, where he earned a doctorate, and began to write and teach in the field of constitutional government and politics. He gained national stature while president of Princeton from 1902 until 1910; he became the Democratic governor of New Jersey in 1911 and, two years later, president of the United States. Wilson's main objective at the peace conference after World War I was to create a League of Nations to help keep the peace. In 1919 during an intensive speechmaking campaign to arouse public support for the League, Wilson suffered a debilitating stroke. He died in Washington, D.C., in 1924.

Questions to consider. Note, in reading the following message, that although Woodrow Wilson believed in the unique and superior character of American institutions, he was willing to enter into alliances with European powers—hence, presumably, the length and passionate tone of his address to Congress. (Compare it, for example, with Franklin D. Roosevelt's address to Congress in 1941—Document 29). What are the four principal grounds on which Wilson was willing to reverse the American diplomatic tradition? Which of these did he seem to take most seriously? Were there other American interests that he might have stressed but did not? What reasons might Wilson have had for stressing so strongly America's attachment to Germany's people as opposed to its government? Might Wilson's arguments and rhetoric have served to prolong rather than to shorten the war?

―――――

Address to Congress (1917)
Woodrow Wilson

I have called the Congress into extraordinary session because there are serious, very serious choices of policy to be made, and made immediately, which it was neither right nor constitutionally permissible that I should assume the responsibility of making.

On the third of February last I officially laid before you the extraordinary announcement of the Imperial German Government that on and after the first day of February it was its purpose to put aside all restraints of law or of humanity and use its submarines to sink every vessel that sought to approach either the ports of Great Britain and Ireland or the western coasts of Europe or any of the ports controlled by the enemies of Germany within the Mediterranean. . . .

I was for a little while unable to believe that such things would in fact be done by any government that had hitherto subscribed to the humane practices of civilized nations. International law had its origin in the attempt to set up some law which would be respected and observed upon the seas, where no nation had right of dominion and where lay the free highways of the world. . . . This minimum of right the German Government has swept aside under the plea of retaliation and necessity and because it had no weapons which it could use at sea except these which it is impossible to employ as it is employing them without throwing to the winds all scruples of humanity or of respect for all understandings that were supposed to underlie the intercourse of the world. I am not now thinking of the loss of property involved, immense and serious as that is, but only of the wanton and wholesale destruction of the lives of non-combatants, men, women, and children, engaged in pursuits which have always, even in the darkest periods of modern history, been deemed innocent and legitimate. Property can be paid for; the lives of peaceful and innocent people cannot be. The present German submarine warfare against commerce is a warfare against mankind.

From the **New York Times**, April 3, 1917.

It is a war against all nations. American ships have been sunk, American lives taken, in ways which it has stirred us very deeply to learn of, but the ships and people of other neutral and friendly nations have been sunk and overwhelmed in the waters in the same way. There has been no discrimination. The challenge is to all mankind. Each nation must decide for itself how it will meet it. The choice we make for ourselves must be made with a moderation of counsel and a temperateness of judgement befitting our character and our motives as a nation. We must put excited feeling away. Our motive will not be revenge or the victorious assertion of the physical might of the nation, but only the vindication of right, of human right, of which we are only a single champion. . . .

With a profound sense of the solemn and even tragical character of the step I am taking and of the grave responsibilities which it involves, but in unhesitating obedience to what I deem my constitutional duty, I advise that the Congress declare the recent course of the Imperial German Government to be in fact nothing less than war against the government and people of the United States; that it formally accept the status of belligerent which has thus been thrust upon it; and that it take immediate steps not only to put the country in a more thorough state of defense but also to exert all its power and employ all its resources to bring the Government of the German Empire to terms and end the war. . . .

We have no quarrel with the German people. We have no feeling towards them but one of sympathy and friendship. It was not upon their impulse that their government acted in entering this war. It was not with their previous knowledge or approval. It was a war determined upon as wars used to be determined upon in the old, unhappy days when peoples were nowhere consulted by their rulers and wars were provoked and waged in the interest of dynasties or of little groups of ambitious men who were accustomed to use their fellow men as pawns and tools. . . .

We are accepting this challenge of hostile purpose because we know that in such a Government, following such methods, we can never have a friend; and that in the presence of its organized power, always lying in wait to accomplish we know not what purpose, there can be no assured security for the democratic Governments of the world. We are now about to accept gauge of battle with this natural foe to liberty and shall, if necessary, spend the whole force of the nation to check and nullify its pretensions and its power. We are glad, now that we see the facts with no veil of false pretense about them, to fight thus for the ultimate peace of the world and for the liberation of its peoples, the German peoples included: for the rights of nations great and small and the privilege of men everywhere to choose their way of life and of obedience. The world must be made safe for democracy. Its peace must be planted upon the tested foundations of political liberty. We have no selfish ends to serve. We desire no conquest, no dominion. We seek no indemnities for ourselves, no material compensation for the sacrifices we shall freely make. We are but one of the champions of the rights of mankind. We shall be satisfied when those rights have been made as secure as the faith and the freedom of nations can make them. . . .

It will be all the easier for us to conduct ourselves as belligerents in a high spirit of right and fairness because we act without animus, not in enmity towards a people or with the desire to bring any injury or disadvantage upon them, but only in armed opposition to an irresponsible government which has thrown aside all considerations of humanity and of right and is running amuck. We are, let me say again, the sincere friends of the German people, and shall desire nothing so much as the early reestablishment of intimate relations of mutual advantage between us,—however hard it may be for them, for the time being, to believe that this is spoken from our hearts. We have borne with their present Government through all these bitter months because of that friendship,—exercising a patience and forbearance which would otherwise have been impossible. We shall, happily, still have an opportunity to prove that friendship in our daily attitude and actions towards the millions of men and women of German birth and native sympathy who live amongst us and share our life, and we shall be proud to prove it towards all who are in fact loyal to their neighbors and to the Government in the hour of test. They are, most of them, as true and loyal Americans as if they had never known any other fealty of allegiance. They will be prompt to stand with us in rebuking and restraining the few who may be of a different mind and purpose. If there should be disloyalty, it will be dealt with with a firm hand of stern repression; but, if it lifts its head at all, it will lift it only here and there and without countenance except from a lawless and malignant few.

It is a distressing and oppressive duty, Gentlemen of the Congress, which I have performed in thus addressing you. There are, it may be, many months of fiery trial and sacrifice ahead of us. It is a fearful thing to lead this great peaceful people into war, into the most terrible and disastrous of all wars, civilization itself seeming to be in the balance. But the right is more precious than peace, and we shall fight for the things which we have always carried nearest our hearts,—for democracy, for the right of those who submit to authority to have a voice in their own Governments, for the rights and liberties of small nations, for a universal dominion of right by such a concert of free peoples as shall bring peace and safety to all nations and make the world itself at last free. To such a task we can dedicate our lives and our fortunes, everything that we have, with the pride of those who know that the day has come when America is privileged to spend her blood and her might for the principles that gave her birth and happiness and the peace which she has treasured. God helping her, she can do no other.

25.

SKEPTICS

Many Americans found great glory in World War I. After all, the doughboys, as the American infantrymen were called, had turned the tide against Germany, and John ("Black Jack") Pershing, commander of the U.S. forces, emerged from the conflict a national hero. But the human price had been stiff: 100,000 Americans dead and 200,000 wounded. American casualties in World War I were low compared with European casualties (almost 2 million Germans and 1 million British died) or with U.S. losses in the Civil War (600,000) or in World War II (400,000). But the American losses were hardly insignificant, particularly since the country was in the war for only eighteen months and mobilized only about 4 million men. Much of the dying occurred in the appalling conditions of the Argonne Forest, where years of trenching and shelling had created a veritable wasteland of death.

Justifying such remarkable carnage would have taken remarkable results—something on the order of the new international order that Woodrow Wilson had promised (Document 24). But this, of course, the president had not been able to deliver, nor even his own country's membership in the League of Nations. So the skepticism that had attended U.S. entry into the war persisted, engendering a somber, even cynical mood beneath the boisterous patriotic surface. One source of this dark mood was the **Chicago Tribune,** which was the most influential newspaper in the Midwest and contained persistent editorials criticizing Wilsonian interventionism. The **Tribune** editorial of November 13, 1921, reprinted below, is in response to a wave of recrimination, social unrest, and small-scale military skirmishes in Europe and also the growing European calls for U.S. financial aid. This editorial is an expression of characteristic midwestern Republican views on the foolishness of idealism, the evils of European politics, and the folly of war.

A variant of these views also pervaded the major fiction of the period. Many writers of the early twentieth century were probably predisposed to skepticism about the war effort because they felt alienated and estranged from "bourgeois" America, with its perpetual striving for status and possessions, and some had pacifist leanings even before the United States entered World War I in 1917. Actual participation in the war confirmed the pacifist inclinations of several writers. Such books as E. E. Cummings's **The Enormous Room,** John Dos Passos's **Three Soldiers,** William Faulkner's **Soldier's Pay,** and Ernest Hemingway's **A Farewell to Arms** depicted the war as murderous and meaningless. Hemingway worked the war most deeply into his fiction. The excerpts below come from **In Our Time,** a collection of stories both about the war and about life in upstate Michigan strung together with brief mood-setting paragraphs; all the paragraphs reprinted here are this kind of paragraph, each with its own characters and locale. Hemingway wrote in a spare, detached style that was widely imitated in the postwar years and won him almost as much acclaim as his plots and characters. The disillusionment that pervaded his work was imitated, too, so much so that finally it seemed almost incredible that the United States could have participated in the war. Americans who sought an explanation for U.S. entry in World War I increasingly found some mixture of self-righteousness, bumbling stupidity, and the machinations of the arms dealers, and resolved never to go to war again—and did not until Pearl Harbor.

The editor and publisher of the **Chicago Tribune** when the editorial below was published was Robert R. McCormick, a graduate of Yale University and Northwestern University's law school and nephew of Cyrus H. McCormick of mechanical reaper fame. Forty-one years old in 1921, Robert McCormick had already held political office in Chicago and served as both a **Tribune** war correspondent and an artillery officer in France. Under McCormick's direction the **Tribune** company had a fivefold increase in newspaper circulation and also had acquired vast nonnewspaper business holdings. McCormick died in Illinois in 1955, with his formidable suspicions of idealists and Europeans still intact. His fellow Chicagoan, Ernest Hemingway, was born in 1899 into a middle-class family. Having skipped college to become a newspaper reporter, he spent the war years with a volunteer ambulance unit in Italy and after the war joined the growing colony of expatriate Americans in Paris. Hemingway received the Nobel Prize for Literature in 1954. He died at his home in Ketchum, Idaho, in 1961.

Questions to consider. The 1921 **Tribune** editorial painted a gloomy picture of European conditions three years after the end of the war. Does the editorial seem to express surprise at this state of affairs? What or whom did the writer hold most responsible? Had the war, then, been utterly futile and valueless? What actions did the writer advise the United States to take, or not to take? With whom was the editorial arguing? Does it include statements with which you agree? In the Hemingway paragraphs, what seems to be the dominant mood? Anger? Pity? Sarcasm? Are there any common features in these Hemingway scenes? Why might people of the 1920s have found them startling, even shocking? Do they still have shock power? Why or why not?

Unregenerate Europe (1921)
The Chicago Tribune

It is natural that pacifists and excited humanitarians should stress the evil consequences of the world war at this time. It is equally natural that foreign statesmen and public agencies should join them in keeping this phase of the European situation [of famine and insurrections] before us. It gives a tremendous momentum to the pacifist propaganda, and it relieves the governments and peoples of Europe of a large part of their responsibility for the present condition of their affairs.

But the American mind should clear itself on this point. No one will deny that the war is responsible directly for a vast wastage of life and property. But what needs recognition and emphasis at this moment . . . is that had common sense and self-control governed the policies of the governments and the sentiments of the peoples of Europe their affairs would not be tottering now on the rim of chaos.

On the contrary, were there wisdom and courage in the statesmanship of Europe, were there the same selfless devotion in chancelleries and parliaments as was exhibited on the battlefield, Europe would have been today well on the way to recovery.

The expenditures of the war and the intensification of long existing animosities and jealousies undoubtedly have complicated the problems of statecraft and of government. Undoubtedly the temporary depletion of man power and the temporary exhaustion of body and spirit among the war worn peoples were a burden which recovery has had to assume. Undoubtedly the wastage of wealth and diversion of productive agencies were a handicap to expeditious restoration.

But that these are chiefly responsible for the present state of Europe we do not admit and the future judgment of history, we are confident, will deny.

It is chiefly the folly which has been persistently demonstrated by governments and people since the war that is responsible for Europe's condition today. It is because the moment hostilities ceased and the enemy was disarmed, victors and vanquished turned their backs on the healing and constructive principles they had solemnly asserted from time to time when matters were going against them at the battle front, that the European nations almost without exception have been going down hill. There never in history has been a more perfect illustration of the ancient sarcasm: "When the devil is sick, the devil a monk would be; when the devil is well, the devil a monk is he."

If we wish to know why Europe is in the present state, we cannot do better than to draw a parallel between the assertions of purpose and principle of the allies and "associated" powers in 1916, '17, and '18, and what has actually happened since Nov. 11, 1918.

The war was a gigantic folly and waste. No one will deny that. But it was not so foolish nor so wasteful as the peace which has followed it. The European governments, those who come at our invitation and those who remain away, would have us believe they are mere victims of the war. They say nothing of what the war did for them. We might remind them that they profited as well as lost by the war. Many of them were freed from age long tyranny. They got rid of kaisers and saber clattering aristocracies. They were given freedom, and their present state shows how little they have known how to profit by it. They have been given new territories and new resources, and they have shown how little they deserve their food fortune. The last three years in Europe have been given not to sane efforts to heal wounds, remove hostilities, develop cooperation for the common economic restoration which is essential to the life of each. On the contrary, they have been marked by new wars and destruction, by new animosities and rivalries, by a refusal to face facts, make necessary sacrifices and compromises for financial and economic recovery, by greedy grabbing of territory and new adventures in the very imperialism which brought about the war.

It is well for Americans and their representatives to keep this in mind. The appeal to America's disinterestedness is unfairly fortified by the assumption that Europe is the innocent victim of one egotist's or one nation's ruthless ambition. We can take due account of the disastrous effects of the Prussian effort at dominance, but that should not overshadow the stubborn errors which began over again on the very threshold of peace, and which have made the peace more destructive than the war. When the European governments and peoples are ready to make a real peace, which cannot arrive until they give over the policies and attitudes that produced the world war, America will then not fail to give generous aid. But America would be foolish to contribute to the support of present methods or give any encouragement to the spirit which now prevails in the old world.

In Our Time (1925)
Ernest Hemingway

Minarets stuck up in the rain out of Adrianople [Turkey] across the mud flats. The carts were jammed for thirty miles along the Karagatch road. Water buffalo and cattle were hauling carts through the mud. There was no end and no beginning. Just carts loaded with everything they owned. The old men and women, soaked through, walked along keeping the cattle moving. The Maritza [River] was running yellow almost up to the bridge. Carts were jammed solid on the bridge with camels bobbing along through them. Greek cavalry herded along the procession. The women and children were in the carts, crouched with mattresses, mirrors, sewing machines, bundles. There was a woman having a baby with a young girl holding a blanket over her and crying. Scared sick looking at it. It rained all through the evacuation. . . .

We were in a garden in Mons [Belgium]. Young Buckley came in with his patrol from across the river The first German I saw climbed up over the garden wall. We waited till he got one leg over and then potted him. He had so much equipment on and looked awfully surprised and fell down into the garden. Then three more came over further down the wall. We shot them. They all came just like that. . . .

It was a frightfully hot day. We'd jammed an absolutely perfect barricade across the bridge. It was simply priceless. A big old wrought-iron grating from the front of a house. Too heavy to lift and you could shoot through it and they would have to climb over it. It was absolutely topping. They tried to get over it, and we potted them from forty yards. They rushed it, and officers came out alone and worked on it. It was an absolutely perfect obstacle. Their officers were very fine. We were frightfully put out when we heard the flank had gone, and we had to fall back. . . .

They shot the six cabinet ministers at half-past six in the morning against the wall of a hospital. There were pools of water in the courtyard. There were wet dead leaves on the paving of the courtyard. It rained hard. All the shutters of the hospital were nailed shut. One of the ministers was sick with typhoid. Two soldiers carried him downstairs and out into the rain. They tried to hold him up against the wall but he sat down in a puddle of water. The other five stood very quietly against the wall. Finally the officer told the soldiers it was no good trying to make him stand up. When they fired the first volley he was sitting down in the water with his head on his knees.

Nick sat against the wall of the church where they had dragged him to be clear of machine gun fire in the street. Both legs stuck out awkwardly. He had been hit in the spine. His face was sweaty and dirty. The sun shone on his face. The day was very hot. Rinaldi, big backed, his equipment sprawling, lay face downward against the wall. Nick looked straight ahead brilliantly. The pink wall of the house opposite had fallen out from the roof, and an iron bedstead hung twisted toward the street. Two Austrian dead lay in the rubble in the shade of the house. Up the street were other dead. Things were getting forward in the town. It was going well. Stretcher bearers would be along any time now. Nick turned his head and looked down at Rinaldi. "Senta Rinaldo; Senta. You and me we've made a separate peace." Rinaldi lay still in the sun,

A doughboy in France, 1918. World War I battlefields had three memorable features: long open fields filled with barbed wire that soldiers had to cross in the face of withering machine-gun fire; vast areas of landscape so cratered and devastated by artillery fire that nothing green or living remained; and mud, particularly in the trenches, where soldiers tried to escape the machine guns, and in the roads, where soldiers tried to march calf-deep in muck. These conditions produced 10 million dead and 5 million wounded, an unusually high ratio of wounded to dead and one that made an indelible impression on medical corps personnel, such as Ernest Hemingway. (National Archives)

breathing with difficulty. "We're not patriots." Nick turned his head away, smiling sweatily. Rinaldi was a disappointing audience. . . .

While the bombardment was knocking the trench to pieces at Fossalta [Italy], he lay very flat and sweated and prayed, "Oh Jesus Christ get me out of here. Dear Jesus, please get me out. Christ, please, please, please, Christ. If you'll only keep me from getting killed I'll do anything you say. I believe in you and I'll tell everybody in the world that you are the only thing that matters. Please, please, dear Jesus." The shelling moved further up the line. We went to work on the trench and in the morning the sun came up and the day was hot and muggy and cheerful and quiet. The next night back at Mestre he did not tell the girl he went upstairs with at the Villa Rossa about Jesus. And he never told anybody.

COUNTERPOINT IV

Economics and Empire

Senator Albert Beveridge demanded the taking of the Philippines because, he said, the islands were rich in their own resources and also commanded the trade routes to China and other Asian countries. Beveridge mentioned race and national prestige. But his main argument was economic. Was he right? Would the commercial payoff really justify the conquest and subjugation of the islands? Would the Philippines in fact funnel the riches of the East to America?

Bonifacio Salamanca shows that the United States did reap some benefits from the islands themselves. First, the Filipinos substantially increased their purchases of American-made goods. They imported almost eight times as much from abroad in 1912 as in 1901; of this larger amount, two-fifths came from the United States as against a tenth in 1901 (table A.1). Much the same was true for exports, which grew almost as rapidly. For example, Americans increased their purchase of Philippine tobacco products, an island mainstay, from practically nothing in 1901 to almost 40 percent in 1912 (table A.2), and did the same for sugar, which was beginning to dominate the local economy, taking 71 percent of the total sugar exports (table A.3). In fact, tobacco and sugar together made up virtually all the Philippine exports to the United States. The new American possession, in other words, was not just a colony. It was, increasingly, a plantation colony, its economy geared increasingly to agricultural production for the benefit of U.S. investors in the islands and U.S. consumers at home.

Yet the dollar value of this commerce was less than $10 million each for imports and exports as late as 1912—hardly enough, it would seem, to serve as the catalyst for transoceanic imperialism. Remember, though, that Senator Beveridge never claimed that the Philippines alone were the goal. He also saw the islands as "a self-supporting, dividend-paying fleet" for controlling the Pacific Ocean—an extension, in effect, of the U.S.-occupied Hawaiian islands five thousand miles to the east as well as a springboard to East Asia a thousand miles north by northwest. Hawaii had been a special trading partner of the United States since the 1870s and a protectorate since 1894, so that when the Americans formally annexed it in early 1898, trade was already substantial and growing, as Merze Tate's figures indicate (table B). By 1915, Hawaii was importing more goods than the Philippines, almost all from the United States, and was exporting four times as much as the Philippines, mostly in the form of sugar, again virtually all to the United States. Hawaii's economy was entirely export-oriented, as Tate's final column shows, the epitome of a plantation colony and undoubtedly a model for American activity in the Philippines. U.S.-Hawaiian trade, moreover, continued to expand rapidly into the 1920s, justifying hopes for similar Filipino growth.

What of Beveridge's other concern, East Asia? Data compiled by Warren Cohen and James Reed cast doubt on economics as a motive for U.S. imperialism. U.S. exports to Japan and China in 1905 were less than a tenth of all American exports—half the share of Canada and Mexico—and remained less than a tenth until the 1930s (table C.1). Imports from China and Japan were more important, but not much more, and the lion's share of that came not from China, as Beveridge had expected, but from Japan (table C.2). Finally, even if direct U.S. investments in Chinese railroads, ships, and utilities are added, both the actual amounts and the share of all U.S. foreign investment remained low (table C.3).

In view of these figures, does an economic interpretation of imperialism have any merit? Perhaps to a modest degree. Total U.S. exports to the whole western Pacific basin—China, Japan, and Hawaii as well as the Philippines—totaled $150 million as of 1912–1913, plus another $50 million in direct investment; and imports reached nearly $200 million. These were significant sums, even for a country like the United States whose economy was still oriented to domestic production and sales. Beveridge and other expansionists, moreover, were concerned with the future, not the present. Trade might be modest now, but tomorrow would be another day.

If economics was not the motive here, what was? James Reed suggests that at least for Asia proper, missionaries rather than businessmen may have been the driving force behind expansion. In 1906 there were 1,631 Protestant missionaries in China and Japan, with China having about two times the number of missionaries that Japan had (table D.1). By 1916 there were 3,720 missionaries, with China having more than three times the number of missionaries that Japan had. This was several times the number of American businessmen that Reed found in East Asia. As measured by correspondence, the missionaries were more aggressive in making their views known than any other group (table D.2). Wanting to "civilize the heathen and save their souls" might well have been as crucial to the age of imperialism as buying and selling. If once civilized and saved the heathens went on to trade with Americans, then in the U.S. view so much the better.

A. Philippine Trade

1. Philippine Trade with the United States

	Total Imports	U.S. Percentage of Total Imports	Total Exports	U.S. Percentage of Total Exports
1901	$ 3,500,000	12%	$ 4,500,000	18%
1907	5,000,000	17	10,500,000	31
1912	24,500,000	39	23,000,000	41

2. Philippine Tobacco Product Exports

	To All Countries	To United States	
	Value	*Value*	*Percentage of Total Tobacco Exports*
1901	$2,500,000	$ 500	.02%
1907	2,500,000	25,000	1.00
1912	5,500,000	2,000,000	38.00

3. Philippine Sugar Exports

	To All Countries		To United States	
	Tons	*Percentage of Total Philippine Exports*	*Tons*	*Percentage of Total Sugar Exports*
1901	60,000	10%	5,000	14%
1907	130,000	13	11,000	10
1912	200,000	18	135,000	71

SOURCE: From *The Filipino Reaction to American Rule, 1901–1913* by Bonifacio S. Salamanca (Shoe String Press, Hamden, Conn., 1968), pp. 135–139; reprint by New Day Publishers, Quezon City, Philippines, 1984. Reprinted by permission of the author.

B. Hawaiian Trade

	Total Imports	Total Exports	Domestic Produce Exported
1880	$ 4,000,000	$ 5,000,000	$ 5,000,000
1890	7,000,000	13,000,000	13,000,000
1899	16,000,000	23,000,000	23,000,000
1915	26,000,000	62,000,000	62,000,000
1925	82,000,000	106,000,000	106,000,000

SOURCE: Adapted from Merze Tate: *Hawaii: Reciprocity or Annexation* (Michigan State University Press, East Lansing, Michigan, 1968), p. 272. Reprinted by permission.

C. U.S. Exports and Trade and Investment in Asia

1. U.S. Exports to Leading Markets (Percentage of Total U.S. Exports)

	Great Britain and France	Canada and Mexico	Japan and China
1890	58%	6%	1%
1905	39	12	7
1920	30	14	6
1935	24	17	11

2. U.S. Trade with China and Japan, 1913

China		Japan	
Exports	*Imports*	*Exports*	*Imports*
$21,000,000	$39,000,000	$58,000,000	$92,000,000

3. U.S. Direct Investment in China

	U.S. Investment in China	Percentage of Total U.S. Foreign Investment
1902	$ 20,000,000	1.2%
1914	50,000,000	1.4
1931	200,000,000	1.3

SOURCE: Sections 1 and 3 from *America's Response to China: An Interpretative History of Sino-American Relations,* second edition, by Warren I. Cohen. Copyright 1980. Reprinted by permission of Alfred A. Knopf, Inc. Section 2 from James Reed, *The Missionary Mind and American East Asia Policy, 1911–1915* (Cambridge, Council on East Asian Studies, Harvard University, 1983), p. 42.

D. U.S. Preoccupation with Asia: Growth in Missionary Activity and State Department Correspondence

1. U.S. Missionaries to China and Japan

	China	Japan	Total Number to China and Japan
1906	1,037	594	1,631
1911	1,812	771	2,583
1916	2,862	858	3,720

2. State Department Correspondence Regarding China, 1911–1913, According to Occupations of Opinion Leaders

Missionaries, ministers, religious workers	30%
Businessmen	17
Lawyers	9
Academics	8
Editors, journalists	3
Others	13
Unidentifiable	20

SOURCE: From James Reed, *The Missionary Mind and American East Asia Policy, 1911–1915* (Cambridge, Council on East Asian Studies, Harvard University, 1983), pp. 18, 146.

The Great Depression. The Depression affected all Americans in varying degree. Many people lost everything—jobs, homes, household goods—and had to travel the country seeking employment. (Library of Congress)

CHAPTER FIVE

Crises and Victories

26.

THE GREAT COLLAPSE

American industrialization meant not only surging production but also periodic business "busts"—in the 1870s, the 1890s, 1907, and 1919–1921—when prices, profits, and employment all plunged and remained low until its basic strength moved the economy again to higher levels. But no previous bust matched the depression that descended on the nation in the early 1930s. From 1929, when Herbert C. Hoover became the third consecutive Republican president since World War I, until 1933, when Franklin D. Roosevelt, a Democrat, succeeded him, the economy all but collapsed. Stocks and bonds lost three-fourths of their value, bank failures increased from 500 to 4,000 a year, farm income fell by half, and unemployment rose from 4 percent to almost 25 percent.

In the light of this unprecedented cataclysm, Roosevelt's inaugural address, excerpted below, might appear moderate, with its call for confidence, honest labor, the protection of agriculture and land, organized relief, and a bit of economic planning. Only its castigation of the "money changers" and its plea for executive authority to meet the crisis seemed to prefigure the sweeping liberalism that many observers instinctively associate with the Roosevelt years. Yet the address was charged with emotion and a sense of mission, and its moderation reflected both the confusion of the times, when few people understood the nation's problems and still fewer had solutions, and the personal conservatism of Roosevelt, who was ultimately American capitalism's savior as well as its reformer.

Franklin Delano Roosevelt, a distant cousin of Theodore Roosevelt, was born in 1882 to a wealthy New York family, attended exclusive schools and colleges, and practiced law in New York City. He married his cousin Eleanor in 1905, entered Democratic politics—serving in the state senate from 1910 to 1913—and became assistant secretary of the navy in 1913. After running (and losing) as the Democrats' vice-presidential candidate in 1920, he contracted polio, which left him permanently crippled. Nevertheless, he remained active in politics, serving as governor of New York from 1928 to 1932, when he defeated Hoover for the presidency. During the 1932 campaign Roosevelt criticized Hoover for excessive government spending and an unbalanced budget, but after entering the White House Roosevelt also was obliged to adopt a spending policy in order to help those who were starving, to put people to work, and to revive the economy. His New Deal stressed economic recovery as well as relief and reform. Roosevelt's New Deal, backed by the great Democratic majorities that he forged, mitigated many of the effects of the Great Depression, though the depression never actually ended until the advent of World War II. Roosevelt achieved reelection in 1936, 1940, and 1944 (a record unequaled then and unconstitutional since 1951) and died, still in office, in 1945 in Warm Springs, Georgia.

Questions to consider. In his first inaugural address Roosevelt placed great emphasis on candor, honesty, and truth. Why did he do this? Did he display these qualities himself in discussing the crisis? In what ways did he try to reassure the American people? What reasons did he give for the Great Depression? Do they seem convincing? What values did he think were important for sustaining the nation in a time of trouble? What did he single out as the first and most pressing task of his administration? What solutions did he propose for meeting the economic crisis? Do they seem adequate? How did he regard his authority to act under the Constitution? How would you have reacted to his address if you had been an unemployed worker, a hard-pressed farmer, or a middle-class citizen who had lost your home through foreclosure?

━━━━━

First Inaugural Address (1933)
Franklin D. Roosevelt

This is a day of national consecration, and I am certain that my fellow-Americans expect that on my induction into the Presidency I will address them with a candor and a decision which the present situation of our nation impels. This is pre-eminently the time to speak the truth, the whole truth, frankly and boldly. Nor need we shrink from honestly facing conditions in our country today. This great nation will endure as it has endured, will revive and will prosper.

So first of all let me assert my firm belief that the only thing we have to fear is fear itself—nameless, unreasoning, unjustified terror which paralyzes needed efforts to convert retreat into advance. In every dark hour of our national life a leadership of frankness and vigor has met with that understanding and support of the people themselves which is essential to victory. I am convinced that you will again give that support to leadership in these critical days.

In such a spirit on my part and on yours we face our common difficulties. They concern, thank God, only material things. Values have shrunken to

From the **New York Times,** March 5, 1933.

fantastic levels; taxes have risen; our ability to pay has fallen; government of all kinds is faced by serious curtailment of income; the means of exchange are frozen in the currents of trade; the withered leaves of industrial enterprise lie on every side; farmers find no markets for their produce; the savings of many years in thousands of families are gone.

More important, a host of unemployed citizens face the grim problem of existence, and an equally great number toil with little return. Only a foolish optimist can deny the dark realities of the moment.

Yet our distress comes from no failure of substance. We are stricken by no plague of locusts. Compared with the perils which our forefathers conquered because they believed and were not afraid, we have still much to be thankful for. Nature still offers her bounty and human efforts have multiplied it. Plenty is at our doorstep, but a generous use of it languishes in the very sight of the supply. Primarily, this is because the rulers of the exchange of mankind's goods have failed through their own stubbornness and their own incompetence, have admitted their failure and abdicated. Practices of the unscrupulous money changers stand indicted in the court of public opinion, rejected by the hearts and minds of men.

True, they have tried, but their efforts have been cast in the pattern of an outworn tradition. Faced by failure of credit, they have proposed only the lending of more money. Stripped of the lure of profit by which to induce our people to follow their false leadership, they have resorted to exhortations, pleading tearfully for restored confidence. They know only the rules of a generation of self-seekers. They have no vision, and when there is no vision the people perish.

The money changers have fled from their high seats in the temple of our civilization. We may now restore that temple to the ancient truths. The measure of the restoration lies in the extent to which we apply social values more noble than mere monetary profit.

Happiness lies not in the mere possession of money; it lies in the joy of achievement, in the thrill of creative effort. The joy and moral stimulation of work no longer must be forgotten in the mad chase of evanescent profits. These dark days will be worth all they cost us if they teach us that our true destiny is not to be ministered unto but to minister to ourselves and to our fellow-men.

Recognition of the falsity of material wealth as the standard of success goes hand in hand with the abandonment of the false belief that public office and high political position are to be valued only by the standards of pride of place and personal profit; and there must be an end to a conduct in banking and in business which too often has given to a sacred trust the likeness of callous and selfish wrongdoing. Small wonder that confidence languishes, for it thrives only on honesty, on honor, on the sacredness of obligations, on faithful protection, on unselfish performance. Without them it cannot live.

Restoration calls, however, not for changes in ethics alone. This nation asks for action, and action now.

Bread line.   The Depression forced unemployed men into the bread line at the Central Union Mission in Washington, D.C., and into a thousand other relief lines like it. In 1932 when the misery was most widespread, much of the nation's resentment focused on the administration of Herbert Hoover, who seemed personally responsible for the nation's mushrooming "Hoovervilles" of shanties and mass poverty. Franklin D. Roosevelt, who offered jaunty optimism and a fresh face, was the natural political beneficiary. (National Archives)

Our greatest primary task is to put people to work. This is no unsolvable problem if we face it wisely and courageously. It can be accomplished in part by direct recruiting by the Government itself, treating the task as we would treat the emergency of war, but at the same time, through this employment, accomplishing greatly needed projects to stimulate and reorganize the use of our natural resources.

Hand in hand with this, we must frankly recognize the overbalance of population in our industrial centers and, by engaging on a national scale in the redistribution, endeavor to provide a better use of the land for those best fitted for the land. The task can be helped by definite efforts to raise the values of agricultural products and with this the power to purchase the output of our cities. It can be helped by preventing realistically the tragedy of the growing loss, through foreclosure, of our small homes and our farms. It can be helped by insistence that the Federal, State and local governments act forthwith on the demand that their cost be drastically reduced. It can be helped by the unifying of relief activities which today are often scattered, uneconomical and unequal. It can be helped by national planning for a supervision of all forms of transportation and of communications and other utilities which have a definitely public character. There are many ways in which it can be helped, but it can never be helped merely by talking about it. We must act, and act quickly. . . .

. . . This I propose to offer, pledging that the larger purposes will bind upon us all as a sacred obligation with a unity of duty hitherto evoked only in the time of armed strife.

With this pledge taken, I assume unhesitatingly the leadership of this great army of our people, dedicated to a disciplined attack upon our common problems.

Action in this image and to this end is feasible under the form of government which we have inherited from our ancestors. Our Constitution is so simple and practical that it is possible always to meet extraordinary needs by changes in emphasis and arrangement without loss of essential form. That is why our constitutional system has proved itself the most superbly enduring political mechanism the modern world has produced. It has met every stress of vast expansion of territory, of foreign wars, of bitter internal strife, of world relations.

It is to be hoped that the normal balance of executive and legislative authority may be wholly adequate to meet the unprecedented task before us. But it may be that an unprecedented demand and need for undelayed action may call for temporary departure from that normal balance of public procedure.

I am prepared under my constitutional duty to recommend the measures that a stricken nation in the midst of a stricken world may require. These measures, or such other measures as the Congress may build out of its experience and wisdom, I shall seek, within my constitutional authority, to bring to speedy adoption.

But in the event that the Congress shall fail to take one of these two courses, and in the event that the national emergency is still critical, I shall not evade the clear course of duty that will then confront me. I shall ask the Congress for the one remaining instrument to meet the crisis—broad Executive power to wage a war against the emergency as great as the power that would be given me if we were in fact invaded by a foreign foe.

For the trust reposed in me I will return the courage and the devotion that befit the time. I can do no less. . . .

27.

A SAFETY NET

The New Deal was a grab bag of efforts to cope with the ravages of the Great Depression. "It is common sense to take a method and try it," said Franklin Roosevelt. "If it fails, admit it frankly and try another. But above all, try something." Gradually, however, administration officials began to categorize New Deal measures in terms of their objectives: relief (emergency public works and aid to the poor); recovery (business price supports and low-interest loans); and reform (business regulation, progressive taxation, public housing, and electric power).

No legislation of Roosevelt's first administration was more significant than the Social Security Act of 1935, which provided for old-age pensions, unemployment compensation, and aid to the blind, crippled, and other dependents. Adopted in part to appease such radical critics as Senator Huey P. Long of Louisiana, the social security program actually represented a fusion of all three New Deal goals. It expanded the relief effort, spurred recovery a bit by giving consumers more purchasing power, and laid the groundwork for a new system of economic security. Early benefits were low and coverage limited, as Secretary of Labor Frances Perkins acknowledged in the radio address reprinted below, and the system was funded by a "regressive" tax on wages and payrolls. Even so, the measure embodied the unprecedented and far-reaching idea that society should provide (as a Democratic congressman put it) "security of the individual from birth to death." With the Social Security Act, the "welfare state" in a real sense began.

Frances Perkins was born in Boston in 1882. A college graduate and one-time schoolteacher and church worker, Perkins took advanced degrees in economics and worked from 1911 to 1933 in various New York agencies related to consumer protection and industrial safety. As one of Roosevelt's first and most important cabinet appointees, she became the first woman cabinet member in American history. A strong advocate and defender of innovative welfare and labor measures, Perkins was surrounded by controversy throughout her twelve-year tenure. Despite this, or perhaps because of it, she became one of the president's most trusted lieutenants. She died in New York City in 1965.

Questions to consider. In her speech discussing the Social Security Act (which she helped draft), Perkins attempted to make a new departure in the American system sound natural and reasonable. Do you think she succeeded in her objective? How was unemployment handled in

America before the New Deal? To what extent would the states be involved in the social security system established by the new legislation? Was Perkins correct in saying that the Social Security Act preserved "the benefits of local administration and national leadership"? How did she relate the Social Security Act to other New Deal measures? What, according to Perkins, were the act's basic objectives? To what progress in American thinking did she allude in the last part of her address?

The Social Security Act (1935)
Frances Perkins

People who work for a living in the United States of America can join with all other good citizens on this forty-eighth anniversary of Labor Day in satisfaction that the Congress has passed the Social Security Act. This act establishes unemployment insurance as a substitute for haphazard methods of assistance in periods when men and women willing and able to work are without jobs. It provides for old-age pensions which mark great progress over the measures upon which we have hitherto depended in caring for those who have been unable to provide for the years when they no longer can work. It also provides security for dependent and crippled children, mothers, the indigent disabled and the blind.

Old people who are in need, unemployables, children, mothers and the sightless, will find systematic regular provisions for needs. The Act limits the Federal aid to not more than $15 per month for the individual, provided the State in which he resides appropriates a like amount. There is nothing to prevent a State from contributing more than $15 per month in special cases and there is no requirement to allow as much as $15 from either State or Federal funds when a particular case has some personal provision and needs less than the total allowed.

Following essentially the same procedure, the Act as passed provides for Federal assistance to the States in caring for the blind, a contribution by the States of up to $15 a month to be matched in turn by a like contribution by the Federal Government. The Act also contains provision for assistance to the States in providing payments to dependent children under sixteen years of age. There also is provision in the Act for cooperation with medical and health organizations charged with rehabilitation of physically handicapped children. The necessity for adequate service in the fields of public and maternal health and child welfare calls for the extension of these services to meet individual community needs.

From Frances Perkins, "The Social Security Act," **Vital Speeches** (September 2, 1935).

A social security poster.   The federal social security system initiated in the 1930s was one of a long series of changes in the way Americans dealt with the needy. In the eighteenth century, towns and counties were the principal disbursers of assistance, augmented in the nineteenth century by churches and individual charity and in the early twentieth by state governments and large-scale private philanthropy. The magnitude of the Great Depression dwarfed all previous economic crises, however, creating a level of need far beyond what all the existing sources of charity could provide. The Roosevelt administration took the logical next step: a new federal role for a deep national need.

Consider for a moment those portions of the Act which, while they will not be effective this present year, yet will exert a profound and far-reaching effect upon millions of citizens. I refer to the provision for a system of old-age benefits supported by the contributions of employer and employees, and to the section which sets up the initial machinery for unemployment insurance.

Old-age benefits in the form of monthly payments are to be paid to individuals who have worked and contributed to the insurance fund in direct proportion to the total wages earned by such individuals in the course of their employment subsequent to 1936. The minimum monthly payment is to be $10, the maximum $85. These payments will begin in the year 1942 and will be to those who have worked and contributed. . . .

Federal legislation was framed in the thought that the attack upon the problems of insecurity should be a cooperative venture participated in by both the Federal and State Governments, preserving the benefits of local adminis-tration and national leadership. It was thought unwise to have the Federal Government decide all questions of policy and dictate completely what the States should do. Only very necessary minimum standards are included in the Federal measure leaving wide latitude to the States. . . .

The social security measure looks primarily to the future and is only a part of the administration's plan to promote sound and stable economic life. We cannot think of it as disassociated from the Government's program to save the homes, the farms, the businesses and banks of the Nation, and especially must we consider it a companion measure to the Works Relief Act which does undertake to provide immediate increase in employment and corresponding stimulation to private industry by purchase of supplies.

While it is not anticipated as a complete remedy for the abnormal condi-tions confronting us at the present time, it is designed to afford protection for the individual against future major economic vicissitudes. . . .

Our social security program will be a vital force working against the recurrence of severe depressions in the future. We can, as the principle of sustained purchasing power in hard times makes itself felt in every shop, store and mill, grow old without being haunted by the spectre of a poverty-ridden old age or of being a burden on our children. . . .

The passage of this act with so few dissenting votes and with so much intelligent public support is deeply significant of the progress which the American people have made in thought in the social field and awareness of methods of using cooperation through government to overcome social hazards against which the individual alone is inadequate. . . .

28.

ORGANIZING THE MASSES

Economic conditions in the 1930s had a tremendous impact on American labor. The Great Depression wreaked havoc with the lives of working people. By 1932, New York had a million jobless and Chicago another 600,000; 50 percent of Cleveland's work force was unemployed, as was 60 percent of Akron's and 80 percent of Toledo's. Even those who still had jobs saw their wages and hours decline dramatically, and things did not greatly improve as the decade wore on.

The New Deal gave labor unions an opportunity to replenish their membership, which had plummeted to half of its World War I strength. The chief piece of legislation affecting unions was the Labor Relations Act of 1935, which established a national board to keep employers from interfering with labor organizers or union members and to supervise union elections. Thus encouraged, leaders of several large unions bolted the conservative American Federation of Labor (AFL) to form the Committee for Industrial Organization, which soon became the Congress of Industrial Organizations (CIO). The AFL emphasized craft unions (which were made up of workers in a given trade); the CIO insisted that industrial unions (which included all industrial workers, skilled and unskilled, in an industry) were essential in the great mass-production industries in which labor previously had been unorganized. In 1936 and 1937 the CIO, led by John L. Lewis, president of the United Mine Workers, mounted successful, though bloody, organizing campaigns to establish unions in the steel, rubber, electrical, automobile, and other basic industries. The AFL soon responded with organizing drives of its own. Thus, total union membership had tripled by 1940. The New Deal facilitated the rise of Big Labor as it did the welfare state, all the while preserving the country's basic economic system.

John L. Lewis, the forceful CIO leader, was born near Lucas, Iowa, in 1880 to a Welsh immigrant family. Leaving school after the seventh grade, Lewis worked briefly with his father in the coal fields and then wandered across the West for several years before returning to the mines in about 1905. He soon became active in union affairs and in 1920 was elected president of the United Mine Workers. Although he was originally associated with the AFL, Lewis spearheaded the formation of the CIO after the passage of the Labor Relations Act of 1935 and presided vigorously and dramatically for the next few years over the violent struggle for industrial unionism. In the 1940s he repeatedly quarreled with leaders of the CIO, the AFL, and the federal government, called several bitter coal strikes, and was twice held in contempt of court for ignoring anti-strike injunctions. He nonetheless remained a revered labor spokesman. He was president of the United Mine Workers until 1960 and chairman of its retirement fund until his death in Washington, D.C., in 1969.

Questions to consider. John L. Lewis, perhaps America's most important labor leader in the twentieth century, had great gifts as an orator ("He can use his voice like a policeman's billy," said one commentator, "or like a monk at orisons [prayer]"), as well as a striking physical appearance (he had a mass of reddish hair, bushy eyebrows, and piercing blue eyes). But his effectiveness as a speaker also depended on his choice of words. In the 1937 radio speech reprinted below he was trying to justify the CIO to an American public that was still not particularly friendly to organized labor. Do you think his style of speech was likely to win the understanding and sympathy of middle-class Americans? How "radical" was the position taken in his speech? How did he link the CIO to traditional American values and institutions? How extensive, according to Lewis, was resistance to the CIO's organizing drive in the big unorganized industries of the country? How did he implicate the federal government in this resistance? In what ways did he distinguish the CIO's philosophy from that of "alien" doctrines like communism? What did he have to say about politics? Do you find any notable and quotable phrases in his speech?

═══════

The Steelworkers Organization Campaign (1936)
John L. Lewis

Out of the agony and travail of economic America, the Committee for Industrial Organization was born. To millions of Americans, exploited without stint by corporate industry and socially debased beyond the understanding of the fortunate, its coming was as welcome as the dawn to the night watcher. To a lesser group of Americans, infinitely more fortunately situated, blessed with larger quantities of the world's goods and insolent in their assumption of privilege, its coming was heralded as a harbinger of ill, sinister of purpose, of unclean methods and non-virtuous objectives.

From **John L. Lewis and the International Union, United Mine Workers of America: The Story from 1917 to 1952** (United Mine Workers of America, Washington, D.C., 1952), 43–49. Reprinted by permission of the United Mine Workers of America.

The workers of the nation were tired of waiting for corporate industry to right their economic wrongs, to alleviate their social agony and to grant them their political rights. Despairing of fair treatment, they resolved to do something for themselves. They, therefore, have organized a new labor movement, conceived within the principles of the national Bill of Rights and committed to the proposition that the workers are free to assemble in their own forums, voice their own grievances, declare their own hopes, and contract on even terms with modern industry, for the sale of their only material possession—their labor.

The Committee for Industrial Organization has a numerical enrollment of 3,718,000 members. It has thirty-two affiliated national and international unions. Of this number, eleven unions account for 2,765,000 members. This group is organized in the textile, auto, garment, lumber, rubber, electrical manufacturing, power, steel, coal and transport industries. The remaining membership exists in the maritime, oil production and refining, shipbuilding, leather, chemical, retail, meat packing, vegetable canning, metalliferous mining, miscellaneous manufacturing, agricultural labor, and service and miscellaneous industries. Some 200 thousand workers are organized into 506 chartered local unions not yet attached to a national industrial union. Much of this progress was made in the face of violent and deadly opposition which reached its climax in the slaughter of workers paralleling the massacres of Ludlow [Colorado, 1914] and Homestead [Pennsylvania, 1892].

In the steel industry, the corporations generally have accepted collective bargaining and negotiated wage agreements with the Committee for Industrial Organization. Eighty-five per cent of the industry is thus under contract and a peaceful relationship exists between the management and the workers. Written wage contracts have been negotiated with 399 steel companies covering 510 thousand men. One thousand thirty-one local lodges in 700 communities have been organized.

Five of the corporations in the steel industry elected to resist collective bargaining and undertook to destroy the steel workers' union. These companies filled their plants with industrial spies, assembled depots of guns and gas bombs, established barricades, controlled their communities with armed thugs, leased the police power of cities and mobilized the military power of a state to guard them against the intrusion of collective bargaining within their plants.

During this strike, eighteen steel workers were either shot to death or had their brains clubbed out by police or armed thugs in the pay of the steel companies. In Chicago, Mayor [Edward V.] Kelly's police force was successful in killing ten strikers before they could escape the fury of the police, shooting eight of them in the back. One hundred sixty strikers were maimed and injured by police clubs, riot guns and gas bombs and were hospitalized. Hundreds of strikers were arrested, jailed, treated with brutality while incarcerated and harassed by succeeding litigation. None but strikers were murdered, gassed, injured, jailed or maltreated. No one had to die except the

Strike pickets. During the winter of 1936–1937 the Congress of Industrial Organizations climaxed its drive to unionize America's basic industries with a series of strikes that caused conflict in some communities and tensions in many others. In this artwork, workers picket for bargaining rights and higher wages in late 1937. A year later, total union membership had zoomed to almost 8 million. Workers were responding to CIO organizers who sang, "You'll win. What I mean. . . . Take it easy . . . but take it!" ("We Demand" by Joe Jones; The Butler Institute of American Art)

workers who were standing for the right guaranteed them by the Congress and written in the law.

The infamous Governor [Martin L.] Davey of Ohio, successful in the last election because of his reiterated promises of fair treatment to labor, used the military power of the commonwealth on the side of the Republic Steel Co. and the Youngstown Sheet and Tube Co. Nearly half of the staggering military expenditure incident to the crushing of this strike in Ohio was borne by the federal government through the allocation of financial aid to the military establishment of the state.

The steel workers have now buried their dead, while the widows weep and watch their orphaned children become objects of public charity. The murder of these unarmed men has never been publicly rebuked by any authoritative officer of the state or federal government. Some of them, in extenuation, plead lack of jurisdiction, but murder as a crime against the moral code can always be rebuked without regard to the niceties of legalistic jurisdiction by those who profess to be the keepers of the public conscience.

Shortly after Kelly's police force in Chicago had indulged in their bloody orgy, Kelly came to Washington looking for political patronage. That patronage was forthcoming and Kelly must believe that the killing of the strikers is no liability in partisan politics.

The men in the steel industry who sacrificed their all were not merely aiding their fellows at home but were adding strength to the cause of their comrades in all industry. Labor was marching toward the goal of industrial democracy and contributing constructively toward a more rational arrangement of our domestic economy.

Labor does not seek industrial strife. It wants peace, but a peace with justice. In the long struggle for labor's rights, it has been patient and forebearing. Sabotage and destructive syndicalism have had no part in the American labor movement. Workers have kept faith in American institutions. Most of the conflicts which have occurred have been when labor's right to live has been challenged and denied.

Fascist organizations have been launched and financed under the shabby pretext that the CIO movement is communistic. The real breeders of discontent and alien doctrines of government and philosophies subversive of good citizenship are such as these who take the law into their own hands.

No tin-hat brigade of goose-stepping vigilantes or Bible-babbling mob of blackguarding and corporation-paid scoundrels will prevent the onward march of labor, or divert its purpose to play its natural and rational part in the development of the economic, political and social life of our nation.

Unionization, as opposed to communism, presupposes the relation of employment; it is based upon the wage system and it recognizes fully and unreservedly the institution of private property and the right to investment profit.

The organized workers of America, free in their industrial life, conscious partners in production, secure in their homes and enjoying a decent standard of living, will prove the finest bulwark against the intrusion of alien doctrines of government.

Do those who have hatched this foolish cry of communism in the CIO fear the increased influence will be cast on the side of shorter hours, a better system of distributed employment, better homes for the under-privileged, social security for the aged, a fairer distribution of the national income?

Certainly labor wants a fairer share in the national income. Assuredly labor wants a larger participation in increased productivity efficiency. Obviously the population is entitled to participate in the fruits of the genius of our men of achievement in the field of the material sciences.

Under the banner of the Committee for Industrial Organization, American labor is on the march. Its objectives today are those it had in the beginning: to strive for the unionization of our unorganized millions of workers and for the acceptance of collective bargaining as a recognized American institution.

The objectives of this movement are not political in a partisan sense. Yet it is true that a political party which seeks the support of labor and makes pledges of good faith to labor must, in equity and good conscience, keep that faith and redeem those pledges.

The spectacle of august and dignified members of the Congress, servants of the people and agents of the republic, skulking in hallways and closets, hiding their faces in a party caucus to prevent a quorum from acting upon a labor measure, is one that emphasizes the perfidy of politicians and blasts the confidence of labor's millions in politicians' promises and statesmen's vows.

Labor next year cannot avoid the necessity of a political assay of the work and deeds of its so-called friends and its political beneficiaries. It must determine who are its friends in the arena of politics as elsewhere. It feels that its cause is just and that its friends should not view its struggle with neutral detachment or intone constant criticism of its activities.

Those who chant their praises of democracy, but who lose no chance to drive their knives into labor's defenseless back, must feel the weight of labor's woe even as its open adversaries must ever feel the thrust of labor's power.

Labor, like Israel, has many sorrows. Its women weep for their fallen and they lament for the future of the children of the race. It ill behooves one who has supped at labor's table and who has been sheltered in labor's house to curse with equal fervor and fine impartiality both labor and its adversaries when they become locked in deadly embrace.

29.

A DAY OF INFAMY

The United States did not completely isolate itself from other nations after the disillusionment of World War I. During the 1920s the U.S. government negotiated arms-limitations pacts, sought to preserve the Open Door in China, encouraged massive bank loans to a war-ravaged Europe, and maintained troops in Latin America. Yet throughout the 1920s and into the 1930s the United States held steady on two key matters. It refused to enter military or defense alliances with any nation and to spend heavily on armies and armaments. During the 1930s the American public was probably more opposed to war than at any other time in U.S. history.

The rise of aggressive governments in Nazi Germany, Fascist Italy, and imperial Japan gradually changed America's sense of detachment. But the shift to involvement was slow. Not until German forces subdued France in 1940 did President Franklin Roosevelt promise "everything short of war" to a beleaguered England. And not until Japan, which saw America's presence in the Pacific as a threat to its own ambitions there, conducted devastating attacks on the American fleet and naval base at Pearl Harbor, Hawaii, and on the Philippines on December 7, 1941, did Roosevelt ask Congress for a declaration of war. The president's emphasis on the surprise element in this "day of infamy" and on the need henceforth to guard against "treachery" presaged not only the vast wartime military build-up to come but also the maintenance of a large military establishment after the war was over. Roosevelt's address in 1941 thus shaped America's perceptions of its international position just as Woodrow Wilson's had in 1917 (Document 24), though in a profoundly different direction.

Questions to consider. Several questions arise from a reading of Roosevelt's announcement of war. How comparable was the sinking of American ships by Japanese airplanes in 1941 to the sinking of American ships by German submarines in 1917? Did this difference in the nature of the weaponry perhaps add to the impact of Roosevelt's announcement? Note, too, that Roosevelt did not attach a lengthy declaration of large goals for humanity to his message, as Wilson had done. Why not? Did the facts actually "speak for themselves," as Roosevelt stated? How could the president assert that the American people had "already formed their opinion"? Did the notions of American exceptionalism and the redemption of humanity sneak into the message despite its brevity?

Finally, consider the announcement within the contexts of both foreign and domestic policy. To what extent might the attack on Pearl Harbor and the U.S. response to it be seen as logical consequences of the victories and acquisitions of U.S. involvement in China (Document 21) and of the Spanish-American War (Document 22)? To what extent, alternatively, were they consequences of the restrictive immigration measures from the 1880s to the 1920s (Document 12)?

Address to Congress (1941)
Franklin D. Roosevelt

Yesterday, December 7, 1941—a date which will live in infamy—the United States of America was suddenly and deliberately attacked by naval and air forces of the Empire of Japan.

The United States was at peace with that nation and, at the solicitation of Japan, was still in conversation with its Government and its Emperor looking toward the maintenance of peace in the Pacific. Indeed, one hour after Japanese air squadrons had commenced bombing in Oahu, the Japanese Ambassador to the United States and his colleague delivered to the Secretary of State a formal reply to a recent American message. While this reply stated that it seemed useless to continue the existing diplomatic negotiations, it contained no threat or hint of war or armed attack.

It will be recorded that the distance of Hawaii from Japan makes it obvious that the attack was deliberately planned many days or even weeks ago. During the intervening time the Japanese Government has deliberately sought to deceive the United States by false statements and expressions of hope for continued peace.

The attack yesterday on the Hawaiian Islands has caused severe damage to American naval and military forces. Very many American lives have been lost. In addition American ships have been reported torpedoed on the high seas between San Francisco and Honolulu.

Yesterday the Japanese Government also launched an attack against Malaya. Last night Japanese forces attacked Hong Kong. Last night Japanese forces attacked Guam. Last night Japanese forces attacked the Philippine Islands. Last night the Japanese attacked Wake Island. This morning the Japanese attacked Midway Island.

From the **New York Times**, December 9, 1941.

Pearl Harbor, December 1941.   The Japanese attack on Pearl Harbor sank or damaged eighteen major warships, including these two destroyers and the lightly damaged battleship, the **Pennsylvania,** in the background. The raid also destroyed 180 aircraft and killed more than 2,000 Americans. Yet the assault left vital oil storage and repair facilities undamaged. (National Archives)

Japan has, therefore, undertaken a surprise offensive extending throughout the Pacific area. The facts of yesterday speak for themselves. The people of the United States have already formed their opinions and well understand the implications to the very life and safety of our nation.

As Commander-in-Chief of the Army and Navy, I have directed that all measures be taken for our defense.

Always will we remember the character of the onslaught against us.

No matter how long it may take us to overcome this premeditated invasion, the American people in their righteous might will win through to absolute victory.

I believe I interpret the will of the Congress and of the people when I assert that we will not only defend ourselves to the uttermost but will make very certain that this form of treachery shall never endanger us again.

Hostilities exist. There is no blinking at the fact that our people, our territory and our interests are in grave danger.

With confidence in our armed forces—with the unbounded determination of our people—we will gain the inevitable triumph—so help us God.

I ask that the Congress declare that since the unprovoked and dastardly attack by Japan on Sunday, December seventh, a state of war has existed between the United States and the Japanese Empire.

30.

DESTROYER OF WORLDS

American strategy in the Pacific war was to "island-hop" toward Japan, occupying undefended atolls where possible and taking others by amphibious assault where necessary. This oceanic march began in 1942 with a painful, costly victory at Guadalcanal, northeast of Australia, and culminated in 1945 at Okinawa, off southern Japan, in a gruesome fight that produced 150,000 casualties. Meanwhile, the United States had proved its new air capability with the victories of its carrier-based planes over Japanese fleets at Midway and the Coral Sea in 1942 and with long-range bombing of the Japanese mainland after 1943. In mid-1945, finally, as American soldiers grouped to invade Japan, President Harry S Truman warned the Japanese that unless they surrendered by August 3 they would face "prompt and utter destruction." When they did not surrender, he ordered that an atomic bomb be dropped on Hiroshima on August 6 and another on Nagasaki on August 9.

The concept of the atomic bomb was brought to the United States by scientists fleeing Nazi Germany and Fascist Italy. In 1939, after suggestions from scientist Albert Einstein that the Germans might develop nuclear weapons, President Roosevelt authorized a National Defense Research Committee, which in turn led to the top-secret Manhattan Project for developing the bomb. By 1945, nuclear plants in Tennessee and Washington had produced enough fissionable material to construct a test bomb, which was exploded spectacularly in the New Mexico desert in July. One of the first decisions, therefore, that President Truman faced upon succeeding Roosevelt in office concerned using the bomb against Japan. Whether he did so to avoid a bloody land assault, as he claimed, an assault that would have undoubtedly cost many American and Japanese lives, or to demonstrate American power to the Russians, as a few historians suggest, continues to be debated. But the effects of the bomb itself were soon clear. More than 100,000 Japanese died from the two blasts.

While on assignment in late 1945 and 1946, John Hersey, a journalist covering the Far East for major American periodicals, prepared an account of how the bomb affected individual Japanese. Though most Allied leaders regarded the atomic bomb as just another big bomb, the excerpts from Hersey's **Hiroshima** reprinted below make clear that in its capacity for devastation the bomb dwarfed all other weapons of war.

John Hersey was born in 1914 in Tientsin, China, to American missionary parents, and became a journalist in the late 1930s after study at Yale University and Cambridge University in England. His first major work was **Men on Bataan** (1942), based on a series of interviews. A stream of books based on interviews and news clippings soon followed, including **Into the Valley** (1943), about a company of marines on Guadalcanal, and **Hiroshima** (1946). Hersey won the Pulitzer Prize for **A Bell for Adano** (1944), a story about the American occupation of Italy.

Questions to consider. Hiroshima probably continues to be the most widely read and influential study of the effects of the dropping of the bomb. What clues in the excerpts below help explain this popularity? Is it strictly a consequence of Hersey's strategy of focusing on individuals? Might his style of writing—the measured, somewhat reserved quality of his prose—also be a factor? What about the power of particular scenes? Why, for example, does Hersey tell us about the blind soldiers? Is it the blindness that moves us, or the fact that these blind are soldiers? Why did Hersey choose to make two of his six main characters, Dr. Fujii and Dr. Sasaki, medical men? Why is one of the six, Father Kleinsorge, not Japanese? Some U.S. officials were upset, even angry, that **Hiroshima** was so popular. What passage in the excerpts might have caused such official distress? How would you respond to Father Siemes's final query about the moral significance of modern warfare?

———

Hiroshima (1946)
John Hersey

The lot of Drs. Fujii, Kanda, and Machii right after the explosion—and, as these three were typical, that of the majority of the physicians and surgeons of Hiroshima—with their offices and hospitals destroyed, their equipment scattered, their own bodies incapacitated in varying degrees, explained why so many citizens who were hurt went untended and why so many who might have lived died. Of a hundred and fifty doctors in the city, sixty-five were already dead and most of the rest were wounded. Of 1,780 nurses, 1,654 were dead or too badly hurt to work. In the biggest hospital, that of the Red Cross, only six doctors out of thirty were able to function, and only ten nurses out of more than two hundred. The sole uninjured doctor on the Red Cross Hospital staff was Dr. Sasaki. After the explosion, he hurried to a storeroom to fetch bandages. This room, like everything he had seen as he ran through the hospital, was chaotic—bottles of medicines thrown off shelves and broken, salves spattered on the walls, instruments strewn everywhere. He grabbed up some bandages and an unbroken bottle of mercurochrome, hurried back to the chief surgeon, and bandaged his cuts. Then he went out into the corridor and began patching up the wounded patients and the doctors and nurses there. He blundered so without his glasses that he took a pair off the face of a wounded nurse, and although they only approximately compensated for the errors of his vision, they were better than nothing. (He was to depend on them for more than a month.)

Dr. Sasaki worked without method, taking those who were nearest him first, and he noticed soon that the corridor seemed to be getting more and more crowded. Mixed in with the abrasions and lacerations which most people in the hospital had suffered, he began to find dreadful burns. He realized then that casualties were pouring in from outdoors. There were so many that he began to pass up the lightly wounded; he decided that all he could hope to do was to stop people from bleeding to death. Before long, patients lay and crouched on the floors of the wards and the laboratories and all the other rooms, and in the corridors, and on the stairs, and in the front hall, and under the portecochère, and on the stone front steps, and in the driveway and court-yard, and for blocks each way in the streets outside. Wounded people supported maimed people; disfigured families leaned together. Many people were vom-iting. A tremendous number of schoolgirls—some of those who had been taken from their classrooms to work outdoors, cleaning fire lanes—crept into the hospital. In a city of two hundred and forty-five thousand, nearly a hundred thousand people had been killed or doomed at one blow; a hundred thousand more were hurt. At least ten thousand of the wounded made their way to the best hospital in town, which was altogether unequal to such a trampling, since it had only six hundred beds, and they had all been occupied. The people in the suffocating crowd inside the hospital wept and cried, for Dr. Sasaki to hear, "*Sensei!* Doctor!" and the less seriously wounded came and pulled at his sleeve and begged him to go to the aid of the worse wounded. Tugged here and there in his stockinged feet, bewildered by the numbers, staggered by so much raw flesh, Dr. Sasaki lost all sense of the profession and stopped working as a skillful surgeon and a sympathetic man; he became an automaton, mechan-ically wiping, daubing, winding, wiping, daubing, winding. . . .

Mr. Tanimoto found about twenty men and women on the sandspit. He drove the boat onto the bank and urged them to get aboard. They did not move and he realized that they were too weak to lift themselves. He reached down and took a woman by the hands, but her skin slipped off in huge, glovelike pieces. He was so sickened by this that he had to sit down for a moment. Then he got out into the water and, though a small man, lifted several of the men and women, who were naked, into his boat. Their backs and breasts were clammy, and he remembered uneasily what the great burns he had seen during the day had been like: yellow at first, then red and swollen, with the skin sloughed off, and finally, in the evening, suppurated and smelly. With the tide risen, his bamboo pole was now too short and he had to paddle most of the way across with it. On the other side, at a higher spit, he lifted the slimy living bodies out and carried them up the slope away from the tide. He had to keep consciously repeating to himself, "These are human beings." It took him three trips to get them all across the river. When he had finished, he decided he had to have a rest, and he went back to the park.

As Mr. Tanimoto stepped up the dark bank, he tripped over someone, and someone else said angrily, "Look out! That's my hand." Mr. Tanimoto, ashamed of hurting wounded people, embarrassed at being able to walk up-right, suddenly thought of the naval hospital ship, which had not come (it never did), and he had for a moment a feeling of blind, murderous rage at the crew of the ship, and then at all the doctors. Why didn't they come to help these people? . . .

The morning, again, was hot. Father Kleinsorge went to fetch water for the wounded in a bottle and a teapot he had borrowed. He had heard that it was possible to get fresh tap water outside Asano Park. Going through the rock gardens, he had to climb over and crawl under the trunks of fallen pine trees; he found he was weak. There were many dead in the gardens. At a beautiful moon bridge, he passed a naked, living woman who seemed to have been burned from head to toe and was red all over. Near the entrance to the park, an Army doctor was working, but the only medicine he had was iodine, which he painted over cuts, bruises, slimy burns, every-thing—and by now everything he painted had pus on it. Outside the gate of the park, Father Kleinsorge found a faucet that still worked—part of the plumbing of a vanished house—and he filled his vessels and returned. When he had given the wounded the water, he made a second trip. This time, the woman by the bridge was dead. On his way back with the water, he got lost on a detour around a fallen tree, and as he looked for his way through the woods, he heard a voice ask from the underbrush, "Have you anything to drink?" He saw a uniform. Thinking there was just one soldier, he approached with the water. When he had penetrated the bushes, he saw there were about twenty men, and they were all in exactly the same nightmarish state: their faces were wholly burned, their eyesockets were hollow, the fluid from their melted eyes had run down their cheeks. (They must have had their faces upturned when the bomb went off; perhaps they were anti-aircraft personnel.) Their mouths were mere swollen, pus-covered wounds, which they could not bear to stretch enough to admit the spout of the teapot. So Father Kleinsorge got a large piece of grass and draw out the stem so as to make a straw, and gave them all water to drink that way. One of them said, "I can't see any-thing." Father Kleinsorge answered, as cheerfully as he could, "There's a doctor at the entrance to the park. He's busy now, but he'll come soon and fix your eyes, I hope." . . .

Early that day, August 7th, the Japanese radio broadcast for the first time a succinct announcement that very few, if any, of the people most concerned with its content, the survivors in Hiroshima, happened to hear: "Hiroshima suffered considerable damage as the result of an attack by a few B-29s. It is believed that a new type of bomb was used. The details are being investigated." Nor is it probable that any of the survivors happened to be tuned in on a short-wave rebroadcast of an extraordinary announcement by the President of the United States, which identified the new bomb as atomic: "That bomb had more power than twenty thousand tons of TNT. It had more than two thousand times the blast power of the British Grand Slam, which is the largest bomb ever yet used in the history of warfare." Those victims who were able to worry at all about what had happened thought of it and discussed it in more primitive, childish terms—gasoline sprinkled from an airplane, maybe, or some combustible gas, or a big cluster of incendiaries, or the work of parachutists; but, even if they had known the truth, most of them were too busy or too weary or too badly hurt to care that they were the objects of the first great experiment in the use of atomic power, which (as the voices on the short wave shouted) no country except the United States, with its industrial know-how, its willingness to throw two billion gold dollars into an important wartime gamble, could possibly have developed. . . .

Dr. Sasaki and his colleagues at the Red Cross Hospital watched the unprecedented disease unfold and at last evolved a theory about its nature. It had, they decided, three stages. The first stage had been all over before the doctors even knew they were dealing with a new sickness; it was the direct reaction to the bombardment of the body, at the moment when the bomb went off, by neutrons, beta particles, and gamma rays. The apparently uninjured people who had died so mysteriously in the first few hours or days had succumbed in this first stage. It killed ninety-five per cent of the people within a half mile of the center, and many thousands who were farther away. The doctors realized in retrospect that even though most of these dead had also suffered from burns and blast effects, they had absorbed enough radiation to kill them. The rays simply destroyed body cells—caused their nuclei to degenerate and broke their walls. Many people who did not die right away came down with nausea, headache, diarrhea, malaise, and fever, which lasted several days. Doctors could not be certain whether some of these symptoms were the result of radiation or nervous shock. The second stage set in ten or fifteen days after the bombing. Its first symptom was falling hair. Diarrhea and fever, which in some cases went as high as 106, came next. Twenty-five to thirty days after the explosion, blood disorders appeared: gums bled, the white-blood-cell count dropped sharply, and *petechiae* [eruptions] appeared on the

Hiroshima. After three years and $2 billion of secret research, the United States exploded the first atomic bomb at Alamogordo, New Mexico, on the morning of July 16, 1945. A scientist who was there said it was as if the "earth had opened" and the "skies had split," or like the moment of creation when God said, "Let there be light." Although the catastrophic power of the weapon was clear, President Truman never really considered not using it against Japan. After the bloody battle of Okinawa in mid-1945, few Americans would have decided differently. (National Archives)

skin and mucous membranes. The drop in the number of white blood corpuscles reduced the patient's capacity to resist infection, so open wounds were unusually slow in healing and many of the sick developed sore throats and mouths. The two key symptoms, on which the doctors came to base their prognosis, were fever and the lowered white-corpuscle count. If fever remained steady and high, the patient's chances for survival were poor. The white count almost always dropped below four thousand; a patient whose count fell below one thousand had little hope of living. Toward the end of the second stage, if the patient survived, anemia, or a drop in the red blood count, also set in. The third stage was the reaction that came when the body struggled to compensate for its ills—when, for instance, the white count not only returned to normal but increased to much higher than normal levels. In this stage, many patients died of complications, such as infections in the chest cavity. Most burns healed with deep layers of pink, rubbery scar tissue, known as keloid tumors. The duration of the disease varied, depending on the patient's constitution and the amount of radiation he had received. Some victims recovered in a week; with others the disease dragged on for months.

As the symptoms revealed themselves, it became clear that many of them resembled the effects of overdoses of X-ray, and the doctors based their therapy on that likeness. They gave victims liver extract, blood transfusions, and vitimins, especially B_1. The shortage of supplies and instruments hampered them. Allied doctors who came in after the surrender found plasma and penicillin very effective. Since the blood disorders were, in the long run, the predominant factor in the disease, some of the Japanese doctors evolved a theory as to the seat of the delayed sickness. They thought that perhaps gamma rays, entering the body at the time of the explosion, made the phosphorus in the victims' bones radioactive, and that they in turn emitted beta particles, which, though they could not penetrate far through flesh, could enter the bone marrow, where blood is manufactured, and gradually tear it down. Whatever its source, the disease had some baffling quirks. Not all the patients exhibited all the main symptoms. People who suffered flash burns were protected, to a considerable extent, from radiation sickness. Those who had lain quietly for days or even hours after the bombing were much less liable to get sick than those who had been active. Gray hair seldom fell out. And, as if nature were protecting man against his own ingenuity, the reproductive processes were affected for a time; men became sterile, women had miscarriages, menstruation stopped. . . .

A surprising number of the people of Hiroshima remained more or less indifferent about the ethics of using the bomb. Possibly they were too terrified by it to want to think about it at all. Not many of them even bothered to find out much about what it was like. Mrs. Nakamura's conception of it—and awe of it—was typical. "The atom bomb," she would say when asked about it, "is the size of a matchbox. The heat of it is six thousand times that of the sun. It exploded in the air. There is some radium in it. I don't know just how it works, but when the radium is put together, it explodes." As for the use of the bomb, she would say, "It was war and we had to expect it." And then she would add, "*Shikata ga nai*," a Japanese expression as common as, and corresponding to, the Russian word, "*nichevo*": "It can't be helped. Oh, well. Too bad." Dr. Fujii said approximately the same thing about the use of the bomb to Father Kleinsorge one evening, in German: "*Da ist nichts zu machen.* There's nothing to be done about it."

Many citizens of Hiroshima, however, continued to feel a hatred for Americans which nothing could possibly erase. "I see," Dr. Sasaki once said, "that they are holding a trial for war criminals in Tokyo just now. I think they ought to try the men who decided to use the bomb and they should hang them all."

Father Kleinsorge and the other German Jesuit priests, who, as foreigners, could be expected to take a relatively detached view, often discussed the ethics of using the bomb. One of them, Father Siemes, who was out at Nagatsuka [Hiroshima suburb] at the time of the attack, wrote in a report to the Holy See in Rome: "Some of us consider the bomb in the same category as poison gas and were against its use on a civilian population. Others were of the opinion that in total war, as carried on in Japan, there was no difference between civilians and soldiers, and that the bomb itself was an effective force tending to end the bloodshed, warning Japan to surrender and thus to avoid total destruction. It seems logical that he who supports total war in principle cannot complain of a war against civilians. The crux of the matter is whether total war in its present form is justifiable, even when it serves a just purpose. Does it not have material and spiritual evil as its consequences which far exceed whatever good might result? When will our moralists give us a clear answer to this question?"

COUNTERPOINT V

Leadership and Labor

The Great Depression was the American labor movement's finest hour. Assisted by the National Labor Relations Act (1935), which made large-scale organizing possible, driven by the deep suffering that made organizing imperative, and inspired by the new Congress of Industrial Organizations, organizers like John L. Lewis attracted hundreds of thousands to the cause, many from industries in which no unions had existed before. By the early 1940s, organized labor was a major force in national economic and political life, and its leaders—Lewis on behalf of the United Mine Workers, Sidney Hillman of the Amalgamated Clothing Workers, Phil Murray of the United Steel Workers, and Walter Reuther of the United Auto Workers—were men of prominence and clout.

Lewis and labor's other great figures proclaimed themselves to be labor's legitimate voice not only by virtue of their union work but by virtue of their background. On the whole their claims were justified. Reuther, for example, was an apprentice machinist at age sixteen and finished high school and attended college at night. Phil Murray, like Lewis, left school at an early age to mine coal, and David Dubinsky of the Ladies Garment Workers was a baker's apprentice at age ten. But did the hundreds of lower-level union activists resemble the leadership? Were they too "sons of labor," reflecting the characteristics of the mass of American workers whom they claimed to represent? Or were they an overeducated, elite group—perhaps some version, in fact, of the outside agitators so often blamed by the owners for stirring up the work force?

Walter Licht and Hal Seth Barron have tried to answer these questions by analyzing the backgrounds of several hundred lower-level labor officers of the early 1940s, when the immense organizing drives had borne full fruit. According to Licht and Barron more labor leaders were foreign born and city bred than Americans generally—but not by much (table A.1). The overwhelming majority of the officials were born in the United States (as were most Americans); and a clear majority were, like their compatriots, from towns and not cities (table A.2). Not surprisingly, therefore, two-thirds of the laborites were either "old stock American" (English, Dutch, Scottish, and French) or Irish and German, earliest of the nineteenth-century immigrant groups (table A.3). Irish and Jews were slightly overrepresented, and blacks significantly underrepresented, according to their percentage of the total population. The 1940 census did not collect information on ethnicity. But except for the Irish, Jews, and blacks, the ethnic portrait of these union officeholders was probably quite similar to that of the country as a whole.

This sort of material, though interesting, is tangential to the central question: did labor officials have working-class backgrounds? Were they, like their famous chiefs, really "sons of labor"? Not entirely, suggests the evidence. A fifth had professional or businessman-manager fathers, twice the proportion that the population in general had, and only half as many officials had semiskilled or unskilled fathers as the general population had (table B.1). The high proportion of officials with skilled-labor fathers partially redressed the balance, and the "farmer" fathers may well have been debt-ridden sons of toil. But the fact remains that only half the union officials had proletarian beginnings. Officials also had better schooling than the general population, as the educational data (table B.2) shows. Around 30 percent had attended grade school only, whereas the proportion for the total population was double that figure. But a third of the officials had some higher education versus just a tenth of the total population. Although labor's men were not exactly the effete corps of impudent class rebels that businessmen commonly made them out to be, neither did they rise uniformly from laboring families and the shop floor.

Business executives considered the industrial unions of the CIO to be far more radical and dangerous than the older, more familiar AFL craft unions and therefore far more alien and disreputable and open to attack. Did significant differences exist between CIO and AFL leaders? Virtually none, argue Licht and Barron, as regards place of birth and education. As regards ethnicity, father's occupation, and age, quite a bit. The ethnic differences are fairly modest. A third of the CIO men were from "new immigrant stock" versus a fifth of the AFLers (table C.1). The differences in fathers' occupations are more striking (table C.2). Slightly more than half the CIO men had working-class fathers compared with slightly under half of the AFL men. More significantly, over a third of the CIO men had semiskilled or unskilled fathers—twice as many as did the AFLers.

Labors' opponents, then, appear to have been partially correct. The secondary leaders of the CIO, like the top national leadership, may have been less proletarian than the general U.S. population, but they were a lot more proletarian and "new" (more were younger and from new immigrant stock) than the AFL leadership. Two-thirds of the CIO leaders were under age forty-five (meaning that they had been under forty during the great organizing drives of the 1930s in contrast to one-third of the AFL leaders (table C.3).

Unskilled fathers. New stock families. The aggressive energy of youth. These factors formed a volatile combination, making the men of the CIO highly visible to adversaries and allies alike. Both groups painted these union leaders in the starkest colors—chiefly varying shades of black and white with touches of "red" thrown in. But their distinctive backgrounds also combined to make them tremendous successes.

A. Labor Officials: Regional, Community, and Ethnic Backgrounds

1. Regional Origins of Labor Officials

Region of Birth	Number	Percentage	U.S. Population Percentage (1940 Census)
New England	25	6%	5%
Middle Atlantic	89	22	19
Midwest	113	29	29
South	86	22	32
West	25	6	6
Foreign born	59	15	9
Total	397	100	100

2. Types of Communities in Which Labor Officials Were Born

Community	Population Base	Number	Percentage	U.S. Population Percentage (1910 Census)
Rural–small town	Less than 5,000	144	40%	58%
Large town	5,000–24,999	65	18	11
Small city	25,000–99,999	42	12	9
Large city	More than 100,000	110	30	22
Total		361	100	100

3. Ethnic Backgrounds of Labor Officials

Ethnic Group	Number	Percentage
Old stock American	131	39%
Irish-American	54	16
German-American	44	13
Jewish	34	10
Slavic-American	17	5
Italian-American	16	5
Negro	13	4
British-American	11	3
French-Canadian	10	3
Other	8	2
Total	338	100

Source: Walter Licht and Hal Seth Barron, "Labor's Men: A Collective Biography of Union Officialdom During the New Deal Era," *Labor History* 19 (Fall 1978), reprinted by permission.

B. Labor Officials: Their Fathers' Occupational Status and Their Educational Background

1. Occupational Status of Fathers of Labor Officials

Fathers' Occupational Status	Number	Percentage	U.S. Population Percentage (1910) Census)
Professional	41	12%	5%
Businessman-manager	29	9	7
Small proprietor–white-collar worker	31	9	9
Skilled worker	75	23	12
Semiskilled-unskilled worker	91	27	50
Farmer	68	20	17
Total	335	100	100

2. Educational Background of Labor Officials

Educational Level	Number	Percentage	U.S. Population Percentage (1940 Census)
Grade school	109	29%	60%
Some high school	25	7	
High school graduate	115	30	30
Technical-business school	37	10	
Some college	32	8	
College graduate	30	8	10
Professional school graduate	29	8	
Total	377	100	100

SOURCE: Walter Licht and Hal Seth Barron, "Labor's Men: A Collective Biography of Union Officialdom During the New Deal Era," *Labor History* 19 (Fall 1978), reprinted by permission.

C. Labor Leaders: Their Ethnicity, Father's Occupation, and Age

1. Ethnicity of AFL and CIO Leaders

	Number	Old Stock American	Old Immigrant Stock	New Immigrant Stock
AFL	160	43%	38%	19%
CIO	167	33	37	30

2. Occupation of AFL and CIO Leaders' Fathers

	Number	White Collar	Skilled Worker	Semiskilled or Unskilled Worker	Farmer
AFL	167	29%	28%	19%	24%
CIO	159	31	16	37	16

3. Age of AFL and CIO Leaders

	Number	Under 45	Over 45
AFL	191	35%	65%
CIO	187	65	35

SOURCE: Walter Licht and Hal Seth Barron, "Labor's Men: A Collective Biography of Union Officialdom During the New Deal Era," *Labor History* 19 (Fall 1978), reprinted by permission.

An F-4 Phantom Fighter with an array of its weaponry.   (McDonnell Douglas-
St. Louis)

CHAPTER SIX

Postwar Conflict and Hope

31.

CONTAINMENT

When Germany invaded Poland in September 1939, Britain and France came to Poland's aid, and World War II began. But the surrender of Germany in May 1945 did not mean a free and independent Poland. Instead, when the war ended, the Soviet Union took over most of eastern Europe, including Poland, and installed regimes of its own choosing, backed by military force. The Russians had suffered severely in both World War I and World War II from invasions from the West and were determined to surround themselves with a ring of friendly states after the war. But American policymakers, shocked by the ruthlessness with which the Russians had accomplished their purpose, interpreted Soviet policy as expansionist rather than defensive in nature and began to fear that the Soviet Union had designs on western Europe as well. The United States therefore sponsored economic aid (the Marshall Plan) as well as military aid (the Truman Doctrine) to nations in Europe that seemed threatened by Soviet aggression; it also persuaded the nations of western Europe to organize the North Atlantic Treaty Organization (NATO). Thus was born the cold war between the Soviet Union and the United States.

In July 1947 an article entitled "The Sources of Soviet Conduct" appeared in **Foreign Affairs,** an influential journal published in New York. The author, identified only as "X," was later revealed to be George F. Kennan, head of the policy-planning staff of the State Department, so the article may have reflected official American views on Soviet foreign policy. Pointing out that the Soviet Union based its policies on a firm belief in the "innate antagonism between capitalism and socialism," Kennan warned that the Russians were going to be difficult to deal with for a long time. He added that the Kremlin was "under no ideological compulsion to accomplish its purposes in a hurry" and that the only wise course for the United States to follow as that of "a long-term, patient but firm and vigilant containment of Russian expansionist tendencies." Kennan's article, which is excerpted below, shaped as well as reflected American policy. By providing a rationale for the "containment" policy that dominated American diplomacy after World War II, Kennan produced what was surely the most influential piece of journalism since Thomas Paine's **Common Sense.**

George F. Kennan was born in Milwaukee, Wisconsin, in 1904. After graduating from Princeton University in 1925, he joined the foreign service, in which he specialized in Russian affairs while serving in minor

European posts. In 1933, he went to Moscow when the United States extended diplomatic recognition to the Soviet Union and opened an embassy there. Kennan served elsewhere in the late 1930s, but he returned to the Soviet Union during World War II and was appointed U.S. ambassador there in 1952. Kennan continued to write extensively on Russian and American diplomacy even after leaving the foreign service in the late 1950s. He came to deplore the excessively military application of the containment doctrine he had outlined in 1947, and in his later books and articles he made various proposals for demilitarization and disengagement that might diminish cold war tensions and lessen the chances of nuclear war.

   Questions to consider. In assigning responsibility for the cold war to a combination of Marxist ideology, the Kremlin's desire for power, and the world communist movement, Kennan was also arguing, of course, that the West was largely defensive and even innocent. What evidence from twentieth-century history might be introduced to counter this argument? Kennen argued, similarly, that the Soviet threat was likely to last, practically speaking, forever. Given his views on Soviet objectives, were social or political changes conceivable that might alter these objectives or the Soviet capacity to pursue them? Did changes of this type in fact occur? Again, Kennan's article outlined his notions of Soviet society clearly enough. What assumptions, according to the evidence of the article, was Kennan making about American society? How did his own ideology compare with that of, say, Woodrow Wilson in 1917 (Document 24)? Finally, Kennan wrote his essay to mold American policy. One can imagine, however, various policies flowing from this analysis: an effort to roll back Russian power in Europe, an armed "garrison" state in the United States, intense economic or propaganda competition, and even a pre-emptive nuclear strike. Which of these did Kennan himself hope to see? Were Harry Truman on Korea (Document 33) and John Foster Dulles on "massive retaliation" (Document 34) equally the descendants of containment?

The Sources of Soviet Conduct (1947)
George F. Kennan

The political personality of Soviet power as we know it today is the product of ideology and circumstances: ideology inherited by the present Soviet leaders from the movement in which they had their political origin, and circumstances of the power which they now have exercised for nearly three decades in Russia. There can be few tasks of psychological analysis more difficult than to try to trace the interaction of these two forces and the relative role of each in the determination of official Soviet conduct. Yet the attempt must be made if that conduct is to be understood and effectively countered.

It is difficult to summarize the set of ideological concepts with which the Soviet leaders came into power. Marxian ideology, in its Russian-Communist projection, has always been in process of subtle evolution. The materials on which it bases itself are extensive and complex. But the outstanding features of Communist thought as it existed in 1916 may perhaps be summarized as follows: (a) that the central factor in the life of man, the fact which determines the character of public life and the "physiognomy of society," is the system by which material goods are produced and exchanged; (b) that the capitalist system of production is a nefarious one which inevitably leads to the exploitation of the working class by the capital-owning class and is incapable of developing adequately the economic resources of society or of distributing fairly the material goods produced by human labor; (c) that capitalism contains the seeds of its own destruction and must, in view of the inability of the capital-owning class to adjust itself to economic change, result eventually and inescapably in a revolutionary transfer of power to the working class; and (d) that imperialism, the final phase of capitalism, leads directly to war and revolution.

The rest may be outlined in Lenin's own words: "Unevenness of economic and political development is the inflexible law of capitalism. It follows from this that the victory of Socialism may come originally in a few capitalist countries or even in a single capitalist country. The victorious proletariat of that country, having expropriated the capitalists and having organized Socialist production at home, would rise against the remaining capitalist world, drawing to itself in the process the oppressed classes of other countries." It must be noted that there was no assumption that capitalism would perish without proletarian revolution. A final push was needed from a revolutionary proletariat movement in order to tip over the tottering structure. But it was regarded as inevitable that sooner or later that push be given. . . .

Now the outstanding circumstance concerning the Soviet regime is that down to the present day this process of political consolidation has never been

From **Foreign Affairs** (July 1947), 25: 566–582. Reprinted by permission of Foreign Affairs, July 1947. Copyright 1947 by the Council on Foreign Relations, Inc.

completed and the men in the Kremlin have continued to be predominantly absorbed with the struggle to secure and make absolute the power which they seized in November 1917. They have endeavored to secure it primarily against forces at home, within Soviet society itself. But they have also endeavored to secure it against the outside world. For ideology, as we have seen, taught them that the outside world was hostile and that it was their duty eventually to overthrow the political forces beyond their borders. The powerful hands of Russian history and tradition reached up to sustain them in this feeling. Finally, their own aggressive intransigence with respect to the outside world began to find its own reaction; and they were soon forced, to use another Gibbonesque[1] phrase, "to chastise the contumacy" which they themselves had provoked. It is an undeniable privilege of every man to prove himself right in the thesis that the world is his enemy; for if he reiterates it frequently enough and makes it the background of his conduct he is bound eventually to be right.

Now it lies in the nature of the mental world of the Soviet leaders, as well as in the character of their ideology, that no opposition to them can be officially recognized as having any merit or justification whatsoever. Such opposition can flow, in theory, only from the hostile and incorrigible forces of dying capitalism. As long as remnants of capitalism were officially recognized as existing in Russia, it was possible to place on them, as an internal element, part of the blame for the maintenance of a dictatorial form of society. But as these remnants were liquidated, little by little, this justification fell away; and when it was indicated officially that they had been finally destroyed, it disappeared altogether. And this fact created one of the most basic of the compulsions which came to act upon the Soviet regime: since capitalism no longer existed in Russia and since it could not be admitted that there could be serious or widespread opposition to the Kremlin springing spontaneously from the liberated masses under its authority, it became necessary to justify the retention of the dictatorship by stressing the menace of capitalism abroad. . . .

As things stand today, the rulers can no longer dream of parting with these organs and suppression. The quest for absolute power, pursued now for nearly three decades with a ruthlessness unparalleled (in scope at least) in modern times, has again produced internally as it did externally, its own reaction. The excesses of the police apparatus have fanned the potential opposition to the regime into something far greater and more dangerous than it could have been before those excesses began.

But least of all can the rulers dispense with the fiction by which the maintenance of dictatorial power has been defended. For this fiction has been canonized in Soviet philosophy by the excesses already committed in its name; and it is now anchored in the Soviet structure of thought by bonds far greater than those of mere ideology. . . .

---

[1] This refers to Edward Gibbon, English historian (1737–1794).—Eds.

So much for the historical background. What does it spell in terms of the political personality of Soviet power as we know it today?

Of the original ideology, nothing has been officially junked. Belief is maintained in the basic badness of capitalism, in the inevitability of its destruction, in the obligation of the proletariat to assist in that destruction and to take power into its own hands. But stress has come to be laid primarily on those concepts which relate most specifically to the Soviet regime itself: to its position as the sole truly Socialist regime in a dark and misguided world, and to the relationships of power within in.

The first of these concepts is that of the innate antagonism between capitalism and Socialism. We have seen how deeply that concept has become imbedded in foundations of Soviet power. It has profound implications for Russia's conduct as a member of international society. It means that there can never be on Moscow's side any sincere assumption of a community of aims between the Soviet Union and powers which are regarded as capitalism. It must invariably be assumed in Moscow that the aims of the capitalist world are antagonistic to the Soviet regime and, therefore, to the interests of the peoples it controls. If the Soviet Government occasionally sets its signature to documents which would indicate the contrary, this is to be regarded as a tactical maneuver permissible in dealing with the enemy (who is without honor) and should be taken in the spirit of *caveat emptor* [let the buyer beware]. Basically, the antagonism remains. It is postulated. And from it flow many of the phenomena which we find disturbing in the Kremlin's conduct of foreign policy: the secretiveness, the lack of frankness, the duplicity, the war suspiciousness, and the basic unfriendliness of purpose. These phenomena are there to stay, for the foreseeable future. There can be variations of degree and of emphasis. When there is something the Russians want from us, one or the other of these features of their policy may be thrust temporarily into the background; and when that happens there will always be Americans who will leap forward with gleeful announcements that "the Russians have changed," and some who will even try to take credit for having brought about such "changes." But we should not be misled by tactical maneuvers. These characteristics of Soviet policy, like the postulate from which they flow, are basic to the internal nature of Soviet power, and will be with us, whether in the foreground or the background, until the internal nature of Soviet power is changed.

This means that we are going to continue for a long time to find the Russians difficult to deal with. It does not mean that they should be considered as embarked upon a do-or-die program to overthrow our society by a given date. The theory of the inevitability of the eventual fall of capitalism has the fortunate connotation that there is no hurry about it. The forces of progress can take their time in preparing the final *coup de grace*. Meanwhile, what is vital is that the "Socialist fatherland"—that oasis of power which has been already won for Socialism in the person of the Soviet Union—should be cherished and defended by all good Communists at home and abroad, its

Berlin apartment block.   The U.S. Congress approved the first $5 billion for the European Recovery Program (as the Marshall Plan was officially called) in 1948 with the stipulation that most of the funds would go to purchase American-made products. Goods began to arrive in Europe soon afterward. Much of the early aid went, in fact, for agricultural assistance and housing construction to stave off the malnutrition and homelessness that haunted Europe after World War I. (UPI/Bettmann Newsphoto)

fortunes promoted, its enemies badgered and confounded. The promotion of premature, "adventuristic" revolutionary projects abroad which might embarrass Soviet power in any way would be an inexcusable, even a counter-revolutionary act. The cause of Socialism is the support and promotion of Soviet power, as defined in Moscow.

This brings us to the second of the concepts important to contemporary Soviet outlook. This is the infallibility of the Kremlin. The Soviet concept of power, which permits no focal points of organization outside the Party itself, requires that the Party leadership remain in theory the sole repository of truth.

For if truth were to be found elsewhere, there would be justification for its expression in organized activity. But it is precisely that which the Kremlin cannot and will not permit.

The leadership of the Communist Party is therefore always right, and has been always right ever since in 1929 Stalin formalized his personal power by announcing that decisions of the Politburo were being taken unanimously.

On the principle of infallibility there rests the iron discipline of the Communist Party. In fact, the two concepts are mutually self-supporting. Perfect discipline requires recognition of infallibility. Infallibility requires the observance of discipline. And the two together go far to determine the behaviorism of the entire Soviet apparatus of power. But their effect cannot be understood unless a third factor be taken into account: namely, the fact that the leadership is at liberty to put forward for tactical purposes any particular thesis which it finds useful to the cause at any particular moment and to require the faithful and unquestioning acceptance of that thesis by the members of the movement as a whole. This means that truth is not a constant but is actually created, for all intents and purposes, by the Soviet leaders themselves. It may vary from week to week, from month to month. It is nothing absolute and immutable— nothing which flows from objective reality. It is only the most recent manifestation of the wisdom of those in whom the ultimate wisdom is supposed to reside, because they represent the logic of history. The accumulative effect of these factors is to give to the whole subordinate apparatus of Soviet power an unshakeable stubbornness and steadfastness in its orientation. This orientation can be changed at will by the Kremlin but by no other power. Once a given party line has been laid down on a given issue of current policy, the whole Soviet governmental machine, including the mechanism of diplomacy, moves inexorably along the prescribed path, like a persistent toy automobile wound up and headed in a given direction, stopping only when it meets with some unanswerable force. The individuals who are the components of this machine are unamenable to argument or reason which comes to them from outside sources. Their whole training has taught them to mistrust and discount the glib persuasiveness of the outside world. Like the white dog before the phonograph, they hear only the "master's voice." And if they are to be called off from the purposes last dictated to them, it is the master who must call them off. Thus the foreign representative can not hope that his words will make any impression on them. The most that he can hope is that they will be transmitted to those at the top, who are capable of changing the party line. But even those are not likely to be swayed by any normal logic in the words of the bourgeois representative. Since there can be no appeal to common purposes, there can be no appeal to common mental approaches. For this reason, facts speak louder than words to the ears of the Kremlin; and words carry the greatest weight when they have the ring of reflecting, or being backed up by, facts of unchallengeable validity.

But we have seen that the Kremlin is under no ideological compulsion to accomplish its purposes in a hurry. Like the Church, it is dealing in ideological concepts which are of long-term validity, and it can afford to be patient. It has no right to risk the existing achievements of the revolution for the sake of vain baubles of the future. The very teachings of Lenin himself require great caution and flexibility in the pursuit of Communist purposes. Again, these precepts are fortified by the lessons of Russian history: of centuries of obscure battles between nomadic forces over the stretches of a vast unfortified plain. Here caution, circumspection, flexibility and deception are the valuable qualities; and their value finds natural appreciation in the Russian or the oriental mind. Thus the Kremlin has no compunction about retreating in the face of superior force. And being under the compulsion of no timetable, it does not get panicky under the necessity for such a retreat. Its political action is a fluid stream which moves constantly, wherever it is permitted to move, toward a given goal. Its main concern is to make sure that it has filled every nook and cranny available to it in the basin of world power. But if it finds unassailable barriers in its path, it accepts these philosophically and accommodates itself to them. The main thing is that there should always be pressure, unceasing constant pressure, toward the desired goal. There is no trace of any feeling in Soviet psychology that that goal must be reached at any given time.

These considerations make Soviet diplomacy at once easier and more difficult to deal with than the diplomacy of individual aggressive leaders like Napoleon and Hitler. On the one hand it is more sensitive to contrary force, more ready to yield on individual sectors of the diplomatic front when that force is felt to be too strong, and thus more rational in the logic and rhetoric of power. On the other hand it cannot be easily defeated or discouraged by a single victory on the part of its opponents. And the patient persistence by which it is animated means that it can be effectively countered not by sporadic acts which represent the momentary whims of democratic opinion but only by intelligent long-range policies on the part of Russia's adversaries—policies no less steady in their purpose, and no less variegated and resourceful in their application, than those of the Soviet Union itself.

In these circumstances it is clear that the main element of any United States policy toward the Soviet Union must be that of a long-term, patient but firm and vigilant containment of Russian expansive tendencies. It is important to note, however, that such a policy has nothing to do with outward histrionics: with threats or blustering or superfluous gestures of outward "toughness." While the Kremlin is basically flexible in its reaction to political realities, it is by no means unamenable to considerations of prestige. Like almost any other government, it can be placed by tactless and threatening gestures in a position where it cannot afford to yield even though this might be dictated by its sense of realism. The Russian leaders are keen judges of human psychology, and as such they are highly conscious that loss of temper and of self-control is never a source of strength in political affairs. They are quick to exploit such evidence of weakness. For these reasons, it is a *sine qua non* of successful dealing with Russia that the foreign government in question should remain at all times cool and collected and that its demands on Russian policy should be put forward in such a manner as to leave the way open for a compliance not too detrimental to Russian prestige. . . .

It is clear that the United States cannot expect in the foreseeable future to enjoy political intimacy with the Soviet regime. It must continue to regard the Soviet Union as a rival, not a partner, in the political arena. It must continue to expect that Soviet policies will reflect no abstract love of peace and stability, no real faith in the possibility of a permanent happy coexistence of the Socialist and capitalist worlds, but rather a cautious, persistent pressure toward the disruption and weakening of all rival influence and rival power.

Balanced against this are the fact that Russia, as opposed to the Western world in general, is still by far the weaker party, that Soviet policy is highly flexible, and that Soviet society may well contain deficiencies which will eventually weaken its own total potential. This would of itself warrant the United States entering with reasonable confidence upon a policy of firm containment, designed to confront the Russians with unalterable counterforce at every point where they show signs of encroaching upon the interests of a peaceful and stable world.

But in actuality the possibilities for American policy are by no means limited to holding the line and hoping for the best. It is entirely possible for the United States to influence by its actions the internal developments, both within Russia and throughout the international Communist movement, by which Russian policy is largely determined. This is not only a question of the modest measure of informational activity which this government can conduct in the Soviet Union and elsewhere, although that, too, is important. It is rather a question of the degree to which the United States can create among the peoples of the world generally the impression of a country which knows what it wants, which is coping successfully with the problems of its internal life and with the responsibilities of a World Power, and which has a spiritual vitality capable of holding its own among the major ideological currents of the time. To the extent that such an impression can be created and maintained, the aims of Russian Communism must appear sterile and quixotic, the hopes and enthusiasm of Moscow's supporters must wane, and added strain must be imposed on the Kremlin's foreign policies. For the palsied decrepitude of the capitalist world is the keystone of Communist philosophy. Even the failure of the United States to experience the early economic depression which the ravens of the Red Square have been predicting with such complacent confidence since hostilities ceased would have deep and important repercussions throughout the Communist world.

By the same token, exhibitions of indecision, disunity and internal disintegration within this country have an exhilarating effect on the whole Communist movement. At each evidence of these tendencies, a thrill of hope and excitement goes through the Communist world; a new jauntiness can be noted in the Moscow tread; now groups of foreign supporters climb on to what they can only view as the band wagon of international politics; and Russian pressure increases all along the line in international affairs.

It would be an exaggeration to say that American behavior unassisted and alone could exercise a power of life and death over the Communist movement and bring about the early fall of Soviet power in Russia. But the United States has it in its power to increase enormously the strains under which Soviet policy must operate, to force upon the Kremlin a far greater degree of moderation and circumspection than it has had to observe in recent years, and in this way to promote tendencies which must eventually find their outlet in either the breakup or the gradual mellowing of Soviet power. For no mystical, Messianic movement—and particularly not that of the Kremlin—can face frustration indefinitely without eventually adjusting itself in one way or another to the logic of that state of affairs.

Thus the decision will really fall in large measure in this country itself. The issue of Soviet-American relations is in essence a test of the overall worth of the United States as a nation among nations. To avoid destruction the United States need only measure up to its own best traditions and prove itself worthy of preservation as a great nation.

Surely, there was never a fairer test of national quality than this. In the light of these circumstances, the thoughtful observer of Russian-American relations will find no cause for complaint in the Kremlin's challenge to American society. He will rather experience a certain gratitude to a Providence which, by providing the American people with this implacable challenge, has made their entire security as a nation dependent on their pulling themselves together and accepting the responsibilities of moral and political leadership that history plainly intended them to bear.

32.

SEEING REDS

In 1946, Joseph R. McCarthy defeated Progressive Senator Robert M. LaFollette, Jr., in the Republican primary in Wisconsin and went on to win election to the U.S. Senate that fall. During the primary contest he was supported by Wisconsin Communists who were infuriated by LaFollette's pre–Pearl Harbor anti-interventionism and by his criticisms of Soviet dictator Joseph Stalin. Asked about the support the Communists were giving him against LaFollette, McCarthy said airily, "The Communists have votes, too, don't they?" Four years later he became the leader of an impassioned crusade against communism, and the word **McCarthyism** came to mean a reckless and demagogic assault on domestic dissent.

McCarthyism did not operate in a vacuum. Revelations of Communist spy activity in Canada, England, and the United States after World War II produced demands for counterespionage measures, and in 1947 President Truman inaugurated a loyalty program to ferret out Communists in government. Meanwhile, a series of "spy" cases hit the headlines: the trial and conviction of eleven Communist leaders under the Smith Act for conspiring to advocate the violent overthrow of the government; the conviction of former State Department official Alger Hiss, denounced as a Communist spy, for perjury; and the trial and execution of Julius and Ethel Rosenberg, government workers charged with passing atomic secrets to the Russians. For many Americans, the distinction between the expression of unpopular ideas (like Stalinism) and deliberate conspiratorial activity on behalf of a foreign power (like Stalinist Russia) became increasingly blurred. In 1950, Senator McCarthy obliterated the distinction.

In a radio speech (excerpted below) given in Wheeling, West Virginia, in February 1950, McCarthy announced that he had in his hand a list of Communists in the State Department "known to the Secretary of State" and "still working and making policy." Overnight McCarthy became a national figure, and although he never showed anyone his famous "list" and was increasingly vague about the precise number of names it contained (205 or 81 or 57 or "a lot"), he came to exercise great influence in the U.S. Senate and in the nation. In July 1950 a Senate subcommittee headed by Maryland's Millard Tydings dismissed McCarthy's charges as "a fraud and a hoax." But when Tydings, a conservative Democrat, ran for re-election that fall, McCarthy's insinuations that he was pro-Communist helped defeat him. Similar accusations helped defeat Connecticut Democrat William Benton in 1952.

In 1951, McCarthy charged that George C. Marshall, President Truman's former secretary of state and of defense, was part of "a conspiracy so immense and infamy so black as to dwarf any previous venture in the history of man." During the 1952 presidential campaign McCarthy talked ominously of "twenty years of treason" under the Democrats, and his followers identified Roosevelt's New Deal, Truman's Fair Deal, and, indeed, all efforts for social reform since the Great Depression, as Communist inspired. In 1953, as chairman of the Senate Committee on Government Operations, McCarthy launched a series of investigations of federal agencies, including the Voice of America, the International Information Agency, and the Army Signal Corps installation at Fort Monmouth, New Jersey. When the army decided to fight back, McCarthyism reached its climax in a series of televised Senate hearings in the spring of 1954. During these hearings, the Wisconsin senator's accusations and defamations of character gradually alienated all but his most devoted followers. On July 30, Republican Senator Ralph Flanders of Vermont introduced a resolution of censure; in December, the Senate voted, 67 to 32, to censure McCarthy for his behavior. McCarthy's personal influence ended at this point, but its effect on the nation lingered long after.

Joseph R. McCarthy was born in Grand Chute, Wisconsin, in 1908 to middle-class Roman Catholic parents. He graduated from Marquette University and entered the legal profession in Wisconsin in 1935. Originally a Democrat, he won his first political race (for a local judgeship) as a Republican in 1939. After serving as a Marine from 1942 to 1944, he became a state Republican power with his defeat of LaFollette in the 1946 senatorial race. McCarthy's strongest bases of support were Wisconsin's small business owners and voters of German heritage; they re-elected him in 1952 and largely continued their support even after his fall from national popularity. He died at the Bethesda Naval Hospital in Maryland in 1957.

Questions to consider. A number of questions arise about McCarthy's speech. Why did McCarthy launch his attack in 1950 rather than in 1949 or 1951? What area of the world most concerned him, and what had happened there to give his message impact? Why did he attack from an out-of-the-way place (Wheeling, West Virginia) rather than from Washington or even his home state, Wisconsin, and why, moreover, on the radio? Why did McCarthy single out the State Department for attack, as opposed to, say, the Department of Defense or the Department of Justice? In view of the fact that seven twentieth-century presidents and more secretaries of state had attended just four private colleges (Yale, Harvard, Princeton, and Amherst) was there perhaps a certain logic in men such as McCarthy trying to link the Communist conspiracy with the conspiracy of "those who have had all the benefits"? Finally, McCarthy spoke earlier in the speech of "enemies from within." Have any democracies ever actually become Communist? Was there ever a time or place in American history when forces "from within" might be said to have "destroyed democracy"? Was this what McCarthy had in mind?

Lincoln Day Address (1950)
Joseph R. McCarthy

Ladies and gentlemen, tonight as we celebrate the one hundred and forty-first birthday of one of the greatest men in American history, I would like to be able to talk about what a glorious day today is in the history of the world. As we celebrate the birth of this man who with his whole heart and soul hated war, I would like to be able to speak of peace in our time, of war being outlawed, and of worldwide disarmament. These would be truly appropriate things to be able to mention as we celebrate the birthday of Abraham Lincoln.

Five years after a world war has been won, men's hearts should anticipate a long peace, and men's minds should be free from the heavy weight that comes with war. But this is not such a period—for this is not a period of peace. This is a time of the "cold war." This is a time when all the world is split into two vast, increasingly hostile armed camps—a time of a great armaments race.

Today we are engaged in a final, all-out battle between communistic atheism and Christianity. The modern champions of communism have selected this as the time. And, ladies and gentlemen, the chips are down—they are truly down.

Six years ago, at the time of the first conference to map out the peace— Dumbarton Oaks—there was within the Soviet orbit 180 million people. Lined up on the antitotalitarian side there were in the world roughly 1,625 million people. Today, only six years later, there are 800 million people under the absolute domination of soviet Russia—an increase of over 400 percent. On our side, the figure has shrunk to around 500 million. In other words, in less than six years the odds have changed from 9 to 1 in our favor to 8 to 5 against us. This indicates the swiftness of the tempo of Communist victories and American defeats in the cold war. As one of our outstanding historical figures once said, "When a great democracy is destroyed, it will not be because of enemies from without, but rather because of enemies from within."

From the **Congressional Record**, 81st Congress, v. 96, part 2 (February 20, 1950).

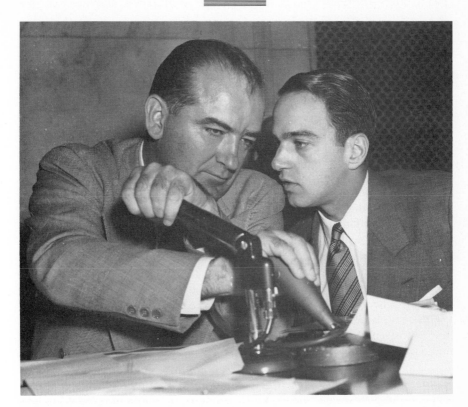

Joseph R. McCarthy and Roy Cohn.   Senator McCarthy covers the microphones in front of him as he confers with his chief counsel during the Army-McCarthy Senate Hearings in 1954. Because the hearings were televised, millions of Americans saw McCarthy in action. Perceived by many as an evasive bully, perpetually obstructing the proceedings with his shouts of "Point of order," McCarthy's star faded rapidly. Television comedians poked fun at him. Within the year, his colleagues had censured him for "conduct unbecoming" to a senator. (Wide World Photo)

The truth of this statement is becoming terrifyingly clear as we see this country each day losing on every front. . . .

The reason why we find ourselves in a position of impotency is not because our only powerful potential enemy has sent men to invade our shores, but rather because of the traitorous actions of those who have been treated so well by this Nation. It has not been the less fortunate or members of minority groups who have been selling this Nation out, but rather those who have had all the benefits that the wealthiest nation on earth has had to offer—the finest homes, the finest college education, and the finest jobs in Government we can give.

This is glaringly true in the State Department. There the bright young men who are born with silver spoons in their mouths are the ones who have been worst. . . .

When Chiang Kai-shek was fighting our war, the State Department had in China a young man named John S. Service. His task, obviously, was not to work for the communization of China. Strangely, however, he sent official reports back to the State Department urging that we torpedo our ally Chiang Kai-shek and stating, in effect, that communism was the best hope for China.

Later, this man—John Service—was picked up by the Federal Bureau of Investigation for turning over to the Communists secret State Department information. Strangely, however, he was never prosecuted. However, Joseph Grew, the Under Secretary of State, who insisted on his prosecution, was forced to resign. Two days after Grew's successor, Dean Acheson, took over as Under Secretary of State, this man—John Service—who had been picked up by the FBI and who had previously urged that communism was the best hope of China, was not only reinstated in the State Department but promoted. And finally, under Acheson, placed in charge of all placements and promotions.

Today, ladies and gentlemen, this man Service is on his way to represent the State Department and Acheson in Calcutta—by far and away the most important listening post in the Far East. . . .

This, ladies and gentlemen, gives you somewhat of a picture of the type of individuals who have been helping to shape our foreign policy. In my opinion the State Department, which is one of the most important government departments, is thoroughly infested with Communists.

I have in my hand 57 cases of individuals who would appear to be either card carrying members or certainly loyal to the Communist Party, but who nevertheless are still helping to shape our foreign policy.

One thing to remember in discussing the Communists in our Government is that we are not dealing with spies who get 30 pieces of silver to steal the blueprints of a new weapon. We are dealing with a far more sinister type of activity because it permits the enemy to guide and shape our policy. . . .

As you hear this story of high treason, I know that you are saying to yourself, "Well, why doesn't the Congress do something about it?" Actually, ladies and gentlemen, one of the important reasons for the graft, the corruption, the dishonesty, the disloyalty, the treason in high Government positions—one of the most important reasons why this continues is a lack of moral uprising on the part of the 140 million American people. In the light of history, however, this is not hard to explain.

It is the result of an emotional hangover and a temporary moral lapse which follows every war. It is the apathy to evil which people who have been subjected to the tremendous evils of war feel. As the people of the world see mass murder, the destruction of defenseless and innocent people, and all of the crime and lack of morals which go with war, they become numb and apathetic. It has always been thus after war.

However, the morals of our people have not been destroyed. They still exist. This cloak of numbness and apathy has only needed a spark to rekindle them. Happily, this spark has finally been supplied.

As you know, very recently the Secretary of State [Dean Acheson] proclaimed his loyalty to a man [Alger Hiss] guilty of what has always been considered as the most abominable of all crimes—of being a traitor to the people who gave him a position of great trust. The Secretary of State in attempting to justify his continued devotion to the man who sold out the Christian world to the atheistic world, referred to Christ's Sermon on the Mount as a justification and reason therefor, and the reaction of the American people to this would have made the heart of Abraham Lincoln happy.

When this pompous diplomat in striped pants, with a phony British accent, proclaimed to the American people that Christ on the Mount endorsed communism, high treason, and betrayal of a sacred trust, the blasphemy was so great that it awakened the dormant indignation of the American people.

He has lighted the spark which is resulting in a moral uprising and will end only when the whole sorry mess of twisted, warped thinkers are swept from the national scene so that we may have a new birth of national honesty and decency in Government.

33.

A COLD WAR TURNS HOT

During and after World War II, the Soviet Union under Joseph Stalin moved into eastern Europe, taking over Poland, East Germany, Czecho-slovakia, Rumania, and Bulgaria; these countries were transformed into Soviet satellites, and Stalinist regimes were imposed. Only Yugoslavia, under the determined leadership of Marshal Tito, successfully resisted Soviet control.

The Truman administration gave Tito economic support and also sent aid to the nations of western Europe. Truman and his advisers looked on Soviet action in eastern Europe as preliminary to a drive to the Atlantic rather than as defensive in nature. They also regarded the triumph of communism in China in 1949 under Mao Zedong (Tse-tung) as Russian inspired, even though Mao won power mainly on his own. Increasingly, American leaders regarded colonial revolts against Western rule everywhere, if led by radicals, as ultimately the work of Stalin. Ameri-can policy after the war, therefore, came to be centered on thwarting the Russians at all points: economic and military aid to western Europe, technological assistance to the so-called Third World, and military sup-port for anticommunist governments facing domestic insurrections.

In 1950 the cold war between the United States and the Soviet Union turned hot in Korea. Korea, a peninsula abutting China, had been freed from Japanese rule at the end of World War II, divided at the 38th parallel, and occupied by Russian troops in the north and by American troops in the south. The Russians installed a friendly regime in North Korea and then withdrew; the United States did the same in South Korea. On June 25, 1950, the North Korean armies suddenly crossed the thirty-eighth parallel and launched a full-scale invasion of South Korea. President Truman, seeing the hand of China and therefore of the Soviet Union behind this move, promptly committed American troops to the defense of South Korea, won the backing of the United Nations for his action, and, in the following radio and television address, announced American determination to support anticommunist governments throughout East Asia. The Korean War lasted from June 1950 until the armistice of July 1953. Under U.N. auspices, sixteen nations participated in the conflict against North Korea. South Korea remained independent, but the Korean War cost the United States $22 billion and 34,000 dead.

Harry S Truman was born on a farm near Independence, Missouri, in 1884. After graduating from high school, he worked as a farmer and a bank clerk, and during World War I saw action in France as a captain in the field artillery. After the war he entered the clothing business and then went into politics in 1922. After serving as county judge and presiding judge of Jackson County, Missouri, he was elected senator in 1934 and served in the Senate until his election as vice president in 1944. As a senator he supported Roosevelt's New Deal policies and won a national reputation as chairman of a Senate committee that sought to end favoritism and waste in defense spending. His presidency from 1945 to 1953 was characterized by futile efforts to ram progressive Fair Deal legislation through a conservative Congress and, increasingly, by an anticommunist domestic and foreign policy. Popularly remembered for his integrity, combativeness, and sense of responsibility—"The buck," he said, "stops here"—Truman died at his home in Independence, Missouri, in 1972.

Questions to consider. Compare Truman's speech with the war messages of Franklin D. Roosevelt in 1941 (Document 29) and Woodrow Wilson in 1917 (Document 24). How do Roosevelt's and Truman's messages differ in tone, length, and detail? What was there about the attack and response in Korea, as opposed to Pearl Harbor, that forced Truman to deliver this kind of speech? Actually, the address was far closer in many ways to Wilson's. Both spoke at length in order to justify sending American soldiers into a foreign war; they employed the rhetoric of "universal peace and freedom" for the same reason. Even here, though, there were important differences, most notably in Truman's lengthy references to the economy. Why did Truman feel obliged to address this point in 1950, whereas Wilson had not in 1917? How helpful are Tables A.8, A.11, and A.12 in the Statistical Appendix in accounting for this difference?

━━━━━━

Address on Korea (1950)
Harry S Truman

At noon today I sent a message to the Congress about the situation in Korea. I want to talk to you tonight about that situation, and about what it means to the security of the United States and to our hopes for peace in the world.

Korea is a small country, thousands of miles away, but what is happening there is important to every American.

On Sunday, June 25th, Communist forces attacked the Republic of Korea.

From **Public Papers of the Presidents of the United States: Harry S Truman** (Government Printing Office, Washington, D.C., 1961–1966), 1950: 537–540.

This attack has made it clear, beyond all doubt, that the international Communist movement is willing to use armed invasion to conquer independent nations. An act of aggression such as this creates a very real danger to the security of all free nations.

The attack upon Korea was an outright breach of the peace and a violation of the Charter of the United Nations. By their actions in Korea, Communist leaders have demonstrated their contempt for the basic moral principles on which the United Nations is founded. This is a direct challenge to the efforts of the free nations to build the kind of world in which men can live in freedom and peace.

This challenge has been presented squarely. We must meet it squarely. . . .

The Communist invasion was launched in great force, with planes, tanks, and artillery. The size of the attack, and the speed with which it was followed up, make it perfectly plain that it had been plotted long in advance.

As soon as word of the attack was received, Secretary of State [Dean] Acheson called me at Independence, Mo., and informed me that, with my approval, he would ask for an immediate meeting of the United Nations Security Council. The Security Council met just 24 hours after the Communist invasion began.

One of the main reasons the Security Council was set up was to act in such cases as this—to stop outbreaks of aggression in a hurry before they develop into general conflicts. In this case the Council passed a resolution which called for the invaders of Korea to stop fighting, and to withdraw. The Council called on all members of the United Nations to help carry out this resolution. The Communist invaders ignored the action of the Security Council and kept right on with their attack.

The Security Council then met again. It recommended that members of the United Nations help the Republic of Korea repel the attack and help restore peace and security in that area.

Fifty-two of the 59 countries which are members of the United Nations have given their support to the action taken by the Security Council to restore peace in Korea.

These actions by the United Nations and its members are of great importance. The free nations have now made it clear that lawless aggression will be met with force. The free nations have learned the fateful lesson of the 1930's. That lesson is that aggression must be met firmly. Appeasement leads only to further aggression and ultimately to war.

The principal effort to help the Koreans preserve their independence, and to help the United Nations restore peace, has been made by the United States. We have sent land, sea, and air forces to assist in these operations. We have done this because we know that what is at stake here is nothing less than our own national security and the peace of the world.

So far, two other nations—Australia and Great Britain—have sent planes to Korea; and six other nations—Australia, Canada, France, Great Britain, the Netherlands, and New Zealand—have made naval forces available.

Under the flag of the United Nations a unified command has been established for all forces of the members of the United Nations fighting in Korea. Gen. Douglas MacArthur is the commander of this combined force.

The prompt action of the United Nations to put down lawless aggression, and the prompt response to this action by free peoples all over the world, will stand as a landmark in mankind's long search for a rule of law among nations.

Only a few countries have failed to endorse the efforts of the United Nations to stop the fighting in Korea. The most important of these is the Soviet Union. The Soviet Union has boycotted the meetings of the United Nations Security Council. It has refused to support the actions of the United Nations with respect to Korea.

The United States requested the Soviet Government, 2 days after the fighting started, to use its influence with the North Koreans to have them withdraw. The Soviet Government refused.

The Soviet Government has said many times that it wants peace in the world, but its attitude toward this act of aggression against the Republic of Korea is in direct contradiction of its statements.

For our part, we shall continue to support the United Nations action to restore peace in the world.

We know that it will take a hard, tough fight to halt the invasion, and to drive the Communists back. The invaders have been provided with enough equipment and supplies for a long campaign. They overwhelmed the lightly armed defense forces of the Korean Republic in the first few days and drove southward.

Now, however, the Korean defenders have reorganized and are making a brave fight for their liberty, and an increasing number of American troops have joined them. Our forces have fought a skillful, rearguard delaying action, pending the arrival of reinforcements. Some of these reinforcements are now arriving; others are on the way from the United States. . . .

Furthermore, the fact that Communist forces have invaded Korea is a warning that there may be similar acts of aggression in other parts of the world. The free nations must be on their guard, more than ever before, against this kind of sneak attack. . . .

When we have worked out with other free countries an increased program for our common defense, I shall recommend to the Congress that additional funds be provided for this purpose. This is of great importance. The free nations face a worldwide threat. It must be met with a worldwide defense. The United States and other free nations can multiply their strength by joining with one another in a common effort to provide this defense. This is our best hope for peace.

The things we need to do to build up our military defense will require considerable adjustment in our domestic economy. We have a tremendously rich and productive economy, and it is expanding every year.

Our job now is to divert to defense purposes more of that tremendous productive capacity—more steel, more aluminum, more of a good many things.

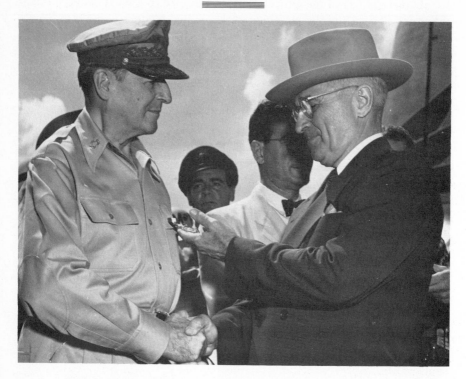

General Douglas MacArthur. On June 29, 1950, the American government ordered combat troops into Korea under the command of General MacArthur. Three months later, MacArthur's forces engineered a brilliant landing behind North Korean lines and quickly overran the northern half of the country. This position proved untenable because, contrary to MacArthur's prediction, Chinese troops entered the war and pushed the Americans far into the south—one of the longest retreats in U.S. history. Here MacArthur, left, receives a decoration from President Harry S Truman—who would soon strip him of his command for insubordination. (UPI/Bettmann Newsphoto)

Some of the additional production for military purposes can come from making fuller use of plants which are not operating at capacity. But many of our industries are already going full tilt, and until we can add new capacity, some of the resources we need for the national defense will have to be taken from civilian uses.

This requires us to take certain steps to make sure that we obtain the things we need for national defense, and at the same time guard against inflationary price rises.

The steps that are needed now must be taken promptly.

In the message which I sent to the Congress today, I described the economic measures which are required at this time.

First, we need laws which will insure prompt and adequate supplies for military and essential civilian use. I have therefore recommended that the Congress give the Government power to guide the flow of materials into essential uses, to restrict their use for nonessential purposes, and to prevent the accumulation of unnecessary inventories.

Second, we must adopt measures to prevent inflation and to keep our Government in a sound financial condition. One of the major causes of inflation is the excessive use of credit. I have recommended that the Congress authorize the Government to set limits on installment buying and to curb speculation in agricultural commodities. In the housing field, where Government credit is an important factor, I have already directed that credit restraints be applied, and I have recommended that the Congress authorize further controls.

As an additional safeguard against inflation, and to help finance our defense needs, it will be necessary to make substantial increases in taxes. This is a contribution to our national security that every one of us should stand ready to make. As soon as a balanced and fair tax program can be worked out, I shall lay it before the Congress. This tax program will have as a major aim the elimination of profiteering.

Third, we should increase the production of goods needed for national defense. We must plan to enlarge our defense production, not just for the immediate future, but for the next several years. This will be primarily a task for our businessmen and workers. However, to help obtain the necessary increases, the Government should be authorized to provide certain types of financial assistance to private industry to increase defense production.

Our military needs are large, and to meet them will require hard work and steady effort. I know that we can produce what we need if each of us does his part—each man, each woman, each soldier, each civilian. This is a time for all of us to pitch in and work together. . . .

We have the resources to meet our needs. Far more important, the American people are unified in their belief in democratic freedom. We are united in detesting Communist slavery.

We know that the cost of freedom is high. But we are determined to preserve our freedom—no matter what the cost.

I know that our people are willing to do their part to support our soldiers and sailors and airmen who are fighting in Korea. I know that our fighting men can count on each and every one of you.

Our country stands before the world as an example of how free men, under God, can build a community of neighbors, working together for the good of all.

That is the goal we seek not only for ourselves, but for all people. We believe that freedom and peace are essential if men are to live as our Creator intended us to live. It is this faith that has guided us in the past, and it is this faith that will fortify us in the stern days ahead.

34.

THE SWORD OF DAMOCLES

The administration of Dwight D. Eisenhower, who became president in 1953 after a sweeping electoral victory, successfully arranged the armistice in Korea, which public-opinion polls showed the American public deeply desired. Yet the settlement left more than fifty thousand U.S. troops in South Korea to protect the local government, and, in general, Eisenhower's advisers took the same view of the Communist threat that Truman did. The main difference was that the new administration was Republican and therefore more concerned with curtailing federal spending and balancing the federal budget than its predecessors had been. The Eisenhower administration was anxious to keep military spending under control.

Eisenhower's fiscal conservatism produced two significant modifications in American diplomacy. First, this policy led to a system of military alliances with noncommunist nations on the perimeters of China and the Soviet Union whereby these nations would receive military aid and presumably do much of the fighting should the cold war again turn hot. Second, the Eisenhower administration placed greater emphasis on atomic weapons, taking the position that they offered "more bang for a buck" than conventional forces. Thus was born the doctrine of "massive retaliation," outlined below by Secretary of State John Foster Dulles, and also (since the Russians quickly matched the American nuclear build-up) the ominous concept of the "balance of terror" as a means of preserving world peace.

John Foster Dulles, chief architect of the massive retaliation doctrine, was born in Washington, D.C., in 1888. After graduating from Princeton University, he joined a New York law firm, becoming its head in 1927. Utilizing the experience he gained at the peace conference in Paris after World War I, he figured prominently in the organization of the United Nations in 1945 and served as chief U.S. delegate to the U.N. General Assembly until 1949. As Eisenhower's secretary of state, Dulles promoted a larger nuclear arsenal and an elaborate system of anticommunist alliances in East Asia and the Middle East. He also talked about the "liberation" of eastern Europe from Soviet domination and championed "brinkmanship," that is, going to the very edge of nuclear war in order to prevent further Russian territorial gains in the world. More than most American officials after World War II, Dulles (together with his brother Allen, who headed the Central Intelligence Agency) moralized the struggle with the Soviet Union and presented it as a struggle between the forces of good and evil throughout the globe. Yet when there were uprisings against Soviet domination in eastern Europe in the 1950s, the United States refrained from intervening, and the rebels were quickly suppressed by Russian forces. Bad health forced Dulles's resignation in April 1959. He died in Washington a month later.

Questions to consider. Dulles took great pains at the beginning of his statement to place the United States within a historical framework— in this case the period from the end of the Napoleonic wars to the present—and then a few paragraphs later noted that the Soviets, too, think in terms of "an entire historical era." What impressions did Dulles hope to make on his readers by constructing his argument this way? What international traditions seem to have been most crucial in his thinking? Did he think the Soviet system could ever change? Would ever change? Dulles was also careful to argue that the United States needs "collective security" as well as the capacity for "massive atomic and thermonuclear retaliation." On what specific grounds did he press for collective security arrangements? The United States and the Soviet Union had comparable populations. Why, then, did Dulles assume that the United States could never field armies as large as those of the Soviet Union? What does this suggest about the ultimate motives behind the development of a nuclear arsenal? What is the "sword of Damocles"? Under the circumstances, was this an appropriate metaphor?

Security and Peace (1954)
John Foster Dulles

During the nineteenth century the maintenance of peace and order depended largely on Great Britain, with its Navy and the system of naval bases which enabled it to operate with mobility and flexibility throughout the world. By suitable commercial, investment and monetary policies, Great Britain and other nations with surplus capital stimulated economic growth in under-developed areas. The French Revolution had aroused men to respect and promote human rights and fundamental freedoms. The United States also made its contribution. Our people devoted their energies largely to domestic matters, not because they lacked concern for others but believing that what our founders called "the conduct and example" of freedom would exert a liberating

From **Department of State Bulletin** (January 1954).

influence everywhere. In fact, it did so. The "great American experiment" was a source of hope and inspiration to men everywhere, and especially to those living under despotism. Our dynamic example of freedom drew many to our shores and inspired others, in the old world and the new, to emulate our course.

All of these influences contributed to giving the world relative peace and security for the 100 years between the ending of the Napoleonic wars and the beginning of the First World War. During this period there were many advances in the practice of political liberty, and generally throughout the world there was a great advance in material and social well-being.

The events of the twentieth century, and especially the two World Wars and their aftermaths, have created an entirely new situation. In large measure the United States has inherited a responsibility for leadership which, in the past, has been shared by several nations. Today there rests upon us, to a unique degree, the threefold task of providing insurance against another world war; of demonstrating the good fruits of freedom which undermine the rule of despots by contrast; and of providing a major part of the effort required for the healthy growth of underdeveloped areas.

The Eisenhower Administration inherited security policies that had much worth. Many of these policies were bipartisan in character. They reflected a national recognition of the peril facing the civilized world, a united determination to meet it, and an acceptance of the rôle of leadership thrust on us by events. We had helped to reëstablish the economies of other countries shattered by the war. We had taken a major part in resisting the aggression in Korea. In the face of the Soviet threat we were engaged in rebuilding our military strength and that of other free countries. . . .

The Soviet menace does not reflect the ambitions of a single ruler, and cannot be measured by his life expectancy. There is no evidence that basic Soviet policies have been changed with the passing of Stalin. Indeed, the Berlin Conference of last February gave positive evidence to the contrary. The Soviet Communists have always professed that they are planning for what they call "an entire historical era."

The assets behind this threat are vast. The Soviet bloc of Communist-controlled countries—a new form of imperialist colonialism—represents a vast central land mass with a population of 800,000,000. About 10,000,000 men are regularly under arms, with many more trained millions in reserve. This land force occupies a central position which permits striking at any one of about 20 countries along a perimeter of some 20,000 miles. It is supplemented by increasing air power, equipped with atomic weapons, able to strike through northern Arctic routes which bring our industrial areas in range of quick attack.

The threat is not merely military. The Soviet rulers dispose throughout the world the apparatus of international Communism. It operates with trained agitators and a powerful propaganda organization. It exploits every area of discontent, whether it be political discontent against "colonialism" or social discontent against economic conditions. It seeks to harass the existing order and pave the way for political coups which will install communist-controlled régimes. . . .

. . . The cornerstone of security for the free nations must be a collective system of defense. They clearly cannot achieve security separately. No single nation can develop for itself defensive power of adequate scope and flexibility. In seeking to do so, each would become a garrison state and none would achieve security.

This is true of the United States. Without the coöperation of allies, we would not even be in a position to retaliate massively against the war industries of an attacking nation. That requires international facilities. Without them, our air striking power loses much of its deterrent power. With them, strategic air power becomes what Sir Winston Churchill called the "supreme deterrent." He credited to it the safety of Europe during recent years. But such power, while now a dominant factor, may not have the same significance forever. Furthermore, massive atomic and thermonuclear retaliation is not the kind of power which could most usefully be evoked under all circumstances.

Security for the free world depends, therefore, upon the development of collective security and community power rather than upon purely national potentials. Each nation which shares the security should contribute in accordance with its capabilities and facilities. The Inter-American Treaty of Reciprocal Assistance (Rio Pact) of 1947 set a postwar example in establishing the principle that an armed attack against one would be considered as an attack against all. The North Atlantic Treaty is based on the same principle. Its members have gone much further in organizing joint forces and facilities as a part of the integrated security system. NATO provides essential air and naval bases, to which its various members can contribute—each according to its means and capabilities. It provides the planes and ships and weapons which can use these bases. It provides so many points from which an aggressor could be harassed, in so many different ways, that he cannot prudently concentrate his forces for offense against a single victim.

While NATO best exemplifies this collective security concept, there are other areas where the same concept is evolving, although as yet in a more rudimentary form. An example is the Western Pacific, where the United States has a series of collective security treaties which now embrace Australia, New Zealand, the Philippines, Japan and Korea. Collective arrangements are now in the making in the Middle East, with Turkey-Pakistan as the nucleus. These developments show the growing acceptance of the collective security concept we describe. . . .

. . . The question remains: How should collective defense be organized by the free world for maximum protection at minimum cost? The heart of the problem is how to deter attack. This, we believe, requires that a potential aggressor be left in no doubt that he would be certain to suffer damage outweighing any possible gains from aggression.

This result would not be assured, even by collective measures, if the free world sought to match the potential Communist forces, man for man and tank for tank, at every point where they might attack. The Soviet-Chinese bloc does not lack manpower and spends it as something that is cheap. If an aggressor knew he could always prescribe the battle conditions that suited him and engage us in struggles mainly involving manpower, aggression might be encouraged. He would be tempted to attack in places and by means where his manpower superiority was decisive and where at little cost he could impose upon us great burdens. If the free world adopted that strategy, it could bankrupt itself and not achieve security over a sustained period.

The free world must devise a better strategy for its defense, based on its own special assets. Its assets include, especially, air and naval power and atomic weapons which are now available in a wide range, suitable not only for strategic bombing but also for extensive tactical use. The free world must make imaginative use of the deterrent capabilities of these new weapons and mobilities and exploit the full potential of collective security. Properly used, they can produce defensive power able to retaliate at once and effectively against any aggression. . . .

A would-be aggressor will hesitate to commit aggression if he knows in advance that he thereby not only exposes those particular forces which he chooses to use for his aggression, but also deprives his other assets of "sanctuary" status. That does not mean turning every local war into a world war. It does not mean that if there is a Communist attack somewhere in Asia, atom or hydrogen bombs will necessarily be dropped on the great industrial centers of China or Russia. It does mean that the free world must maintain the collective means and be willing to use them in the way which most effectively makes aggression too risky and expensive to be tempting. . . .

. . . We do not, of course, claim to have found some magic formula that ensures against all forms of Communist successes. Despotism is entrenched as never before. It remains aggressive, particularly in Asia. In Europe, its purposes remain expansive, as shown by Mr. Molotov's[1] plans at the Berlin Conference for Germany, Austria and all Europe. However, time and fundamentals will work for us, if only we will let them.

The dictators face an impossible task when they set themselves to suppress, over a vast area and for a long time, the opportunities which flow from freedom. We can be sure that there is going on, even within the Soviet empire, a silent test of strength between the powerful rulers and the multitudes of human beings. Each individual seems by himself to be helpless in this struggle. But their aspirations in the aggregate make up a mighty force. There are some signs that the Soviet rulers are, in terms of domestic policy, bending to some of the human desires of their people. There are promises of more food, more household goods, more economic freedom. This does not prove that the dictators have themselves been converted. It is rather that they may be dimly perceiving that there are limits to their power **indefinitely** to suppress the human spirit.

---

[1]Vyacheslav Molotov, USSR Foreign Minister.—Eds.

That is a truth which should not be lost sight of as we determine our own policies. Our national purpose is not merely to survive in a world fraught with appalling danger. We want to end this era of danger. We shall not achieve that result merely by developing a vast military establishment. That serves indispensably to defend us and to deter attack. But the sword of Damocles remains suspended. The way to end the peril peacefully is to demonstrate that freedom produces not merely guns, but the spiritual, intellectual and material richness that all men want.

35.

THE MILITARY-INDUSTRIAL COMPLEX

During Dwight D. Eisenhower's eight years as president, the United States ended the Korean War and moved to replace expensive conventional armaments with "cheap" nuclear weapons. Moreover, though the Eisenhower administration landed troops briefly in Lebanon, sent military aid to Indochina, and helped overthrow radical governments in Iran and Guatemala, the United States managed to stay out of war in other parts of the world. There was intense cold war. But there was also peace.

Despite all the years of peace under Eisenhower, the United States in 1960 still kept 2,500,000 military personnel on active duty, poured $51 billion into the defense budget—10 percent of the entire gross national product—and threw every scientific resource into creating sophisticated weapons systems. So striking was this development that President Eisenhower, himself a former general and a probusiness Republican, felt compelled in his 1961 farewell address to warn the public against the rise of a "military-industrial complex" in the land. Since military spending never in fact receded after Eisenhower, the concept and the phrase entered permanently into the political vocabulary, thus becoming somewhat ironic Eisenhower legacies to the people.

Born in Texas in 1890, Dwight D. Eisenhower grew up in Kansas in modest circumstances. A West Point graduate of 1915, he served at various army posts in the United States and Asia and under General Douglas MacArthur during the 1930s; his abilities were also perceived by General George Marshall, and he won promotion to brigadier general in 1941. Commander of the Allied forces in western Europe, he oversaw Allied invasions of North Africa, Italy, and France during World War II, demonstrating impressive diplomatic and administrative skills, and returned to America in late 1945 as a five-star general and a vastly popular hero. It was largely these skills and this reputation, plus his disarming grin and the irresistible slogan "I like Ike," that propelled him to landslide presidential victories in 1952 and 1956. After 1961, Eisenhower eased quickly into retirement and discovered that, much like his nemesis Harry Truman, he had become one of America's beloved political figures. He died in Washington, D.C., in 1969.

Questions to consider. Two aspects of President Eisenhower's striking address deserve special attention. First, Eisenhower was warning not only against the influence of the military and the arms industry, as represented by huge military budgets, but also against the rise of a scientific-technological elite, as symbolized by the growing control of scholarship by Washington. Of these two tendencies, which did he seem to see as the greater threat? Second, although Eisenhower said plainly that these forces—the military-industrial and the scientific-technological—represented a danger to our liberties and democratic processes, he was vague about how exactly the forces did endanger them and especially about what might, in a concrete way, be done to prevent such threats. Was Eisenhower, a former general, perhaps tacitly urging that soldiers and defense contractors be restricted in their political activities—in campaign contributions, for example, or lobbying efforts—or that defense budgets be scrutinized and slimmed down with special rigor? How realistic were these hints? What connection, if any, was he making at the end of his speech between disarmament and democracy?

Farewell Address (1961)
Dwight D. Eisenhower

A vital element in keeping the peace is our military establishment. Our arms must be mighty, ready for instant action, so that no potential aggressor may be tempted to risk his own destruction.

Our military organization today bears little relation to that known by any of my predecessors in peacetime, or indeed by the fighting men of World War II or Korea.

Until the latest of our world conflicts, the United States had no armaments industry. American makers of plowshares could, with time and as required, make swords as well. But now we can no longer risk emergency improvisation of national defense; we have been compelled to create a permanent armaments industry of vast proportions. Added to this, three and a half million men and women are directly engaged in the defense establishment. We annually spend on military security more than the net income of all United States corporations.

This conjunction of an immense military establishment and a large arms industry is new in the American experience. The total influence—economic, political, even spiritual—is felt in every city, every statehouse, every office of the federal government. We recognize the imperative need for this development. Yet we must not fail to comprehend its grave implications. Our toil, resources, and livelihood are all involved; so is the very structure of our society.

From the **New York Times**, January 18, 1961.

President Eisenhower's farewell address. This January 17, 1961, photograph shows Dwight D. Eisenhower flashing his famous grin just before starting his farewell television-radio address to the nation. Because of America's international influence and the crucial role of the presidency in foreign affairs, the Eisenhower White House acquired an unprecedented pomp and grandeur. Sensing this shift in power, the world's press flocked around Ike. Reflecting the same shift, the White House staff grew as well, eventually challenging both formal cabinets and "kitchen" cabinets alike in the formulation of policy. (Wide World Photo)

In the councils of government, we must guard against the acquisition of unwarranted influence, whether sought or unsought, by the military-industrial complex. The potential for the disastrous rise of misplaced power exists and will persist.

We must never let the weight of this combination endanger our liberties or democratic processes. We should take nothing for granted. Only an alert and knowledgeable citizenry can compel the proper meshing of the huge industrial and military machinery of defense with our peaceful methods and goals, so that security and liberty may prosper together.

Akin to, and largely responsible for the sweeping changes in our industrial-military posture, has been the technological revolution during recent decades.

In this revolution, research has become central; it also becomes more formalized, complex, and costly. A steadily increasing share is conducted for, by, or at the direction of, the federal government. . . .

The prospect of domination of the nation's scholars by federal employ-ment, project allocations, and the power of money is ever present—and is gravely to be regarded.

Yet, in holding scientific research and discovery in respect, as we should, we must also be alert to the equal and opposite danger that public policy could itself become the captive of a scientific-technological elite.

It is the task of statesmanship to mold, to balance, and to integrate these and other forces, new and old, within the principles of our democratic sys-tem—ever aiming toward the supreme goals of our free society.

Another factor in maintaining balance involves the element of time. As we peer into society's future, we—you and I, and our government—must avoid the impulse to live only for today, plundering, for our own ease and convenience, the precious resources of tomorrow. We cannot mortgage the material assets of our grandchildren without risking the loss also of their political and spiritual heritage. We want democracy to survive for all genera-tions to come, not to become the insolvent phantom of tomorrow.

Down the long lane of the history yet to be written America knows that this world of ours, ever growing smaller, must avoid becoming a community of dreadful fear and hate, and be, instead, a proud confederation of mutual trust and respect.

Such a confederation must be one of equals. The weakest must come to the conference table with the same confidence as do we, protected as we are by our moral, economic, and military strength. That table, though scarred by many past frustrations, cannot be abandoned for the certain agony of the battlefield.

Disarmament, with mutual honor and confidence, is a continuing impera-tive. Together we must learn how to compose differences, not with arms, but with intellect and decent purpose. Because this need is so sharp and apparent I confess that I lay down my official responsibilities in this field with a definite sense of disappointment. As one who has witnessed the horror and the linger-ing sadness of war—as one who knows that another war could utterly destroy this civilization which has been so slowly and painfully built over thousands of years—I wish I could say tonight that a lasting peace is in sight.

Happily, I can say that war has been avoided. Steady progress toward our ultimate goal has been made. But, so much remains to be done. As a private citizen, I shall never cease to do what little I can to help the world advance along that road. . . .

36.

THE DEFENSE OF FREEDOM

Although the New Frontier of President John F. Kennedy had a significant domestic component centering on civil rights and social welfare programs, Kennedy's primary emphasis, as his inaugural address, reprinted below, makes clear, was on the development of a vigorous foreign policy. Kennedy perceived the Soviet threat in much the same way that Richard M. Nixon, his Republican opponent, had perceived it during the 1960 presidential campaign: as ubiquitous and unremitting and therefore to be countered at every turn. But Kennedy's views held significant differences from the policy pursued by the Eisenhower administration.

Kennedy was more willing than Eisenhower to increase defense spending; he was also more skeptical than John Foster Dulles about the value of responding to revolutions in the Third World by threatening thermonuclear war. Departing from the policies of his predecessor, Kennedy moved toward a doctrine of "flexible response" that stressed conventional forces over atomic weapons and emphasized international propaganda and public relations over armaments. At once idealistic and demanding, like the 1961 inaugural address itself, Kennedy's views led to the signing of treaties with the Soviet Union that banned atmospheric nuclear testing and to the establishment of emergency communications between the White House and the Kremlin. But these same views also led to the sending of more and more military personnel to South Vietnam, to prevent Ho Chi Minh, the Communist leader of North Vietnam, from unifying Vietnam under his rule.

John F. Kennedy was born in 1917 to a wealthy Irish-American family. After graduating with honors from Harvard in 1940, he served for a time as secretary to his father, who was then U.S. ambassador to Great Britain. **Why England Slept**—his best-selling book on British military policies during the 1930s—was published in 1940. During World War II he served in the U.S. Navy and won the Navy and Marine Corps Medal for his heroism. After the war he entered politics in Massachusetts, winning election to the House of Representatives in 1946 and to the Senate in 1952. His book **Profiles in Courage,** published in 1956, won the Pulitzer Prize, and in 1960 he narrowly bested Richard Nixon in a contest for the presidency. The youngest man and the only Roman Catholic ever elected president, Kennedy projected an image of intelligence, vitality, and sophistication. Worldwide mourning occurred after he was assassinated in Dallas, Texas, on November 22, 1963.

Questions to consider. Some historians have argued that in this address Kennedy formally shifted the focus of the cold war from Europe to the nonaligned or economically underdeveloped part of the world. Do you agree or disagree? If you agree, do you also believe there was a connection between this shift and Kennedy's emphasis on feeding and clothing the world—on winning by doing good? Was there perhaps also a connection between this shift and Kennedy's preference for invoking human rights instead of democracy? Historians have also read the address as an unprecedented fusion of Harry Truman's adversarialism (Document 33) with Woodrow Wilson's universalism (Document 24). Again, do you agree or disagree? Was this fusion connected with Kennedy's sense of facing an "hour of maximum danger" in which Americans might have to "pay any price" for liberty? On closer inspection, do you think that Kennedy was in fact trying to invoke sentiments or feelings expressed by Wilson in 1917 (Document 24), by Franklin Roosevelt in 1941 (Document 29), or by Truman in 1950 (Document 33)? If you believe Kennedy was trying to imitate Roosevelt in 1941, was he justified and responsible in doing so?

Inaugural Address (1961)
John F. Kennedy

We observe today not a victory of party but a celebration of freedom—symbolizing an end as well as a beginning—signifying renewal as well as change. For I have sworn before you and Almighty God the same solemn oath our forbears prescribed nearly a century and three-quarters ago.

The world is very different now. For man holds in his mortal hands the power to abolish all forms of human poverty and all forms of human life. And yet the same revolutionary beliefs for which our forbears fought are still at issue around the globe—the belief that the rights of man come not from the generosity of the state but from the hand of God.

We dare not forget today that we are the heirs of that first revolution. Let the word go forth from this time and place, to friend and foe alike, that the torch has been passed to a new generation of Americans—born in this century, tempered by war, disciplined by a hard and bitter peace, proud of our ancient heritage—and unwilling to witness or permit the slow undoing of those human rights to which this nation has always been committed, and to which we are committed today at home and around the world.

From the **New York Times**, January 21, 1961.

Let every nation know, whether it wishes us well or ill, that we shall pay any price, bear any burden, meet any hardship, support any friend, oppose any foe to assure the survival and the success of liberty.

This much we pledge—and more.

To those old allies whose cultural and spiritual origins we share, we pledge the loyalty of faithful friends. United, there is little we cannot do in a host of co-operative ventures. Divided, there is little we can do—for we dare not meet a powerful challenge at odds and split asunder.

To those new states whom we welcome to the ranks of the free, we pledge our word that one form of colonial control shall not have passed away merely to be replaced by a far more iron tyranny. We shall not always expect to find them supporting our view. But we shall always hope to find them strongly supporting their own freedom—and to remember that, in the past, those who foolishly sought power by riding the back of the tiger ended up inside.

To those people in the huts and villages of half the globe struggling to break the bonds of mass misery, we pledge our best efforts to help them help themselves, for whatever period is required—not because the Communists may be doing it, not because we seek their votes, but because it is right. If a free society cannot help the many who are poor, it cannot save the few who are rich.

To our sister republics south of our border, we offer a special pledge—to convert our good words into good deeds—in a new alliance for progress—to assist free men and free governments in casting off the chains of poverty. But this peaceful revolution of hope cannot become the prey of hostile powers. Let all our neighbors know that we shall join with them to oppose aggression or subversion anywhere in the Americas. And let every other power know that this hemisphere intends to remain the master of its own house.

To that world assembly of sovereign states, the United Nations, our last best hope in an age where the instruments of war have far outpaced the instruments of peace, we renew our pledge of support—to prevent it from becoming merely a forum for invective—to strengthen its shield of the new and the weak—and to enlarge the area in which its writ may run.

Finally, to those nations who would make themselves our adversary, we offer not a pledge but a request: that both sides begin anew the quest for peace, before the dark powers of destruction unleashed by science engulf all humanity in planned or accidental self-destruction.

We dare not tempt them with weakness. For only when our arms are sufficient beyond doubt can we be certain beyond doubt that they will never be employed.

But neither can two great and powerful groups of nations take comfort from our present course—both sides overburdened by the cost of modern weapons, both rigidly alarmed by the steady spread of the deadly atom, yet both racing to alter that uncertain balance of terror that stays the hand of mankind's final war.

So let us begin anew—remembering on both sides that civility is not a sign of weakness, and sincerity is always subject to proof. Let us never negotiate out of fear. But let us never fear to negotiate.

Let both sides explore what problems unite us instead of belaboring those problems which divide us.

Let both sides, for the first time, formulate serious and precise proposals for the inspection and control of arms—and bring the absolute power to destroy other nations under the absolute control of all nations.

Let both sides seek to invoke the wonders of science instead of its terror. Together let us explore the stars, conquer the deserts, eradicate disease, tap the ocean depths, and encourage the arts and commerce.

Let both sides unite to heed in all corners of the earth the command of Isaiah—to "undo the heavy burdens . . . [and] let the oppressed go free."

And if a beachhead of co-operation may push back the jungle of suspicion, let both sides join in creating a new endeavor, not a new balance of power, but a new world of law, where the strong are just and the weak secure and the peace preserved.

All this will not be finished in the first one hundred days. Nor will it be finished in the first one thousand days, nor in the life of this administration, nor even perhaps in our lifetime on this planet. But let us begin.

In your hands, my fellow citizens, more than mine, will rest the final success or failure of our course. Since this country was founded, each generation of Americans has been summoned to give testimony to its national loyalty. The graves of young Americans who answered the call to service surround the globe.

Now the trumpet summons us again—not as a call to bear arms, though arms we need—not as a call to battle, though embattled we are—but a call to bear the burden of a long twilight struggle, year in and year out, "rejoicing in hope, patient in tribulation"—a struggle against the common enemies of man: tyranny, poverty, disease, and war itself.

Can we forge against these enemies a grand and global alliance, North and South, East and West, that can assure a more fruitful life for all mankind? Will you join in that historic effort?

In the long history of the world, only a few generations have been granted the role of defending freedom in its hour of maximum danger. I do not shrink from this responsibility—I welcome it. I do not believe that any of us would exchange places with any other people or any other generation. The energy, the faith, the devotion which we bring to this endeavor will light our country and all who serve it—and the glow from that fire can truly light the world.

And so, my fellow Americans: ask not what your country can do for you—ask what you can do for your country.

My fellow citizens of the world: ask not what America will do for you, but what together we can do for the freedom of man.

Finally, whether you are citizens of America or citizens of the world, ask of us here the same high standards of strength and sacrifice which we ask of you. With a good conscience our only sure reward, with history the final judge of deeds, let us go forth to lead the land we love, asking His blessing and His help, but knowing that here on earth God's work must truly be our own.

37.

AGONY IN ASIA

American involvement in Vietnam began modestly enough with a promise in 1945 to help France restore colonial rule there. The United States backed France because Ho Chi Minh, leader of the struggle for Vietnamese independence, was a Communist. American policymakers were more impressed by Ho's communism than by his nationalism; they looked upon him as a tool of the Kremlin, although he had the backing of many non-Communists in Indochina who wanted freedom from French control. In 1954, Ho's forces defeated the French at Dien Bien Phu, and the French decided to withdraw from Vietnam. At this point the United States stepped in, backed a Korean-style partition of Vietnam, and gave aid to the South Vietnamese government in Saigon. American policy continued to be based on the belief that communism in Vietnam was inspired by China or the Soviet Union, if not both. If Vietnam went Communist, Washington warned, other countries in Asia might topple like so many dominoes, and Communist influence in the world would grow at the expense of America's.

U.S. military personnel entered the Vietnamese conflict between North and South in 1961, President Kennedy's first year in office; American bombers began raiding North Vietnam in 1965, after the re-election of Kennedy's successor, Lyndon B. Johnson. By 1969, American troops in South Vietnam numbered around 550,000, and American planes had dropped more bombs in Vietnam than were dropped on Germany and Japan during World War II. Yet the Vietcong (the South Vietnamese insurgents), aided by the North Vietnamese Communists, seemed stronger than ever, and international opinion was turning against the United States.

The escalation of American involvement in Vietnam provoked perhaps the greatest wartime opposition in American history. By the end of 1965, the first draft card burnings had occurred, and students in major universities throughout the country had organized teach-ins to discuss the nature of the war and had held the first antiwar march on Washington. By 1967, protest rallies drew hundreds of thousands, there was widespread evasion of the draft among middle- and upper-middle-class students, and some of the country's most prominent leaders, including the Reverend Martin Luther King, Jr., were vehemently criticizing the Johnson administration for its Vietnam policy. The speech reprinted below, delivered by King at Riverside Church in New York City, indicates the links that many people had begun to see between international violence and domestic violence, war spending and social poverty, and the suppression of independence movements abroad and minority aspirations at home.

Martin Luther King's stance had special force because of his stature as an advocate of peace and human rights. Born in Atlanta, Georgia, in 1929, the son of a Baptist clergyman, King entered college at the age of fifteen and eventually received a doctorate in theology from Boston University. In 1954 he became minister of a church in Montgomery, Alabama, and in 1955 he became a leader in the successful effort to integrate the local bus system. Calling upon this experience and on his philosophy of nonviolence, King was soon promoting demonstrations against segregation throughout the South. In August 1963 he spoke to 250,000 people in the nation's capital on behalf of black voting rights, the first so-called March on Washington and a model for later antiwar protests. In 1964 he won the Nobel Peace Prize. In April 1968, having broken with the Johnson administration over the Vietnam War and on the eve of a vast "Poor People's Campaign" for economic justice, King was assassinated in Memphis, Tennessee. The death of the apostle of nonviolence triggered massive race riots in the nation's cities. His funeral attracted 150,000 mourners. The inscription on his tombstone, taken from his 1963 Washington speech, reads: "Free at Last, Free at Last, Thank God Almighty, I'm Free at Last."

Questions to consider. Of the seven reasons King gave for deciding to "break silence" over Vietnam, which—as measurable by the rank and emphasis he gave them and by his rhetorical style—seem to have mattered most to him? Was he concerned more with domestic or with nondomestic factors? With race or with violence? With American blacks, with American society, or with humanity? In considering these questions, note how King inveighed first against racial injustice, then against violence, and finally against both together. Was he right to link the two so closely? Would any perceptive critic of injustice have done so, or did this constant intertwining reflect King's particular way of seeing things and his personal experience in the civil rights movement? Many historians believe that this speech marked a sharp leftward political shift by King away from the struggle for civil rights toward a broader struggle for economic justice and social transformation. Is there evidence for this interpretation in the speech? If so, was the shift a logical one, given King's concerns? Was it inevitable? Was it necessary? Why **did** King wait until 1967 to attack American policy in Vietnam publicly? Why was he careful to call his silence, rather than his attack, a "betrayal"?

A Time to Break Silence (1967)
Martin Luther King, Jr.

I come to this magnificent house of worship tonight because my conscience leaves me no other choice. I join with you in this meeting because I am in deepest agreement with the aims and work of the organization which has brought us together: Clergy and Laymen Concerned About Vietnam. The recent statement of your executive committee are the sentiments of my own heart and I found myself in full accord when I read its opening lines: "A time comes when silence is betrayal." That time has come for us in relation to Vietnam. . . .

Over the past two years, as I have moved to break the betrayal of my own silences and to speak from the burnings of my own heart, as I have called for radical departures from the destruction of Vietnam, many persons have questioned me about the wisdom of my path. At the heart of their concerns this query has often loomed large and loud: Why are you speaking about the war, Dr. King? Why are you joining the voices of dissent? Peace and civil rights don't mix, they say. Aren't you hurting the cause of your people, they ask? And when I hear them, though I often understand the source of their concern, I am nevertheless greatly saddened, for such questions mean that the inquirers have not really known mè, my commitment or my calling. Indeed, their questions suggest that they do not know the world in which they live.

In the light of such tragic misunderstanding, I deem it of signal importance to try to state clearly, and I trust concisely, why I believe that the path from Dexter Avenue Baptist Church—the church in Montgomery, Alabama, where I began my pastorate—leads clearly to this sanctuary tonight. . . .

Since I am a preacher by trade, I suppose it is not surprising that I have seven major reasons for bringing Vietnam into the field of my moral vision. There is at the outset a very obvious and almost facile connection between the war in Vietnam and the struggle I, and others, have been waging in America. A few years ago there was a shining moment in that struggle. It seemed as if there was a real promise of hope for the poor—both black and white—through the Poverty Program. There were experiments, hopes, new beginnings. Then came the build-up in Vietnam and I watched the program broken and eviscerated as if it were some idle political plaything of a society gone mad on war, and I knew that America would never invest the necessary funds or energies in rehabilitation of its poor so long as adventures like Vietnam continued to draw men and skills and money like some demonic destructive suction tube. So I was increasingly compelled to see the war as an enemy of the poor and to attack it as such.

From **Freedomways** (Spring 1967), 103–117. Reprinted by permission of Joan Daves. Copyright © 1967 by Martin Luther King, Jr.

Perhaps the more tragic recognition of reality took place when it became clear to me that the war was doing far more than devastating the hopes of the poor at home. It was sending their sons and their brothers and their husbands to fight and to die in extraordinarily high proportions relative to the rest of the population. We were taking the black young men who had been crippled by our society and sending them 8,000 miles away to guarantee liberties in Southeast Asia which they had not found in Southwest Georgia and East Harlem. So we have been repeatedly faced with the cruel irony of watching negro and white boys on TV screens as they kill and die together for a nation that has been unable to seat them together in the same schools. So we watch them in brutal solidarity burning the huts of a poor village, but we realize that they would never live on the same block in Detroit. I could not be silent in the face of such cruel manipulation of the poor.

My third reason moves to an even deeper level of awareness, for it grows out of my experience in the ghettos of the north over the last three years— especially the last three summers. As I have walked among the desperate, rejected and angry young men I have told them that Molotov cocktails and rifles would not solve their problems. I have tried to offer them my deepest compassion while maintaining my conviction that social change comes most meaningfully through nonviolent action. But they asked—and rightly so— what about Vietnam? They asked if our own nation wasn't using massive doses of violence to solve its problems, to bring about the changes it wanted. Their questions hit home, and I knew that I could never again raise my voice against the violence of the oppressed in the ghettos without having first spoken clearly to the greatest purveyor of violence in the world today—my own government. For the sake of those boys, for the sake of this government, for the sake of the hundreds of thousands trembling under our violence, I cannot be silent.

For those who ask the question, "Aren't you a Civil Rights leader?" and thereby mean to exclude me from the movement for peace, I have this further answer. In 1957 when a group of us formed the Southern Christian Leadership Conference, we chose as our motto: "To save the soul of America." We were convinced that we could not limit our vision to certain rights for black people, but instead affirmed the conviction that America would never be free or saved from itself unless the descendants of its slaves were loosed completely from the shackles they still wear. In a way we were agreeing with Langston Hughes, that black bard of Harlem, who had written earlier:

> O, yes
> I say it plain,
> America never was America to me,
> And yet I swear this oath—
> America will be![1]

---

[1] Reprinted by permission of Harold Ober Associates Incorporated. Copyright 1938 by Langston Hughes. Copyright renewed 1965 by Langston Hughes.

Now, it should be incandescently clear that no one who has any concern for the integrity and life of America today can ignore the present war. If America's soul becomes totally poisoned, part of the autopsy must read Vietnam. It can never be saved so long as it destroys the deepest hopes of men the world over. So it is that those of us who are yet determined that America will be are led down the path of protest and dissent, working for the health of our land.

As if the weight of such a commitment to the life and health of America were not enough, another burden of responsibility was placed upon me in 1964; and I cannot forget that the Nobel Prize for Peace was also a commission—a commission to work harder than I had ever worked before for "the brotherhood of man." This is a calling that takes me beyond national allegiances, but even if it were not present I would yet have to live with the meaning of my commitment to the ministry of Jesus Christ. To me the relationship of this ministry to the making of peace is so obvious that I sometimes marvel at those who ask me why I am speaking against the war. Could it be that they do not know that the good news was meant for all men—for communists and capitalists, for their children and ours, for black and for white, for revolutionary and conservative? Have they forgotten that my ministry is in obedience to the one who loved his enemies so fully that he died for them? What then can I say to the "Viet Cong" or to Castro or to Mao as a faithful minister of this one? Can I threaten them with death or must I not share with them my life?

Finally, as I try to delineate for you and for myself the road that leads from Montgomery to this place I would have offered all that was most valid if I simply said that I must be true to my conviction that I share with all men the calling to be a son of the Living God. Beyond the calling of race or nation or creed is this vocation of sonship and brotherhood, and because I believe that the Father is deeply concerned especially for his suffering and helpless and outcast children, I come tonight to speak for them. . . .

And as I ponder the madness of Vietnam and search within myself for ways to understand and respond to compassion my mind goes constantly to the people of that peninsula. I speak now not of the soldiers of each side, not of the junta in Saigon, but simply of the people who have been living under the curse of war for almost three continuous decades now. I think of them too because it is clear to me that there will be no meaningful solution there until some attempt is made to know them and hear their broken cries. . . .

They languish under our bombs and consider us—not their fellow Vietnamese—the real enemy. They move sadly and apathetically as we herd them off the land of their fathers into concentration camps where minimal social needs are rarely met. They know they must move or be destroyed by our bombs. So they go—primarily women and children and the aged.

They watch as we poison their water, as we kill a million acres of their crops. They must weep as the bulldozers roar through their areas preparing to destroy the precious trees. They wander into the hospitals, with at least 20 casualties from American firepower for one "Viet Cong-inflicted injury. So

The Vietnam War. *The faces of a mother and her children reflect the misery of war as they struggle across a river to escape bombardment of their South Vietnamese village in this 1965 photo. The picture won a Pulitzer Prize for photographer Kyoichi Sawada. (UPI/Bettmann Newsphoto)*

far we may have killed a million of them—mostly children. They wander into the towns and see thousands of the children, homeless, without clothes, running in packs on the streets like animals. They see the children degraded by our soldiers as they beg for food. They see the children selling their sisters to our soldiers, soliciting for their mothers.

What do the peasants think as we ally ourselves with the landlords and as we refuse to put any action into our many words concerning land reform? What do they think as we test out our latest weapons on them, just as the Germans tested out new medicine and new tortures in the concentration camps of Europe? Where are the roots of the independent Vietnam we claim to be building? Is it among these voiceless ones?

We have destroyed their two most cherished institutions: the family and the village. We have destroyed their land and their crops. We have cooperated in the crushing of the nation's only non-communist revolutionary political force—the unified Buddhist Church. We have supported the enemies of the peasants of Saigon. We have corrupted their women and children and killed their men. What liberators! . . .

At this point I should make it clear that while I have tried in these last few minutes to give a voice to the voiceless on Vietnam and to understand the arguments of those who are called enemy, I am as deeply concerned about our own troops there as anything else. For it occurs to me that what we are submitting them to in Vietnam is not simply the brutalizing process that goes on in any war where armies face each other and seek to destroy. We are adding cynicism to the process of death, for they must know after a short period there that none of the things we claim to be fighting for are really involved. Before long they must know that their government has sent them into a struggle among Vietnamese, and the more sophisticated surely realize that we are on the side of the wealthy and the secure while we create a hell for the poor.

Somehow this madness must cease. We must stop now. I speak as a child of God and brother to the suffering poor of Vietnam. I speak for those whose land is being laid waste, whose homes are being destroyed, whose culture is being subverted. I speak for the poor of America who are paying the double price of smashed hopes at home and death and corruption in Vietnam. I speak as a citizen of the world, for the world as it stands aghast at the path we have taken. I speak as an American to the leaders of my own nation. The great initiative in this war is ours. The initiative to stop it must be ours. . . .

There is something seductively tempting about stopping there and sending us all off on what in some circles has become a popular crusade against the war in Vietnam. I say we must enter the struggle, but I wish to go on now to say something even more disturbing. The war in Vietnam is but a symptom of a far deeper malady within the American spirit, and if we ignore this sobering reality we will find ourselves organizing clergy and laymen-concerned committees for the next generation. They will be concerned about Guatemala and Peru. They will be concerned about Thailand and Cambodia. They will be concerned about Mozambique and South Africa. We will be marching for these and a dozen other names and attending rallies without end unless there is a significant and profound change in American life and policy. Such thoughts take us beyond Vietnam, but not beyond our calling as sons of the living God.

In 1957 a sensitive American official overseas said that it seemed to him that our nation was on the wrong side of a world revolution. During the past 10 years we have seen emerge a pattern of suppression which now has justified the presence of U.S. military "advisors" in Venezuela. This need to maintain social stability for our investments accounts for the counter-revolutionary action of American forces in Guatemala. It tells why American helicopters are being used against guerrillas in Colombia and why American napalm and green beret forces have already been active against rebels in Peru. It is with such activity in mind that the words of the late John F. Kennedy come back to haunt us. Five years ago he said, "Those who make peaceful revolution impossible will make violent revolution inevitable."

Increasingly, by choice or by accident, this is the role our nation has taken—the role of those who make peaceful revolution impossible by refusing to give up the privileges and the pleasures that come from the immense profits of overseas investment.

I am convinced that if we are to get on the right side of the world revolution, we as a nation must undergo a radical revolution of values. We must rapidly begin the shift from a "thing-oriented" society to a "person-oriented" society. When machines and computers, profit motives and property rights are considered more important than people, the giant triplets of racism, materialism, and militarism are incapable of being conquered.

A true revolution of values will soon cause us to question the fairness and justice of many of our past and present policies. On the one hand we are called to play the Good Samaritan on life's roadside; but that will be only an initial act. One day we must come to see that the whole Jericho Road must be transformed so that men and women will not be constantly beaten and robbed as they make their journey on Life's highway. True compassion is more than flinging a coin to a beggar; it is not haphazard and superficial. It comes to see that an edifice which produces beggars needs re-structuring. A true revolution of values will soon look uneasily on the glaring contrast of poverty and wealth. With righteous indignation, it will look across the seas and see individual capitalists of the West investing huge sums of money in Asia, Africa and South America, only to take the profits out with no concern for the social betterment of the countries, and say: "This is not just." It will look at our alliance with the landed gentry of Latin America and say: "This is not just." The Western arrogance of feeling that it has everything to teach others and nothing to learn from them is not just. A true revolution of values will lay hands on the world order and say of war: "This way of settling differences is not just." This business of burning human beings with napalm, of filling our nation's homes with orphans and widows, of injecting poisonous drugs of hate into the veins of peoples normally humane, of sending men home from dark and bloody battlefields physically handicapped and psychologically de-ranged, cannot be reconciled with wisdom, justice and love. A nation that continues year after year to spend more money on military defense than on programs of social uplift is approaching spiritual death. . . .

Now let us begin. Now let us re-dedicate ourselves to the long and bitter—but beautiful—struggle for a new world. This is the calling of the sons of God, and our brothers wait eagerly for our response. Shall we say the odds are too great? Shall we tell them the struggle is too hard? Will our message be that the forces of American life militate against their arrival as full men, and we send our deepest regrets? Or will there be another message, of longing, of hope, of solidarity with their yearnings, of commitment to their cause, whatever the cost? The choice is ours, and though we might prefer it otherwise we must choose in this crucial moment of human history.

COUNTERPOINT VI

War and Disorder

The United States Army that left Vietnam in 1973 was only a shadow of the proud and aggressive force that had arrived there eight years earlier. In the closing years of American involvement, amid widespread cynicism and a general breakdown of discipline, desertions and combat refusals reached unprecedented levels. In the same land, the French had earlier fought just as long and unsuccessfully—a war (the French Indo-China War) that became as unpopular in France as the Vietnam War later became in the United States. The French forces that withdrew from Vietnam in 1954, however, showed much of the same esprit that they had at the war's outset.

What happened to U.S. forces in Vietnam? A great deal, according to data compiled from congressional hearings and Department of Defense studies by military analysts Paul Savage and Richard Gabriel. Desertion rates, for example, were fairly low in 1965 at the beginning of the massive troop buildup ordered by President Lyndon Johnson, but after 1966 they started to escalate sharply (table A.1). By 1968 the desertion rate was nearly twice as high as the original rate, and by 1971 about five times as high. Moreover, the number of attacks by soldiers on officers and noncommissioned officers (NCOs) by a method called "fragging" (because of the deadly fragments of exploding shells) more than doubled from 1969 to 1970 (table A.2). Drug use also reached incredible proportions (table A.3). By 1971 one of every two U.S. soldiers in Vietnam used marijuana; one of every three used stimulants or psychedelics, including cocaine and LSD; and more than one in four used narcotics, including heroin.

As usual, describing what went on is easier than explaining why it went on. Explanations therefore abound. Savage and Gabriel point to what they believe was a faulty command structure (table B). During World War II, in which discipline and morale were fairly high, the Army had one officer for every thirteen enlisted (or conscripted) soldiers. This ratio changed in Korea, with fewer enlisted men for each officer, particularly for the ranks above captain. In Vietnam there were even fewer enlisted men per officer, in particular for all the ranks above lieutenant. Savage and Gabriel conclude somberly that the Army was badly over-officered in the Vietnam War, that ordinary soldiers could see that it was overofficered, and that the soldiers reacted with anger, cynicism, and violence—against their own leaders, not the enemy.

Critics of Savage and Gabriel's thesis have responded by noting that similar trends in officer/enlisted ratios in Korea did not have similar, dire consequences, and that drug use was rampant everywhere in the Army, not just in Vietnam. Edward Bernard Glick argues that race was a factor, just as Martin Luther King, Jr., said it was in 1967 (Document 37). The evidence is not overwhelming, to be sure. Blacks were not overrepresented in the military; they made up about 10 percent of the total U.S. population and about the same percentage of the Army (table C.1). The percentage of black soldiers who died in Vietnam from January to September 1968 is somewhat higher than the percentage of blacks in either the Army or the total U.S. population, but only by about 3 percent (table C.2). Two points, though, are worth noting. First, blacks were seriously underrepresented at the officer level: only 3 percent of Army officers and under 2 percent in the other services (table C.1). Second, blacks made up 15 percent of the Army deaths in Vietnam from 1961 to 1968, more than their share in the total U.S. or Army populations (table C.2). Although the proportion of blacks killed in Vietnam was highest before 1967—before rates of desertion, fragging, and drug use skyrocketed—it remained high, and the 1,057 dead in the first nine months of 1968 was the highest absolute number to that time. Even so, says Glick, racial animosity was probably only a modest factor in overall Army deterioration.

Elwin Powell adds a third element to the disruptive climate: the general rise in criminal and violent behavior in the United States during the same years. Rates for both property crime and violent crime, Powell shows, climbed steadily throughout the 1960s (figure D.1), as did virtually all types of serious violent crime (table D.2). The categories of crimes against property—robbery, burglary, larceny—had greater increases than violent crimes against individuals, but these crimes also rose markedly during 1960–1968; the murder rate increased by 40 percent, from 5.0 to 6.9, and the rates of both rape and aggravated assault increased by 75 percent. Powell speculates that this climate of violence and lawlessness probably seeped into the Vietnam War effort, leading to poorer discipline and more extreme alienation. But the violence, he suggests, almost certainly seeped the other way as well. The bigger the war and the more men involved, in other words, the greater the likelihood that war violence would lead to domestic violence. Nor was this only a Vietnam phenomenon, writes Powell; America's wars have always created a violent domestic climate (table D.3). Vietnam was an extreme case, but World Wars I and II had comparable effects, creating circular, escalating convolutions of fundamentally antisocial behavior.

A. Indications of Breakdown in Army Discipline

1. Desertion Rates and Combat Deaths, 1965–1973

Year	Strength of the Army (Global)		Total Ground Forces Strength in Vietnam	Deaths Due to Hostile Action	U.S. Army Desertion Rate per 1,000	U.S. Army Deserters
	Officers	*Enlisted*				
1965	111,541	1,079,750	184,300		15.7	1.10% (n = 13,177)
1966	117,205	1,296,600	385,300		14.7	3.12 (n = 44,244)
1967	142,964	1,401,750	485,600	8,581 (1961–1967)	21.4	1.73 (n = 26,782)
1968	165,569	1,357,000	543,400	9,387	29.1	2.58 (n = 39,321)
1969	171,182	1,153,000	475,200	7,043	42.4	4.27 (n = 56,608)
1970	160,814	1,161,444	343,600	3,911	52.3	6.07 (n = 76,643)
1971	144,595	962,605	139,000	1,449	73.4	7.13 (n = 79,027)
1972	120,982	686,692	25,200	195	53.2	5.52 (n = 44,643)
1973	117,860	703,031	—	—	37.3	3.95 (n = 32,500)
						(Total n = 380,445)

2. Assaults with Explosive Devices on Officers and NCOs, 1969–1972

Combat Year	Total Incidents	Actual Assaults[a]	Possible Assaults[b]	Deaths	Injuries	Intended Victim	
						OFF/NCO	Other
1969	126 (239)[c]	96	30	37	191	70	56
1970	271 (386)	209	62	34	306	154	117
1971	333	222	111	12	198	158	175
1972	58	27	31	3	19	31	31
Total	788 (1,016)	554	234	86	714	413	379

3. Drug Usage in the U.S. Army, 1971

Service Location	Type of Drug				
	Marijuana	Other Psychedelic Drugs	Stimulants	Depressants	Narcotic Drugs
Continental United States	41.3%	28.4%	28.9%	21.5%	20.1%
Europe	40.2	33.0	23.0	14.0	13.1
Vietnam	50.9	30.8	31.9	25.1	28.5
Other Southeast Asia	42.0	23.2	24.7	18.1	17.6
Total	42.7	29.4	28.0	20.4	20.1

[a]Motive determined as intent to kill, do bodily harm, or to intimidate.
[b]Possible motive determined as intent to kill, do bodily harm, or to intimidate.
[c]Figures in parentheses obtained from congressional hearings.

SOURCE: From Paul L. Savage and Richard A. Gabriel, "Cohesion and Disintegration in the American Army in Vietnam," *Armed Forces and Society 2* (May 1976), 340–376. Reprinted by permission of the Inter-University Seminar on Armed Forces and Society and Sage Publications.

B. Officer/Enlisted Ratios in World War II, Korea, and Vietnam

Rank	World War II (1945)	Korea (1953)	Vietnam (1971)
General	1:4,916	1:2,953	1:1,952
Colonel	1:672	1:274	1:163
Lieutenant Colonel	1:258	1:108	1:67
Major	1:118	1:77	1:44
Captain	1:42	1:44	1:20
First Lieutenant	1:35	1:42	1:41
Second Lieutenant	1:76	1:45	1:71
All officers[a]	1:13	1:11	1:8

[a]Excluding warrant officers.

SOURCE: From Paul L. Savage and Richard A. Gabriel, "Cohesion and Disintegration in the American Army in Vietnam," *Armed Forces and Society* 2 (May 1976), 340–376. Reprinted by permission of the Inter-University Seminar on Armed Forces and Society and Sage Publications.

C. Blacks in the U.S. Armed Forces: Participation and Vietnam Casualties

1. Number and Percentage of Blacks in the United States Active Armed Forces (September 1968)

Service	Officers	Enlisted	Total
Army	5,646 (3.4%)	153,516 (11.4%)	159,162 (10.5%)
Navy	352 (0.4)	31,809 (4.8)	32,161 (4.3)
Marine Corps	196 (0.8)	32,055 (11.3)	32,251 (10.5)
Air Force	2,461 (1.8)	78,422 (10.3)	80,883 (9.0)
Total	8,655 (2.1)	295,802 (9.7)	304,457 (8.8)

2. Deaths of Blacks by Hostile Action in Vietnam

Service	1961 to 1966 Total	Blacks	1967 Total	Blacks
Army	4,156	832 (20.0%)	5,443	733 (13.5%)
Navy	199	1 (0.5)	311	9 (2.9)
Marine Corps	2,027	223 (11.0)	3,452	441 (12.8)
Air Force	262	4 (1.5)	172	9 (5.2)
Total	6,644	1,060 (16.0)	9,378	1,192 (12.7)

Service	Jan.–Sept. 1968 Total	Blacks	1961–1968 Total	Blacks
Army	7,941	1,057 (13.3%)	17,540	2,622 (14.9%)
Navy	390	10 (2.6)	900	20 (2.2)
Marine Corps	4,055	576 (14.2)	9,534	1,240 (13.0)
Air Force	153	2 (1.3)	587	15 (2.6)
Total	12,540	1,645 (13.1)	28,562	3,897 (13.6)

SOURCE: From *Soldiers, Scholars and Society* by Edward Bernard Glick (Goodyear Publishing Company, Pacific Palisades, 1971). Reprinted by permission of the author.

D. Crime and Violence in the United States

1. The Increase of Crime in the 1960s

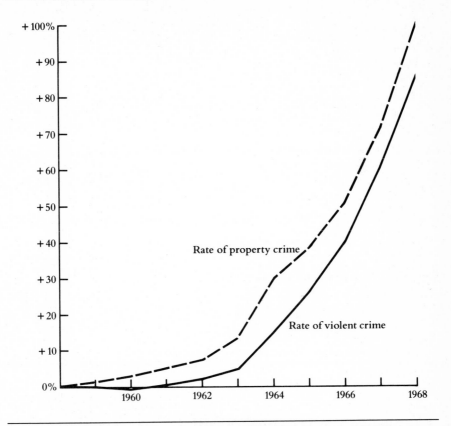

2. Index of Crime in the United States, 1960–1967 (Rate per 100,000)

	Murder	Rape	Robbery	Aggravated Assault	Burglary	Larceny
1960	5.0	9.4	59.9	84.7	500.5	282.3
1961	4.7	9.2	58.1	84.4	510.6	288.9
1962	4.5	9.3	59.4	87.3	256.4	308.4
1963	4.5	9.2	61.5	91.0	566.9	344.0
1964	4.8	11.0	67.9	104.5	623.8	382.6
1965	5.1	11.9	71.3	109.5	651.0	408.0
1966	5.6	12.9	80.3	118.4	708.3	456.8
1967	6.1	13.7	102.1	128.0	811.5	529.2
1968	6.9	16.5	147.3	147.1	981.5	684.1

(continued)

Table D continued

3. Correlation Between War and Racial Disturbance in the United States, 1900–1967

Years	Number of Disturbances
1900–1904	0
1905–1909	2
1910–1914	0
1915–1919	22
1920–1924	4
1925–1929	1
1930–1934	0
1935–1939	1
1940–1944	18
1945–1949	0
1950–1954	0
1955–1959	0
1960–1964	11
1965–1967	150

SOURCE: From *The Design of Discord* by Elwin H. Powell (Oxford University Press, New York, 1970). Reprinted by permission of the author.

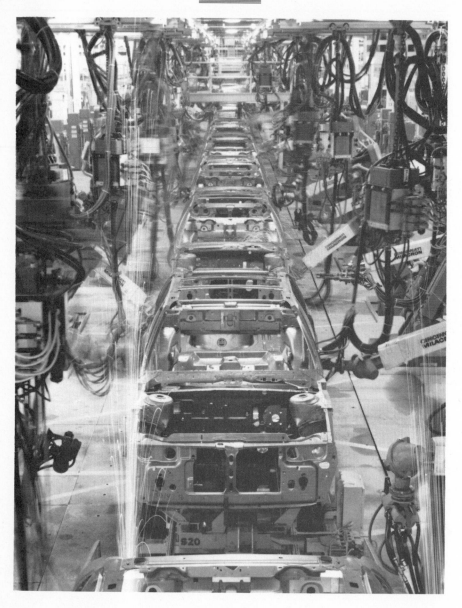

Automation in industry. An automobile assembly line at Chrysler's plant at Sterling Heights, Michigan, shows robotic equipment at work. The increased use of computer-controlled robots in industries means fewer workers are needed, giving a cost advantage to up-to-date factories. But the layoffs that follow the conversion from labor-intensive production to automated production place tremendous stresses on the work force. (Courtesy Chrysler Corporation)

CHAPTER SEVEN

Contemporary America

38.

DESEGREGATION BEGINS

Racial segregation was a fact of life everywhere in the South until the middle of this century. Organizations such as the National Association for the Advancement of Colored People (NAACP) and the Congress of Racial Equality (CORE) fought hard against segregation and its hand-maiden, disfranchisement of blacks. But in 1896 the Supreme Court had ruled in **Plessy** v. **Ferguson** (Document 9) that separate facilities for blacks and whites were legal, and there seemed little recourse from this decree, especially given the unsympathetic racial views of the national government in this period. Only in 1947 did some tentative preliminary change come with the integration of major-league baseball for commercial reasons, the integration of the armed forces by presidential order, and the integration of Southern law schools by a Supreme Court decision that year arguing that such schools were inherently unequal because they denied opportunities to those excluded.

Then, in 1954, in an NAACP lawsuit entitled **Brown** v. **The Board of Education of Topeka,** the Supreme Court extended its reasoning from law schools to the entire segregated school system, thereby reversing the "separate-but-equal" doctrine some sixty years after its adoption. Written by Chief Justice Earl Warren on behalf of a unanimous Court, at first this momentous decision, reprinted below, was met with bitter resentment and resistance from most Southern whites. Yet it marked the beginning of the end for legally segregated schools in the nation. Together with the massive civil rights movement led by Martin Luther King, Jr., and others, it outlawed all segregated public facilities, whether buses, beaches, lunch counters, voting booths, or schools.

Earl Warren was born in Los Angeles in 1891. After he was graduated from the University of California at Berkeley, he practiced law in the San Francisco area until joining the army during World War I. In the 1920s Warren embarked on a successful political career in California, serving as district attorney, state attorney general, and governor. His only electoral defeat came as Republican vice-presidential candidate in 1948. When President Eisenhower appointed him chief justice in 1953, Warren was considered a rather traditional Republican moderate. His leadership of the Court, however, brought an unexpected burst of judicial activism that strengthened not only minority rights but also the rights of voters, trial defendants, and witnesses before congressional committees. Warren resigned from the Court in 1969 and died in Washington in 1974.

Questions to consider. Compare Earl Warren's assumptions and reasoning in this case with those of Henry Billings Brown in **Plessy** v. **Ferguson** (1896) (Document 9). Note, for example, that Warren virtually disregarded what Brown had believed to be so crucial—the actual differences between the races. Note, too, that Warren read very large public purposes into the bountiful commitment of local governments to public education: good citizenship, values, training, and social adjustment. Were these two factors—colorblindness and purposeful public education—enough to account for the Court's 1954 decision? If so, why did Warren introduce psychological studies into his argument? Was it merely a reflection of the findings of modern social science? Or was it because Brown had already reasoned from psychological effects in **Plessy**? In what other areas besides education might modern courts attempt to use the equal protection clause of the Fourteenth Amendment as construed by the Warren Court?

Brown *v.* The Board of Education of Topeka (1954)

These cases come to us from the States of Kansas, South Carolina, Virginia, and Delaware. They are premised on different facts and different local conditions, but a common legal question justifies their consideration together in this consolidated opinion.

In approaching this problem, we cannot turn the clock back to 1868 when the Amendment was adopted, or even to 1896 when Plessy v. Ferguson was written. We must consider public education in the light of its full development and its present place in American life throughout the Nation. Only in this way can it be determined if segregation in public schools deprives these plaintiffs of the equal protection of the laws.

Today, education is perhaps the most important function of state and local governments. Compulsory school attendance laws and the great expenditures for education both demonstrate our recognition of the importance of education to our democratic society. It is required in the performance of our most basic public responsibilities, even service in the armed forces. It is the very foundation of good citizenship. Today it is a principal instrument in awakening the child to cultural values, in preparing him for later professional training, and in helping him to adjust normally to his environment. In these days, it is doubtful that any child may reasonably be expected to succeed in

Brown v. The Board of Education of Topeka, 347 U.S. 483 (1954).

Eyes on the prize. Although school boards were cautious and reluctant to desegregate segregated schools, eventually court pressure and federal prodding forced them to. The result was an extended series of white riots against the black children who tried to enter the school buildings. One of the earliest and worst confrontations took place in 1957 in Little Rock, Arkansas, where Governor Orval Faubus attempted to use the Arkansas National Guard to prevent desegregation. President Eisenhower was personally unhappy with the Supreme Court decision in **Brown** v. **The Board of Education of Topeka.** But as a former five-star general and the U.S. commander-in-chief, he disliked this challenge to his and the Court's authority. He therefore assumed command of the Arkansas Guards units and sent 1,000 paratroopers to prevent further violence. Black students then started attending classes. (Wide World Photo)

life if he is denied the opportunity of an education. Such an opportunity, where the state has undertaken to provide it, is a right which must be made available to all on equal terms.

We come then to the question presented: Does segregation of children in public schools solely on the basis of race, even though the physical facilities and other "tangible" factors may be equal, deprive the children of the minority group of equal educational opportunities? We believe that it does.

In Sweatt v. Painter, . . . in finding that a segregated law school for Negroes could not provide them equal educational opportunities, this Court relied in large part on "those qualities which are incapable of objective measurement but which make for greatness in a law school." In McLaurin v. Oklahoma State Regents, . . . the Court, in requiring that a Negro admitted to a white graduate school be treated like all other students, again resorted to intangible considerations: ". . . his ability to study, to engage in discussions and exchange views with other students, and, in general, to learn his profession." Such considerations apply with added force to children in grade and high schools. To separate them from others of similar age and qualifications solely because of their race generates a feeling of inferiority as to their status in the community that may affect their hearts and minds in a way unlikely ever to be undone. The effect of this separation on their educational opportunities was well stated by a finding in the Kansas case by a court which nevertheless felt compelled to rule against the Negro plaintiffs:

> Segregation of white and colored children in public schools has a detrimental effect upon the colored children. The impact is greater when it has the sanction of the law; for the policy of separating the races is usually interpreted as denoting the inferiority of the Negro group. A sense of inferiority affects the motivation of a child to learn. Segregation with the sanction of the law, therefore, has a tendency to retard the educational and mental development of Negro children and to deprive them of some of the benefits they would receive in a racially integrated school system.

Whatever may have been the extent of psychological knowledge at the time of Plessy v. Ferguson, this finding is amply supported by modern authority. Any language in Plessy v. Ferguson contrary to this finding is rejected.

We conclude that in the field of public education the doctrine of "separate but equal" has no place. Separate educational facilities are inherently unequal. Therefore, we hold that the plaintiffs and others similarly situated for whom the actions have been brought are, by reason of the segregation complained of, deprived of the equal protection of the laws guaranteed by the Fourteenth Amendment. . . .

39.

NONVIOLENCE AND PROTEST

When the Supreme Court ordered public schools desegregated in 1954, the country's leading civil rights organizations—the NAACP, CORE, and the National Urban League—were all situated in the North. They drew their strength mainly from teachers, journalists, lawyers, students, businesspeople, and other persons who made up the tiny black middle class, and challenged racial oppression mostly through lawsuits and political lobbying. The initiatives of these organizations might affect Southern blacks and change the lives of black rural and urban workers, who comprised most blacks, because most blacks still lived in the South and did manual labor. But the organizations themselves were not based on this Southern black majority and so were unable to involve these blacks in the civil rights struggle or to mount direct challenges to racial injustice in the section of the country where it mattered most.

By the late 1950s the situation was changing. In part this resulted from efforts to implement the **Brown** decision, particularly in New Orleans, Louisiana, and Little Rock, Arkansas. There militant whites met black students with violence, prompting not only federal intervention but black demonstrations in support of desegregation. Southern NAACP chapters now grew rapidly, giving that organization a regional strength it had not enjoyed before. Even more important were the direct actions against segregated public facilities led by the Reverend Martin Luther King, Jr., and the civil rights group he founded in 1957, the Southern Christian Leadership Conference (SCLC). The first of these actions was precipitated by an incident in Montgomery, Alabama, in December 1955, when a woman named Rosa Parks refused to move from her seat at the front of the bus to one at the back, where bus regulations required blacks to sit. When Parks was arrested, Montgomery blacks, acting under King's general leadership, began a boycott of the bus system that involved unprecedented mass meetings in local black churches and lasted until the city finally desegregated its public transportation a year later. This success spurred similar actions elsewhere against the racial caste system and propelled King and the SCLC to the forefront of civil rights protest.

In the early 1960s CORE sent "freedom riders" on bus trips into the South to find out whether interstate bus facilities were integrated. A new group, the Student Nonviolent Coordinating Committee (SNCC), organized sit-ins in segregated cafes, stand-ins at segregated theaters, and swim-ins at segregated beaches. Then in early 1963, King and the SCLC

organized boycotts and marches in the industrial city of Birmingham,
Alabama, during which thousands of black men, women, and children
were beaten, shot at, attacked by dogs, sprayed with hoses, and imprisoned. Among the imprisoned was King; while in jail, in answer to an
"open letter" by several white clergymen, he wrote a statement, reprinted below, on the goals and methods of the civil rights movement
and SCLC's controversial philosophy of nonviolent protest. The Birmingham protests ended after important city business and civic leaders
pledged to begin the process of local desegregation. (For a sketch of
King's life, see the introduction to Document 37.)

Questions to consider. King organized his famous letter around
points that local ministers had raised in an open letter critical of the
demonstrations. Do you find his responses compelling? Is his explanation of the philosophy of nonviolence adequate? King himself acknowledged that many in the black community, especially in the North, found
nonviolence too passive, deferential, and submissive. Were they likely to
find his letter satisfactory? To defend lawbreaking, King divided laws
into two categories and attempted to distinguish between why he ad-
vocated breaking unjust laws and opposed breaking just ones. Is his
distinction valid? Finally, what evidence can you find in the style of the
letter that it was written in jail? By a minister?

Letter from Birmingham Jail (1963)
Martin Luther King, Jr.

My Dear Fellow Clergymen:

While confined here in the Birmingham city jail, I came across your
recent statement calling my present activities "unwise and untimely." . . .

I think I should indicate why I am here in Birmingham, since you have
been influenced by the view which argues against "outsiders coming in." I
have the honor of serving as president of the Southern Christian Leadership
Conference, an organization operating in every southern state, with headquarters in Atlanta, Georgia. We have some eighty-five affiliated organizations
across the South, and one of them is the Alabama Christian Movement for
Human Rights. Frequently we share staff, educational and financial resources

with our affiliates. Several months ago the affiliate here in Birmingham asked us to be on call to engage in a nonviolent direct-action program if such were deemed necessary. We readily consented, and when the hour came we lived up to our promise. So I, along with several members of my staff, am here because I was invited here. I am here because I have organizational ties here.

But more basically, I am in Birmingham because injustice is here. Just as the prophets of the eighth century B.C. left their villages and carried their "thus saith the Lord" far beyond the boundaries of their home towns, and just as the Apostle Paul left his village of Tarsus and carried the gospel of Jesus Christ to the far corners of the Greco-Roman world, so am I compelled to carry the gospel of freedom beyond my own home town. Like Paul, I must constantly respond to the Macedonian call for aid.

Moreover, I am cognizant of the interrelatedness of all communities and states. I cannot sit idly by in Atlanta and not be concerned about what happens in Birmingham. Injustice anywhere is a threat to justice everywhere. We are caught in an inescapable network of mutuality, tied in a single garment of destiny. Whatever affects one directly, affects all indirectly. Never again can we afford to live with the narrow, provincial "outside agitator" idea. Anyone who lives inside the United States can never be considered an outsider any-where within its bounds.

You deplore the demonstrations taking place in Birmingham. But your statement, I am sorry to say, fails to express a similar concern for the condi-tions that brought about the demonstrations. I am sure that none of you would want to rest content with the superficial kind of social analysis that deals merely with effects and does not grapple with underlying causes. It is unfortunate that demonstrations are taking place in Birmingham, but it is even more unfortunate that the city's white power structure left the Negro community with no alternative.

In any nonviolent campaign there are four basic steps: collection of the facts to determine whether injustices exist; negotiation; self-purification; and direct action. We have gone through all these steps in Birmingham. There can be no gainsaying the fact that racial injustice engulfs this community. Bir-mingham is probably the most thoroughly segregated city in the United States. Its ugly record of brutality is widely known. Negroes have experienced grossly unjust treatment in the courts. There have been more unsolved bomb-ings of Negro homes and churches in Birmingham than in any other city in the nation. These are the hard, brutal facts of the case. On the basis of these conditions, Negro leaders sought to negotiate with the city fathers. But the latter consistently refused to engage in good-faith negotiation. . . .

As in so many past experiences, our hopes had been blasted, and the shadow of deep disappointment settled upon us. We had no alternative except to prepare for direct action, whereby we would present our very bodies as a means of laying our case before the conscience of the local and the national community. Mindful of the difficulties involved, we decided to undertake a process of self-purification. We began a series of workshops on nonviolence, and we repeatedly asked ourselves: "Are you able to accept blows without retaliating?" "Are you able to endure the ordeal of jail?" We decided to schedule our direct-action program for the Easter season, realizing that except for Christmas, this is the main shopping period of the year. . . .

You may well ask: "Why direct action? Why sit-ins, marches and so forth? Isn't negotiation a better path?" You are quite right in calling for negotiation. Indeed, this is the very purpose of direct action. Nonviolent direct action seeks to create such a crisis and foster such a tension that a community which has constantly refused to negotiate is forced to confront the issue. It seeks so to dramatize the issue that it can no longer be ignored. My citing the creation of tension as part of the work of the nonviolent-resister may sound rather shocking. But I must confess that I am not afraid of the word "tension." I have earnestly opposed violent tension, but there is a type of constructive, nonviolent tension which is necessary for growth. Just as Socrates [Greek philosopher] felt that it was necessary to create a tension in the mind so that individuals could rise from the bondage of myths and half-truths to the unfettered realm of creative analysis and objective appraisal, so must we see the need for nonviolent gadflies to create the kind of tension in society that will help men rise from the dark depths of prejudice and racism to the majestic heights of understanding and brotherhood.

The purpose of our direct-action program is to create a situation so crisis-packed that it will inevitably open the door to negotiation. I therefore concur with you in your call for negotiation. Too long has our beloved Southland been bogged down in a tragic effort to live in monologue rather than dialogue. . . .

We know through painful experience that freedom is never voluntarily given by the oppressor; it must be demanded by the oppressed. Frankly, I have yet to engage in a direct-action campaign that was "well timed" in the view of those who have not suffered unduly from the disease of segregation. For years now I have heard the word "Wait!" It rings in the ear of every Negro with piercing familiarity. This "Wait" has almost always meant "Never." We must come to see, with one of our distinguished jurists, that "justice too long delayed is justice denied."

We have waited for more than 340 years for our constitutional and God-given rights. The nations of Asia and Africa are moving with jetlike speed toward gaining political independence, but we still creep at horse-and-buggy pace toward gaining a cup of coffee at a lunch counter. Perhaps it is easy for those who have never felt the stinging darts of segregation to say, "Wait." But when you have seen vicious mobs lynch your mothers and fathers at will and drown your sisters and brothers at whim; when you have seen hate-filled policemen curse, kick and even kill your black brothers and sisters; when you see the vast majority of your twenty million Negro brothers smothering in an airtight cage of poverty in the midst of an affluent society; when you suddenly find your tongue twisted and your speech stammering as you seek to explain to your six-year-old daughter why she can't go to the public amusement park that has just been advertised on television, and see tears welling up in her eyes when she is told that Funtown is closed to colored children, and see ominous clouds of inferiority beginning to form in her little mental sky, and see her beginning to distort her personality by developing an unconscious bitterness toward white people; when you have to concoct an answer for a five-year-old son who is asking: "Daddy, why do white people treat colored people so mean?"; when you take a cross-country drive and find it necessary to sleep night after night in the uncomfortable corners of your automobile because no motel will accept you; when you are humiliated day in and day out by nagging signs reading "white" and "colored"; when your first name becomes "nigger," your middle name becomes "boy" (however old you are) and your last name becomes "John," and your wife and mother are never given the respected title "Mrs."; when you are harried by day and haunted by night by the fact that you are a Negro, living constantly at tiptoe stance, never quite knowing what to expect next, and are plagued with inner fears and outer resentments; when you are forever fighting a degenerating sense of "nobodiness"—then you will understand why we find it difficult to wait. There comes a time when the cup of endurance runs over, and men are no longer willing to be plunged into the abyss of despair. I hope, sirs, you can understand our legitimate and unavoidable impatience.

You express a great deal of anxiety over our willingness to break laws. This is certainly a legitimate concern. Since we so diligently urge people to obey the Supreme Court's decision of 1954 [*Brown* v. *The Board of Education of Topeka*] outlawing segregation in the public schools, at first glance it may seem rather paradoxical for us consciously to break laws. One may well ask: "How can you advocate breaking some laws and obeying others?" The answer lies in the fact that there are two types of laws: just and unjust. I would be the first to advocate obeying just laws. One has not only a legal but a moral responsibility to obey just laws. Conversely, one has a moral responsibility to disobey unjust laws. I would agree with St. Augustine that "an unjust law is no law at all."

Now, what is the difference between the two? How does one determine whether a law is just or unjust? A just law is a man-made code that squares with the moral law or the law of God. An unjust law is a code that is out of harmony with the moral law. To put it in the terms of St. Thomas Aquinas [Catholic theologian]: An unjust law is a human law that is not rooted in eternal law and natural law. Any law that uplifts human personality is just. Any law that degrades human personality is unjust. All segregation statutes are unjust because segregation distorts the soul and damages the personality. It gives the segregator a false sense of superiority and the segregated a false sense of inferiority. Segregation, to use the terminology of the Jewish philosopher Martin Buber, substitutes an "I-it" relationship for an "I-thou" relationship and ends up relegating persons to the status of things. Hence segregation is not only politically, economically and sociologically unsound, it is morally wrong and sinful. Paul Tillich [Protestant theologian] has said that sin is separation. Is not segregation an existential expression of man's tragic separation, his awful estrangement, his terrible sinfulness? Thus it is that I can urge men to obey the 1954 decision of the Supreme Court, for it is morally right; and I can urge them to disobey segregation ordinances, for they are morally wrong. . . .

March on Washington.   In August 1963, some 250,000 demonstrators gathered
at the foot of the Washington Monument to press the federal government for
action on the civil rights front. Highlighted by Martin Luther King's dramatic "I
have a dream" speech envisioning a land without prejudice, the march was
notable in three ways in addition to its size. First, it was integrated. Second, it
was orderly. Third, it had a limited goal: congressional action to protect constitutional rights. It was practically the last of the great demonstrations of the 1960s
with all these characteristics. (Wide World Photo)

I hope you are able to see the distinction I am trying to point out. In no
sense do I advocate evading or defying the law, as would the rabid segregationist. That would lead to anarchy. One who breaks an unjust law must
do so openly, lovingly, and with a willingness to accept the penalty. I submit
that an individual who breaks a law that conscience tells him is unjust, and
who willingly accepts the penalty of imprisonment in order to arouse the

conscience of the community over its injustice, is in reality expressing the highest respect for the law. . . .

In your statement you assert that our actions, even though peaceful, must be condemned because they precipitate violence. But is this a logical assertion? Isn't this like condemning a robbed man because his possession of money precipitated the evil act of robbery? Isn't this like condemning Socrates because his unswerving commitment to truth and his philosophical inquiries precipitated the act by the misguided populace in which they made him drink hemlock? Isn't this like condemning Jesus because his unique God-consciousness and never-ceasing devotion to God's will precipitated the evil act of crucifixion? We must come to see that, as the federal courts have consistently affirmed, it is wrong to urge an individual to cease his efforts to gain his basic constitutional rights because the quest may precipitate violence. Society must protect the robbed and punish the robber. . . .

You speak of our activity in Birmingham as extreme. At first I was rather disappointed that fellow clergymen would see my nonviolent efforts as those of an extremist. I began thinking about the fact that I stand in the middle of two opposing forces in the Negro community. One is a force of complacency, made up in part of Negroes who, as a result of long years of oppression, are so drained of self-respect and a sense of "somebodiness" that they have adjusted to segregation; and in part of a few middle-class Negroes who, because of a degree of academic and economic security and because in some ways they profit by segregation, have become insensitive to the problems of the masses. The other force is one of bitterness and hatred, and it comes perilously close to advocating violence. It is expressed in the various black nationalist groups that are springing up across the nation, the largest and best-known being Elijah Muhammad's Muslim movement. Nourished by the Negro's frustration over the continued existence of racial discrimination, this movement is made up of people who have lost faith in America, who have absolutely repudiated Christianity, and who have concluded that the white man is an incorrigible "devil."

I have tried to stand between these two forces, saying that we need emulate neither the "do-nothingism" of the complacent nor the hatred and despair of the black nationalist. For there is the more excellent way of love and nonviolent protest. I am grateful to God that, through the influence of the Negro church, the way of nonviolence became an integral part of our struggle. . . .

. . . [T]hough I was initially disappointed at being categorized as an extremist, as I continued to think about the matter I gradually gained a measure of satisfaction from the label. Was not Jesus an extremist for love: "Love your enemies, bless them that curse you, do good to them that hate you, and pray for them which despitefully use you, and persecute you." Was not Amos an extremist for justice: "Let justice roll down like waters and righteousness like an ever-flowing stream." Was not Paul an extremist for the Christian gospel: "I bear in my body the marks of the Lord Jesus." Was not Martin Luther an extremist: "Here I stand: I cannot do otherwise, so help me God." And John Bunyan: "I will stay in jail to the end of my days before I make a butchery of my conscience." And Abraham Lincoln: "This nation cannot survive half slave and half free." And Thomas Jefferson: "We hold these truths to be self-evident, that all men are created equal . . ." So the question is not whether we will be extremists, but what kind of extremists we will be. Will we be extremists for hate or for love? Will we be extremists for the preservation of injustice or for the extension of justice? . . .

Before closing I feel impelled to mention one other point in your statement that has troubled me profoundly. You warmly commended the Birmingham police force for keeping "order" and "preventing violence." I doubt that you would have so warmly commended the police force if you had seen its dogs sinking their teeth into unarmed, nonviolent Negroes. I doubt that you would so quickly commend the policemen if you were to observe their ugly and inhumane treatment of Negroes here in the city jail; if you were to watch them push and curse old Negro women and young Negro girls; if you were to see them slap and kick old Negro men and young boys; if you were to observe them, as they did on two occasions, refuse to give us food because we wanted to sing our grace together. I cannot join you in your praise of the Birmingham police department. . . .

I wish you had commended the Negro sit-inners and demonstrators of Birmingham for their sublime courage, their willingness to suffer and their amazing discipline in the midst of great provocation. One day the South will recognize its real heroes. They will be the James Merediths,[1] with the noble sense of purpose that enables them to face jeering and hostile mobs, and with the agonizing loneliness that characterizes the life of the pioneer. They will be old, oppressed, battered Negro women, symbolized in a seventy-two-year-old woman in Montgomery, Alabama, who rose up with a sense of dignity and with her people decided not to ride segregated buses, and who responded with ungrammatical profundity to one who inquired about her weariness: "My feets is tired, but my soul is at rest." They will be the young high school and college students, the young ministers of the gospel and a host of their elders, courageously and nonviolently sitting in at lunch counters and willingly going to jail for conscience' sake. One day the South will know that when these disinherited children of God sat down at lunch counters, they were in reality standing up for what is best in the American dream and for the most sacred values in our Judaeo-Christian heritage, thereby bringing our nation back to those great wells of democracy which were dug deep by the founding fathers in their formulation of the Constitution and the Declaration of Independence.

Never before have I written so long a letter. I'm afraid it is much too long to take your precious time. I can assure you that it would have been much shorter if I had been writing from a comfortable desk, but what else can one do when he is alone in a narrow jail cell, other than write long letters, think long thoughts and pray long prayers?

---

[1] James Meredith was the first black student at the University of Mississippi. His efforts to enter the university in 1962 were met by white demonstrations and violence.—Eds.

40.

A TURN TO MILITANCY

The civil rights movement began in earnest with **Brown** v. **The Board of Education** (Document 38) in 1954 and the Montgomery bus boycott in 1955. For the next few years two groups provided the movement with leadership: the NAACP, which worked mainly through the courts and enjoyed a national membership; and the SCLC, which was based in the Southern churches and used the tactics of nonviolent demonstrations and boycotts. Though differing in methods, the two organizations shared important characteristics. Their chief objective was the integration of public facilities, including schools. And although they both had predominantly black membership, they accepted white support and participation.

In the early 1960s, however, the civil rights movement began to change. Its primary focus moved from efforts to integrate public facilities to efforts to secure black voting rights. This brought fierce white resistance and much violence, particularly during the "freedom summers" of 1964 and 1965, when black and white college students ran voter registration campaigns in various parts of the South. The violence and the racially selective nature of the registration drives in turn sparked a reaction among young black activists against white participation in the movement. The new militant black position—articulated by the Student Nonviolent Coordinating Committee in the following 1966 position paper—gained plausibility from the outbreak of rioting in the black slums of Northern cities and from the example of liberation struggles in the Third World. After 1966, then, the civil rights movement became increasingly ethnocentric, militant, and fragmented. By 1970 it hardly existed in its original form.

SNCC had been founded in 1960 at a conference called by Martin Luther King, Jr., who imbued its early members with his philosophy of nonviolence. The decisive shift in position occurred early in 1966 when Stokely Carmichael, the principal author of the position paper reprinted below, became chairman. Carmichael was born in 1941 on the West Indian island of Trinidad. After moving with his family to New York City, he lived first in mostly black Harlem and then in the mostly white Bronx. He attended the High School of Science in the Bronx and Howard University in Washington, D.C., and went to jail twenty-seven times during the Southern civil rights campaigns. Under Carmichael, SNCC dropped "Nonviolent" from its name, and its leaders urged angry blacks to undertake a militant black-power position. Carmichael himself later married singer Miriam Makeba and moved to West Africa, where he took the name Kwame Ture and announced, "Africa is my home. I'm staying."

Questions to consider. The SNCC paper on black power prompted vigorous debate. Those distressed by the statement characterized it as belligerent, damaging, and despairing. Sympathizers called it necessary, determined, and reasonable. Does one set of adjectives seem more accurate than the other in assessing this statement? (Recently, scholars have used both sets of adjectives simultaneously in judging it!) Consider, too, the following points. Was it accurate to say in 1966 that no black could ever "represent" Americans and no white could ever "relate" to blacks? Did the paper propose to change this or accept it as a fact of life? Why were there so many references to popular culture in so political a paper? Why did the paper conclude by stressing the task of "identification"? Where did SNCC expect to find new sources of identity? In light of, say, William McKinley's statement on the Philippines (Document 22), was this a valid expectation?

Position Paper of the Student Nonviolent Coordinating Committee (1966)

The myth that the Negro is somehow incapable of liberating himself, is lazy, etc., came out of the American experience. In the books that children read, whites are always "good" (good symbols are white), blacks are "evil" or seen as savages in movies, their language is referred to as a "dialect," and black people in this country are supposedly descended from savages.

Any white person who comes into the movement has these concepts in his mind about black people if only subconsciously. He cannot escape them because the whole society has geared his subconscious in that direction.

Miss America coming from Mississippi has a chance to represent all of America, but a black person from either Mississippi or New York will never represent America. So that white people coming into the movement cannot relate to the black experience, cannot relate to the word "black," cannot relate to the "nitty gritty," cannot relate to the experience that brought such a word into being, cannot relate to chitterlings, hog's head cheese, pig feet, hamhocks, and cannot relate to slavery, because these things are not a part of their experience. They also cannot relate to the

Published by the Student Nonviolent Coordinating Committee. Reprinted by permission.

Black power.   By 1968 the black-power movement had reached its most militant phase. Here Stokely Carmichael (left) and H. Rap Brown talk to newsmen about the takeover of five Columbia University buildings by sit-in demonstrators (rear). Brown and Carmichael had had to avoid a police cordon at the campus entrance to join the protesters. Brown, who once argued that violence is as "American as cherry pie," attacked the "racist policies" of Columbia, which was situated at the edge of Harlem, and called the occupied buildings "a black fortress." (United Press International)

black religious experience, nor to the black church unless, of course, this church has taken on white manifestations.

Negroes in this country have never been allowed to organize themselves because of white interference. As a result of this, the stereotype has been reinforced that blacks cannot organize themselves. The white psychology that blacks have to be watched, also reinforces this stereotype. Blacks, in fact, feel intimidated by the presence of whites, because of their knowledge of the power that whites have over their lives. One white person can come into a meeting of black people and change the complexion of that meeting, whereas one black person would not change the complexion of that meeting unless he was an obvious Uncle Tom. People would immediately start talking about "brotherhood," "love," etc.; race would not be discussed.

If people must express themselves freely, there has to be a climate in which they can do this. If blacks feel intimidated by whites, then they are not liable to vent the rage that they feel about whites in the presence of whites—especially not the black people whom we are trying to organize, i.e. broad masses of black people. A climate has to be created whereby blacks can express themselves. The reason that whites must be excluded is not that one is anti-white, but because the efforts that one is trying to achieve cannot succeed because whites have an intimidating effect. Oftentimes the intimidating effect is in direct proportion to the amount of degradation that black people have suffered at the hands of white people. How do blacks relate to other blacks as such? How do we react to Willie Mays as against Mickey Mantle? What is our response to Mays hitting a home run against Mantle performing the same deed? One has to come to the conclusion that it is because of black participation in baseball. Negroes still identify with the Dodgers because of Jackie Robinson's efforts with the Dodgers. Negroes would instinctively champion all-black teams if they opposed all-white or predominantly white teams. The same principle operates for the movement as it does for baseball: a mystique must be created whereby Negroes can identify with the movement.

Thus an all-black project is needed in order for the people to free themselves. This has to exist from the beginning. This relates to what can be called "coalition politics." There is no doubt in our minds that some whites are just as disgusted with this system as we are. But it is meaningless to talk about coalition if there is no one to align ourselves with, because of the lack of organization in the white communities. There can be no talk of "hooking up" unless black people organize blacks and white people organize whites. If these conditions are met then perhaps at some later date—and if we are going in the same direction—talks about exchange of personnel, coalition, and other meaningful alliances can be discussed.

These facts do not mean that whites cannot help. They can participate on a voluntary basis. We can contract work out to them, but in no way can they participate on a policy-making level.

The charge may be made that we are "racists," but whites who are sensitive to our problems will realize we must determine our own destiny.

In an attempt to find a solution to our dilemma, we propose that our organization (S.N.C.C.) should be black-staffed, black-controlled and black-financed. We do not want to fall into a similar dilemma that other civil rights organizations have fallen into. If we continue to rely upon white financial support we will find ourselves entwined in the tentacles of the white power complex that controls this country. It is also important that a black organization (devoid of cultism) be projected to our people so that it can be demonstrated that such organizations are viable.

More and more we see black people in this country being used as a tool of the white liberal establishment. Liberal whites have not begun to address themselves to the real problem of black people in this country; witness their bewilderment, fear and anxiety when nationalism is mentioned concerning black people. An analysis of their (white liberal) reaction to the word alone (nationalism) reveals a very meaningful attitude of whites of any ideological persuasion toward blacks in this country. It means previous solutions to black problems in this country have been made in the interests of those whites dealing with these problems and not in the best interests of black people in this country. Whites can only subvert our true search and struggle for self-determination, self-identification, and liberation in this country. Re-evaluation of the white and black roles must NOW take place not so that black people play but rather black people define white people's roles.

Too long have we allowed white people to interpret the importance and meaning of the cultural aspects of our society. We have allowed them to tell us what was good about our Afro-American music, art and literature. How many black critics do we have on the "jazz" scene? How can a white person who is not a part of the black psyche (except in the oppressor's role) interpret the meaning of the blues to us who are manifestations of the songs themselves? It must also be pointed out that on whatever level of contact that blacks and whites come together, that meeting or confrontation is not on the level of the whites. This only means that our everyday contact with whites is a reinforcement of the myth of white supremacy. Whites are the ones who must try to raise themselves to our humanistic level. We are not, after all, the ones who are responsible for a genocidal war in Vietnam; we are not the ones who are responsible for neocolonialism in Africa and Latin America; we are not the ones who held a people in animalistic bondage over 400 years. We reject the American dream as defined by white people and must work to construct an American reality defined by Afro-Americans.

One of the criticisms of white militants and radicals is that when we view the masses of white people we view the over-all reality of America, we view the racism, the bigotry, and the distortion of personality, we view man's inhumanity to man; we view in reality 180 million racists. The sensitive white intellectual and radical who is fighting to bring about change is conscious of this fact, but does not have the courage to admit this. When he admits this reality, then he must also admit his involvement because he is a part of the collective white America. It is only to the extent that he recognizes this that he will be able to change his reality.

Another concern is how does the white radical view the black community and how does he view the poor white community in terms of organizing. So far we have found that most white radicals have sought to escape the horrible reality of America by going into the black community and attempting to organize black people while neglecting the organization of their own people's racist communities. How can one clean up someone else's yard when one's own yard is untidy?

A thorough re-examination must be made by black people concerning the contributions that we have made in shaping this country. If this re-examination and re-evaluation is not made and black people are not given their proper due and respect, then the antagonisms and contradictions are going to become more and more glaring, more and more intense until a national explosion may result.

When people attempt to move from these conclusions it would be faulty reasoning to say they are ordered by racism, because, in this country and in the West, racism has functioned as a type of white nationalism when dealing with black people. We all know the habit that this has created throughout the world and particularly among nonwhite people in this country.

Therefore any re-evaluation that we must make will, for the most part, deal with identification. Who are black people, what are black people; what is their relationship to America and the world?

It must be repeated that the whole myth of "Negro citizenship," perpetuated by the white elite, has confused the thinking of radical and progressive blacks and whites in this country. The broad masses of black people react to American society in the same manner as colonial peoples react to the West in Africa and Latin America, and had the same relationship—that of the colonized toward the colonizer.

41.

THE AGE OF AQUARIUS

The 1969 Woodstock Music Festival in Bethel, New York, marked the climax of the "youth culture" phenomenon of the 1960s. Partly a result of the unusually high proportion of Americans between the ages of fifteen and twenty-five and of their concentration in the country's burgeoning university system, the youth culture also represented a reaction against certain tendencies in post-Eisenhower America, particularly (in the words of the youth movement itself) authoritarianism, conformity, repression, and individual isolation. Radical politics, communal living, sexual spontaneity, and heavy drug use characterized the youth culture of the 1960s, along with long hair, blue jeans, and obscene language. But its real center of gravity, the cement holding it together, was almost certainly rock music.

Rock music, with its heavy beat, amplified electric guitars, and social lyrics, derived from the folk music of the 1950s and from the rhythm and blues of black musicians. One early synthesis came when folksinger Bob Dylan used an electric guitar and drums at the Newport Folk Festival of 1964; another came when the Beatles created an "acid rock" sound through distorted guitar amplification aimed at listeners under the influence of drugs. The outdoor rock concert, with its aura of natural community, soon became immensely popular, reaching a climax at the Woodstock Festival. By the early 1970s the youth culture was in decline, a victim in part of the backlash against drug abuse, the entertainment world's rampant commercialism, and the aging of its participants. Rock music lived on in a sanitized, nonpolitical form.

Patrick Lydon, a student at Yale University in 1969, was the New Haven correspondent of the **Boston Globe** at the time of Woodstock. In April 1970, while covering a New Haven rally of the controversial Black Panther party, Lydon had his notes confiscated by members of the Connecticut National Guard.

Questions to consider. Patrick Lydon's account of the Woodstock Festival is reprinted below. What aspects of the festival were most remarkable to Lydon: its musical brilliance, the size of the crowd, the crowd's camaraderie and good humor, or its sharing and spontaneous behavior? Why did he call police kindness and army food-drops "miracles"? Why did he believe the festival began as a symbolic protest? What was it protesting? What did it symbolize? What did Lydon's description of the Bethel townspeople and their reactions reveal about the festival's meaning? At the time, writers compared the spirit of Woodstock to that of (among other things) Massachusetts Bay Colony (Vol. 1, Document 4), Brook Farm (Vol. 1, Document 28), and the newly formed CIO (Document 28). Why were these various comparisons made? How valid were they?

═══════════

A Joyful Confirmation That Good Things *Can* Happen Here (1969)
Patrick Lydon

It all happened up at the farm and everything happened. Half a million kids—hippies, rock people, and even straights—ran up to the farm for a long weekend of rock 'n' roll music mixed with mud, no sleep, rain, drugs, more mud, and even more smiles. Too many people came to the Woodstock Festival but they came high and they only got higher.

It started on Route 17, hip cars passing bread to the cycle riders and waving "V" signs everywhere. Bethel townspeople gazed in awe at the streams of hippies, but they murmured "Peace" to the visitors, offered free water, and returned smiles. Everyone arrived to find the whole show was free. As the weekend went on, the miracles kept coming—the kindness of the scattered police, the "food-drop" by an Army helicopter and flowers from the sky. Yet faith makes miracles and it was the astonishing peace and joy of the youthful masses that brought happy results.

Before it became the greatest hippie demonstration of unity, the music was the focus of the festival. Friday was the folk night but the playing was plagued by rain and delays. Every artist was received with warmth because they all played well and because the listeners were glad of any music. Joan Baez closed the evening in the rain, but she roused the masses to join her in "We Shall Overcome."

Saturday brought continued rain, some despair, and greater crowds. The roads toward the site were jammed with cars—cars full of sleepers. Fields and forests of motley tents stretched on every side. As the morning wore on, the weather cleared and good energy seemed to come with the sun. The music started not long after one o'clock and slowly built in intensity and excellence. Once again the crowd gave every group a standing ovation. Saturday's closing series of the Grateful Dead, Creedence Clearwater Revival, Janis Joplin, Sly and the Family Stone, The Who and the Jefferson Airplane must be one of

Woodstock. Four hundred thousand people attended the Woodstock Festival in upstate New York, surviving rain and primitive facilities. The biggest names in popular music appeared, including Joan Baez, who started as a folk singer, Jimi Hendrix, one of the few black performers who made it big in the rock world, and the Jefferson Airplane, who epitomized rock's closeness to drugs and revolt. (Wide World Photo)

the great shows of rock 'n' roll history. Sly had the whole audience chanting "Higher" and raising "V" signs with their fingers. Pete Townshend of The Who had it spellbound with his dynamic finale. The Who brought in the dawn. The Airplane did not finish until after eight o'clock in the morning— over eighteen hours after the day's start.

The Sunday show was meant to start at 1 o'clock and most people slept on the field before the stage. In the easy atmosphere of timeless togetherness, waits didn't seem long. The show didn't begin until shortly before 3 and the cruel rain stopped it not long after 4. The site had dried slowly since Saturday morning, but it was quickly mud again. The rain came down hard for an hour but spirits held out bravely. A large part of the crowd took up tonic cans and banged them together, danced and chanted at the sky—"Sun's Comin'." By the time the sun was ready to come back, it had nearly set and the music was on again. The intensity of Saturday night was never recaptured, the rain and sleepless hours had drained off some enthusiasm, and drugs were running out. But each group played hard and well—the bands all seemed genuinely thrilled to be there. The long night ended with the humor of Sha-Na-Na and a disappointing set by Jimi Hendrix's new band. Even then, at 10 o'clock on Monday morning, there was universal good heart.

The music on stage was only a part of the weekend's activity. The art exhibit of painting and sculpture was rather small but interesting. Followers of Meher Baba, the Avatar, sat nude on a suspended rock testifying their faith. The Grateful Dead gave two independent concerts at the nearby Hog Farm. Despite the bad weather, hundreds of people went swimming.

Although it was consistently excellent, the music will not be what participants remember best. It was natural that a huge crowd should arrive in good spirits, laughing, getting together in the music that brought them, but that their good vibrations never broke was extraordinary. As the announcer on stage praised the crowd, and as the bands registered their excitement at playing for such a gathering, the crowd felt an increasing sense of good in itself. The free food given by the people of the Hog Farm held body and soul together, the Red Cross Station took care of those who were ill, and a special tent treated those who were on bum acid trips.

There was the joy of confirmation, the delight in accenting what others would give. Hippies had never been quite so successful together, never before had they so impressed the world that watched. The strength of the crowd seemed strongest in the hard rain on Sunday afternoon. To the banging of the cans, dancing hippies gave all of themselves. Instead of despairing at the discomfort of rain and mud, the crowd rejoiced in its power to resist the weather. One boy stood covered with mud, ornamented with refuse he found in it, yet overjoyed that he could make happiness for others.

Out of the mud came dancers, out of electrical failure came music, out of hunger came generosity. What began as a symbolic protest against American society ended as a joyful confirmation that good things can happen here, that Army men can raise a "V" sign, that country people can welcome city hippies. One of Hendrix's last numbers was "The Star Spangled Banner." Yes, most everything happened up on the farm.

42.

A COLD WAR BREAKTHROUGH

American diplomacy has centered on China as much as on the Soviet Union. A thriving China trade was a minor goal in America's war for independence and a major motive for acquiring California and its harbors during the Mexican War. China was also the main focus of John Hay's Open Door policy and helped determine America's Pacific strategy in the Spanish-American War. Finally, a prime U.S. concern after the Russian Revolution of 1917 was to avoid "losing China" to communism, either from internal insurrection or from Russian intervention. When the Chinese Communists did seize power in 1949, Washington took it as a major defeat for the United States and therefore a commensurate victory for the Soviets, a view apparently confirmed when the Soviet Union and China jointly supported North Korea and North Vietnam during the wars in Korea and Vietnam. Never did international communism seem more aggressively monolithic than in the years immediately after 1949, when the United States sought to isolate China internationally and backed one dictator after another in South Korea, South Vietnam, and Taiwan (Republic of China), all in the name of "containment."

Yet nationalism eventually reasserted itself, and before long a bitter falling-out between the Russian and the Chinese dictatorships occurred. By the 1960s the Soviet Union and China had resumed their historic national rivalry. Clearly, Communist China was no mere extension of the Kremlin and never had been. During the same decade the Chinese and the Russians competed bitterly for influence in the Third World and among European Communist parties, jockeyed for power in the Far East, and vilified each other. By 1970, more Russian troops guarded the Soviet border against China than against Western Europe. The way was open to rapprochement between the United States and China. In 1972, President Richard M. Nixon, seeking to end the Vietnamese conflict and find a possible counterweight to the Soviet Union, abandoned America's nonrecognition policy by visiting the People's Republic of China and paving the way for the establishment of friendly relations. The results of the trip were modest, as the following communiqué shows. But the trip represented a profound shift toward flexibility in dealing with Communist nations. By 1981, American corporations were investing in China, and the U.S. government was speaking of military aid. The close desire for relations with Beijing (Peking) quickly became an important feature of American diplomacy. One aspect of the cold war of the 1950s appeared to be over.

The new China policy was all the more dramatic because of Richard Nixon's reputation as a militant anticommunist. Born in 1913 to a middle-class California family, Nixon graduated from Whittier College in 1934 and from Duke University School of Law in 1937. He practiced law for several years and served in the U.S. Navy during World War II. In 1946 he defeated a Democratic incumbent for Congress by implying that the Communists secretly supported the man. In the House of Representatives he was zealous in investigating communism in government, and in 1950 he was elected to the Senate from California after again implying that the Communists supported his opponent. Two years later he became Dwight Eisenhower's running mate. He served as vice president for eight years and in 1960 lost the election for the presidency to John Kennedy. Then, in 1968, in an impressive comeback, he captured the Republican presidential nomination and went on to defeat the Democratic candidate in November. In 1971, he initiated U.S. troop withdrawal from Vietnam to de-escalate the war; a cease-fire was signed in 1973. In 1972 he won overwhelmingly in his bid for re-election. Nixon's administration was marked chiefly by bold foreign-policy initiatives, such as the China trip, and efforts to reach agreements with the Soviet Union on strategic arms limitations. In 1974, however, threatened with impeachment for abusing his powers of office, he was forced to resign.

Questions to consider. The United States–China communiqué is illuminating in its efforts to lay out acceptable differences and areas of common ground. In studying the American statement, for example, note the order in which the points are listed, beginning with security from aggression and the need for better communications despite different ideologies, then moving fairly briefly to Vietnam and Korea, and concluding finally with Japan, India, and Pakistan. Compare this and the cautious language in which it was laid out with the response by China. What were the most striking differences in the two lists and the language used? Why, for instance, did China's tone on Japan differ so radically from America's? What differences seem to have been most crucial? In the next section, what was the significance of the final sentence concerning "collusion" and "spheres of influence"? What guest, so to speak, threatened to crash the banquet? Taiwan presented perhaps the thorniest problem of all, greater even than Korea or Vietnam. What circumstances of the post–World War II era made Taiwan so delicate an issue? In Washington, many conservatives would attack the language of the communiqué as a "sellout" on the Taiwan question. Was it? Finally, compare this document with the U.S.–China Treaty of 1894 (Document 7) and the Rockhill memorandum of 1899 (Document 21). What does such a comparison say about the positions of China and the United States in the world today?

The United States–China
Communiqué of 1972

President Richard Nixon of the United States of America visited the People's Republic of China at the invitation of Premier Chou En-lai of the People's Republic of China from Feb. 21 to Feb. 28, 1972. Accompanying the President were Mrs. Nixon, U.S. Secretary of State William Rogers, Assistant to the President Dr. Henry Kissinger, and other American officials.

President Nixon met with Chairman Mao Tse-tung of the Communist party of China on Feb. 21. The two leaders had a serious and frank exchange of views on Sino-U.S. relations and world affairs.

During the visit, extensive, earnest and frank discussions were held between President Nixon and Premier Chou En-lai on the normalization of relations between the United States of America and the People's Republic of China, as well as on other matters of interest to both sides. In addition, Secretary of State William Rogers and Foreign Minister Chi Peng-fei held talks in the same spirit.

President Nixon and his party visited Peking and viewed cultural, industrial and agricultural sites, and they also toured Hangchow and Shanghai where, continuing discussions with Chinese leaders, they viewed similar places of interest.

The leaders of the People's Republic of China and the United States of America found it beneficial to have this opportunity, after so many years without contact, to present candidly to one another their views on a variety of issues. They reviewed the international situation in which important changes and great upheavals are taking place and expounded their respective positions and attitudes.

The U.S. side stated:

Peace in Asia and peace in the world requires efforts both to reduce immediate tensions and to eliminate the basic causes of conflict. The United States will work for a just and secure peace: just, because it fulfills the aspirations of peoples and nations for freedom and progress; secure, because it removes the danger of foreign aggression. The United States supports individual freedom and social progress for all the peoples of the world, free of outside pressure or intervention.

The United States believes that the effort to reduce tensions is served by improving communications between countries that have different ideologies so as to lessen the risks of confrontation through accident, miscalculation or misunderstanding. Countries should treat each other with mutual respect and

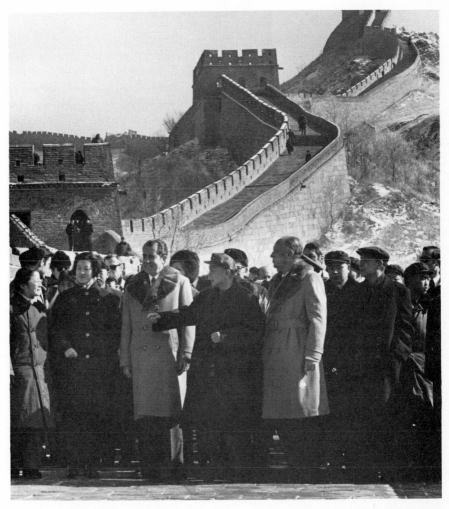

Richard Nixon in China. This photograph shows President Nixon (left center) with Chinese Deputy Premier Li Hsien-Nien (gesturing) at the Great Wall during Nixon's historic visit to the People's Republic of China in February 1972. Conceived partly to help end the Vietnam conflict and partly to balance Nixon's forthcoming trip to the Soviet Union, the China visit signaled U.S. acceptance of the Communist government in Beijing. It led to Chinese admission to the United Nations, Sino-American economic and cultural exchanges, and the eventual exchange of ambassadors. To the right of Li Hsien-Nien is Secretary of State William P. Rogers; absent is a key architect of the China initiative, National Security Adviser Henry Kissinger. (United Press International)

be willing to compete peacefully, letting performance be the ultimate judge. No country should claim infallibility and each country should be prepared to reexamine its own attitudes for the common good.

The United States stressed that the peoples of Indochina should be allowed to determine their destiny without outside intervention; its constant primary objective has been a negotiated solution; the eight-point proposal put forward by the Republic of Vietnam and the United States on Jan. 27, 1972, represents the basis for the attainment of that objective; in the absence of a negotiated settlement the United States envisages the ultimate withdrawal of all U.S. forces from the region consistent with the aim of self-determination for each country of Indochina.

The United States will maintain its close ties with and support for the Republic of Korea. The United States will support efforts of the Republic of Korea to seek a relaxation of tension and increase communications in the Korean peninsula. The United States places the highest value on its friendly relations with Japan; it will continue to develop the existing close bonds. Consistent with the United Nations Security Council Resolution of Dec. 21, 1971, the United States favors the continuation of the cease-fire between India and Pakistan and the withdrawal of all military forces to within their own territories and to their own sides of the cease-fire line in Jammu and Kashmir; the United States supports the right of the peoples of South Asia to shape their own future in peace, free of military threat, and without having the area become the subject of big-power rivalry.

The Chinese side stated:
Wherever there is oppression, there is resistance. Countries want independence, nations want liberation and the people want revolution—this has become the irresistible trend of history. All nations, big or small, should be equal; big nations should not bully the small and strong nations should not bully the weak. China will never be a superpower and it opposes hegemony and power politics of any kind.

The Chinese side stated that it firmly supports the struggles of all oppressed people and nations for freedom and liberation and that the people of all countries have the right to choose their social systems according to their own wishes and the right to safeguard the independence, sovereignty and territorial integrity of their own countries and oppose foreign aggression, interference, control and subversion. All foreign troops should be withdrawn to their own countries.

The Chinese side expressed its firm support to the peoples of Vietnam, Laos and Cambodia in their efforts for the attainment of their goals and its firm support to the seven-point proposal of the Provisional Revolutionary Government of the Republic of South Vietnam and the elaboration of February this year on the two key problems in the proposal, and to the Joint Declaration of the Summit Conference of the Indochinese Peoples.

It firmly supports the eight-point program for the peaceful unification of Korea put forward by the Government of the Democratic People's Republic of Korea on April 12, 1971, and the stand for the abolition of the "U.N. Commission for the Unification and Rehabilitation of Korea." It firmly opposes the revival and outward expansion of Japanese militarism and firmly supports the Japanese people's desire to build an independent Japan. It firmly maintains that India and Pakistan should, in accordance with the United Nations resolutions on the India-Pakistan question, immediately withdraw all their forces to their respective territories and to their own sides of the cease-fire line in Jammu and Kashmir and firmly supports the Pakistan Government and people in their struggle to preserve their independence and sovereignty and the people of Jammu and Kashmir in their struggle for the right of self-determination.

There are essential differences between China and the United States in their social systems and foreign policies. However, the two sides agreed that countries, regardless of their social systems, should conduct their relations on the principles of respect for the sovereignty and territorial integrity of all states, nonaggression against other states, noninterference in the internal affairs of other states, equality and mutual benefit, and peaceful coexistence. International disputes should be settled on this basis, without resorting to the use or threat of force. The United States and the People's Republic of China are prepared to apply these principles to their mutual relations.

With these principles of international relations in mind the two sides stated that:

Progress toward the normalization of relations between China and the United States is in the interests of all countries.

Both wish to reduce the danger of international military conflict.

Neither should seek hegemony in the Asia-Pacific region and each is opposed to the efforts by any other country or group of countries to establish such hegemony; and

Neither is prepared to negotiate on behalf of any third party or to enter into agreements or understandings with the other directed at other states.

Both sides are of the view that it would be against the interests of the peoples of the world for any major country to collude with another against other countries, or for major countries to divide up the world into spheres of interest.

The sides reviewed the long-standing serious disputes between China and the United States.

The Chinese side reaffirmed its position: The Taiwan question is the crucial question obstructing the normalization of relations between China and the United States; the Government of the People's Republic of China is the sole legal government of China; Taiwan is a province of China which has long been returned to the motherland; the liberation of Taiwan is China's internal affair in which no other country has the right to interfere; and all U.S. forces and military installations must be withdrawn from Taiwan. The Chinese government firmly opposes any activities which aim at the creation of "one China, one Taiwan," "one China, two governments," "two Chinas" and "Independent Taiwan" or advocate that "the status of Taiwan remains to be determined."

The U.S. side declared: The United States acknowledges that all Chinese on either side of the Taiwan Strait maintain there is but one China and that Taiwan is a part of China. The United States Government does not challenge that position. It reaffirms its interest in a peaceful settlement of the Taiwan question by the Chinese themselves. With this prospect in mind, it affirms the ultimate objective of the withdrawal of all U.S. forces and military installations from Taiwan. In the meantime, it will progressively reduce its forces and military installations on Taiwan as the tension in the area diminishes.

The two sides agreed that it is desirable to broaden the understanding between the two peoples. To this end, they discussed specific areas in such fields as science, technology, culture, sports and journalism, in which people-to-people contacts and exchanges would be mutually beneficial. Each side undertakes to facilitate the further development of such contacts and exchanges.

Both sides view bilateral trade as another area from which mutual benefits can be derived, and agree that economic relations based on equality and mutual benefit are in the interest of the peoples of the two countries. They agree to facilitate the progressive development of trade between their two countries.

The two sides agree that they will stay in contact through various channels, including the sending of a senior U.S. representative to Peking from time to time for concrete consultations to further the normalization of relations between the two countries and continue to exchange views on issues of common interest.

The two sides expressed the hope that the gains achieved during this visit would open up new prospects for the relations between the two countries. They believe that the normalization of relations between the two countries is not only in the interest of the Chinese and American peoples but also contributes to the relaxation of tension in Asia and the world.

President Nixon, Mrs. Nixon and the American party express their appreciation for the gracious hospitality shown them by the government and people of the People's Republic of China.

43.

WATERGATE

On June 17, 1972, five men were arrested for rifling the files and tapping the telephones of the Democratic National Committee in the Watergate office building in Washington, D.C. Thus was born the Watergate affair that transfixed the nation for the next two years. All five burglars, it turned out, were former agents of the Central Intelligence Agency (CIA). Two of the men, James McCord and G. Gordon Liddy, were currently working for the Committee to Re-elect the President (CRP or, popularly, CREEP), an independent organization supporting President Richard Nixon's bid for re-election. McCord and Liddy had connections with another former CIA agent, E. Howard Hunt, who, like Liddy, now served as a White House aide. The other burglars were Cubans who had been associated with the Bay of Pigs operation in Cuba.

After the trial and conviction of the five burglars, McCord broke silence by indicating, first, that the head of CRP himself, none other than former Attorney General John N. Mitchell, had approved the break-in and, second, that White House agents had paid "hush money" to the burglars. Newspaper reporters, the Federal Bureau of Investigation, and a special Senate committee on campaign practices opened investigations and soon learned that CRP had used extortionist tactics to raise an illegal slush fund from businesspersons and corporations for the 1972 presidential campaign, and that CRP had used this fund to pay for burglaries, wiretaps, forgeries, phony demonstrations, and other "dirty tricks" to discredit and punish Nixon critics.

By the summer of 1973 it was clear that President Nixon's closest aides, including advisers H. R. Haldeman and John D. Ehrlichman and counsel John W. Dean, had tried to interfere with the Watergate investigations and were withholding valuable evidence, notably tapes of White House conversations during the period under question. When the Senate committee, wondering who (including President Nixon) knew what, requested access to the tapes, Nixon pleaded executive privilege and refused to release them; and when Archibald Cox, a special Watergate prosecutor whom Nixon had appointed, asked for the tapes, the president ordered Cox's dismissal, even though several Justice Department officials resigned in protest.

During the next few months more than thirty former Nixon advisers were indicted for federal crimes, including Dean, Ehrlichman, Haldeman, Mitchell, and former Secretary of Commerce and CRP finance chairman Maurice Stans. The House Judiciary Committee began preparing articles of impeachment against the president. On August 4, 1974, the Supreme Court ordered Nixon to release the tapes, which investigators, hoping to unearth the "smoking pistol" (direct evidence, if it existed, that the president himself had authorized the cover-up), were eager to examine.

As suggested in the brief excerpts reprinted below, the tapes did indeed provide such evidence. According to the June 1972 conversations, Nixon knew of the Watergate break-in forty-eight hours after it happened; he also withheld evidence, authorized bribes, and used the FBI and the CIA to thwart Congressional investigators. The September 1972 excerpt suggests Nixon's intent, in the aftermath of Watergate, to use the FBI and the Justice Department against the administration's enemies. In March 1973, the president elaborated on the nature of his enemies. A week later, in response to Dean's concern about washing money—"the sort of thing Mafia people can do"—for paying blackmail, Nixon replied that the money could be obtained. With such conversations made public and facing almost certain impeachment, Richard Nixon announced his resignation of the presidency on August 8, 1974. In the end, Nixon's bold diplomacy in foreign affairs seemed swallowed up by domestic sordidness.

Questions to consider. The Watergate episode, as revealed in these tape transcriptions, illustrated the remarkable size and complexity of the White House staff and executive bureaucracy in the last third of this century; the constant, almost casual resort to the new technology of wiretapping and secret surveillance; and the phenomenal importance of money in high-level politics and the apparent ease of raising it. Might these features of the modern presidency have tended in themselves to promote the kind of domineering mentality that characterized the Nixon White House? Did the fact that Nixon felt assailed (not unlike Senator Joseph McCarthy—Document 32) by "upper intellectual types" and a "dying" establishment affect his actions? How prominently did activist, Kennedy-style cold war attitudes and habits—the use of CIA operatives, references to the Bay of Pigs and national security—figure in the episode? Do future Watergate threats lie mainly in the nature of the modern presidency, or mainly in a special combination of anticommunism and status anxiety that may have been unique to Richard Nixon?

White House Conversations (1972–1973)

June 23, 1972

HALDEMAN: Now, on the investigation, you know the Democratic breakin thing, we're back in the problem area because the FBI is not under control, because [Director Patrick] Gray doesn't exactly know how to control it and they have—their investigation is now leading into some productive areas. . . . They've been able to trace the money—not through the money itself—but through the bank sources—the banker. And it goes in some directions we don't want it to go. Ah, also there have been some [other] things—like an informant came in off the street to the FBI in Miami who was a photographer or has a friend who is a photographer who developed some films through this guy [Bernard] Barker and the films had pictures of Democratic National Committee letterhead documents and things. So it's things like that that are filtering in. . . . [John] Mitchell came up with yesterday, and John Dean analyzed very carefully last night and concludes, concurs now with Mitchell's recommendation that the only way to solve this . . . is for us to have [CIA Assistant Director Vernon] Walters call Pat Gray and just say, "Stay to hell out of this—this is ah, [our] business here. We don't want you to go any further on it." That's not an unusual development, and ah, that would take care of it.

PRESIDENT: What about Pat Gray—you mean Pat Gray doesn't want to?

HALDEMAN: Pat does want to. He doesn't know how to, and he doesn't have any basis for doing it. Given this, he will then have the basis. He'll call [FBI Assistant Director] Mark Felt in, and the two of them—and Mark Felt wants to cooperate because he's ambitious—

PRESIDENT: Yeah.

HALDEMAN: He'll call him in and say, "We've got the signal from across the river to put the hold on this." And that will fit rather well because the FBI agents who are working the case, at this point, feel that's what it is.

PRESIDENT: This is CIA? They've traced the money? Who'd they trace it to?

HALDEMAN: Well, they've traced it to a name, but they haven't gotten to the guy yet.

PRESIDENT: Would it be somebody here?

HALDEMAN: Ken Dahlberg.

PRESIDENT: Who the hell is Ken Dahlberg?

HALDEMAN: He gave $25,000 in Minnesota and, ah, the check went directly to this guy Barker.

PRESIDENT: It isn't from the Committee though, from [Maurice] Stans?

HALDEMAN: Yeah. It is. It's directly traceable and there's some more through some Texas people that went to the Mexican bank which can also be traced to the Mexican bank—they'll get their names today.

From **Hearings Before the Committee on the Judiciary,** House of Representatives, 93rd Congress, 2nd Session (Government Printing Office, Washington, D.C., 1974).

PRESIDENT: Well, I mean, there's no way—I'm just thinking if they don't cooperate, what do they say? That they were approached by the Cubans? That's what Dahlberg has to say, the Texans too.

HALDEMAN: Well, if they will. But then we're relying on more and more people all the time. That's the problem and they'll [the FBI] . . . stop if we could take this other route.

PRESIDENT: All right.

HALDEMAN: [Mitchell and Dean] say the only way to do that is from White House instructions. And it's got to be to [CIA Director Richard] Helms and to—ah, what's his name? . . . Walters.

PRESIDENT: Walters.

HALDEMAN: And the proposal would be that . . . [John] Ehrlichman and I call them in, and say, ah—

PRESIDENT: All right, fine. How do you call him in—I mean you just—well, we protected Helms from one hell of a lot of things.

HALDEMAN: That's what Ehrlichman says.

PRESIDENT: Of course; this [Howard] Hunt [business.] That will uncover a lot of things. You open that scab there's a hell of a lot of things and we just feel that it would be very detrimental to have this thing go any further. This involves these Cubans, Hunt, and a lot of hanky-panky that we have nothing to do with ourselves. Well, what the hell, did Mitchell know about this?

HALDEMAN: I think so. I don't think he knew the details, but I think he knew.

PRESIDENT: He didn't know how it was going to be handled though—with Dahlberg and the Texans and so forth? Well who was the asshole that did? Is it [G. Gordon] Liddy? Is that the fellow? He must be a little nuts!

HALDEMAN: He is.

PRESIDENT: I mean he just isn't well screwed on, is he? Is that the problem?

HALDEMAN: No, but he was under pressure, apparently, to get more information, and as he got more pressure, he pushed the people harder.

PRESIDENT: Pressure from Mitchell?

HALDEMAN: Apparently. . . .

PRESIDENT: All right, fine, I understand it all. We won't second-guess Mitchell and the rest. Thank God it wasn't [special White House counsel Charles] Colson.

HALDEMAN: The FBI interviewed Colson yesterday. They determined that would be a good thing to do. To have him take an interrogation, which he did, and the FBI guys working the case concluded that there were one or two possibilities—one, that this was a White House (they don't think that there is anything at the Election Committee) they think it was either a White House operation and they had some obscure reasons for it—non-political, or it was a—Cuban [operation] and [involved] the CIA. And after their interrogation of Colson yesterday, they concluded it was not the White House, but are now convinced it is a CIA thing, so the CIA turnoff would—

PRESIDENT: Well, not sure of their analysis, I'm not going to get that involved. I'm (unintelligible).

HALDEMAN: No, sir, we don't want you to.

PRESIDENT: You call them in.

HALDEMAN: Good deal.

PRESIDENT: Play it tough. That's the way they play it and that's the way we are going to play it. . . .

*   *   *

PRESIDENT: O.K. . . . Just say (unintelligible) very bad to have this fellow Hunt, ah, he knows too damned much. . . . If it gets out that this is all involved, the Cuba thing, it would be a fiasco. It would make the CIA look bad, it's going to make Hunt look bad, and it is likely to blow the whole Bay of Pigs thing which we think would be very unfortunate—both for CIA, and for the country, at this time, and for American foreign policy. Just tell him to lay off. Don't you [think] so?

HALDEMAN: Yep. That's the basis to do it on. Just leave it at that. . . .

September 15, 1972

PRESIDENT: We are all in it together. This is a war. We take a few shots and it will be over. We will give them a few shots and it will be over. Don't worry. I wouldn't want to be on the other side right now. Would you?

DEAN: Along that line, one of the things I've tried to do, I have begun to keep notes on a lot of people who are emerging as less than our friends because this will be over some day and we shouldn't forget the way some of them have treated us.

PRESIDENT: I want the most comprehensive notes on all those who tried to do us in. They didn't have to do it. If we had had a very close election and they were playing the other side I would understand this. No—they were doing this quite deliberately and they are asking for it and they are going to get it. We have not used the power in this first four years, as you know. We have never used it. We have not used the Bureau, and we have not used the Justice Department, but things are going to change now. And they are either going to do it right or go.

DEAN: What an exciting prospect.

PRESIDENT: Thanks. It has to be done. We have been (adjective deleted) fools for us to come into this election campaign and not do anything with regard to the Democratic Senators who are running, et cetera. And who the hell are they after? They are after us. It is absolutely ridiculous. It is not going to be that way any more.

March 13, 1973

PRESIDENT: How much of a crisis? It will be—I am thinking in terms of—the point is, everything is a crisis. (expletive deleted) it is a terrible lousy

President Nixon's resignation. Richard M. Nixon, with his wife and daughter at his side, gives a thumbs-up sign to members of his staff on August 9, 1974. On that day his resignation from the presidency as a result of the Watergate affair took effect. Though departing solely to avoid impeachment and still facing possible criminal prosecution, Nixon spent this day insisting on his service to America and recalling his great diplomatic triumphs. In September, Gerald Ford, having assumed the presidency, granted Nixon a full pardon for "offenses" against the United States. Nixon's top three aides went to prison. (Wide World Photo)

thing—it will remain a crisis among the upper intellectual types, the soft heads, our own, too—Republicans—and the Democrats and the rest. Average people won't think it is much of a crisis unless it affects them. (unintelligible)

DEAN: I think it will pass. I think after the [Senator Sam] Ervin hearings, they are going to find so much—there will be some new revelations. I don't think that the thing will get out of hand. I have no reason to believe it will.

PRESIDENT: As a matter of fact, it is just a bunch of (characterization deleted). We don't object to such damn things anyway. On, and on and on.

No, I tell you this it is the last gasp of our hardest opponents. They've just got to have something to squeal about it.

DEAN: It is the only thing they have to squeal—

PRESIDENT: (Unintelligible) They are going to lie around and squeal. They are having a hard time now. They got the hell kicked out of them in the election. There is not a Watergate around in this town, not so much our opponents, even the media, but the basic thing is the establishment. The establishment is dying, and so they've got to show that despite the successes we have had in foreign policy and in the election, they've got to show that it is just wrong, just because of this. They are trying to use this as the whole thing.

March 21, 1973

DEAN: So that is it. That is the extent of the knowledge. So where are the soft spots on this? Well, first of all, there is the problem of the continued blackmail which will not only go on now, but it will go on while these people are in prison, and it will compound the obstruction of justice situation. It will cost money. It is dangerous. People around here are not pros at this sort of thing. This is the sort of thing Mafia people can do: washing money, getting clean money, and things like that. We just don't know about those things, because we are not criminals and not used to dealing in that business.

PRESIDENT: That's right.

DEAN: It is a tough thing to know how to do.

PRESIDENT: Maybe it takes a gang to do that.

DEAN: That's right. There is a real problem as to whether we could even do it. Plus there is a real problem in raising money. Mitchell has been working on raising some money. He is one of the ones with the most to lose. But there is no denying the fact that the White House, in Ehrlichman, Haldeman and Dean, are involved in some of the early money decisions.

PRESIDENT: How much money do you need?

DEAN: I would say these people are going to cost over a million dollars over the next two years.

PRESIDENT: We could get that. On the money, if you need the money you could get that. You could get a million dollars. You could get it in cash. I know where it could be gotten. It is not easy, but it could be done. But the question is who the hell would handle it? Any ideas on that?

DEAN: That's right. Well, I think that is something that Mitchell ought to be charged with.

PRESIDENT: I would think so too.

44.

WOMEN'S LIBERATION

No recent movement has had greater impact than the campaign for women's rights. After its bright triumph of the early 1920s, interest in the movement had lagged. Probably the resurgence started because of a trend in the work force: 27 percent of adult women worked outside the home in 1940, 33 percent in 1960, and 50 percent in 1980. With so many women in the work force, their concerns began to be heard: equal pay for equal work; managerial positions in heretofore all-male dominated companies; and elimination of sexual and physical harassment. Over half of these women workers, moreover, were married, and almost a third had children. Working wives, it turned out, often strained traditional male-dominant marriages, and both the divorce rate and the need for new childcare arrangements increased. Also, married or not, working women saw their lives turning less exclusively around children and domesticity; they therefore looked increasingly to modern birth control devices and to abortion (the Supreme Court declared abortion legal in 1973). The birth rate decreased 50 percent from 1960 to 1980.

The true feminist or women's liberation movement came, however, with the addition of "consciousness raising" to these socioeconomic trends. Thus Betty Friedan's **Feminine Mystique,** published in 1963, attacked the mass media for brainwashing women into models of domesticity, and the National Organization for Women (NOW), created in 1966, pressed for the elimination of all discriminatory legal sexual distinctions. Politics witnessed (a half-century after the suffrage amendment) major gains: women governors in Washington, Kentucky, Vermont, and Connecticut; senators from Florida and Kansas; mayors in Chicago, San Francisco, and Houston; three cabinet officers in the Carter administration and one in the Reagan administration; a Supreme Court justice; and a Democratic party vice-presidential candidate.

Some feminists, meanwhile, labored to erase cultural stereotypes, such as producing schoolbooks in which men sometimes did housework and women flew airplanes, or substituting the word **chair** for **chairman** at meetings. Others took a more exclusive route, forming women's support groups to deal with women's concerns, particularly health care and sexuality. Reprinted below, representing the latter trend, is the preface by Vilunya Diskin and Wendy Coppedge Sanford to **Our Bodies, Ourselves: A Book by and for Women,** first published commercially in 1973 by the Boston Women's Health Book Collective. Already translated into eight languages, with massive clinic and public sales, the book is arguably the most influential ever published in terms of explaining the female body to women and in helping women deal with their femaleness; the preface explains the ideas and experiences that produced the book.

Vilunya Diskin graduated from the University of California at Los Angeles in 1963 and from the Harvard School of Public Health in 1981. She lives in Lexington, Massachusetts, and in addition to writing, she has served on the boards of the American Public Health Association and the Population Association of America. Wendy Coppedge Sanford graduated from Radcliffe in 1967 and the Harvard Divinity School in 1980. She lives in Cambridge, Massachusetts, where she writes on health and sexuality. Both Diskin and Sanford continue to be active in the Boston Women's Health Book Collective, which operates a women's health information center.

Questions to consider. Consider, in studying this preface, the clear, quiet tone of the writing, so different from the strident, alienating rhetoric of some feminists of the time. Why did the authors take such care to maintain this calm, straightforward style? In what ways was this tone essential to their purpose? Consider, too, the group's early rejection of doctor-patient or teacher-student relationships. Why was it important to avoid these? Was a "collective"—leaderless, consensual, mutually supportive—the best or only means to do so? Or did the spirit of the times (recall here Stokely Carmichael [Document 40] and Patrick Lydon [Document 41]) virtually dictate the "collective" response? Note also the authors' justification of their women-only approach. Was it understandable? Justifiable? Persuasive? Finally, why did this path of "body discovery" prove so liberating for the authors and, presumably, for millions of readers?

Preface to *Our Bodies, Ourselves* (1973)
Vilunya Diskin and Wendy Coppedge Sanford

The history of this book, *Our Bodies, Ourselves,* is lengthy and satisfying.

It began in a small discussion group on "women and their bodies" which was part of a women's conference held in Boston in the spring of 1969, one of the first gatherings of women meeting specifically to talk with other women. For many of us it was the very first time we had joined together with other women to talk and think about our lives and what we could do about them. Before the conference was over, some of us decided to keep on meeting as a group to continue the discussion, and so we did.

In the beginning we called ourselves "the doctors group." We had all experienced similar feelings of frustration and anger toward specific doctors and the medical maze in general, and initially we wanted to do something about those doctors who were condescending, paternalistic, judgmental and non-informative. As we talked and shared our experiences with one another, we realized just how much we had to learn about our bodies. So we decided on a summer project—to research those topics which we felt were particularly pertinent to learning about our bodies, to discuss in the group what we had learned, then to write papers individually or in groups of two or three, and finally to present the results in the fall as a course for women on women and their bodies.

As we developed the course we realized more and more that we really *were* capable of collecting, understanding and evaluating medical information. Together we evaluated our reading of books and journals, our talks with doctors and friends who were medical students. We found we could discuss, question and argue with each other in a new spirit of cooperation rather than competition. We were equally struck by how important it was for us to be able to open up with one another and share our feelings about our bodies. The process of talking was as crucial as the facts themselves. Over time the facts and feelings melted together in ways that touched us very deeply, and that is reflected in the changing titles of the course and then the book—from *Women and Their Bodies* to *Women and Our Bodies* to, finally, *Our Bodies, Ourselves*.

When we gave the course we met in any available free space we could get—in day schools, in nursery schools, in churches, in our homes. We wanted the course to stimulate the same kind of talking and sharing that we who had prepared the course had experienced. We had something to say, but we had a lot to learn as well; we did not want a traditional teacher-student relationship. At the end of ten to twelve sessions—which roughly covered the material in the current book—we found that many women felt both eager and competent to get together in small groups and share what they had learned with other women. We saw it as a never-ending process always involving more and more women.

After the first teaching of the course, we decided to revise our initial papers and mimeograph them so that other women could have copies as the course expanded. Eventually we got them printed and bound together in an inexpensive edition published by the New England Free Press. It was fascinating and very exciting for us to see what a constant demand there was for our book. It came out in several editions, a larger number being printed each time, and the time from one printing to the next becoming shorter. The growing volume of requests began to strain the staff of the New England Free Press. Since our book was clearly speaking to many people, we wanted to reach beyond the audience who lived in the area or who were acquainted with the New England Free Press. For wider distribution it made sense to publish our book commercially.

You may want to know who we are. Our ages range from twenty-five to forty-one, most of us are from middle-class backgrounds and have had at least some college education, and some of us have professional degrees. Some of us are married, some of us are separated, and some of us are single. Some of us have children of our own, some of us like spending time with children, and others of us are not sure we want to be with children. In short, we are both a very ordinary and a very special group, as women are everywhere. We can describe only what life has been for us, though many of our experiences have been shared by other women. We realize that poor and nonwhite women have had greater difficulty in getting accurate information and adequate health care, and have most often been mistreated in the ways we describe in this book. Learning about our womanhood from the inside out has allowed us to cross over some of the socially created barriers of race, color, income and class, and to feel a sense of identity with all women in the experience of being female.

We are eleven individuals and we are a group. (The group has been ongoing for three years, and some of us have been together since the beginning. Others came in at later points. Our current collective has been together for one year.) We know each other well—our weaknesses as well as our strengths. We have learned through good times and bad how to work together (and how not to, as well). We recognize our similarities and differences and are learning to respect each person for her uniqueness. We love each other.

Many, many other women have worked with us on the book. A group of gay women got together specifically to do the chapter on lesbianism. Other chapters were done still differently. For instance, the mother of one woman in the group volunteered to work on menopause with some of us who have not gone through that experience ourselves. Other women contributed thoughts, feelings and comments as they passed through town or passed through our kitchens or workrooms. There are still other voices from letters, phone conversations, and a variety of discussions that are included in the chapters as excerpts of personal experiences. Many women have spoken for themselves in this book, though we in the collective do not agree with all that has been written. Some of us are even uncomfortable with part of the material. We have included it anyway, because we give more weight to accepting that we differ than to our uneasiness. We have been asked why this is exclusively a book about women, why we have restricted our course to women. Our answer is that we are women and, as women, do not consider ourselves experts on men (as men through the centuries have presumed to be experts on us). We are not implying that we think most twentieth-century men are much less alienated from their bodies than women are. But we know it is up to men to explore that for themselves as we have done. We would like to read a book about men and their bodies.

We are offering a book that can be used in many different ways—individually, in a group, for a course. Our book contains real material about our bodies and ourselves that isn't available elsewhere, and we have tried to present it in a new way—an honest, humane and powerful way of thinking about ourselves and our lives. We want to share the knowledge and power that come with this way of thinking, and we want to share the feelings we have for each other—supportive and loving feelings that show we can indeed help one another grow.

From the very beginning of working together, first on the course that led to this book and then on the book itself, we have felt exhilarated and energized by our new knowledge. Finding out about our bodies and our bodies' needs, starting to take control over that area of our lives, has released for us an energy that has overflowed into our work, our friendships, our relationships with men and women, and for some of us, our marriages and our parenthood. In trying to figure out why this has had such a life-changing effect on us, we have come up with several important ways in which this kind of body education has been liberating for us and may be a starting point for the liberation of many other women.

First, we learned what we learned equally from professional sources—textbooks, medical journals, doctors, nurses—and from our own experiences. The facts were important, and we did careful research to get the information we had not had in the past. As we brought the facts to one another we learned a good deal, but in sharing our personal experiences relating to those facts we learned still more. Once we had learned what the "experts" had to tell us, we found that we still had a lot to teach and to learn from one another. For instance, many of us had "learned" about the menstrual cycle in science or biology classes—we had perhaps even memorized the names of the menstrual hormones and what they did. But most of us did not remember much of what we had learned. This time when we read in a text that the onset of menstruation is a normal and universal occurrence in young girls from ages ten to eighteen, we started to talk about our first menstrual periods. We found that, for many of us, beginning to menstruate had not felt normal at all, but scary, embarrassing, mysterious. We realized that what we had been told about menstruation and what we had not been told—even the tone of voice it had been told in—had all had an effect on our feelings about being female. Similarly, the information from enlightened texts describing masturbation as a normal, common sexual activity did not really become our own until we began to pull up from inside ourselves and share what we had never before expressed—the confusion and shame we had been made to feel, and often still felt, about touching our bodies in a sexual way.

Learning about our bodies in this way is an exciting kind of learning, where information and feelings are allowed to interact. It makes the difference between rote memorization and relevant learning, between fragmented pieces of a puzzle and the integrated picture, between abstractions and real knowledge. We discovered that people don't learn very much when they are just passive recipients of information. We found that each individual's response to information was valid and useful, and that by sharing our responses we could develop a base on which to be critical of what the experts tell us. Whatever we need to learn now, in whatever area of our lives, we know more how to go about it.

A second important result of this kind of learning is that we are better prepared to evaluate the institutions that are supposed to meet our health needs—the hospitals, clinics, doctors, medical schools, nursing schools, public health departments, Medicaid bureaucracies and so on. For some of us it was the first time we had looked critically, and with strength, at the existing institutions serving us. The experience of learning just how little control we had over our lives and bodies, the coming together out of isolation to learn from each other in order to define what we needed, and the experience of supporting one another in demanding the changes that grew out of our developing critique—all were crucial and formative political experiences for us. We have felt our potential power as a force for political and social change.

The learning we have done while working on *Our Bodies, Ourselves* has been a good basis for growth in other areas of life for still another reason. For women throughout the centuries, ignorance about our bodies has had one major consequence—pregnancy. Until very recently pregnancies were all but inevitable, biology *was* our destiny—that is, because our bodies are designed to get pregnant and give birth and lactate, that is what all or most of us did. The courageous and dedicated work of people like Margaret Sanger started in the early twentieth century to spread and make available birth control methods that women could use, thereby freeing us from the traditional lifetime of pregnancies. But the societal expectation that a woman above all else will have babies does not die easily. When we first started talking to each other about this, we found that that old expectation had nudged most of us into a fairly rigid role of wife-and-motherhood from the moment we were born female. Even in 1969, when we first started the work that led to this book, we found that many of us were still getting pregnant when we didn't want to. It was not until we researched carefully and learned more about our reproductive systems, about birth-control methods and abortion, about laws governing birth control and abortion, and not until we put all this information together with what it meant to us to be female, that we began to feel we could truly set out to control whether and when we would have babies.

This knowledge has freed us to a certain extent from the constant, energy-draining anxiety about becoming pregnant. It has made our pregnancies better because they no longer happen to us, but we actively choose them and enthusiastically participate in them. It had made our parenthood better because it is our choice rather than our destiny. This knowledge has freed us from playing the role of mother if it is not a role that fits us. It has given us a sense of a larger life space to work in, an invigorating and challenging sense of time and room to discover the energies and talents that are in us, to do the work we want to do. And one of the things we most want to do is to help make this freedom of choice, this life span, available to every woman. This is why people in the women's movement have been so active in fighting against the inhumane legal restrictions, the imperfections of available contraceptives, the poor sex education, the highly priced and poorly administered health care that keep too many women from having this crucial control over their bodies.

There is a fourth reason why knowledge about our bodies has generated so much new energy. For us, body education is core education. Our bodies are the physical bases from which we move out into the world; ignorance, uncertainty—even, at worst, shame—about our physical selves create in us an alienation from ourselves that keeps us from being the whole people that we could be. Picture a woman trying to do work and to enter into equal and satisfying relationships with other people—when she feels physically weak because she has never tried to be strong; when she drains her energy trying to change her face, her figure, her hair, her smells, to match some ideal norm set by magazines, movies and TV; when she feels confused and ashamed of the menstrual blood that every month appears from some dark place in her body; when her internal body processes are a mystery to her and surface only to cause her trouble (an unplanned pregnancy, or cervical cancer); when she does not understand or enjoy sex and concentrates her sexual drives into aimless romantic fantasies, perverting and misusing a potential energy because she has been brought up to deny it. Learning to understand, accept, and be responsible for our physical selves, we are freed of some of these preoccupations and can start to use our untapped energies. Our image of ourselves is on a firmer base, we can be better friends and better lovers, better *people,* more self-confident, more autonomous, stronger and more whole.

45.

TECHNOLOGY UNBOUND

After population growth, cheap land, and bountiful resources, it was technological innovation—the work of creative individuals such as Eli Whitney, Isaac M. Singer, Andrew Carnegie (Document 14), and Henry Ford—that was the driving force of American industrialization. After World War II, modern industries like petrochemicals, aerospace, and electronics helped power an unprecedented twenty-five years of almost uninterrupted growth in real national income. At every hand, it seemed, technology yielded products of prosperity: plastics and pharmaceuticals, satellites and jetliners, televisions and computers.

By the 1970s, however, doubts had appeared concerning the benefits of technology. These doubts stemmed in part from the "oil shocks" of 1973 and 1979, when exploding petroleum prices produced not only stagflation—a combination of high unemployment and rising prices—but concern about whether science could discover usable substitutes for hydrocarbon fuels. Another source of doubt came from fear that technology was destructive as well as creative. Evidenced by a spreading ecology movement, this fear centered chiefly on nuclear-powered electric plants with their radiation dangers and on the petrochemical industry, whose "unnatural" nonbiodegradable products and byproducts polluted the nation's air, water, and soil.

Despite the passage of Clean Air and Water Acts and the establishment of the Environmental Protection Agency (1970) and the Nuclear Regulatory Commission (1975), concern did not reach a peak until early 1979 when the discovery of a toxic chemical dump (called, ironically, Love Canal) led to the partial evacuation of a town in upstate New York and when the near meltdown of the Three Mile Island nuclear plant near Harrisburg, Pennsylvania, sent tremors of anxiety through that region. The first selection below, reprinted from the "Notes and Comment" section of the **New Yorker** magazine, illustrates the public reaction to the Three Mile Island ordeal, which resulted in killing plans to build more nuclear plants and intensified technological fears, at least toward nuclear power.

A final source of technological doubt concerned not whether we could find new energy supplies or could avoid poisoning ourselves but whether, given continuing stagflation and the success of foreign competitors such as Germany and Japan, the United States was technologically competitive—that is, was technological **enough.** The second selection reprinted below (by physicist Robert Jastrow) summarizes these concerns and provides an answer that was characteristic of the early 1980s, when many of the novel technologies Jastrow mentions were first becoming known to the general public.

"Notes and Comment," where the "Three Mile Island" remarks appeared, is a regular anonymous feature of the **New Yorker,** one of America's most literate, stylish, and genteel publications. Robert Jastrow was founder of the Goddard Institute for Space Studies of the National Aeronautics and Space Administration and chairman of the committee that set priorities for the early investigations of the moon. Once called "one of the rare scientists with the gift of making the unimaginable imaginable," Jastrow is currently professor of earth science at Dartmouth College. His books include **Red Giants and White Dwarfs** and **God and the Astronomers.**

Questions to consider. In reading "Three Mile Island," consider why words such as "forever" and "human error" had so great an impact. Consider, too, the relevance to the Three Mile Island affair of the following documents: Patrick Lydon on Woodstock (Document 41), the preface to **Our Bodies, Ourselves** (Document 44), and John Hersey on Hiroshima (Document 30). Remember also that Upton Sinclair had described the ravages of technology as early as 1906 (Document 16). How do the tone and intent of **The Jungle** differ from the tone and intent of "Three Mile Island"?

In reading "Science and the American Dream," consider four questions in particular. First, with whom does it appear that Jastrow was arguing in this essay? Second, can Jastrow be accurately placed within the tradition of probusiness, proindustry writers such as Alexander Hamilton (Vol. 1, Document 15) and Andrew Carnegie (Document 14)? Third, can Jastrow be accurately fitted into the conventional liberal or conservative categories of modern American politics? Finally, if Jastrow's argument is correct, how reassuring are Americans likely to find it? Would his argument reassure some people more than others?

Three Mile Island (1979)

A recent headline in the *Washington Post* concerning the afflicted nuclear power plant on Three Mile Island, in Pennsylvania, read, "Aides Wonder If Contamination May Close Plant Forever." The plant may have been rendered permanently inoperable, the story that followed explained, because of the release into the reactor-containment chamber of large quantities of radioactive isotopes, some of which will remain dangerous for as much as a thousand years. And within the reactor there are damaged fuel rods containing radioactive elements with half-lives of some twenty-four thousand years. That "Forever" stood out on the page; we could not remember having seen the word used in a newspaper headline before. (In human terms, twenty-four thousand years—roughly five times the span of recorded history, or the equivalent of almost a thousand generations of men—is forever.) Journalism has always dealt with what is historical and is therefore transient—even empires rise and decline—but now the papers were discussing a future of incomprehensible remoteness, as though they had given up on human affairs and instead interested themselves in the doings of immortal beings. The appearance in news stories of words like "forever" is one more clear signal, if we still need it, that with the discovery of nuclear energy events of a new order of magnitude, belonging to a new dimension of time, have broken into the stream of history. In unleashing nuclear chain reactions, we have brought a cosmic force, virtually never found in terrestrial nature, onto the earth—a force that, both in its visible, violent form of nuclear explosions and in its invisible, impalpable form of radiation, is alien and dangerous to earthly life, and can, through damage to life's genetic foundation, break the very frame on which the generations of mankind are molded. In the midst of the ups and downs of human fortunes, decisions of everlasting consequence have presented themselves. Last week, these decisions were being made in Pennsylvania. "We all live in Pennsylvania!" West German anti-nuclear demonstrators shouted in an inversion of President Kennedy's famous declaration *"Ich bin ein Berliner."* The danger of extinction is posed above all by nuclear war, but it was nevertheless symbolized during last week's disaster by the evacuation of children and pregnant women—who represent the future generations—from the vicinity of the plant. The lesson was plain: when atomic fission is brought in, the human future is driven out.

Another headline that caught our attention was one in the *News* which read, "Human Error Probed In Leak." The concept of "human error" has cropped up often during the Pennsylvania crisis. The alleged error referred to in the *News* story was an operator's decision to turn off a certain cooling

From "Notes and Comment," **The New Yorker** (April 9, 1979), 25. Reprinted by permission; ©1979 The New Yorker Magazine Inc.

Three Mile Island. The towers of the Three Mile Island nuclear plant near Harrisburg, Pennsylvania, became sinister symbols after they sprang radioactive leaks in the spring of 1979. The Three Mile Island episode probably struck special terror into American hearts because it coincided with the appearance of **The China Syndrome,** a movie about a nuclear power near-disaster. Hollywood, in fact, had conditioned people to fear radiation as early as the 1950s with movies about mutant monsters—giant ants, flies, bees, and locusts, to name a few. (Wide World Photo)

system at an untimely moment, and this was contrasted with possible "technical" errors that could supposedly be made by machinery alone. But, even assuming that operators made mistakes, the question remains of who designed the plant in such a way that one or two untimely decisions could lead to a complete breakdown. Gods did not design the plant; human beings, each one as capable of error as any operator, did. That being so, it appears that the larger human error must lie in the decision to build plants of that design in the first place. But even this conclusion is too narrow—fails to get to the bottom of this matter of human error. The most striking aspect of the Pennsylvania disaster was not that a very unlikely (or "astronomically improbable," as the advocates of nuclear energy used to like to say) series of events occurred but that so many *entirely unpredicted* problems developed, the most important one to date being, of course, the sudden appearance inside the reactor of the explosive hydrogen bubble, which Harold Denton, the chief of reactor regulation for the Nuclear Regulatory Commission, called "a new twist." Events at the plant have turned out to be not at all like the well-ordered scenarios of the nuclear experts but, instead, to be like almost everything else in life—full of new twists. And the surprises within the plant were compounded by rumor and misinformation outside it, so that even when the scientists at the plant were in possession of reliable technical information Governor Richard Thornburgh, who had final responsibility for the lives of the people in the area, often was not. "There are a number of conflicting versions of every event that seems to occur," he observed to reporters at one point. In short, the conditions—reminiscent of New York's blackout two summers ago—that prevailed during this crisis were no different from the ones that prevail in almost every large crisis: erroneous prediction, more or less inadequate preparation, mass confusion and misunderstanding of the facts (accompanied by large amounts of cynicism and black humor), and official sleeplessness and improvisation. The main thing that planners concerned with nuclear power left out of their scenarios was not the correct workings of some valve or control panel. It was the thing that no scenario can take into account: simple human fallibility per se—an ineradicable ingredient in the actions not only of power-plant operators but also of power-plant designers, of government officials, and of the general public as well. What the experts know and most of the rest of us will never know is how to build a nuclear power plant. What we know and they seem to have forgotten is that human imperfection is ingrained in everything that human beings undertake. In almost every enterprise—for example, in air travel—mistakes are somehow tolerated, but in this one case they cannot be, because the losses, which include not only the lives of tens of thousands of people but the habitability of our country and of the earth, are so high, and are "forever." At the deepest level, then, the human error in our nuclear program may be the old Socratic flaw of thinking that we know what we don't know and can't know. The Faustian[1] proposal that the experts make to us is to let them lay their fallible human hands on eternity, and it is unacceptable.

---

[1] Faust was a literary figure modeled after a sixteenth-century alchemist who supposedly promised his immortal soul to Satan in exchange for power in the physical world.—Eds.

Science and the American Dream (1983)
Robert Jastrow

Industrial productivity depends on technical innovations, engineering and general knowhow—areas in which American prowess has been unchallenged. How is it possible that American productivity leveled off in the last 10 years, while the productivity of Japan and Germany increased rapidly? What happened? The experts have given many answers. They all sound convincing, but when I began to look into the situation I found that none passes the test of a comparison with the facts. Here are some frequently heard opinions on the causes of our decline, and the data that test their validity.

American labor has priced itself out of the market. The Japanese have captured our market with cheap labor.

True once but no longer. Japanese wages were pennies an hour in 1950, but factory wages in Japan are now about $10 an hour, nearly the same as in America. Steel and automobile workers in America make more than their counterparts in Japan but that is not true for industry across the board for the two countries.

We spend too much on social welfare, on defense, on government as a whole; the tax burden is oppressive.

The United States spends a smaller fraction of its GNP on social welfare than do its leading industrial competitors, Japan and West Germany. This item is surely not the main brake on American productivity.

And although we spend considerably more on defense than Japan and somewhat more than Germany, during the 1970s defense costs averaged only 5.5 percent of the American GNP—significant, but not large enough to slow down the whole economy.

In general, the United States spends approximately the same fraction of its GNP on government as Japan does—about 30 percent—and a considerably smaller fraction of GNP than West Germany spends.

Federal deficits are excessive; the federal debt has zoomed to astronomical levels.

Deficits in the federal budgets of our main competitors, Japan and Germany, are far greater than ours—three to four times larger as a fraction of GNP in recent years.

The federal debt in the United States has increased only 20 percent since 1954, when corrected for inflation. The astronomical zoom reflects inflated dollars.

Antipollution laws have increased the cost of doing business in America.

True, but no more so than in Japan, and less in some cases. In the steel industry, for example, although Japanese steel manufacturers spent nearly

From Robert Jastrow, "Science and the American Dream," **Science Digest** (March 1983), 46–48. First appeared in **Science Digest,** © 1983 by The Hearst Corporation. Reprinted by permission of the author.

twice as much as we did on pollution control in the 1970s—$3.6 billion versus $1.9 billion between 1971 and 1977—they still had lower prices, and took away much of our market. In the automobile industry, Japanese restrictions on the emission of pollutants in automobile exhausts are far more stringent that the limits set by our own government, yet Japanese auto manufacturing costs are far lower.

American industry is not spending enough on R&D.

U.S. expenditures on industrial R&D are considerably higher than in Japan, as a fraction of GNP. The fraction of scientists and engineers engaged in R&D in industry is also higher. Furthermore, U.S. spending on industrial R&D increased throughout most of the '70s, during the period in which our economic growth was slowing down. This factor cannot explain the poor performance of the U.S. economy in the past decade.

The United States is not training enough engineers.

True; in recent years the Japanese have been turning out twice as many engineers as America in proportion to population. That growing pool of bright young engineers is a time bomb for America. Still, at the moment we lead the world in the number of scientists and engineers engaged in R&D in proportion to the size of the labor force, and we have done so throughout the recent period of slow economic growth in the United States.

Investment in plant and equipment is inadequate.

Total capital investment as a fraction of GNP is low in the United States compared with other countries. However, in the manufacturing industries— such as steel, autos, machines tools—investment in machinery and equipment increased nearly 40 percent as a fraction of total production between 1960 and 1978, just when industrial productivity growth was declining. Many economists favor this explanation, but it cannot be a major factor.

Business gets more help from the government in Japan than in the United States.

Differences between Japan and America in this respect are not as great as generally believed. U.S. government purchases of semiconductors, computers and aircraft for the defense and space agencies in the 1950s and 1960s nurtured the great growth industries in computing, semiconductors and aircraft, when they were weak and struggling, by paying a large part of their R&D costs and buying up most of their products. Between 1955 and 1967 the government bought 57 percent of all computers made in the United States, 40 percent of all semiconductors, and more than half of all aircraft. In America, as in Japan, these hi-tech industries prospered because of government support. . . .

There is no villain. The trauma we are passing through now is not a depression, but a natural interlude between two great waves of economic growth. American industry is shedding its skin, casting off old technologies and developing new ones. But the new skin has not yet hardened. Industries based on the new technologies—mainly computers and microelectronics but also robots, fiber optics, long-distance communications, biotechnology, and exotic new materials—are still young. They have not yet developed to the point where they can take up the slack in employment and industrial output created by the decline of the aging enterprises—the smokestack industries of steel, chemicals, autos, and so on.

The potential for growth in the new hi-tech industries is mind-boggling in terms of new jobs and new wealth. The computing industry alone is expected to grow from its current $50 billion to at least $100 billion and growing at the rate of 18 percent a year. Robots, another major new industry, pack a double wallop. Not only do they increase industrial productivity, but the construction of robots itself is showing phenomenal growth, from $200 million in 1980 to a projected $2 billion by 1985.

Fiber optics is another rapidly growing technology. These light-pipes, made from glass fibers the thickness of a horsehair, can carry voices and data in a stream of tiny laser pulses at the rate of millions of pulses a second. AT&T plans to use a message-carrying light-pipe in a telephone cable between Boston and Richmond. The new cable would have taken 2 million pounds of copper with the old-fashioned wire technology.

There is little question that growth in the hi-tech industries will more than make up for the decline in the smokestack industries. Projected growth of $50 billion in the computing industry alone in the next four years is enough to offset the combined losses in the shrinking steel and auto industries. And new jobs go with the growth—easily sufficient to replace the jobs lost in the smokestack industries. Hewlett-Packard, one of the medium-size hi-tech companies, employs 57,000 people, Xerox more than 100,000. Two more Hewlett-Packards and a Xerox in the 1980s will make up for all the jobs lost in the auto industry.

Other countries will vie with us for a share in the wealth generated by the new technologies. Japan is the most formidable competitor. That nation graduated 87,000 engineers in 1980, compared with 63,000 in the United States, and is rapidly closing the gap in total numbers of scientists and engineers engaged in R&D in industry. The Japanese built their initial successes on technology borrowed from the United States, as we once borrowed our technology from Europe. Now, still following in our tracks, they are working very hard to acquire their own base of innovative research in semiconductors, computing, robotics, fiber optics, superplastics and biotechnology.

I would bet my money on America in this competition. The Japanese have the advantages of long-range planning and very productive management of people. But their industrial organization tends to stifle initiative, especially youthful initiative. "The nail that stands up gets hammered down," says a Japanese proverb. Conformity and respect for elders are highly valued traits in Japan.

We Americans have the advantages of an open society and an upward mobility that gives free rein to the innovativeness and entrepreneurial energy of human beings. This is what counts most of all—human capital, and a society in which it is utilized to its maximum potential.

46.

THE GREAT COMMUNICATOR

Since World War II, the Middle East, with its vast oil reserves, has been of strategic importance to both the United States and the Soviet Union. As a consequence, every modern U.S. president has expended enormous financial and political resources to maintain American influence in that region. There have been some successes. In 1953 President Dwight Eisenhower used the Central Intelligence Agency to replace an unfriendly government with a friendly one in oil-rich Iran; in 1958 he deployed the Sixth Fleet to maintain a friendly government in Lebanon. Jimmy Carter helped bring about the so-called Camp David Accords between Israel and Egypt in 1978.

But there have been many failures too, not the least in the very places where initial policies succeeded. In the late 1970s, Islamic partisans seized control of Iran and its oil fields, taking fifty-two American hostages in the process. President Carter, unable to respond effectively, plummeted in public opinion polls and lost the 1980 election to Ronald Reagan partly over Iran. President Reagan himself then came to grief when Israeli and Syrian invasions of Lebanon shattered that country's unity in 1982. Reagan, concerned about Syrian and Soviet influence, sent marines to Beirut, the Lebanese capital, as part of a peacekeeping force, only to see over two hundred of them killed in a terrorist attack. In the first part of the television address reprinted below, Reagan recounted the incident and explained the imperatives of U.S. policy that had originally placed the troops in Beirut. Just three months later, even though the president had called the American presence "essential," he ordered the withdrawal of the force.

The next part of Reagan's address deals with a more successful initiative—the invasion of the tiny Caribbean island of Grenada. Unlike the Middle East, Central America and the islands of the Caribbean had preoccupied Washington for almost a century because of the proximity to U.S. territory, the location of the Panama Canal, and the extensive U.S. business investments in the Caribbean area. Here, too, there had been failures as well as successes, notably the persistence of a pro-Soviet regime in Cuba and the coming to power in 1979 of a radical government in Nicaragua. The Reagan administration came into office determined to reverse what it saw as these pernicious incursions in a vital sphere of U.S. influence. When Congress, nervous about slipping into another Vietnam-type debacle, proved reluctant to support a counter-revolutionary war against the Nicaraguan government, Reagan took steps of his own. On the one hand, he tried to use the CIA to gain his objectives, much as Eisenhower had in Iran in 1954. On the other hand, he sent American troops to tiny Grenada to halt what appeared to be a Cuban-Soviet effort to gain influence on that island.

President Reagan concluded his address by attempting to link the developments in the Middle East with those in the Caribbean. The Soviet Union, he claimed, was actively supporting anti-American terrorism everywhere in the world, including Lebanon and Grenada, and the United States had to respond accordingly. Ironically, there were more connections than the Soviet one. Midway through Reagan's second term, it was discovered that the administration, contrary to the president's announced policy, had directed the delivery of American arms to the militant Iranian government in a futile effort to free U.S. hostages. Moreover, millions of dollars of the funds used to pay for these weapons wound up illegally supporting the Contras, or Nicaraguan counter-revolutionaries. An investigative commission headed by Republican John Tower called the Iran-Contra activities "case studies in the perils of policy pursued outside the constraints of orderly process." Even so, the Grenada assault stands as perhaps the most significant foreign policy triumph of the Reagan presidency.

Born in 1914, Ronald Reagan won initial fame in Hollywood, where he worked in films and was president of the Screen Actors' Guild. During the 1950s he appeared on television and did publicity for General Electric. In 1964 he campaigned for Republican conservative Barry Goldwater; two years later Reagan was elected to the first of two terms as governor of California. By 1980 he was both a seasoned politician and a seasoned actor—photogenic, comfortable before the cameras, and possessing a mellifluous, compelling voice. No president since Franklin Roosevelt, with whom Reagan has often compared himself, has utilized the electronic media so effectively or to such political advantage. His critics have called him the "Teflon" president because of the way he manages to escape unscathed from policy gaffes. But his friends call him with equal accuracy, and for much the same reasons, the "Great Communicator," perhaps the finest of the century.

Questions to consider. Ronald Reagan's 1983 address is similar to but also different from earlier U.S. attacks on Soviet communism. Compare, for example, the precise detail at the beginning of this talk with the way President Truman introduced his 1950 address on Korea (Document 33). What reasons might Reagan have had for introducing a major foreign policy announcement in this way? Do they seem related chiefly to his speaking abilities, to his special strengths as a communicator with the electorate? Or do the topics themselves seem somehow to require this kind of introduction? If the latter, is the reason for this mainly because Lebanon and Grenada are so far apart? Or is it because the military units involved were small compared with those Truman requested for Korea or with the forces that fought in World War II or Vietnam? Or is it perhaps because this was 1983, almost a decade after the end of the Vietnam conflict, instead of 1950, a half-decade after the war against Germany and Japan? How persuasive is Reagan's argument later in the address that Soviet communism was behind the difficulties in both places? Is Reagan's Communist menace of the 1980s the same one that George Kennan saw in 1947 (Document 31) or John Kennedy in 1961 (Document 36)?

Address on Lebanon and Grenada (1983)
Ronald Reagan

My fellow Americans, . . . in these past several days, violence has erupted again, in Lebanon and Grenada.

In Lebanon we have some 1,600 marines, part of a multinational force that's trying to help the people of Lebanon restore order and stability to that troubled land. Our marines are assigned to the south of the city of Beirut near the only airport operating in Lebanon. Just a mile or so to the north is the Italian contingent and not far from them the French and a company of British soldiers.

This past Sunday, at 22 minutes after 6, Beirut time, with dawn just breaking, a truck looking like a lot of other vehicles in the city approached the airport on a busy main road. There was nothing in its appearance to suggest it was any different than the trucks or cars that were normally seen on and around the airport. But this one was different.

At the wheel was a young man on a suicide mission. The truck carried some 2,000 pounds of explosives, but there was no way our marine guards could know this. Their first warning that something was wrong came when the truck crashed through a series of barriers, including a chain link fence and barbed wire entanglements. The guards opened fire but it was too late.

The truck smashed through the doors of the headquarters building in which our marines were sleeping and instantly exploded. The four-story concrete building collapsed in a pile of rubble.

More than 200 of the sleeping men were killed in that one hideous insane attack. Many others suffered injury and are hospitalized here or in Europe. This was not the end of the horror.

From Ronald Reagan, "Address on Lebanon and Grenada," **Vital Speeches of the Day** 50 (November 15, 1983), 66–69.

At almost the same instant another vehicle on a suicide and murder mission crashed into the headquarters of the French peacekeeping force, an eight-story building, destroying and killing more than 50 French soldiers.

Prior to this day of horror there had been several tragedies for our men in the multinational force; attacks by snipers and mortar fire had taken their toll. I called the bereaved parents and/or widows of the victims to express on behalf of all of us our sorrow and sympathy. Sometimes there were questions. And now many of you are asking: Why should our young men be dying in Lebanon? Why is Lebanon important to us?

Well, it's true Lebanon is a small country more than five and a half thousand miles from our shores, on the edge of what we call the Middle East. But every President who has occupied this office in recent years has recognized that peace in the Middle East is of vital concern to our nation and, indeed, to our allies in Western Europe and Japan. We've been concerned because the Middle East is a powder keg. Four times in the last 30 years the Arabs and Israelis have gone to war and each time the world has teetered near the edge of catastrophe. The area is key to the economic and political life of the West. Its strategic importance, its energy resources, the Suez Canal, the well-being of the nearly 200 million people living there; all are vital to us and to world peace.

If that key should fall into the kinds of a power or powers hostile to the free world, there would be a direct threat to the United States and to our allies.

We have another reason to be involved. Since 1948, our nation has recognized and accepted a moral obligation to assure the continued existence of Israel as a nation. Israel shares our democratic values and is a formidable force an invader of the Middle East would have to reckon with. For several years, Lebanon has been torn by internal strife. Once a prosperous, peaceful nation, its Government had become ineffective in controlling the militias that warred on each other. . . .

Beyond our progress in Lebanon let us remember that our main goal and purpose is to achieve a broader peace in all of the Middle East. The factions and bitterness that we see in Lebanon are just a microcosm of the difficulties that are spread across much of that region. A peace initiative for the entire Middle East . . . still offers the best hope for bringing peace to the region.

Let me ask those who say we should get out of Lebanon: If we were to leave Lebanon now, what message would that send to those who foment instability and terrorism? If Americans were to walk away from Lebanon, what chance would there be for a negotiated settlement producing the unified, democratic Lebanon? If we turned our backs on Lebanon now, what would be the future of Israel? At stake is the fate of only the second Arab country to negotiate a major agreement with Israel. . . .

If terrorism and intimidation succeed, it'll be a devastating blow to the peace process and to Israel's search for genuine security. It won't just be Lebanon sentenced to a future of chaos. Can the United States, or the free world, for that matter, stand by and see the Middle East incorporated into the

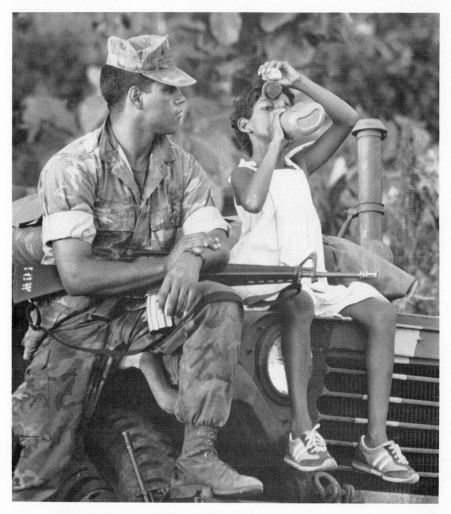

Grenada, October 1983.   A U.S. Marine sergeant shares his water with a nine-year-old in St. George's, the capital city. Except for the U.S. naval base in Cuba, small Army units around the Panama Canal, and advisers directing the Contra rebels in Nicaragua, the United States had not sent soldiers into a country of the Caribbean Basin since President Johnson's dispatch of 200,000 troops to the Dominican Republic in 1965. Prior to this, however, American military forces had entered countries in the area eleven times; in two places, Nicaragua and Haiti, they had stayed twenty years. Viewed in this way, President Ronald Reagan's action in Grenada was not a radical departure in policy, as some critics have contended, but a continuation of a policy pursued systematically by presidents from both political parties. (UPI/Bettmann Newsphoto)

Soviet bloc? What of Western Europe and Japan's dependence on Middle East oil for the energy to fuel their industries? The Middle East is, as I said, vital to our national security and economic well-being.

Brave young men have been taken from us. Many others have been grievously wounded. Are we to tell them their sacrifice was wasted or that they gave their lives in defense of our national security every bit as much as any man who ever died fighting in a war?

We must not strip every ounce of meaning and purpose from their courageous sacrifice. We are a nation with global responsibilities, we're not somewhere else in the world protecting someone else's interest. We're there protecting our own. . . .

Now I know another part of the world is very much on our minds. A place much closer to our shores. Grenada. The island is only twice the size of the District of Columbia with a total population of about 110,000 people. Grenada and a half-dozen other Caribbean islands here were, until recently, British colonies. They are not independent states and members of the British Commonwealth.

While they respect each other's independence they also feel a kinship with each other and think of themselves as one people. In 1979 trouble came to Grenada. Maurice Bishop, a protégé of Fidel Castro, staged a military coup and overthrew the government which had been elected under the constitution left to the people by the British.

He sought the help of Cuba in building an airport, which he claimed was for tourist trade, but which looked suspiciously suitable for military aircraft, including Soviet-built long-range bombers. The six sovereign countries and one remaining colony are joined together in what they call the Organization of Eastern Caribbean States. The six became increasingly alarmed as Bishop built an army greater than all of theirs combined.

Obviously it was not purely for defense. In this last year or so, Prime Minister Bishop gave indications that he might like better relations with the United States. He even made a trip to our country and met with senior officials at the White House and the State Department. Whether he was serious or not we'll never know.

On Oct. 12, a small group in his militia seized him and put him under arrest. They were, if anything, even more radical and more devoted to Castro's Cuba than he had been. Several days later, a crowd of citizens appeared before Bishop's home, freed him and escorted him toward the headquarters of the Military Council. They were fired upon. A number, including some children, were killed and Bishop was seized. He and several members of his Cabinet were subsequently executed and a 24-hour shoot-to-kill curfew was put in effect. Grenada was without a government, its only authority exercised by a self-proclaimed band of military men.

There were then about 1,000 of our citizens on Grenada, 800 of them students in St. George's University Medical School. Concern that they'd be harmed or held as hostages, I ordered a flotilla of ships then on its way to

Lebanon with Marines—part of our regular rotation program—to circle south on a course that would put them somewhere in the vicinity of Grenada in case there should be a need to evacuate our people.

Last weekend I was awakened in the early morning hours and told that six members of the Organization of Eastern Caribbean States joined by Jamaica and Barbados had sent an urgent request that we join them in a military operation to restore order and democracy to Grenada. . . .

The joint chiefs worked around the clock to come up with a plan. They had little intelligence information about conditions on the island. We had to assume that several hundred Cubans working on the airport could be military reserves. As it turned out the number was much larger and they were a military force. Six hundred of them have been taken prisoner and we have discovered a complete base with weapons and communications equipment which makes it clear a Cuban occupation of the island had been planned.

Two hours ago we released the first photos from Grenada. They included pictures of a warehouse of military equipment, one of three we've uncovered so far. This warehouse contained weapons and ammunition stacked almost to the ceiling, enough to supply thousands of terrorists.

Grenada, we were told, was a friendly island paradise for tourism. Well it wasn't. It was a Soviet-Cuban colony being readied as a major military bastion to export terror and undermine democracy.

We got there just in time.

I can't say enough in praise of our military. Army Rangers and paratroopers, Navy Marine and Air Force personnel, those who planned a brilliant campaign and those who carried it out.

Almost instantly our military seized the two airports, secured the campus where most of our students were and they're now in the mopping-up phase.

It should be noted that in all the planning, a top priority was to minimize risk, to avoid casualties to our own men and also the Grenadian forces as much as humanly possible. But there were casualties. And we all owe a debt to those who lost their lives or were wounded. They were few in number but even one is a tragic price to pay.

It's our intention to get our men out as soon as possible. . . .

The events in Lebanon and Grenada, though oceans apart, are closely related. Not only has Moscow assisted and encouraged the violence in both countries, but it provides direct support through a network of surrogates and terrorists. It is no coincidence that when the thugs tried to wrest control of Grenada, there were 30 Soviet advisers and hundreds of Cuban military and paramilitary forces on the island. At the moment of our landing we communicated with the governments of Cuba and the Soviet Union and told them we would offer shelter and security to their people on Grenada. Regrettably, Castro ordered his men to fight to the death and some did. The others will be sent to their homelands.

Now there was a time when our national security was based on a standing army here within our own borders and shore batteries of artillery along our coast, and of course a navy to keep the sea lanes open for the shipping of things necessary to our well being. The world has changed. Today our national security can be threatened in far-away places. It's up to all of us to be aware of the strategic importance of such places and to be able to identify them.

Sam Rayburn [former Speaker of the House] once said that freedom is not something a nation can work for once and win forever. He said it's like an insurance policy: its premiums must be kept up to date. In order to keep it we have to keep working for it and sacrificing for it just as long as we live. If we do not, our children may not know the pleasure of working to keep it for it may not be theirs to keep.

COUNTERPOINT VII

Race, Education, and Achievement

In its landmark **Brown** v. **The Board of Education of Topeka** decision in 1954 (Document 38), the Supreme Court argued that segregated schools were inherently unequal and that because education was becoming more and more essential for future occupational success, schools had to be integrated in order to conform to the equal protection clause of the Fourteenth Amendment. Most discussions of this decision have concerned whether "segregated" always means "unequal" and whether "segregated" means by law only or also by custom. But what about the other part of the Court's argument? Was education really so important, so "essential," as the Court believed? Would more, and more equal, education really produce greater occupational achievement? Why did the plaintiffs believe it would?

The last question is the easiest to answer. Americans from Horace Mann in the mid-1800s to Jane Addams in the early 1900s had preached the value of schooling, and as James Geschwender shows, the correlation between learning and earning still seemed strong in the mid-twentieth century (table A.2). Not only had white males attended school much longer than black males in the 1940s, when the suit leading to the **Brown** decision was begun, they continued to do so throughout the 1950s (table A.1). Both groups, to be sure, had more schooling as of 1960 than they had in 1940. Particularly noticeable is the fact that the percentage of blacks who had no schooling at all was much smaller in 1960 than in 1940 (6.6 percent as opposed to 11.7 percent); the percentage of blacks with six years of elementary school or less had also dropped to 35 percent from 55 percent in 1940. A greater percentage of black men had attended college, too, in 1960 than in 1940 (7.8 percent as against 3.1 percent), although white gains at this level (19.3 percent versus 11.2 percent) were also substantial. Despite these gains, however, blacks still made up over one-fourth of all those with no schooling in 1960, just as they had in 1940. At the time the consequences of these differences seemed self-evident because of data showing that the longer people of all races went to school, the more money they made (table A.2). As whites and nonwhites moved up the educational ladder, however, for those of equal education, the greater the gap in wages became between the two groups. Between whites and nonwhites with some college education the gap in earning power by 1960 was $2,133—more than the total income of nonwhites with less than eight years of schooling!

But Geschwender's figures contain suggestive oddities. If poorly educated whites earned 50 percent more money than poorly educated nonwhites, for example, and college-educated whites made 50 percent more than college-educated nonwhites, why was it argued that equal education alone would produce more equal income? Do, in fact, people need more education in order to perform jobs these days? What connection is there between schooling and work? Not as much as you might think, say Dorothy Newman and several collaborators. For instance, although the proportion of jobs classified as white collar increased to half of all jobs by 1975, only one-fourth of all jobs required a high school diploma or more (table B.1). There were still twice as many white-collar jobs, in other words, as there were high school graduates.

Newman suggests, then, that more education was not necessarily the key to getting or doing better-paying white-collar work. Newman presents further data showing, she feels, that workers in Europe with less education than black Americans are able to fill positions at every economic level (table B.2). If modern work is so complex and demanding as to require more and more education, as Americans have believed, how could the European employment patterns be so different? Even in the United States, white dropouts (those with less than twelve years of school) held one-half of all American jobs in 1950 and 1960, and one-third of them in 1970 (table B.3). If work was too complicated for poorly educated blacks, Newman suggests, how could white dropouts do it? Perhaps Newman's statistics are not complete enough to answer this question, for example, about the quality and level of European education or of the white dropouts. Perhaps as some (including Newman) have always maintained, the basic problem was not inadequate education but discrimination, union membership, or something else.

Remember, though, that the Supreme Court's **Brown** opinion stated that segregated schooling, not just insufficient schooling—quality and not just quantity—produced unequal opportunity. Once the Court had made its decision and school districts began to act on it, then perhaps there would be visible changes in the patterns of career attainment. Indeed, Newman and her colleagues do find some change (table C). In 1947, black families earned slightly more than half as much as white families and in 1957 only a whisker more than that. But by 1967, thirteen years after **Brown**, the ratio was up to just above three-fifths, disappointing, perhaps, but a measurable gain nonetheless. There it seemed to stick. While black income continued to increase, white income did, too, so that the gap in real dollars was as wide in the mid-1970s as it had been a decade before.

Years of schooling, it appears, could not produce the kind of fundamental shift that the principals in the **Brown** case anticipated. The decision's chief impact was perhaps in the realm of justice—"equal protection of the law"—rather than economics—"equal opportunity in the workplace."

A. Levels of Education and Income

1. Level of Education by Color, Males, 1940 and 1960

Level of Education	White			Nonwhite[a]			Nonwhite as Percentage of Total	
	1940	1960	Change	1940	1960	Change	1940	1960
No schooling	3.2%	2.0%	−1.2%	11.7%	6.6%	−5.1%	26.1%	26.3%
Elementary								
1–4 years	8.8	5.5	−3.3	34.5	21.1	−13.4	27.7	28.9
5–6 years	11.1	7.1	−4.0	20.6	14.8	−5.8	15.3	17.9
7 years	7.0	6.6	−0.4	7.5	8.5	+1.0	9.5	11.8
8 years	30.5	18.4	−12.1	11.4	12.3	+0.9	3.5	6.6
High school								
1–3 years	15.1	18.9	+3.8	7.4	17.1	+9.7	4.6	8.7
4 years	13.0	22.1	+9.1	3.8	11.7	+7.9	2.8	5.3
College								
1–3 years	5.3	9.0	+3.7	1.7	4.4	+2.7	3.0	4.9
4 years	5.9	10.3	+4.4	1.4	3.4	+2.0	2.3	3.4

[a]Includes some Hispanic-Americans.

(continued)

Table A continued

2. Median Income by Level of Education and Color, Males 14 and Over, 1961

Level of Education	White	Nonwhite	Difference
Elementary			
Less than 8 years	$2,303	$1,554	$ 749
8 years	3,617	2,505	1,112
High school			
1–3 years	4,090	2,427	1,663
4 years	5,155	3,381	1,774
Some college	6,379	4,246	2,133

SOURCE: Reprinted from *Social Forces* (Vol. 43, December 1964). "Social Structure and the Negro Revolt" by James Geschwender. Copyright © 1964 by The University of North Carolina Press.

B. Distribution of the Labor Force

1. Percentage Distribution of the Labor Force, by Two Occupational Groupings, Decennial Years, 1940–1970, and 1975

Occupational Grouping—Traditional and by Job Requirement	1940	1950	1960	1970	1975
All occupations	100%	100%	100%	100%	100%
Traditional grouping					
White collar	31	37	42	48	50
Blue collar and other[a]	69	63	58	52	50
Job requirement grouping[b]					
Higher (needing high school diploma or more)	15	18	20	23	26
Lower	85	82	80	77	74

[a]Includes service and farm.
[b]Higher are professional, technical, managerial, and administrative.

(continued)

Table B continued

2. Percentage of Workers Who Completed Secondary School and Above, by Occupational Group, in the United States (by Race) and in Selected Developed Countries, Around 1960

Occupational Group	United States		France	Netherlands	Sweden	United Kingdom
	White	*Black*				
All occupations	49%	26%	6%	10%	7%	10%
Professional	91	89	39	59	35	53
Administrative	65	43	36	37	35	30
Clerical	72	69	7	37	8	16
Sales	56	44	5	6	5	9
Crafts and other manual	30	20	1	1	—	2
Farmers	26	6	—	1	1	7

3. White "Dropouts" as a Percentage of the Labor Force in Selected Occupations, 1950, 1960, and 1970

Occupation	Percentage of Total Experienced Civilian Labor Force		
	1950	*1960*	*1970*
All occupations	52%	46%	33%
Professional and technical	10	8	6
Accountants and auditors	11	9	5
Drafting	14	12	8
Elementary and secondary teachers	3	1	1
Clerical	28	27	19
Bank tellers	16	15	11
Secretaries	13	12	8
Telephone operators	40	39	22
Sales	44	43	30
Retail	49	51	37
Crafts	65	59	46
Compositors and typesetters	51	45	30
Electricians	57	51	35
Airplane mechanics	40	40	29
Tool and die makers	58	52	34
Operatives	68	65	52
Bus drivers	69	63	46
Service (excluding protective and private household)	55	54	46
Protective service—police	50	38	19

SOURCE: From *Protest, Politics, and Prosperity: Black Americans and White Institutions, 1940–1975* by Dorothy K. Newman et al. Copyright © 1978 by Dorothy K. Newman. Reprinted by permission of Pantheon Books, a Division of Random House, Inc.

C. Median Family Income by Race, and Black-White Income Gap in Current and Constant 1947 Dollars, 1947–1975

Year	Black Median Family Income	White Median Family Income	Ratio: Black to White	Income Gap (White Minus Black)	Income Gap in Constant Dollars (1947 = 100)
1947	$1,614	$ 3,157	.51	$1,543	$1,543
1948	1,768	3,310	.53	1,542	1,428
1949	1,650	3,232	.51	1,582	1,479
1950	1,869	3,445	.54	1,576	1,459
1951	2,032	3,859	.53	1,827	1,575
1952	2,338	4,114	.57	1,776	1,492
1953	2,466	4,398	.56	1,932	1,610
1954	2,416	4,338	.56	1,922	1,602
1955	2,554	4,613	.55	2,069	1,724
1956	2,632	5,002	.53	2,370	1,943
1957	2,763	5,168	.53	2,405	1,909
1958	2,715	5,300	.51	2,585	2,004
1959	2,915	5,643	.52	2,728	2,098
1960	3,230	5,835	.55	2,605	1,959
1961	3,191	5,981	.53	2,790	2,082
1962	3,328	6,237	.53	2,909	2,155
1963	3,465	6,548	.53	3,083	2,250
1964	3,838	6,858	.56	3,020	2,173
1965	3,993	7,251	.55	3,258	2,311
1966	4,691	7,825	.60	3,134	2,161
1967	5,094	8,234	.62	3,140	2,107
1968	5,360	8,937	.60	3,577	2,293
1969	5,999	9,794	.61	3,727	2,273
1970	6,088	10,236	.61	3,948	2,269
1971	6,440	10,672	.60	4,232	2,338
1972	6,864	11,549	.59	4,685	2,505
1973	7,269	12,595	.58	5,326	2,676
1974	8,006	13,408	.60	5,402	2,444
1975	8,779	14,268	.62	5,489	2,287

SOURCE: From *Protest, Politics, and Prosperity: Black Americans and White Institutions, 1940–1975* by Dorothy K. Newman et al. Copyright © 1978 by Dorothy K. Newman. Reprinted by permission of Pantheon Books, a Division of Random House, Inc.

A STATISTICAL APPENDIX

List of Appendix Tables

All the information in the appendix tables comes from **U.S. Historical Statistics from Colonial Times to 1970,** published by the U.S. Government Printing Office, Washington, D.C., 1975; and **Statistical Abstract of the United States, 1982–83,** also published by the U.S. Government Printing Office, 1984. In the tables a dash (—) means zero; the small letters na mean that figures are **not available.**

Table A.1 U.S. Population and Selected State Populations, 1790–1980

The population of the United States has grown steadily since the nation's founding, just as observers like Gottlieb Mittelberger (Vol. 1, Document 10) and James Madison (Vol. 1, Document 14) thought it would. It has grown faster in some periods than in others, however, and faster in some regions than in others, as shown by the figures for the six states below. Stemming chiefly from economics, immigration, and climate, this regional divergence has had profound political and social consequences—the early prominence of Massachusetts and Virginia statesmen, for example, and the election of two Californians and a Texan to the presidency since 1960.

	Population (in Millions)						
Year	Mass.	N.Y.	Va.	Ill.	Tex.	Cal.	U.S. Total
1790	.4	.3	.7	—	—	—	3.9
1810	.5	1.0	.9	.01	—	—	7.2
1830	.6	1.9	1.0	.2	—	—	12.9
1850	1.0	3.1	1.1	.9	.2	.1	23.2
1870	1.5	4.4	1.2	2.5	.8	.6	39.8
1890	2.2	6.0	1.7	3.8	2.2	1.2	62.9
1910	3.4	9.1	2.1	5.6	3.9	2.4	91.9
1930	4.3	12.6	2.4	7.6	5.8	5.7	122.8
1950	4.7	14.8	3.3	8.7	7.7	10.6	150.7
1970	5.7	18.2	4.6	11.1	11.2	19.9	203.2
1980	5.7	17.6	5.3	11.4	14.2	23.7	226.5

Table A.2 U.S. Population and Breakdown by Urban Population Sizes, 1790–1980

The population of the United States grew rapidly from the start. But as the following figures show, towns and cities grew faster than rural areas even in the early decades of agricultural and frontier expansion. America seems to have been destined to be an urbanized society, which of course it largely was by the twentieth century.

Recently, almost all growth has been urban. But rapid urbanization has not always meant that big cities set the pace. For instance, the population in cities from 25,000 to 250,000 more than doubled from 27.2 million in 1950 to 60.3 million in 1980, while that in cities over 250,000 only went from 34.8 million to 40.6 million, and in the last decade actually lost over a million and a half people. (These figures do not indicate, however, how many cities are in each category nor give how the number of cities increased over the decades.) During the 1950–1980 period, towns of 2,500 and over grew from 96.5 million to 167.1 million in population. Cities of 250,000 and over grew most rapidly in population during 1850–1910, a period of great industrial growth.

	Population (in Millions)				
Year	2,500 and over	2,500– 25,000	25,000– 250,000	250,000 and Over	Total
1790	.2	.14	.06	—	3.9
1810	.5	.3	.2	—	7.2
1830	1.1	.6	.5	—	12.9
1850	3.5	1.3	1.6	.6	23.2
1870	9.9	4.2	2.6	3.1	39.8
1890	22.1	8.1	7.1	6.9	62.9
1910	42.0	13.6	13.0	15.4	91.9
1930	68.9	20.7	20.4	27.8	122.8
1950	96.5	34.5	27.2	34.8	150.7
1970	149.3	58.3	48.8	42.2	203.2
1980	167.1	52.3	60.3	40.6	226.5[a]

[a]Includes 13.9 million in "urbanized areas" that are unincorporated and therefore not distributed in specific city sizes.

Table A.3   U.S. Immigrant Population by Origin, Occupation, Sex, and Age, 1820–1980

The United States has been called a nation of immigrants, and surely few nations were so influenced by newcomers as this one. Immigration, clearly a force behind the great surge in national population, also contributed to the development of cities, social classes, and ethnic and cultural diversity. The make-up of the immigrants themselves changed over time as well, not only in numbers but in nationality, occupational status, and even family structure (as suggested by the shifting proportions of males and of children). For example, in 1910 during industrial expansion, about 70 percent of the immigrants came from eastern and southern European countries, and about 60 percent were laborers or servants. In 1980, the same area provided less than 10 percent of the immigrants, while over 40 percent came from the Americas and 40 percent from Asia; the occupational skills had also shifted, with only 10 percent in the laborer and servant categories, and 20 percent being professionals or skilled workers.

Thus, not only do the totals below ebb and flow according to the coming of war or peace, prosperity or depression, tolerance or persecution, in both the country of origin and the United States, but later immigrants seldom possessed the same characteristics as their counterparts who came one, two, or three generations earlier. Here one may find, among other things, a context for James T. Farrell's portrait in the excerpt from **Young Lonigan** (Vol. 2, Document 11), the Chinese Exclusion Act (Vol. 2, Document 7), and the current debate over further immigration restriction.

	1820	1850	1880	1910	1940	1970	1980
Total[a]	10,311	324,098	457,257	1,041,570	70,756	373,326	460,000
Northern Europe[b]	7,467	307,044	310,213	202,198	37,520	35,375	24,700
Eastern and southern Europe	224	1,279	38,478	724,083	11,976	75,278	34,800
Asia	5	7	5,839	23,533	2,050	90,215	183,000
The Americas	387	15,768	101,692	89,534	17,822	161,727	198,000
Professional-commercial	1,038	7,318	9,699	36,639	18,578	68,497	63,400
Skilled workers and farmers	1,964	69,242	97,133	133,640	6,557	50,461	21,100
Laborers	334	46,640	105,012	505,654	2,372	18,480	39,700
Servants	139	3,203	18,580	105,735	3,940	19,751	8,600
None	6,836	188,931	217,446	260,002	39,409	216,137	275,400
Males	7,197	196,138	287,623	736,038	33,460	176,990	219,500
Under age 15	1,313	62,543	87,154	120,509	9,602	104,880	110,900

[a]Includes immigrants from Africa, Australasia, France, and the Low Countries as well as areas of origin listed below.
[b]Great Britain, Ireland, Scandinavia, and Germany.

Table A.4   U.S. Workers by Economic Sectors (Agriculture, Manufacturing, Construction, and Trade), 1810–1980

This table sorts American workers into four basic sectors of the economy. Here we see evidence of (among other things) the decline in the number of farmers after 1919 (though agricultural production has risen—see Table A.6), the growth of manufacturing before 1900 and its pre-eminence by 1950, the strong showing of construction for a hundred years and its subsequent slower growth (close to the low level of agriculture), and the steady advance of the trade and finance sector to have more than 5 million more workers than in the manufacturing sector. We thus pass from the "farmer's age" to the "workshop of the world" to, at last, the "service economy." Observe how the rise of manufacturing and trade parallels the growth of cities (Table A.2) and how decline in agriculture and slow growth in construction show up in the occupations of the immigrants (Table A.3).

Year	Workers (in Millions)				
	Agriculture	*Manufacturing*	*Construction*	*Trade/Finance*	*Total*
1810	1.9	.08	na	na	2.3
1830	2.9	na	na	na	4.2
1850	4.5	1.2	.4	.5	8.3
1870	6.8	2.5	.8	1.3	12.9
1890	10.0	4.4	1.5	2.9	23.3
1910	11.8	8.3	1.9	5.3	37.5
1930	10.6	9.9	2.0	8.1	48.8
1950	7.9	15.7	3.0	12.2	65.5
1970	3.7	19.4	3.4	18.6	85.9
1980	3.5	20.3	4.2	25.4	109.0

Table A.5 Growth of U.S. Transportation (Ship, Railroad, Airplane, and Automobile), 1790–1980

The following figures illustrate the evolution of transportation in the United States. Each new type of transportation has represented a technological advance—steam power, the internal combustion engine, heavier-than-air flight—and thus mirrors the progress of the Industrial Revolution. Each type has also coincided with a phase of national development: post-Revolutionary foreign trade, the winning of the West, suburbanization, and the modern aerospace era. The hugeness of the transportation system as a whole suggests both the size of the country and the frequency and speed with which Americans have tended to move themselves and their commodities. The individual columns show when each part of the system really took off—or, as in ship tonnage in the age of the supertanker, when it took off anew.

Year	Ship Tonnage into U.S. Ports (in Millions)	Railroad Track Miles (in Thousands)	Motor-Vehicle Registration (in Millions)	Scheduled Commercial Air Routes (in Thousands of Miles)
1790	.6	—	—	—
1810	1.0	—	—	—
1830	1.1	—	—	—
1850	3.7	9	—	—
1870	9.2	53	—	—
1890	18.1	200	—	—
1910	40.2	352	.5	—
1930	81.3	430	22.1	30
1950	86.6	396	49.2	77
1970	254.2	350	108.4	172
1980	492.0	320	155.9	317

Table A.6 U.S. Production of Selected Commodities, 1870–1980

Whether industrialization advanced in a spurt after the Civil War, as Terence Powderly (Vol. 2, Document 13) and Upton Sinclair (Vol. 2, Document 16) believed, or steadily throughout the nineteenth century, as the occupational and transportation data in Tables A.4 and A.5 hint, there is no doubt that the process was very far along by the early twentieth century. The figures below show American gains in the production of a number of important commodities. All of them have gone up sharply over the past century. Yet the listing of the items in pairs highlights divergent growth rates of some interest. Production of sugar in 1970 was twenty times the amount produced in 1870, while that of flour was only three times what was produced a century earlier. The rates of growth of rayon and cigarettes are extraordinarily high when compared with those for cotton and cigars. The number of pairs of shoes produced for women was less than that for men in 1910, but in 1980, women's shoes were 40 percent higher than the number made for men. In most cases the difference in growth rates comes at a particular point in time rather than steadily. What causes the various differences? What does it say about American society that industry begins to produce typewriters and light bulbs? Does the speeding up or slowing down of production growth rates have to do more with technological change or with shifts in consumption habits?

Commodity	Production (in Millions)						
	1870	*1890*	*1910*	*1930*	*1950*	*1970*	*1980*
Flour (barrels)	48	83	107	120	115	129	na
Sugar (lbs.)	1.2	3.2	7.3	12	14.7	20.8	20.1
Bricks[a]	2.8	8	9.9	5.1	6.3	6.7	na
Steel (tons)	.08	4.8	28.3	44.6	96.8	131.5	111.8
Beer (barrels)	7	28	59.5	3.7	88.8	134.7	193
Liquor (gals.)	72	111	164	—	194	355	236
Cotton (bales)	3	8.6	11.6	13.9	10	10.2	11.1
Rayon (lbs.)	—	—	2	118	957	851	438
Cigars	1	4.2	6.8	5.9	5.5	8.0	4.9
Cigarettes	.02	2.5	9.8	124.2	392	562	702
Men's shoes (pairs)	na	na	98	77	103	100	102
Women's shoes (pairs)	na	na	87	112	195	230	143
Typewriters	—	na	.2	.9	1.4	1.4	1.5
Light bulbs	—	na	70	350	1,200	1,582	1,780

[a]Billions.

Table A.7   Growth of U.S. Commercial Banks and U.S. Bank Assets, 1790–1980

The increase in the number of banks and in bank assets provides one measure of American economic growth, especially of growth as related to credit and money transactions—exactly the sort of thing that concerned Benjamin Franklin (Vol. 1, Document 11) and Andrew Jackson (Vol. 1, Document 22). Comparison of the two columns in the table below shows, too, that while bank assets grew steadily from 1790 to 1980, the number of banks shot up all through the era of territorial expansion (1830–1890) and early urbanization (1850–1910), then fell off after 1910 and especially after 1930. This, of course, reflects the ravages of the Great Depression, when so many banks failed that President Franklin Roosevelt declared a bank holiday. But the decline after 1930 reflects a trend that this table does not fully encompass: a pattern of consolidation, takeover, and merger whereby fewer firms dominate **many** important sectors of the American economy.

Year	Number of Commercial Banks	Bank Assets (in Millions of Dollars)
1790	na	na
1810	80	na
1830	330	350
1850	824	532
1870	1,937	1,781
1890	8,201	6,358
1910	25,151	22,922
1930	24,273	74,290
1950	14,676	179,165
1970	14,187	611,305
1980	14,870	1,543,500

Table A.8 U.S. Consumer Price Index and Average Daily Wages of Construction, Manufacturing, and Unskilled Laborers, 1790–1980

The figures here provide a rough view of how ordinary laboring people fared under capitalism from 1790 to 1980. Although wages did not rise quickly for any group until well into the twentieth century, prices also remained fairly steady before that time, and therefore workers may have done better than first appears. The table shows the comparative advantage enjoyed by construction workers over other workers, and the smaller advantage of those in manufacturing over the unskilled. Observe that periods of steady or falling wages usually coincided with periods of heavy immigration (see Table A.3). Table A.8 does not reveal how the work day grew gradually shorter, particularly after 1890. But shown very clearly is the sharp wage increase after 1930, in part the handiwork of labor organizers such as John L. Lewis (Vol. 2, Document 28), whose successes were all the more important because of the tremendous recent growth of the manufacturing sector of the economy.

All the money figures, of course, must be viewed in light of changes in the cost of living over the decades. The consumer price index, which is based on the arbitrary assignment of the value 100 to 1967 prices, provides a rough measure of this cost-of-living change. Construction wages fell in the years from 1830 to 1850, for example. But the cost of living fell even more. Construction workers, therefore, fared better than might appear at first glance. Manufacturing workers made twice as much in 1930 as in 1910. But prices almost doubled, too, so that workers' gains were actually slight.

Year	Price Index[b]	Daily Wage (in Current Dollars)[a]		
		Construction	*Manufacturing*	*Unskilled Labor*
1790	na	1.00	na	.50
1810	47	1.70	na	1.00
1830	32	1.75	na	1.00
1850	25	1.50	na	.90
1870	38	2.50	na	1.75
1890	27	3.00	2.00	1.50
1910	28	4.00	2.40	2.00
1930	50	5.00	5.50	na
1950	72	16.00	12.00	na
1970	116	42.00	27.00	na
1980	247	79.00	58.00	38.00

[a]Wages for 1790–1830 are from the Philadelphia area, for 1850–1870 from the Erie Canal area, and for 1890–1980 from the entire nation. "Current dollars" means the actual wage, *not* adjusted for cost-of-living changes over the years.

[b]A price index assigns a base year (in this case 1967) a value of 100 to represent the price of important commodities (rent, food, clothing, and so forth), then assigns values to other years that relate to 100 as the prices of the same commodities in those years relate to prices in the base year. A glance at the index tells us instantly, therefore, that it cost approximately half as much to live in 1850 as it had in 1810, but about five times as much in 1980 as in 1930.

Table A.9 Selected Religious Affiliations of the U.S. Population (Methodist, Presbyterian, Southern Baptist, Episcopalian, and Roman Catholic), 1790–1980

Religious diversity became a hallmark of American society, just as Roger Williams (Vol. 1, Document 5) hoped it would. But the United States has remained a broadly Christian land despite its diversity, and a heavily Protestant one despite its broad Christianity. The figures here show the growth of four important Protestant denominations and also of the Roman Catholic Church.

Methodism and Presbyterianism, both intimately intertwined with the great reform movements of the nineteenth century, have grown steadily over the decades. Methodism tripled from 1850 to 1890 and tripled again from 1890 to 1980; the Presbyterians in this latter period quadrupled their numbers. The Southern Baptists, born partly in reaction to Northern antislavery agitation before the Civil War, almost quadrupled their membership from 1930 to 1980. Episcopalianism, initially prominent in the South and later attractive to wealthy industrialists, in contrast had a much smaller increase after 1930 and a decline after 1970.

Membership in the Roman Catholic Church increased two and a half times from 1890 to 1930, but it took a longer time period, from 1930 to 1980, for the same increase to take place again. The great Catholic tide thus coincided with the great tide of immigration. Within a quarter-century, Catholics, though still a minority in the United States, outnumbered the combined membership of all the four large Protestant denominations listed in Table A.9. Comparison with the totals for the United States population in Table A.1 will reveal, however, that all but one of these Protestant denominations grew at a pace faster than the population for the period from 1930 to 1980—perhaps a surprising development in what has often been called an age of materialism.

	Number of Members (in Thousands)				
Year	Methodist[a]	Presbyterian	Southern Baptist	Episcopalian	Roman Catholic
1790	58	na	—	na	na
1810	175	na	—	na	na
1830	478	173	—	na	na
1850	1,186	207	400[b]	na	na
1870	1,822	445	na	na	na
1890	3,442	761	1,236	na	8,000[b]
1910	5,073	1,315	2,332	na	14,347
1930	7,319	1,937	3,850	1,939	20,204
1950	8,936	2,364	7,080	2,541	27,766
1970	10,672	3,096	11,629	3,475	47,872
1980	10,372	3,353	13,600	2,786	50,450

[a]Beginning with 1890 figures, the table lists United Methodist Church membership only.
[b]Estimate.

Table A.10 U.S. School Enrollments of School-Age Populations by Race and Sex, 1850–1980

Americans have always prized education, the Puritans, for example, to encourage Bible reading, Franklin and Jefferson to make good citizens. But modern public schools really began only after 1830 when reformers sought to use free schools to reduce social dislocations and foster unity. Enrollments grew rapidly, although mostly for Northern white males at that time. By 1890, however, about the same percentage of girls as boys went to school and a third of the country's black children were in school, which suggests that the Southern educational system was growing. This expansion of Southern schools and black education was one positive result of the Reconstruction effort. The expansion of education generally is testimony to the strength of American local government.

Year	Whites Only	Blacks Only	Males Only	Females Only	Total[a]
1850	56%	2%	50%	45%	47%
1870	54	10	50	47	48
1890	58	33	55	54	54
1910	61	45	59	59	59
1930	71	60	70	70	70
1950	79	75	79	78	79
1970	88	85	89	87	88
1980	86	84	83	86	85

[a]School-age has varied according to time and place over this period, but may generally be understood to mean from about six years old to the mid-teens.

Table A.11 U.S. Federal Civilian Employees (Total) and Numbers Employed by the U.S. Postal Service and the Department of Defense, 1816–1980

The growth of the federal government has been of great interest and concern to Americans recently. In the early nineteenth century, the central government employed only 0.5 percent of the nation's work force; in the early twentieth century, a full 1 percent; and by 1970, more than 3 percent. The table shows the main sources of this rising federal percentage: the post office, which loomed large from the start and then grew with the country; and nonuniformed military personnel, who have been the dominant federal presence for several decades. The decline in the number of employees after 1970 stems mainly from the use of automation equipment in the postal service and the reduction in defense personnel after the end of the Vietnam War.

Year	Post Office	Defense	Total Government Civilian Employees
1816	3,341	190	4,837
1831	8,764	377	11,491
1851	21,391	403	26,274
1871	36,696	1,183	51,020
1891	95,449	20,561	157,442
1910	209,005	58,320	388,708
1930	297,895	103,462	601,319
1950	484,679	753,149	1,960,708
1970	741,216	1,219,125	2,981,574
1980	667,000	973,100	2,883,000

Table A.12   U.S. Federal Expenditures (Total) and Selected
             Expenditure Categories (National Defense, Interest
             on the Public Debt, U.S. Postal Service, Veterans'
             Benefits, and Income Security Including General
             Retirement—Social Security and Medicare—and
             Public Assistance), 1791–1980

The federal government was an insignificant force in the economy of the nineteenth century, except perhaps directly after the Civil War, when interest on the
war debt, veterans' pensions, postal spending, and outlays for military reconstruction and the Indian wars all drove the budget higher. Although the budget grew
at a good clip between 1890 and 1930, the real leap came only after World War II.

Interest on the national debt was a key component of federal spending in
the time of George Washington and remains so today: it is the third largest
category, far ahead of veterans' benefits and the post office combined, and is
growing faster than any other part of the budget. Defense spending grew from
25 percent of the total in 1930 to 33 percent in 1950 to 40 percent in 1970, before
falling to 25 percent again after the Vietnam War. If one includes interest and
veterans' benefits, both up mainly because of wars, the total military component
of the budget suddenly rises to one-half. Even so, defense has multiplied less
rapidly than social security, now grown far beyond the expectations (if not the
hopes) of Frances Perkins (Vol. 2, Document 27).

Remember that these figures must be modified for population growth and
inflation. Even so, the federal government is clearly an important part of the
nation's economy—far greater than ever before—because of the unprecedented
mix of welfare and warfare.

	Expenditures (in Millions of Current Dollars)					
Year	Defense	Interest	Post Office	Veterans' Benefits	Social Security	Total Expenditures
1791	.6	2.3	.04	.2	—	4.3
1810	3.9	2.8	.6	.8	—	8.1
1830	8	1.9	1.9	1.4	—	15
1850	17	3.8	5.2	1.9	—	40
1870	79	129	24	28	—	310
1890	67	36	66	107	—	318
1910	313	21	230	161	—	694
1930	839	659	804	221	—	3,320
1950	13,440	5,750	2,223	2,223	784	39,544
1970	78,360	18,340	7,867	8,307	36,835	196,588
1980	135,900	64,500	19,400	21,200	117,100	576,700